Course   COMMUNICATION 316

Course Number   **Em Griffin**

First Look at Communication

Custom Publication for PSU

http://create.mheducation.com

ISBN-10: 1308363672   ISBN-13: 9781308363677

Contents

Credits

A FIRST LOOK AT
COMMUNICATION
THEORY

NINTH EDITION

EM GRIFFIN

ANDREW LEDBETTER

GLENN SPARKS

A FIRST LOOK AT
COMMUNICATION
THEORY

NINTH EDITION

EM GRIFFIN

Wheaton College

ANDREW LEDBETTER

Texas Christian University

GLENN SPARKS

Purdue University

A FIRST LOOK AT COMMUNICATION THEORY, NINTH EDITION

Published by McGraw-Hill Education, 2 Penn Plaza, New York, NY 10121. Copyright © 2015 by McGraw-Hill Education. All rights reserved. Printed in the United States of America. Previous editions © 2012, 2009, and 2006. No part of this publication may be reproduced or distributed in any form or by any means, or stored in a database or retrieval system, without the prior written consent of McGraw-Hill Education, including, but not limited to, in any network or other electronic storage or transmission, or broadcast for distance learning.

Some ancillaries, including electronic and print components, may not be available to customers outside the United States.

This book is printed on acid-free paper.

1 2 3 4 5 6 7 8 9 0 QVS/QVS 1 0 9 8 7 6 5 4

ISBN 978-0-07-352392-7
MHID 0-07-352392-5

Senior Vice President, Products & Markets: *Kurt L. Strand*
Vice President, General Manager, Products & Markets: *Michael Ryan*
Vice President, Content Production & Technology Services: *Kimberly Meriwether David*
Managing Director: *David S. Patterson*
Executive Director of Development: *Lisa Pinto*
Managing Editor: *Penina Braffman*
Associate Marketing Manager: *Alexandra Schultz*
Development Editor: *Adina Lonn*
Director, Content Production: *Terri Schiesl*
Content Project Manager: *Jessica Portz*
Buyer: *Nichole Birkenholz*
Cover Designer: *Studio Montage, St. Louis, MO*
Media Project Manager: *Jennifer Bartell*
Compositor: *Laserwords Private Limited*
Typeface: *10/12 Palatino LT Std Roman*
Printer: *Quad/Graphics*

All credits appearing on page or at the end of the book are considered to be an extension of the copyright page.

Library of Congress Cataloging-in-Publication Data

CIP APPLIED FOR

The Internet addresses listed in the text were accurate at the time of publication. The inclusion of a website does not indicate an endorsement by the authors or McGraw-Hill Education, and McGraw-Hill Education does not guarantee the accuracy of the information presented at these sites.

www.mhhe.com

ABOUT THE AUTHORS

Em Griffin is Professor Emeritus of Communication at Wheaton College in Illinois, where he taught for over 35 years and was chosen Teacher of the Year. He received his M.A. and Ph.D. in communication from Northwestern University; his research interest is in the development of close friendships. Em is the author of three applied communication books: *The Mind Changers* (persuasion), *Getting Together* (group dynamics), and *Making Friends* (close relationships). For three decades, Em has been an active volunteer with Opportunity International, a nonprofit development organization providing financial solutions and training to empower people living in poverty to transform their lives. He also serves as a mediator and coach at the Center for Conflict Resolution in Chicago. Em's wife, Jean, is an artist and a musician. They recently celebrated 50 years of marriage and have two adult children, Jim and Sharon, and six grandchildren, Josh, Amy, Sam, Kyle, Alison, and Dan. You can reach Em at em.griffin@wheaton.edu.

Andrew Ledbetter is an Associate Professor of Communication Studies at Texas Christian University. He received his M.A. and Ph.D. in communication studies from the University of Kansas. His research addresses how people use communication technology to maintain their interpersonal relationships. A related interest concerns how parent–child communication predicts health and well-being. Andrew has published more than 35 articles and received recognition for teaching excellence from both the National Communication Association and Central States Communication Association. His wife, Jessica, is a former attorney who teaches business law at Texas Christian University. With their daughters, Sydney and Kira, they enjoy involvement in their church, playing board and card games, reading, cooking, and following the TCU Horned Frogs and Kansas Jayhawks. You can reach Andrew at a.ledbetter@tcu.edu, visit his blog at www.andrewledbetter.com, or follow him on Twitter via @dr_ledbetter.

Glenn Sparks is a professor in the Brian Lamb School of Communication at Purdue University in Indiana, where he has taught for 28 years. He received his Ph.D. in communication arts from the University of Wisconsin–Madison; his research focuses on the effects of media. Glenn is the author of *Media Effects Research: A Basic Overview* and a personal memoir, *Rolling in Dough: Lessons I Learned in a Doughnut Shop*. He's co-author of *Refrigerator Rights: Our Crucial Need for Close Connection*. Glenn is an avid sports fan and also enjoys trying to increase his skill playing the theremin. He is married to Cheri, a developmental therapist; they have three adult children, David, Erin, and Jordan, and one grandchild, Caleb. You can reach Glenn at sparks@purdue.edu.

DEDICATION

We dedicate this book to our wives, Jeanie, Jessica, and Cheri, who encouraged us to work together, celebrated with us when the process went well, and comforted us when it didn't. Just as they lovingly supported us in this project, we commit to being there for them in what they feel called to do.

Em, Andrew, Glenn

CONTENTS

viii *CONTENTS*

PREFACE FOR INSTRUCTORS

If you're already familiar with *A First Look at Communication Theory* and understand the approach, organization, and main features of the book, you may want to jump ahead to the "Major Changes in the Ninth Edition" section. For those who are new to the text, reading the entire preface will give you a good grasp of what you and your students can expect.

A Balanced Approach to Theory Selection. We've written *A First Look* for students who have no background in communication theory. It's designed for undergraduates enrolled in an entry-level course, regardless of the students' classification. The trend in the field is to offer students a broad introduction to theory relatively early in their program. But if a department chooses to offer its first theory course on the junior or senior level, the course will still be the students' first comprehensive look at theory, so the book will meet them where they are.

Our goal in this text is to present 32 communication theories in a clear and interesting way. After reading about a given theory, students should understand the theory, know the research that supports it, see useful applications in their lives, and be aware of the theory's possible flaws. We hope readers will discover relationships among theories located across the communication landscape—a clear indication that they grasp what they're reading. But that kind of integrative thinking only takes place when students first comprehend what a theorist claims.

With the help of more than 200 instructors, we've selected a range of theories that reflect the diversity within the discipline. Some theories are proven candidates for a Communication Theory Hall of Fame. For example, Aristotle's analysis of logical, emotional, and ethical appeals continues to set the agenda for many public-speaking courses. Mead's symbolic interactionism is formative for interpretive theorists who are dealing with language, thought, self-concept, or the effect of society upon the individual. Berger's uncertainty reduction theory was the first objective theory to be crafted by a social scientist trained in the field. And no student of mediated communication should be ignorant of Gerbner's cultivation theory, which explains why heavy television viewing cultivates fear of a mean and scary world.

It would be shortsighted, however, to limit the selection to the classics of communication. Some of the discipline's most creative approaches are its newest. For example, Sandra Petronio's theory of communication privacy management undergirds much of the research conducted in the field of health communication. Leslie Baxter and Barbara Montgomery's theory of relational dialectics offers insight into the ongoing tensions inherent in personal relationships. And Robert McPhee's communicative constitution of organizations describes how the principle of social construction works in an organizational context.

Organizational Plan of the Book. Each chapter introduces a single theory in 10 to 15 pages. We've found that most undergraduates think in terms of discrete packets of information, so the concentrated coverage gives them a chance to focus their thoughts while reading a single chapter. This way, students can gain an in-depth understanding of important theories rather than acquire only a vague familiarity with a jumble of related ideas. The one-chapter–one-theory arrangement also gives teachers the opportunity to drop theories or rearrange the order of presentation without tearing apart the fabric of the text.

The first four chapters provide a framework for understanding the theories to come. The opening chapter, "Launching Your Study of Communication Theory," presents working definitions of both *theory* and *communication,* and also prepares students for the arrangement of the chapters and the features within them. Chapter 2, "Talk About Theory," lays the groundwork for understanding the differences between objective and interpretive theories. Chapter 3, "Weighing the Words," presents two sets of criteria for determining a good objective or interpretive theory. Based on Robert Craig's (University of Colorado) conception, Chapter 4, "Mapping the Territory," introduces seven traditions within the field of communication theory.

Following this integrative framework, we feature 32 theories in 32 self-contained chapters. Each theory is discussed within the context of a communication topic: interpersonal messages, relationship development, relationship maintenance, influence, group communication, organizational communication, public rhetoric, media and culture, media effects, intercultural communication, or gender and communication. These communication context sections usually contain three theories. Each section's two-page introduction outlines a crucial issue that theorists working in this area address. The placement of theories in familiar contexts helps students recognize that theories are answers to questions they've been asking all along. The final chapter, "Common Threads in Comm Theories," offers students a novel form of integration that will help them discern order in the tapestry of communication theory that might otherwise seem chaotic.

Because all theory and practice has value implications, we briefly explore a dozen ethical principles throughout the book. Consistent with the focus of this text, each principle is the central tenet of a specific ethical theory. Other disciplines may ignore these thorny issues, but to discuss communication as a process that is untouched by questions of good and bad, right and wrong, or questions of character would be to disregard an ongoing concern in our field.

Features of Each Chapter. Most people think in pictures. Students will have a rough time understanding a theory unless they apply its explanations and interpretations to concrete situations. The typical chapter uses an extended example to illustrate the "truth" a theory proposes. We encourage readers to try out ideas by visualizing a first meeting of freshman roommates, responding to conflict in a dysfunctional family, trying to persuade other students to support a zero-tolerance policy on driving after drinking, and many others. We also use speeches of Martin Luther King Jr. and Malcolm X, and scenes from *Mad Men, The Office, The Help, Bend It Like Beckham,* and *Thank You for Smoking* to illustrate principles of the theories. The case study in each chapter follows the pedagogical principle of explaining what students don't yet know in terms of ideas and images already within their experience.

Some theories are tightly linked with an extensive research project. For example, the impact of cognitive dissonance theory was greatly spurred by Festinger's surprising finding in his now classic $1/$20 experiment. And Philipsen's speech codes theory began with a three-year ethnographic study of what it means to speak like a man in "Teamsterville." When such exemplars exist, we describe the research in detail so that students can learn from and appreciate the benefits of grounding theory in systematic observation. In this way, readers of *A First Look* are led through a variety of research designs and data analyses.

Students will encounter the names of Baxter, Berger, Bormann, Burgoon, Burke, Deetz, Fisher, Giles, Kramarae, Pacanowsky, Pearce, Philipsen, Ting-Toomey, Walther, Wood, and many others in later communication courses. We therefore make a concerted effort to link theory and theorist. By pairing a particular theory with its originator, we try to promote both recall and respect for a given scholar's effort.

The text of each chapter concludes with a section that critiques the theory. This represents a hard look at the ideas presented in light of the criteria for a good theory outlined in Chapter 3. Some theorists have suggested that we are "friends" of their theory. We appreciate that because we want to present all of the theories in a constructive way. But after we summarize a theory's strengths, we then discuss its weaknesses, unanswered questions, and possible errors that remain. We try to stimulate a "That makes sense, and yet I wonder . . ." response among students.

We include a short list of thought questions at the end of each chapter. Labeled "Questions to Sharpen Your Focus," these probes encourage students to make connections among ideas in the chapter and also to apply the theory to their everyday communication experience. As part of this feature, words printed in italics remind students of the key terms of a given theory.

Each chapter ends with a short list of annotated readings entitled "A Second Look." The heading refers to resources for students who are interested in a theory and want to go further than a 10- to 15-page introduction allows. The top item is the resource we recommend as the starting point for further study. The other listings identify places to look for material about each of the major issues raised in the chapter. The format is designed to offer practical encouragement and guidance for further study without overwhelming the novice with multiple citations. The sources of quotations and citations of evidence are listed in an "Endnotes" section at the end of the book.

We think professors and students alike will get a good chuckle out of the cartoons we've selected for each chapter and section introduction. The art's main function, however, is to illustrate significant points in the text. As in other editions, we're committed to using quality cartoon art from *The New Yorker* and *Punch* magazines, as well as comic strips such as "Calvin and Hobbes" and "Dilbert." Perceptive cartoonists are modern-day prophets—their humor serves the education process well when it slips through mental barriers or attitudinal defenses that didactic prose can't penetrate.

While no author considers his or her style ponderous or dull, we believe we've presented the theories in a clear and lively fashion. Accuracy alone does not communicate. We've tried to remain faithful to the vocabulary each theorist uses so that the student can consider the theory in the author's own terms, but we also translate technical language into more familiar words. Students and reviewers cite readability and interest as particular strengths of the text. We encourage you to sample a chapter so you can decide for yourself.

In 13 of the chapters, you'll see photographs of the theorists who appear in "Conversations with Communication Theorists," eight-minute video clips of our discussions together. The text that accompanies each picture previews intriguing comments the theorists made so students can watch the interview with a specific purpose in mind. You can find these videos, as well as auto-graded quizzes, theory abstracts, web links, and crossword puzzles on the book's two websites, *www.mhhe.com/griffin9e* and the author-driven *www.afirstlook.com*.

Both sites offer password-protected features for instructors. The most selected resource is Emily Langan's world-class Instructor's Manual, which offers additional commentary, discussion questions, and classroom activities for each chapter. In addition, the McGraw-Hill Online Learning Center contains a test bank, flashcards, and PowerPoint presentations. The *First Look* site offers annotated movie clips that illustrate theories, a comparison chart showing theories covered in major communication theory texts, and chapter-by-chapter changes from the previous edition.

Major Changes in the Ninth Edition. Andrew Ledbetter and Glenn Sparks have become co-authors with Em. They were special consultants for the previous edition, but we now join together as equal partners. Both men are highly recognized scholars in their field—Andrew in computer-mediated communication and family communication; Glenn in media effects and interpersonal communication. Glenn was a student in Em's first persuasion course at Wheaton; Andrew aced the last communication theory class Em taught before he retired from full-time teaching. Despite differences in our ages of up to 45 years, the three of us are close friends and colleagues who have published together before. Each of us vets and edits what the other two write and offers advice on what to cover. We believe this interactive process ensures that students will read up-to-date information presented in the same "voice" that has characterized the book throughout eight editions.

Responding to instructors' desire to have at least one more organizational theory, we've added a chapter on Robert McPhee's theory, the *communicative constitution of organizations*. McPhee's conception of four flows of communication that create and sustain an organization is just one of several versions of CCO, but we think it's the account easiest to understand and most useful for students. In order to make room for McPhee's theory, we've moved our coverage of Delia's *constructivism* to the theory archive at *www.afirstlook.com*.

We've made a concerted effort to update examples that no longer have the explanatory power or appeal they did when introduced in previous editions. References to old films are a case in point. As apt as these movies are to illustrate *symbolic interactionism* or *critical theory of communication in organizations*, the majority of college students aren't familiar with *Nell* or *Erin Brockovich*. We've replaced many of these examples with cultural material more relevant to students.

Half the chapters in the book have undergone major additions, deletions, or alterations. Here's a sample:

- In the **"Talk About Theory"** chapter, Glenn's and Marty's analyses of the most popular commercial of the 2013 Super Bowl telecast highlight the differences between objective and interpretive scholarship.

- In the **"Weighing the Words"** chapter, a discussion of communication apprehension now illustrates the explanation-of-data standard for objective theories.

- The chapter on the *coordinated management of meaning* has been completely rewritten. It's shorter, less complex, and faithful to the new direction the theory has taken. The CMM Institute will use it on its website to introduce the theory.

- In the **"Uncertainty Reduction Theory"** chapter, the section on *anxiety/uncertainty management theory* has been replaced with an in-depth section on the *relational turbulence model,* which is on the cutting-edge of research in the URT tradition.

- The revised chapter on *social information processing theory* begins by referencing the hit 2010 movie *The Social Network* and then uses an ongoing example of a Facebook friendship to illustrate key components of the theory. Walther's hyperpersonal perspective is applied to online dating.

- The "Three State-of-the-Art Revisions" section of the **"Cognitive Dissonance"** chapter has been largely rewritten. The edits more clearly differentiate among the three revisions and use the example of President Obama's struggle with smoking to illustrate those differences.

- In Deetz' **"Critical Theory of Communication"** chapter, there's an extensive elaboration of his Politically Attentive Relational Constructivism (PARC). This is followed by an account of how Deetz applies the theory to his work with the International Atomic Energy Agency to prevent nuclear plant meltdowns.

- We've made a major reorganization of the chapter on Burke's *dramatism.* The order of the first four sections is now (1) an expanded presentation of the dramatistic pentad, (2) a new section on language as the genesis of guilt, (3) the guilt–redemption cycle, and (4) identification as the necessary condition for persuasion to occur.

- In the chapter on *cultural studies,* we rewrote the section on broadcast and print news supporting dominant ideology, using Obamacare as a case study. We then discussed satire as a possible form of resistance to the dominant ideology, using *The Daily Show* and *The Colbert Report* as examples.

- In the **"Genderlect Styles"** chapter, we replaced the *When Harry Met Sally* example with new material on rules of conversation that boys and girls learn early in life, and discuss how childhood speech communities may be the origin of genderlect.

- The revised chapter on *muted group theory* introduces Orbe's co-cultural theory, which charts how muted groups desire assimilation, separation, or accommodation.

Bottom-line numbers on important features of the text are an index of additional changes we've made in this edition. We've created **two** new "Conversations with Communication Theorists" videos—Glenn interviewing Sandra Petronio about her *communication privacy management theory* and Andrew discussing *communication accommodation theory* with Howie Giles. We've selected **six** new application logs that show how students use theories in their lives, and captured **seven** new cartoons that cleverly highlight a crucial claim of a particular theory. You'll also find **50** new annotated citations in the "Second Look" feature at the end of the chapters.

McGraw-Hill Education offers a robust custom publishing program, Create, that you may want to consider. Create enables you to build a book with only the chapters you need, and arrange them in the order you'll teach them. There's also the option of adding materials you prepare or using chapters from other McGraw-Hill books or resources from their library. When you build a Create book, you will receive a complimentary print review copy in just a few days or a complimentary eBook via email in about one hour.

Acknowledgments. We gratefully acknowledge the wisdom and counsel of many generous scholars whose intellectual capital is embedded in every page you'll read. Over the last 27 years, hundreds of communication scholars have gone out of their way to make the book better. People who have made direct contributions to this edition include Ron Adler, Santa Barbara City College; Ed Appel, Lock Haven University; Ryan Bisel, University of Oklahoma; Dan Brown, Grove City College; Kristen Carr, Texas Christian University; Ken Chase, Wheaton College; Stan Deetz, University of Colorado; Chip Eveland, Ohio State University; Darin Garard, Santa Barbara City College; Howard Giles, University of California, Santa Barbara; Cheris Kramarae, University of Oregon; Glen McClish, San Diego State University; Max McCombs, University of Texas; Marty Medhurst, Baylor University; Rebecca Meisenbach, University of Missouri; Melanie Mills, Eastern Illinois University; James Olufowote, Boston College; Mark Orbe, Western Michigan University; Doug Osman, Purdue University; Kim Pearce, CMM Institute for Personal and Social Evolution; Sandra Petronio, University of Indiana–Purdue University Indianapolis; Gerry Philipsen, University of Washington; Russ Proctor, Northern Kentucky University; Linda Putnam, University of California, Santa Barbara; Derrick Rosenoir, Vanguard University; Alan Rubin, Hebrew University of Jerusalem; Christa Sloan, Pepperdine University; Jordan Soliz, University of Nebraska; Stella Ting-Toomey, California State University, Fullerton; Mina Tsay, Boston University; Paul Witt, Texas Christian University; Robert Woods Jr., Spring Arbor University. Without their help, this edition would be less accurate and certainly less interesting.

Em has great appreciation for two Wheaton undergraduate research assistants. David Washko juggled his responsibilities while playing two seasons of varsity football at Wheaton. Laurel Porter constructed the comprehensive index that contains thousands of entries—a task no one should do more than once in life. Glenn is grateful for Lewis Day and Beth Stanley, two Purdue student production assistants who made recording his conversation with Sandra Petronio possible.

Our relationships with the professionals at McGraw-Hill have been highly satisfactory. Susan Gouijnstook was our initial Development Editor, but a maternity leave and well-deserved promotion to Director of Communication brought Adina Lonn to the Development Editor role. Both women were incredibly responsive to our needs, and their care for the entire project matched ours. They were backed up by Lisa Pinto, Executive Director of Development; David Patterson, Managing

Director; Penina Braffman, Managing Editor; Jessica Portz, Project Manager; and Jamie Daron, Brand Coordinator. Other authors are envious when they hear of our experience working with these professionals.

We've been fortunate to work closely with four outside contractors: Jenn Meyer, a commercial computer artist, created and revised figures on 24-hour notice; Judy Brody achieved the impossible by making the extensive permissions process enjoyable; Robyn Tellefsen, freelance writer and editor, was my student research assistant for the fourth edition of the book and proofreader for editions six through eight. When others saw her abilities and thoroughness, they recommended she be the copy editor for this edition. She also edited a book Glenn wrote. Robyn is quite familiar with communication theory and is someone whose edits we trust implicitly. Thus, the book your students read is better than the one we wrote. Rebecca Lazure is a project manager at SPi Global who took our comments on Robyn's edits and guided the manuscript and images through the production process and ultimately turned over the final digital package to the printer. She did it well and with grace.

We offer a special word of appreciation to Emily Langan, Em's former student who now teaches the courses he taught at Wheaton. This edition is Emily's fourth as writer of the ever-evolving Instructor's Manual that is famous among communication theory instructors. Em recalls the time when he first introduced Emily at a National Communication Association short course on teaching communication theory. The participants stood and applauded. Now, at the NCA short courses, she introduces Em. The three of us are grateful for her wisdom, dedication, creativity, and friendship.

Em Griffin
Andrew Ledbetter
Glenn Sparks

Overview

DIVISION ONE

Overview

CHAPTER 1

Launching Your Study of Communication Theory

This is a book about theories—communication theories. After that statement you may already be stifling a yawn. Many college students, after all, regard theory as obscure, dull, and irrelevant. People outside the classroom are even less charitable. An aircraft mechanic once chided a professor: "You academic types are all alike. Your heads are crammed so full of theory, you wouldn't know which end of a socket wrench to grab. Any plane you touched would crash and burn. All Ph.D. stands for is 'piled higher and deeper.'"

The mechanic could be right. Yet it's ironic that even in the process of knocking theory, he resorts to his own theory of cognitive overload to explain what he sees as the mechanical stupidity of scholars. I appreciate his desire to make sense of his world. Here's a man who spends a hunk of his life making sure that planes stay safely in the air until pilots are ready to land. When we really care about something, we should seek to answer the *why* and *what if* questions that always emerge. That was the message I heard from University of Arizona communication theorist Judee Burgoon when I talked with her in my series of interviews, *Conversations with Communication Theorists.*[1] If we care about the fascinating subject of communication, she suggested, we've got to "do theory."

WHAT IS A THEORY AND WHAT DOES IT DO?

In earlier editions I've used *theory* as "an umbrella term for all careful, systematic, and self-conscious discussion and analysis of communication phenomena," a definition offered by the late University of Minnesota communication professor Ernest Bormann.[2] I like this definition because it's general enough to cover the diverse theories presented in this book. Yet the description is so broad that it doesn't give us any direction on how we might construct a theory, nor does it offer a way to figure out when thoughts or statements about communication haven't attained that status. If I call any idea a "theory," does saying it's so make it so?

In my discussion with Judee Burgoon, she suggested that a theory is nothing more than a "set of systematic hunches about the way things operate."[3] Since Burgoon is the most frequently cited female scholar in the field of communication,

© 1986 by Matt Groening Productions, Inc. All Rights Reserved. Reprinted from *The Big Book of Hell*
© 1990 by Pantheon Books, a division of Random House, Inc.

I was intrigued by her unexpected use of the nontechnical term *hunch.* Would it therefore be legitimate to entitle the book you're reading *Communication Hunches?* She assured me that it would, quickly adding that they should be "informed hunches." So for Burgoon, a theory consists of *a set of systematic, informed hunches about the way things work.* In the rest of this section, I'll examine the three key features of Burgoon's notion of a theory. First, I'll focus on the idea that theory consists of a *set of hunches.* But a set of hunches is only a starting point. Second, I'll discuss what it means to say that those hunches have to be *informed.* Last, I'll highlight the notion that the hunches have to be *systematic*. Let's look briefly at the meaning of each of these core concepts of theory.

A Set of Hunches

If a theory is a set of hunches, it means we aren't yet sure we have the answer. When there's no puzzle to be solved or the explanation is obvious, there's no need to develop a theory. Theories always involve an element of speculation, or conjecture. Being a theorist is risky business because theories go beyond accepted wisdom. Once you become a theorist, you probably hope that all thinking people will eventually embrace the trial balloon you've launched. When you first float your theory, however, it's definitely in the hunch category.

Theory
A set of systematic, informed hunches about the way things work.

By referring to a plural "set of hunches" rather than a single "hunch," Burgoon makes it clear that a theory is not just one inspired thought or an isolated idea. The young theorist in the cartoon may be quite sure that dogs and bees can smell fear, but that isolated conviction isn't a theory. A developed theory offers some sort of explanation. For example, how are bees and dogs able to sniff out fright? Perhaps the scent of sweaty palms that comes from high anxiety is qualitatively different than the odor of people perspiring from hard work. A theory will also give some indication of scope. Do only dogs and bees possess this keen sense of smell, or do butterflies and kittens have it as well? Theory construction involves multiple hunches.

Informed Hunches

Bormann's description of creating communication theory calls for a careful, self-conscious analysis of communication phenomena, but Burgoon's definition asks for more. It's not enough to think carefully about an idea; a theorist's hunches should be *informed*. Working on a hunch that a penny thrown from the Empire State Building will become deeply embedded in the sidewalk, the young theorist has a responsibility to check it out. Before developing a theory, there are articles to read, people to talk to, actions to observe, or experiments to run, all of which can cast light on the subject. At the very least, communication theorists should be familiar with alternative explanations and interpretations of the type of communication they are studying. (Young Theorist, have you heard the story of Galileo dropping balls from the Leaning Tower of Pisa?)

Pepperdine University communication professor Fred Casmir's description of theory parallels Burgoon's call for multiple informed hunches:

> Theories are sometimes defined as guesses—but significantly as "educated" guesses. Theories are not merely based on vague impressions nor are they accidental by-products of life. Theories tend to result when their creators have prepared themselves to discover something in their environment, which triggers the process of theory construction.[4]

Hunches That Are Systematic

Most scholars reserve the term *theory* for an integrated *system* of concepts. A theory not only lays out multiple ideas, but also specifies the relationships among them. In common parlance, it connects the dots. The links among the informed hunches are clearly drawn so that a pattern emerges.

None of the young theories in the cartoon rise to this standard. Since most of the nine are presented as one-shot claims, they aren't part of a conceptual framework. One possible exception is the dual speculation that "adults are really Martians, and they're up to no good." But the connecting word *and* doesn't really show the relationship between grown-ups' unsavory activity and their hypothesized other-world origin. To do that, the young theorist could speculate about the basic character of Martians, how they got here, why their behavior is suspicious, and whether today's youth will turn into aliens when they become parents. A theory would then tie all of these ideas together into a unified whole. As you read about any theory covered in this book, you have a right to expect a set of *systematic*, informed hunches.

Images of Theory

In response to the question *What is a theory?* I've presented a verbal definition. Many of us are visual learners as well and would appreciate a concrete image that helps us understand what a theory is and does. So I'll present three metaphors that I find helpful, but will also note how an over-reliance on these representations of theory might lead us astray.

 Theories as Nets: Philosopher of science Karl Popper said that "theories are nets cast to catch what we call 'the world'. . . . We endeavor to make the mesh ever finer and finer."[5] I appreciate this metaphor because it highlights the ongoing labor of the theorist as a type of deep-sea angler. For serious scholars, theories are the tools of the trade. The term *the world* can be interpreted as everything that goes on under the sun—thus requiring a *grand* theory that applies to all communication, all the time. Conversely, catching the world could be construed as calling for numerous *special* theories—different kinds of small nets to capture distinct types of communication in local situations. Either way, the quest for finer-meshed nets is somewhat disturbing because the study of communication is about people rather than schools of fish. The idea that theories could be woven so tightly that they'd snag everything humans think, say, or do strikes me as naive. The possibility also raises questions about our freedom to choose some actions and reject others.

Theories as Lenses: Many scholars see their theoretical constructions as similar to the lens of a camera or a pair of glasses, as opposed to a mirror that accurately reflects the world out there. The lens imagery highlights the idea that theories shape our perception by focusing attention on some features of communication while ignoring other features, or at least pushing them into the background. Two theorists could analyze the same communication event—an argument, perhaps—and, depending on the lens each uses, one theorist may view the speech act as a breakdown of communication or the breakup of a relationship, while the other theorist will see it as democracy in action. For me, the danger of the lens metaphor is that we might regard what is seen through the glass as so dependent on the theoretical stance of the viewer that we abandon any attempt to discern what is real or true.

 Theories as Maps: I use this image when I describe the *First Look* text to others. Within this analogy, communication theories are maps of the way communication works. The truth they depict may have to do with objective behaviors "out there" or subjective meanings inside our heads. Either way, we need to have theory to guide us through unfamiliar territory. In that sense, this book of theories is like a scenic atlas that pulls together 32 must-see locations. It's the kind of travel guide that presents a close-up view of each site. I would caution, however, that the map is not the territory.[6] A static theory, like a still photograph, can never fully portray the richness of interaction between people that is constantly changing, always more varied, and inevitably more complicated than what any theory can chart. As a person intrigued with communication, aren't you glad it's this way?

WHAT IS COMMUNICATION?

To ask this question is to invite controversy and raise expectations that can't be met. Frank Dance, the University of Denver scholar credited for publishing the first comprehensive book on communication theory, cataloged more than 120 definitions of *communication*—and that was more than 40 years ago.[7] Communication scholars have suggested many more since then, yet no single definition has risen to the top and become the standard within the field of communication. When it comes to defining what it is we study, there's little discipline in the discipline.

At the conclusion of his study, Dance suggested that we're "trying to make the concept of communication do too much work for us."[8] Other communication theorists agree, noting that when the term is used to describe almost every kind of human interaction, it's seriously overburdened. Michigan Tech University communication professor Jennifer Slack brings a splash of reality to attempts to draw definitive lines around what it is that our theories and research cover. She declares that "there is no single, absolute essence of communication that adequately explains the phenomena we study. Such a definition does not exist; neither is it merely awaiting the next brightest communication scholar to nail it down once and for all."[9]

Despite the pitfalls of trying to define *communication* in an all-inclusive way, it seems to me that students who are willing to spend a big chunk of their college education studying communication deserve a description of what it is they're looking at. Rather than giving the final word on what human activities can be legitimately referred to as *communication*, this designation would highlight the essential features of communication that shouldn't be missed. So for starters, I offer this working definition:

> *Communication is the relational process of creating and interpreting messages that elicit a response.*

To the extent that there is redeeming value in this statement, it lies in drawing your attention to five features of communication that you'll run across repeatedly as you read about the theories in the field. I'll flesh out these concepts in the rest of this section.

Communication
The relational process of creating and interpreting messages that elicit a response.

1. Messages

Messages are at the core of communication study. University of Colorado communication professor Robert Craig says that communication involves "talking and listening, writing and reading, performing and witnessing, or, more generally, doing anything that involves 'messages' in any medium or situation."[10]

When academic areas such as psychology, sociology, anthropology, political science, literature, and philosophy deal with human symbolic activity, they intersect with the study of communication. The visual image of this intersection of interests has prompted some to refer to communication as a *crossroads discipline.* The difference is that communication scholars are parked at the junction focusing on messages, whereas other disciplines are just passing through on their way to other destinations. All of the theories covered in this book deal specifically with messages.

Communication theorists use the word *text* as a synonym for a message that can be studied, regardless of the medium. This book is a text. So is a verbatim transcript of a conversation with your instructor, a recorded presidential news conference, a silent YouTube video, or a Justin Timberlake song on your iPod. To illustrate the following four parts of the definition, suppose you received this cryptic text message from a close, same-sex friend: "Pat and I spent the night together." You immediately know that the name Pat refers to the person with whom you have an ongoing romantic relationship. An analysis of this text and the context surrounding its transmission provides a useful case study for examining the essential features of communication.

Text
A record of a message that can be analyzed by others; for example, a book, film, photograph, or any transcript or recording of a speech or broadcast.

2. Creation of Messages

This phrase in the working definition of communication indicates that the content and form of a text are usually *constructed, invented, planned, crafted, constituted, selected,* or *adopted* by the communicator. Each of these terms is used in one or more of the theories I describe, and they all imply that the communicator is making a conscious choice of message form and substance. For whatever reason, your friend sent a text message rather than meeting face-to-face, calling you on the phone, sending an email, or writing a note. Your friend also chose the seven words that were transmitted to your cell phone. There is a long history of textual analysis in the field of communication, wherein the rhetorical critic looks for clues in the message to discern the motivation and strategy of the person who created the message.

There are, of course, many times when we speak, write, or gesture in seemingly mindless ways—activities that are like driving on cruise control. These are preprogrammed responses that were selected earlier and stored for later use. In like manner, our repertoire of stock phrases such as *thank you, no problem, whatever,* or a string of swear words were chosen sometime in the past to express our feelings, and over time have become habitual responses. Only when we become more mindful of the nature and impact of our messages will we have the ability to alter them. That's why consciousness-raising is a goal of five or six of the theories I'll present—each one seeks to increase our communication choices.

3. Interpretation of Messages

Messages do not interpret themselves. The meaning that a message holds for the creators and receivers doesn't reside in the words that are spoken, written, or acted out. A truism among communication scholars is that *words don't mean things, people mean things.* Symbolic interactionist Herbert Blumer stated its implication: "Humans act toward people or things on the basis of the meanings they assign to those people or things."[11]

What is the meaning of your friend's text message? Does "spent the night together" mean *talking until all hours? Pulling an all-night study session? Sleeping on the sofa? Making love?* If it's the latter, was Pat a *willing* or *unwilling partner* (perhaps drunk or the victim of acquaintance rape)? How would your friend characterize their sexual liaison? *Recreational sex? A chance hookup? Friends with benefits? Developing a close relationship? Falling in love? The start of a long-term commitment?* Perhaps of more importance to you, how does Pat view it? What emotional meaning is behind the message for each of them? *Satisfaction? Disappointment? Surprise? The morning-after-the-night-before blahs? Gratefulness? Guilt? Ecstasy?* And finally, what does receiving this message through a digital channel mean for you, your friendship, and your relationship with Pat? None of these answers are in the message. Words and other symbols are polysemic—they're open to multiple interpretations.

4. A Relational Process

The Greek philosopher Heraclitus observed that "one cannot step into the same river twice."[12] These words illustrate the widespread acceptance among communication scholars that communication is a *process.* Much like a river, the flow of communication is always in flux, never completely the same, and can only be described with reference to what went before and what is yet to come. This means that the text message "Pat and I spent the night together" is not the whole story. You'll probably contact both your friend and Pat to ask the clarifying questions raised earlier. As they are answered or avoided, you'll interpret the message in a different way. That's because communication is a process, not a freeze-frame snapshot.

In the opening lines of her essay "Communication as Relationality," University of Georgia rhetorical theorist Celeste Condit suggests that the communication process is more about relationships than it is about content.

> Communication is a process of relating. This means it is not primarily or essentially a process of transferring information or of disseminating or circulating signs (though these things can be identified as happening within the process of relating).[13]

Communication is a relational process not only because it takes place between two or more persons, but also because it affects the nature of the connections among those people. It's obvious that the text message you received will influence the triangle of relationships among you, Pat, and your (former?) friend. But this is true in other forms of mediated communication as well. Television viewers and moviegoers have emotional responses to people they see on-screen. And as businesses are discovering, even the impersonal recorded announcement that "this call may be monitored for quality assurance purposes" has an impact on how we regard their corporate persona.

5. Messages That Elicit a Response

This final component of communication deals with the effect of the message upon people who receive it. At the end of his groundbreaking book on communication theory, Dance concludes, "'Communication,' in its broadest interpretation, may be defined as the eliciting of a response."[14] If a message fails to stimulate any cognitive, emotional, or behavioral reaction, it seems pointless to refer to it as *communication.* We often refer to such situations as a message "falling on deaf ears" or the other person "turning a blind eye."

Picture a mother driving her 10-year-old son home from school. He's strapped in the seat behind her playing *Angry Birds* on his smartphone, equipped with earbuds. His mother asks if he has any homework. Is that communication? Not if he doesn't hear the question or see her lips moving. What if he isn't wired for sound and hears her voice? It depends. If he's glued to the screen and totally engrossed in wiping out pigs before they eat eggs, he may literally tune her out—still no communication.

Suppose, however, the boy hears her words and feels *bad* that he has homework, *sad* that his mom's so nosy, *mad* that she broke his game-playing concentration, or *glad* that he finished the assignment in study hall. Although these are internal feelings that his mother may miss, each response would have been triggered by Mom's question and would therefore qualify as communication. And of course any vocal response, even a noncommittal grunt, indicates that some form of communication has occurred.

In like manner, surely you would respond to your friend's cryptic message about the night spent with Pat—one way or another. In fact, the text seems to have been crafted and sent to provoke a response. How closely your thoughts, feelings, words, or actions would match what your friend expected or intended is another matter. Successful or not, the whole situation surrounding the text and context of the message fits the working definition of communication that we hope will help you frame your study of communication theory. *Communication is the relational process of creating and interpreting messages that elicit a response.*

AN ARRANGEMENT OF IDEAS TO AID COMPREHENSION

Now that you have a basic understanding of what a communication theory is, knowing how we've structured the book and arranged the theories can help you grasp their content. That's because we've organized the text to place a given theory in a conceptual framework and situational context before we present it. After this chapter, there are three more integrative chapters in the "Overview" division. For Chapter 2, I've asked co-author Glenn Sparks and another leading communication scholar to analyze a highly acclaimed TV ad in order to illustrate how half the theories in the book are based on *objective* assumptions, while the other half are constructed using an *interpretive* set of principles. Chapter 3 presents criteria for judging both kinds of theory so you can make an informed evaluation of a theory's worth rather than relying solely on your gut reaction. Finally, Chapter 4 describes seven traditions of communication theory and research. When you know the family tree of a theory, you can explain why it has a strong affinity with some theories but doesn't speak the same language as others.

Following this overview, there are 32 chapters that run 10–15 pages apiece, each concentrating on a single theory. we think you'll find that the one-chapter, one-theory format is user-friendly because it gives you a chance to focus on a single theory at a time. This way, they won't all blur together in your mind. These chapters are arranged into four major divisions according to the primary communication context that they address. The theories in Division Two, "Interpersonal Communication," consider one-on-one interaction. Division Three, "Group and Public Communication," deals with face-to-face involvement in collective settings. Division Four, "Mass Communication," pulls together theories that explore electronic and print media. Division Five, "Cultural Context," explores systems of shared meaning that are so all-encompassing that we often fail to realize their impact upon us.

These four divisions are based on the fact that theories are tentative answers to questions that occur to people as they mull over practical problems in specific situations. It therefore makes sense to group them according to the different communication settings that usually prompt those questions. This organizational plan is like having four separately indexed file cabinets. Although there is no natural progression from one division to another, the plan provides a convenient way to classify and retrieve the 32 theories.

Finally, Division Six, "Integration," seeks to distill core ideas that are common to a number of theories. Ideas have power, and each theory is driven by one or more ideas that may be shared by other theories from different communication contexts. For example, in each of the four context divisions, there's at least one theory committed to the force of narrative. They each declare that people respond to stories and dramatic imagery with which they can identify. Reading about key concepts that cut across multiple theories wouldn't mean much to you now, but after you become familiar with a number of communication theories, it can be an eye-opening experience that also helps you review what you've learned.

CHAPTER FEATURES TO ENLIVEN THEORY

In many of the chapters ahead, we use an extended example from life on a college campus, a well-known communication event, or the conversations of characters in movies, books, or TV shows. The main purpose of these illustrations is to provide a mind's-eye picture of how the theory works. The imagery will also make the basic thrust of the theory easier to recall. But if you can think of a situation in your own life where the theory is relevant, that personal application will make it doubly interesting and memorable for you.

You might also want to see how others put the theories into practice. With our students' permission, we've weaved in their accounts of application for almost all the theories featured in the text. We're intrigued by the rich connections these students make—ones we wouldn't have thought of on our own. Some students draw on scenes from short stories, novels, or movies. To see an annotated list of feature film scenes that illustrate the theories, go to the book's website, www.afirstlook.com, and under Theory Resources, click on Suggested Movie Clips. As co-authors of this book, we'll draw upon our life experiences as well. We've been professional colleagues for years and are close friends, so we'd like that warmth to extend to readers by writing in a direct, personal voice. That means using *I*, *my*, and *me* when referring to individual thoughts or stories from our lives. We think that's much better than stating them in the passive voice or referring to ourselves in an arms-length, third-person way. We don't use personal references in every chapter, but when we do, we want you to know whose voice you're "hearing."

The three of us contributed to every chapter and jointly edited the final version. But in each case one of us took the lead and wrote most of the words.

For the first four introductory chapters and more than half of the theory chapters, that was me. So unless you see a reference in a chapter that Andrew or Glenn is sharing his own ideas, feelings, or experiences, you can assume that the "I" refers to Em—just as it does in this chapter.

We also make a consistent effort to link each theory with its author. It takes both wisdom and courage to successfully plant a theoretical flag. In a process similar to the childhood game king-of-the-hill, as soon as a theorist constructs a theory of communication, critics try to pull it down. That's OK, because the value of a theory is discerned by survival in the rough-and-tumble world of competitive ideas. For this reason we always include a section in theory chapters labeled "Critique." Theorists who prevail deserve to have their names associated with their creations.

There is a second reason for tying a theory to its author. Many of you will do further study in communication, and a mastery of names like Deetz, Giles, Walther, Baxter, Berger, and Burke will allow you to enter into the dialogue without being at a disadvantage. Ignoring the names of theorists could prove to be false economy in the long run.

Don't overlook the three features at the end of each chapter. The queries under the title "Questions to Sharpen Your Focus" will help you mull over key points of the theory. They can be answered by pulling together information from this text and from the text of your life. The italicized words in each question highlight terms you need to know in order to understand the theory. Whenever you see a picture of the theorist, it's captured from one of our *Conversations with Communication Theorists* and shown alongside a brief description of what we talked about. You can view these 6- to 8-minute interviews at www.afirstlook .com. And the feature entitled "A Second Look" offers an annotated bibliography of resources should you desire to know more about the theory. You'll find it a good place to start if you are writing a research paper on the theory or are intrigued with a particular aspect of it.

You've already seen the last feature we'll mention. In every chapter and section introduction we include a cartoon for your learning and enjoyment. Cartoonists are often modern-day prophets. Their incisive wit can illustrate a feature of the theory in a way that's more instructive and memorable than a few extra paragraphs would be. In addition to enjoying their humor, you can use the cartoons as minitests of comprehension. Unlike my comments on "Young Theories" earlier in this chapter, we usually don't refer to the art or the caption that goes with it. So if you can't figure out why a particular cartoon appears where it does, make a renewed effort to grasp the theorist's ideas.

Some students are afraid to try. Like travelers whose eyes glaze over at the sight of a road map, they have a phobia about theories that seek to explain human intentions and behavior. We sympathize with their qualms and misgivings, but find that the theories in this book haven't dehydrated life or made it more confusing. On the contrary, they add clarity and provide a sense of competence as we communicate with others. We hope they do that for you as well.

Every so often a student will ask me, "Do you really think about communication theory when you're talking to someone?" My answer is "Yes, but not all the time." Like everyone else, I often speak on autopilot—words, phrases, sentences, descriptions rolling off my tongue without conscious thought. Old habits die hard. But when I'm in a new setting or the conversational stakes are high, I start to think strategically. And that's when the applied wisdom of theories

12   *OVERVIEW*

that fit the situation comes to mind. By midterm, many of our students discover they're thinking that way as well. That's our wish for you as you launch your study of communication theory.

QUESTIONS TO SHARPEN YOUR FOCUS

1. Suppose you share the aircraft mechanic's suspicion that scholars who create theories would be all thumbs working on a plane's ailerons or engine. What would it take to transform your *hunch* into a *theory?*

2. Which *metaphor* of theory do you find most helpful—theory as a *net*, a *lens*, or a *map?* Can you think of another image that you could use to explain to a friend what this course is about?

3. Suppose you want to study the effects of yawns during intimate conversations. Would your research fall under *communication* as defined as the *relational process of creating and interpreting messages to elicit a response?* If not, how would you change the definition to make it include your interest?

4. You come to this course with a vast array of communication experiences in *interpersonal, group and public, mass media,* and *intercultural contexts.* What are the communication *questions* you want to answer, *puzzles* you want to solve, *problems* you want to fix?

A SECOND LOOK

Recommended resource: Gregory Shepherd, Jeffrey St. John, and Ted Striphas (eds.), *Communication as . . . Perspectives on Theory,* Sage, Thousand Oaks, CA, 2006.

Diverse definitions of communication: Frank E. X. Dance, "The Concept of Communication," *Journal of Communication,* Vol. 20, 1970, pp. 201–210.

Communication as human symbolic interaction: Gary Cronkhite, "On the Focus, Scope and Coherence of the Study of Human Communication," *Quarterly Journal of Speech,* Vol. 72, No. 3, 1986, pp. 231–246.

Theories of communication as practical: J. Kevin Barge, "Practical Theory as Mapping, Engaged Reflection, and Transformative Practice," *Communication Theory,* Vol. 11, 2001, pp. 5–13.

Multidimensional view of theory: James A. Anderson and Geoffrey Baym, "Philosophies and Philosophic Issues in Communication, 1995–2004," *Journal of Communication,* Vol. 54, 2004, pp. 589–615.

To access 50 word summaries of theories
featured in the book, see Appendix A or click on
Theory Overview under Theory Resources at
www.afirstlook.com.

CHAPTER 2

Talk About Theory

I met Glenn Sparks and Marty Medhurst my first year teaching at Wheaton College. Glenn and Marty were friends who signed up for my undergraduate persuasion course. As students, both men were interested in broadcast media. After graduating from Wheaton, each went on for a master's degree at Northern Illinois University. Each earned a doctorate at a different university, and both are now nationally recognized communication scholars. Marty is on the faculty at Baylor University; Glenn is at Purdue University and is a co-author of this book.

Despite their similar backgrounds and interests, Glenn and Marty are quite different in their approaches to communication. Glenn calls himself a *behavioral scientist*, while Marty refers to himself as a *rhetorician*. Glenn's training was in empirical research; Marty was schooled in rhetorical theory and criticism. Glenn conducts experiments; Marty interprets texts.

Behavioral scientist
A scholar who applies the scientific method to describe, predict, and explain recurring forms of human behavior.

Rhetorician
A scholar who studies the ways in which symbolic forms can be used to identify with people, or to persuade them toward a certain point of view.

To understand the theories ahead, you need to first grasp the crucial differences between the objective and interpretive approaches to communication. As a way to introduce the distinctions, I asked Glenn and Marty to bring their scholarship to bear on a television commercial that first aired during Super Bowl XLVII, the game where the lights went out. It's a stealth ad for beer that doesn't show booze on a beach, men in a bar flirting with a waitress serving brew, or a guy tapping a keg yelling, "Party all night!" These are typical images that turn off a significant portion of viewers who see them as silly, distasteful, or unethical. That's because those ads appear to promote the dangerous practice of binge drinking among young adults as a way to gain acceptance or get a buzz. Instead, this ad portrays the bond that develops between a shaggy-hooved Clydesdale horse and his young trainer.[1]

TWO COMMUNICATION SCHOLARS VIEW A HEARTWARMING AD

Using no dialogue or voice-over, the Super Bowl commercial tells a visual story in 60 seconds. We see scenes of the newborn foal, his trainer asleep in the sick colt's stall, horseplay between them as the animal gains stature, and the fully grown animal running free alongside the trainer's truck. When it's time for this magnificent animal to become part of a working team of Clydesdales promoting beer, the trainer leads him into the company's horse van and gazes wistfully as it disappears down the road.

Three years later, the man discovers the Clydesdales will be in a Chicago parade and drives to the city to reconnect with his horse. He smiles with pride as the horse prances by, but blinders keep the animal from seeing him. As the trainer walks sadly back to his truck, the harness is removed and the horse catches a glimpse of him. The final shots show the Clydesdale galloping down the street to catch up with his human friend, who then buries his face in the horse's mane as they are reunited.

Since the sponsor spent $7 million to air this one-minute commercial—and more than that to film it—its marketing department obviously believed that featuring this huge draft horse would sell huge amounts of draft beer. There's no doubt that most critics and viewers liked the ad. *Advertising Age* analyst Ken Wheaton concludes, "Weepy, sentimental, nostalgic. I don't care. This is everything I want from a Budweiser Super Bowl spot."[2] Yet as you'll see, social scientist Glenn and rhetorical critic Marty take different theoretical approaches as they analyze the intent of the ad and how it works.

Glenn: An Objective Approach

Objective approach
The assumption that truth is singular and is accessible through unbiased sensory observation; committed to uncovering cause-and-effect relationships.

After the 2013 Super Bowl ended, a research company announced that the Clydesdale ad was the year's commercial winner.[3] The researchers tracked 400 viewers who used a phone app to express their feelings during the broadcast. Viewers' liking for the Clydesdale ad was on par with what they felt when their favorite team scored a touchdown. Social scientists wonder why the commercial produced so much positive sentiment and whether it resulted in action. They want to explain and predict human behavior.

How do scientists satisfy these interests? After observing behavior, we identify or construct a theory that offers insight into what we've observed. In this case, advertising guru Tony Schwartz' *resonance principle of communication* is a promising theoretical idea.[4] Although Schwartz passed away in 2008, his theory lives on.

According to Schwartz, successful persuasive messages evoke past experiences that create *resonance* between the message content and a person's thoughts or feelings. Schwartz believed that resonance leads to persuasion. It's not *arguments* that persuade people as much as it is *memories* of personal experiences triggered by the message.

The heartwarming story of a worker dedicated to a horse he loves may tap into viewers' deep memories of their own devotion to animals they once nurtured. The emotional scene at the end of the ad might stir reminiscence of your pet's excitement when you would return home or the tremendous relief at being reunited with one you thought lost. Once these good feelings are evoked, Schwartz believed people associate them with the advertised product. For beer drinkers, those good feelings may lead to more sales. For viewers who see drinking beer as a health risk, the good feelings may lead to positive thoughts about a company that seems to care not only about selling beer, but also about taking good care of those splendid Clydesdales. In this case, persuasion may be measured both in beer sales and positive thoughts about Budweiser—a company well aware that its success may lead to alcohol abuse among consumers and a bad corporate reputation.

Theories need to be validated. For scientists, it's not enough to identify a theory that seems to apply to the situation. We want an objective test to find out if a theory is faulty. For example, I'd want to discover if commercials that trigger warm emotional memories are better than other ads at selling products or generating good feelings toward the sponsor. Testing audience response is a crucial scientific enterprise. Even though a theory might sound plausible, we can't be sure it's valid until it's been tested. In science, theory and research walk hand in hand.

Marty: An Interpretive Approach

Interpretive approach
The linguistic work of assigning meaning or value to communicative texts; assumes that multiple meanings or truths are possible.

There is more going on here than a simple reunion of man and horse. The entire ad is structured by an archetypal mythic pattern of birth-death-rebirth. Archetypal myths are those that draw upon a universal experience—what psychoanalyst Carl Jung called the "collective unconscious."[5] Deep within the mental makeup of all human beings is the archetype of the birth-death-rebirth cycle. The use of such archetypes, according to rhetorical theorist Michael Osborn, touches off "depth responses" that emotionally resonate at the core of our being.[6] The ad activates these emotions by incorporating the form of the cycle within a mini-narrative.

We first see the newborn colt in the barn as the breeder feeds him, strokes his coat, and even sleeps next to him in the stall. Birth naturally leads to growth, as we watch the colt mature before our eyes. But just as this Clydesdale grows to full stature, the Budweiser 18-wheeler arrives to take away the treasured horse. Symbolically, this is a death because it represents an absence or void. What once was is no more. Then, three years later, the breeder and his horse are reunited in an act of rebirth. The former relationship, which had been shattered by the symbolic death, is now restored with the reunion of man and horse.

It is significant that the passage of time is three years. Just as Christians believe Jesus lay in the tomb for three days before his resurrection, so the horse is gone for three years before he reappears. But once he reemerges, it is as though he never left. That which was lost has been found. The emotions evoked by this ad are strong because we are dealing with life and death, with loss and restoration. All of us unconsciously long for a reunion with those people or things in our lives that have been most important to us. Even the music—"Landslide" by Fleetwood Mac—underscores the archetypal pattern, as it speaks of love, loss, change, and being afraid. Fear of death is a primordial human instinct. It is only through a rebirth that we can reclaim what time and change have taken from us.

The ad subtly suggests that Budweiser beer is our constant mainstay. Life changes and losses happen, but Bud never changes, never disappears. We see that in the shots of the beer bottle on the breeder's table as he reads about the upcoming parade in Chicago. Bud is portrayed as our companion and our comforter, something that will be with us through the dark nights of separation and loss.

OBJECTIVE OR INTERPRETIVE WORLDVIEWS: SORTING OUT THE LABELS

Although both of these scholars focus on the warm feelings viewers have when seeing the Budweiser Clydesdale ad, Glenn's and Marty's approaches to communication study clearly differ in starting point, method, and conclusion. Glenn is a social *scientist* who works hard to be *objective*. When I refer to theorists and researchers like Glenn throughout the book, I'll use the terms *scientist* and *objective scholar* interchangeably. Marty is a *rhetorical critic* who does *interpretive* study. Here the labels get tricky.

16 *OVERVIEW*

While it's true that all rhetorical critics do interpretive analysis, not all interpretive scholars are rhetoricians. Most (including Marty) are *humanists* who study what it's like to be another person in a specific time and place. But a growing number of postmodern communication theorists reject that tradition. These interpretive scholars refer to themselves with a bewildering variety of brand names: hermeneuticists, poststructuralists, deconstructivists, phenomenologists, cultural studies researchers, and social action theorists, as well as combinations of these terms. Writing from this postmodernist perspective, University of Utah theorist James Anderson observes:

Humanistic scholarship
Study of what it's like to be another person in a specific time and place; assumes there are few important panhuman similarities.

> With this very large number of interpretive communities, names are contentious, border patrol is hopeless and crossovers continuous. Members, however, often see real differences.[7]

All of these scholars, including Marty, do interpretive analysis—scholarship concerned with meaning—yet there's no common term like *scientist* that includes them all. So from this point on I'll use the designation *interpretive scholars* or the noun form *interpreters* to refer to the entire group, and use *rhetoricians, humanists, postmodernists,* or *critical scholars* only when I'm singling out a particular subgroup.

The separate worldviews of interpretive scholars and scientists reflect contrasting assumptions about ways of arriving at knowledge, the core of human nature, questions of value, and the purpose of having theory. The rest of this chapter sketches out these differences.

WAYS OF KNOWING: DISCOVERING TRUTH OR CREATING MULTIPLE REALITIES?

How do we know what we know, if we know it at all? This is the central question addressed by a branch of philosophy known as *epistemology*. You may have been in school for a dozen-plus years, read assignments, written papers, and taken tests without ever delving into the issue *What is truth?* With or without in-depth study of the issue, however, we all inevitably make assumptions about the nature of knowledge.

Epistemology
The study of the origin, nature, method, and limits of knowledge.

Scientists assume that Truth is singular. They see a single, timeless reality "out there" that's not dependent on local conditions. It's waiting to be discovered through the five senses of sight, sound, touch, taste, and smell. Since the raw sensory data of the world is accessible to any competent observer, science seeks to be bias-free, with no ax to grind. The evidence speaks for itself. As Galileo observed, anyone could see through his telescope. Of course, no one person can know it all, so individual researchers pool their findings and build a collective body of knowledge about how the world works.

Scientists consider good theories to be those that are faithful representations of the way the world really is. Of the metaphors introduced in Chapter 1, they like the image of theory as a mirror that reflects reality, or a net that captures part of it. Objective theorists are confident that once a principle is discovered and validated, it will continue to hold true as long as conditions remain relatively the same. That's why Glenn believes the theory of resonance can explain why other media messages succeed or fail.

Interpretive scholars seek truth as well, but many interpreters regard that truth as socially constructed through communication. They believe language creates social realities that are always in flux rather than revealing or representing fixed principles or relationships in a world that doesn't change. Knowledge is always viewed from a particular standpoint. A word, a gesture, or an act may have constancy within a given community, but it's dangerous to assume that interpretations can cross lines of time and space.

Texts never interpret themselves. Most of these scholars, in fact, hold that truth is largely subjective—that meaning is highly interpretive. But rhetorical critics like Marty are not relativists, arbitrarily assigning meaning on a whim. They do maintain, however, that objectivity is a myth; we can never entirely separate the knower from the known.

Convinced that meaning is in the mind rather than in the verbal sign, interpreters are comfortable with the notion that a text may have multiple meanings. Rhetorical critics are successful when they get others to view a text through their interpretive lens—to adopt a new perspective on the world. For example, did Marty convince you that the Budweiser ad draws upon a deep-seated pattern of birth-death-rebirth ingrained in all of us? As Anderson notes, "Truth is a struggle, not a status."[8]

HUMAN NATURE: DETERMINISM OR FREE WILL?

Determinism
The assumption that behavior is caused by heredity and environment.

One of the great philosophical debates throughout history revolves around the question of human choice.[9] Hard-line *determinists* claim that every move we make is the result of heredity ("biology is destiny") and environment ("pleasure stamps in, pain stamps out"). On the other hand, free-will purists insist that every human act is ultimately voluntary ("I am the master of my fate: I am the captain of my soul"[10]). Although few communication theorists are comfortable with either extreme, most tend to line up on one side or the other. Scientists stress the forces that shape human behavior; interpretive scholars focus on conscious choices made by individuals.

The difference between these two views of human nature inevitably creeps into the language people use to explain what they do. Individuals who feel like puppets on strings say, "I *had* to . . . ," whereas people who feel they pull their own strings say, "I *decided* to. . . ." The first group speaks in a passive voice: "I was distracted from studying by the argument at the next table." The second group speaks in an active voice: "I stopped studying to listen to the argument at the next table."

In the same way, the language of scholarship often reflects theorists' views of human nature. Behavioral scientists usually describe human conduct as occurring *because of* forces outside the individual's awareness. Their causal explanations tend not to include appeals to mental reasoning or conscious choice. They usually describe behavior as the response to a prior stimulus. Schwartz' theory of resonance posits that messages triggering emotional memories from our past will inevitably affect us. We *will* be swayed by an ad that strikes a responsive chord.

In contrast, interpretive scholars tend to use explanatory phrases such as *in order to* and *so that* because they attribute a person's action to conscious intent. Their word selection suggests that people are free agents who could decide to respond differently under an identical set of circumstances. Marty, for example, uses the language of voluntary *action* rather than knee-jerk *behavior* when he writes, "It is only through a rebirth that we can reclaim what time and change have taken from us." If someone *reclaims* what was lost, it is an act of volition. The trainer decided to go to Chicago. Others who felt loss might not. The consistent interpreter

18   *OVERVIEW*

doesn't ask why this man made that choice. As Anderson explains, "True choice demands to be its own cause and its own explanation."[11]

Human choice is problematic for the behavioral scientist because as individual freedom goes up, predictability of behavior goes down. Conversely, the roots of humanism are threatened by a highly restricted view of human choice. In an impassioned plea, British author C. S. Lewis exposes the paradox of stripping away people's freedom and yet expecting them to exercise responsible choice:

> In a sort of ghastly simplicity we remove the organ and expect of them virtue and enterprise. We laugh at honor and are shocked to find traitors in our midst. We castrate and bid the geldings be fruitful.[12]

Lewis assumes that significant decisions are value laden; interpretive scholars would agree.

THE HIGHEST VALUE: OBJECTIVITY OR EMANCIPATION?

When we talk about values, we are discussing priorities, questions of relative worth.[13] Values are the traffic lights of our lives that guide what we think, feel, and do. The professional values of communication theorists reflect the commitments they've made concerning knowledge and human nature. Since most social scientists hold to a distinction between the "knower" and the "known," they place value on objectivity that's not biased by ideological commitments. Because humanists and others in the interpretive camp believe that the ability to choose is what separates humanity from the rest of creation, they value scholarship that expands the range of free choice.

As a behavioral scientist, Glenn works hard to maintain his objectivity. He is a man with strong moral and spiritual convictions, and these may influence the topics he studies. But he doesn't want his personal values to distort reality or confuse what *is* with what he thinks *ought to be.* As you can see from Glenn's call for objective testing, he is frustrated when theorists offer no *empirical evidence* for their claims or don't even suggest a way in which their ideas could be validated by an independent observer. He is even more upset when he hears of researchers who fudge the findings of their studies to shore up questionable hypotheses. Glenn shares the research values of Harvard sociologist George Homans—to let the evidence speak for itself: "When nature, however stretched out on the rack, still has a chance to say 'no'—then the subject is science."[14]

Empirical evidence
Data collected through direct observation.

Marty is aware of his own ideology and is not afraid to bring his values to bear upon a communication text and come under scrutiny. He doesn't take an overtly critical stance toward advertising or the capitalist system. But his insight of Bud framed as a constant companion and comforter gives us the resource to laugh at the irony of hugging a bottle of beer whenever we feel lonely or a sense of loss.

Critical interpreters value socially relevant research that seeks to liberate people from oppression of any sort—economic, political, religious, emotional, or any other. They decry the detached stance of scientists who refuse to take responsibility for the results of their work. Whatever the pursuit—a Manhattan Project to split the atom, a Genome Project to map human genes, or a class project to analyze the effectiveness of an ad—critical interpreters insist that knowledge is never neutral. "There is no safe harbor in which researchers can avoid the power structure."[15]

In the heading for this section, I've contrasted the primary values of scientific and interpretive scholars by using the labels *objectivity* and *emancipation.* University of Colorado communication professor Stan Deetz frames the issue somewhat differently. He says that every general communication theory has two priorities—*effectiveness* and *participation.*[16] Effectiveness is concerned with successfully communicating information, ideas, and meaning to others. It also includes persuasion. Participation is concerned with increasing the possibility that all points of view will affect collective decisions and individuals being open to new ideas. It also encourages difference, opposition, and independence. The value question is *Which concern has higher priority?* Objective theorists usually foreground effectiveness and relegate participation to the background. Interpretive theorists tend to focus on participation and downplay effectiveness.

Emancipation
Liberation from any form of political, economic, racial, religious, or sexual oppression; empowerment.

PURPOSE OF THEORY: UNIVERSAL LAWS OR INTERPRETIVE GUIDES?

Even if Glenn and Marty could agree on the nature of knowledge, the extent of human autonomy, and the ultimate values of scholarship, their words would still sound strange to each other because they use distinct vocabularies to accomplish different goals. As a behavioral scientist, Glenn is working to pin down universal laws of human behavior that cover a variety of situations. As a rhetorical critic, Marty strives to interpret a particular communication text in a specific context.

If these two scholars were engaged in fashion design rather than research design, Glenn would probably tailor a coat suitable for many occasions that covers everybody well—one size fits all. Marty might apply principles of fashion design to style a coat that makes an individual statement for a single client—a one-of-a-kind, custom creation. Glenn adopts a theory and then tests it to see if it covers everyone. Marty uses theory to make sense of unique communication events.

Since theory testing is the basic activity of the behavioral scientist, Glenn starts with a hunch about how the world works—perhaps the idea that stories are more persuasive than arguments. He then crafts a tightly worded hypothesis that temporarily commits him to a specific prediction. As an empiricist, he can never completely "prove" that he has made the right gamble; he can only show in test after test that his behavioral bet pays off. If repeated studies uphold his hypothesis, he can more confidently predict which media ads will be effective, explain why, and make recommendations on how practitioners can craft messages that stir up memories.

The interpretive scholar explores the web of meaning that constitutes human existence. When Marty creates scholarship, he isn't trying to prove theory. However, he sometimes uses the work of rhetorical theorists like Michael Osborn to inform his interpretation of the aural and visual texts of people's lives. Robert Ivie, former editor of the *Quarterly Journal of Speech,* suggests that rhetorical critics ought to use theory this way:

> We cannot conduct rhetorical criticism of social reality without benefit of a guiding rhetorical theory that tells us generally what to look for in social practice, what to make of it, and whether to consider it significant.[17]

OBJECTIVE OR INTERPRETIVE: WHY IS IT IMPORTANT?

Why is it important to grasp the differences between objective and interpretive scholarship? The first answer is because you can't fully understand a theory if you aren't familiar with its underlying assumptions about *truth, human nature,* the *purpose of the theory,* and its *values.* If you're clueless, things can get confusing fast. It's like the time my wife, Jeanie, and I were walking around the Art Institute of Chicago, enjoying the work of French impressionists who painted realistic scenes that I could recognize. Then I wandered into a room dedicated to abstract expressionism. The paintings seemed bizarre and made no sense to me. I was bewildered and somewhat disdainful until Jeanie, who is an artist, explained the goals these painters had and the techniques they used to achieve them. So too with interpretive and objective communication theories. Right now you are probably more familiar and comfortable with one approach than you are with the other. But when you understand what each type of theorist is about, your comfort zone will expand and your confusion will diminish.

There's another reason to master these *metatheoretical* differences. After exposure to a dozen or more theories, you may find that they begin to blur together in your mind. Classifying them as scientific or interpretive is a good way to keep them straight. It's somewhat like sorting 52 cards into suits—spades, hearts, diamonds, and clubs. In most sophisticated card games, the distinction is crucial. By the end of this course you could have up to 32 cards in your deck of communication theories. Being able to sort them in multiple combinations is a

Metatheory
Theory about theory; the stated or inherent assumptions made when creating a theory.

good way to show yourself and your professor that you've mastered the material. When you can compare and contrast theories on the basis of their interpretive or objective worldview, you've begun an integration that's more impressive than rote memorization.

Understanding the objective/interpretive choice points I've described can also help you decide the direction you want to take in your remaining course work. Some concentrations in the field of communication tend to have either a scientific or an interpretive bias. For example, all the theories we present in the relationship development, influence, and media effects sections of the book are proposed by objective scholars. Conversely, most of the theories we cover in the public rhetoric, media and culture, organizational communication, and gender and communication sections are interpretive. You'll want to see if this is true at your school before you choose the specific route you'll take.

Finally, theorists in both camps hope you'll care because each group believes that its brand of work holds promise for improving relationships and society. The scientist is convinced that knowing the truth about how communication works will give us a clearer picture of social reality. The interpreter is equally sure that unearthing communicator motivation and hidden ideologies will improve society by increasing free choice and discouraging unjust practices.

PLOTTING THEORIES ON AN OBJECTIVE–INTERPRETIVE SCALE

In this chapter I've introduced four important areas of difference between objective and interpretive communication scholars and the theories they create. A basic appreciation of these distinctions will help you understand where like-minded thinkers are going and why they've chosen a particular path to get there. But once you grasp how they differ, it will be helpful for you to realize that not all theorists fall neatly into one category or the other. Many have a foot in both camps. It's more accurate to picture the *objective* and *interpretive* labels as anchoring the ends of a continuum, with theorists spread out along the scale.

Objective _____ **Interpretive**

Figure 2–1 displays our evaluation of where each theory we feature fits on an objective–interpretive continuum. For easier reference to positions on the scale, we've numbered the five columns at the bottom of the chart. In placing a theory, we've tried to factor in choices the theorists have made about ways of knowing, human nature, what they value most, and the purpose of theory. We've consulted a number of scholars in the field to get their "read" on appropriate placements. They didn't always agree, but in most cases the discussion has sharpened our understanding of theory and the issues to be considered in the process of creating one. What we learned is reflected in the chapters ahead.

Of course, the position of each dot won't make much sense to you until you've read about the theory. But by looking at the pattern of distribution, you can see that roughly half the theories have an objective orientation, while the other half reflect an interpretive commitment. This 50–50 split matches the mix of scholarship we see in the field. When talking about relationships among the theories and the common assumptions made by a group of

22   *OVERVIEW*

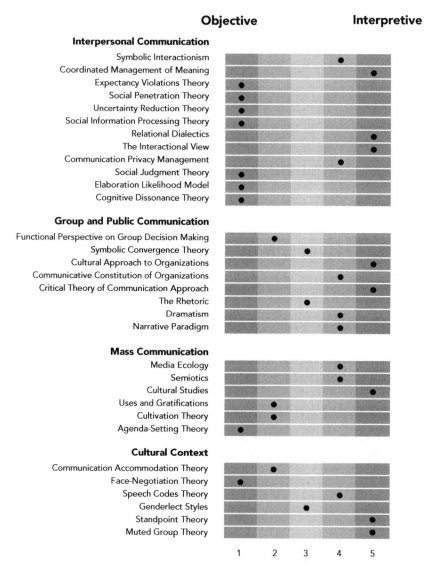

FIGURE 2–1   Classification of Communication Theories According to Objective/ Interpretive Worldview

theorists, your instructor may frequently refer back to this chart. So for easy reference, we reproduce the appropriate "slice" of the chart on the first page of each chapter.

Now that you have an idea of the differences between objective and interpretive theories, you may wonder whether some of these theories are better than others. We think so. Chapter 3, "Weighing the Words," offers a set of six standards you can use to judge the quality of objective theories, and a half dozen alternative criteria to discern the worth of interpretive theories. By applying the appropriate criteria, you can see if you agree with our evaluations.

QUESTIONS TO SHARPEN YOUR FOCUS

1. Compare Glenn Sparks' and Marty Medhurst's approaches to the Clydesdale commercial. Which analysis makes the most sense to you? Why?

2. How do scientists and interpretive scholars differ in their answers to the question *What is truth?* Which perspective do you find more satisfying?

3. How do you account for the wide-ranging diversity among types of interpretive theories (*rhetorical, critical, humanistic, postmodern,* etc.) as compared to the relative uniformity of objective theories?

4. Think of the communication classes you've taken. Did an *objective* or *interpretive* orientation undergird each course? Was this due more to the nature of the subject matter or to the professor's point of view?

A SECOND LOOK

Recommended resource: James A. Anderson and Geoffrey Baym, "Philosophies and Philosophic Issues in Communication 1995–2004," *Journal of Communication,* Vol. 54, 2004, pp. 589–615.

Metatheoretical overview: James A. Anderson, *Communication Theory: Epistemological Foundations,* Guilford, New York, 1996, pp. 13–77.

Metatheory: Robert T. Craig, "Metatheory," in *Encyclopedia of Communication Theory,* Sage, Los Angeles, CA, 2009, pp. 657–661.

Contemporary scientific scholarship: Charles Berger, Michael Roloff, and David Roskos-Ewoldsen (eds.), *Handbook of Communication Science,* 2nd ed., Sage, Los Angeles, CA, 2010.

Contemporary rhetorical scholarship: Sonja Foss, Karen Foss, and Robert Trapp, *Contemporary Perspectives on Rhetoric,* 3rd ed., Waveland, Prospect Heights, IL, 2000.

Defense of empirical scholarship: Robert Bostrom and Lewis Donohew, "The Case for Empiricism: Clarifying Fundamental Issues in Communication Theory," *Communication Monographs,* Vol. 59, 1992, pp. 109–129.

Defense of interpretive scholarship: Arthur Bochner, "Perspectives on Inquiry II: Theories and Stories," in *Handbook of Interpersonal Communication,* 2nd ed., Mark Knapp and Gerald Miller (eds.), Sage, Thousand Oaks, CA, 1994, pp. 21–41.

Scientific research: Glenn Sparks, *Media Effects Research: A Basic Overview,* 4th ed., Wadsworth, Belmont, CA, 2013.

Rhetorical analysis: Martin J. Medhurst, "Mitt Romney, 'Faith in America,' and the Dance of Religion and Politics in American Culture," *Rhetoric & Public Affairs,* Vol. 12, 2009, pp. 195–221.

For a historical perspective on the place of objective and
interpretive theory in the field of communication,
click on Talk about Theory in the Archive
under Theory Resources at
www.afirstlook.com.

CHAPTER 3

Weighing the Words

In Chapter 2 we looked at two distinct approaches to communication theory—objective and interpretive. Because the work of social scientists and interpreters is so different, they often have trouble understanding and valuing their counterparts' scholarship. This workplace tension parallels the struggle between Democrats and Republicans. Members of both political parties study the same financial reports, projected statistics, and potential solutions for fixing the nation's economic woes. Nevertheless, when it comes to proposing a plan of action, the two parties are often miles apart. The distance is usually due to the different assumptions each party uses to guide its thinking. Their philosophies can be so divergent that significant agreement seems impossible, and meaningful compromise only a pipe dream.

In politics, when it gets down to the nitty-gritty of adopting specific proposals and passing concrete laws, the partisan bickering can make the conversation tense. The same can be said of the disputes that are common between objective and interpretive communication scholars. Differences in ways of knowing, views of human nature, values, goals of theory building, and research methods seem to ensure tension and misunderstanding.

Friendly attitudes between empiricists and interpreters are particularly hard to come by when each group insists on applying its own standards of judgment to the work of the other group. As a first-time reader of communication theory, you could easily get sucked into making the same mistake. If you've had training in the scientific method and judge the value of every communication theory by whether it predicts human behavior, you'll automatically reject 50 percent of the theories presented in this book. On the other hand, if you've been steeped in the humanities and expect every theory to help unmask the meaning of a text, you'll easily dismiss the other half.

Regardless of which approach you favor, not all objective or interpretive communication theories are equally good. For each type, some are better than others. Like family members trying to decide which pizza to order, you'll want a way to separate the good, the bad, and the nasty. Since we've included theories originating in the social sciences as well as the humanities, you need to have two separate lenses through which to view their respective claims. This chapter offers that pair of bifocals. We hope by the time you finish you'll be on friendly terms with the separate criteria that behavioral scientists and a wide range of interpretive scholars use to weigh the words of their colleagues. We'll start with the standards that social scientists use to judge the worth of objective theories, and then turn to the criteria that interpretive scholars employ to evaluate their communication theories.

WHAT MAKES AN OBJECTIVE THEORY GOOD?

An objective theory is credible because it fulfills the twin objectives of scientific knowledge. The theory *predicts* some future outcome, and it *explains* the reasons for that outcome. Social scientists of all kinds agree on four additional criteria a theory must meet to be good—*relative simplicity, testability, practical utility,* and *quantifiable research.* As we discuss these standards, we will use the terms *objective* and *scientific* interchangeably.

Scientific Standard 1: Prediction of Future Events

A good objective theory predicts what will happen. Prediction is possible only when we are dealing with things we can see, hear, touch, smell, and taste over and over again. As we repeatedly notice the same things happening in similar situations, we begin to speak of invariable patterns or universal laws. In the realm of the physical sciences, we are seldom embarrassed. Objects don't have a choice about how to respond to a stimulus. The sun can't choose to rise in the west instead of the east.

The social sciences are another matter. Although theories of human behavior often cast their predictions with confidence, a good measure of humility on the part of the theorist is advisable. Even the best theory may only be able to speak about people in general, rather than about specific individuals—and these only in terms of probability and tendencies, not absolute certainty.

What do good scientific communication theories forecast? Some predict that a specific type of communication triggers a particular response. (Mutual self-disclosure creates interpersonal intimacy.) Other theories predict that people will use different types of communication depending upon some pre-existing factor. (People avoid messages that they think will be disagreeable so they won't experience cognitive dissonance.) These claims may or may not be true, but you should regard the scientific theories presented in this book as valuable to the extent that theorists are willing to make confident predictions about communication behavior.

Scientific Standard 2: Explanation of the Data

A good objective theory explains an event or human behavior. Philosopher of science Abraham Kaplan said that theory is a way of making sense out of a disturbing situation.[1] An objective theory should bring clarity to an otherwise jumbled state of affairs; it should draw order out of chaos.

A good social science theory describes the process, focuses our attention on what's crucial, and helps us ignore that which makes little difference. But it also goes beyond raw data and explains *why.* When Willie Sutton was asked why he robbed banks, urban legend says the Depression-era bandit replied, "Because that's where the money is." It's a great line, but as a theory of motivation, it lacks explanatory power. There's nothing in the words that casts light on the internal processes or environmental forces that led Sutton to crack a safe while others tried to crack the stock market.

Sometimes a communication theory can sound great but, upon closer inspection, it doesn't explain much. Years ago, researchers discovered that by having people answer a few key questions about the emotions they felt prior to giving a speech, they could predict which people would be the most nervous or apprehensive during the talk itself. A theory based on the research claimed that *communication apprehension* was a trait only some people possess. The theory had great predictive power in identifying nervous public speakers, but it lacked a good explanation for why some people became nervous and others didn't.[2] It merely suggested that nervous speakers possessed the trait of communication apprehension.

You can probably sense that this circular thinking leaves something to be desired. How do people acquire the trait? Are they born with it? Can they get rid of it through some type of intervention? Over the past few decades, theorists have grappled with the question of how well "trait" theories explain behavior.[3] If the rationale behind why people engage in certain behaviors is simply *That's the kind of people they are,* objective scholars won't be happy with the theory's explanatory power. As a student of communication theory, you shouldn't be either. When you evaluate an objective theory, keep in mind that the *reason* something happens becomes as important as the fact that it does.

Scientific Standard 3: Relative Simplicity

A good objective theory is as simple as possible—no more complex than it has to be. A few decades ago a cartoonist named Rube Goldberg made people laugh by sketching plans for complicated machines that performed simple tasks. His "better mousetrap" went through a sequence of 15 mechanical steps that were triggered by turning a crank and ended with a bird cage dropping over a cheese-eating mouse.

Goldberg's designs were funny because the machines were so needlessly convoluted. They violated the scientific principle called Occam's razor, so named because philosopher William of Occam implored theorists to "shave off" any assumptions, variables, or concepts that aren't really necessary to explain what's going on.[4] When you've concentrated on a subject for a long time, it's easy to get caught up in the grandeur of a theoretical construction. Yet the *rule of parsimony*—another label for the same principle—states that

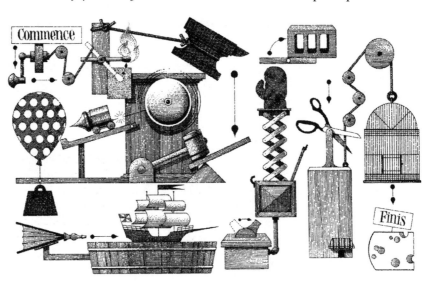

given two plausible explanations for the same event, we should accept the less complex version. Theoretical physicist Albert Einstein put it this way: "Any intelligent fool can make things bigger and more complex. . . . It takes a touch of genius—and a lot of courage—to move in the opposite direction."[5]

Rule of parsimony (Occam's razor)
Given two plausible explanations for the same event, we should accept the simpler version.

Einstein practiced what he preached. His elegant formula ($E = mc^2$) explains the relationships among energy, mass, time, and the speed of light using just three terms, and history credits him with more than a touch of genius. But relative simplicity doesn't necessarily mean *easy to understand*. Trained physicists admit they're still struggling to fully comprehend the theory of relativity. That theory is parsimonious not because it's a no-brainer, but because it doesn't carry the extraneous baggage rival theories carry as they try to explain why time stands still when you approach the speed of light.

Scientific Standard 4: Hypotheses That Can Be Tested

Falsifiability
The requirement that a scientific theory be stated in such a way that it can be tested and disproved if it is indeed wrong.

A good objective theory is testable. If a prediction is wrong, there ought to be a way to demonstrate the error. Karl Popper called this requirement *falsifiability*, and saw it as the defining feature of scientific theory.[6] But some theories are so loosely stated that it's impossible to imagine empirical results that could disprove their hypotheses. And if there is no way to prove a theory false, then any claim that it's true seems hollow. A boyhood example may help illustrate this point.

When I was 12 years old I had a friend named Mike. We spent many hours shooting baskets in his driveway. The backboard was mounted on an old-fashioned, single-car garage with double doors that opened outward like the doors on a cabinet. In order to avoid crashing into them on a drive for a layup, we'd open the doors during play. But since the doors would only swing through a 90-degree arc, they extended about 4 feet onto the court along the baseline.

One day Mike announced that he'd developed a "never-miss" shot. He took the ball at the top of the free-throw circle, drove toward the basket, then cut to the right corner. When he got to the baseline, he took a fade-away jump shot, blindly arcing the ball over the top of the big door. I was greatly impressed as the ball swished through the net. When he boasted that he never missed, I challenged him to do it again, which he did. But his third shot was an air ball—it completely missed the rim.

Before I could make the kind of bratty comment junior high school boys make, he quickly told me that the attempt had not been his never-miss shot. He claimed to have slipped as he cut to the right and therefore jumped from the wrong place. Grabbing the ball, he drove behind the door again and launched a blind arcing shot. Swish. *That*, he assured me, was his never-miss shot.

I knew something was wrong. I soon figured out that any missed attempt was, by definition, not the ballyhooed never-miss shot. When the ball went in, however, Mike heralded the success as added evidence of 100 percent accuracy. I now know that I could have called his bluff by removing the net from the basket so he couldn't hear whether the shot went through. This would have forced him to declare from behind the door whether the attempt was of the never-miss variety. But as long as I played by his rules, there was no way to disprove his claim.

Unfortunately, some theories are stated in a way that makes it impossible to prove them false. They shy away from the put-up-or-shut-up standard—they aren't testable. If it isn't possible to gather clear evidence that goes against a theory's claims, then it's also impossible to collect evidence that clearly supports those claims.

Scientific Standard 5: Practical Utility

Over time, a good objective theory is useful. Since an oft-cited goal of social science is to help people have more control over their daily lives, people facing the type of thorny social situations that the theory addresses should be able to benefit from its wisdom. This requirement is consistent with social psychologist Kurt Lewin's claim that there is nothing as practical as a good theory. A theory that communication practitioners find helpful may not be more valid than one to which few folks turn for guidance, but because of its influence, it may prove to be more valuable.

As you read about theories crafted from an objective perspective, let usefulness be one measure of their worth. A word of caution, however: Most of us can be a bit lazy or shortsighted, having a tendency to consider unimportant anything that's hard to grasp or can't be applied to our lives right now. Before considering a theory irrelevant, make certain you understand it and consider how others have made use of its insight. We'll try to do our part by presenting each theory as clearly as possible and suggesting potential applications. Perhaps you'll be even more interested in how other students have found a theory useful in their lives. That's why we've included a student-written application in almost all of the 32 chapters that feature a specific theory.

Scientific Standard 6: Quantitative Research

As the heading suggests, scientists tend to appeal to *numbers* as they gather evidence to support their theories. Almost all scientific research depends on a *comparison of differences*—this group compared to that group, this treatment as opposed to that treatment, these results versus those results. Since objective theorists aim to mirror reality, it makes sense for them to measure and report what they discover in precise numerical terms rather than in linguistic terms, which are open to interpretation. Enlightenment philosopher David Hume insisted on the superiority of quantitative methods over qualitative research:

> If we take in our hand any volume . . . let us ask: Does it contain any abstract reasoning concerning quantity or number? No. Does it contain any experimental reasoning concerning the matter of fact or existence? No. Commit it then to the flames, for it can contain nothing but sophistry and illusion.[7]

Given the radical nature of Hume's over-the-top pronouncement, we can wryly imagine the English philosopher making daily trips to a used bookstore for fuel to heat his home in winter. But the idea that numbers are more reliable than words does run deep in the scientific community. More than other quantitative methods, objective theorists use *experiments* and *surveys* to test their predictions.

Experiments.   Working under the assumption that human behavior is not random, an experimenter tries to establish a cause-and-effect relationship by

"Are you just pissing and moaning, or can you verify what you're saying with data?"

© Edward Koren/The New Yorker Collection/www.cartoonbank.com

Experiment

A research method that manipulates a variable in a tightly controlled situation in order to find out if it has the predicted effect.

Survey

A research method that uses questionnaires and structured interviews to collect self-reported data that reflects what respondents think, feel, or intend to do.

systematically manipulating one factor (the independent variable) in a tightly controlled situation to learn its effect on another factor (the dependent variable). A laboratory experiment would be an appropriate way to answer the question, *Does greater perceived attitude similarity lead to increased interpersonal attraction?* The experimenter might first identify a range of attitudes held by the participating subjects and then systematically alter the attitude information provided about an experimental confederate before they met. A similarity-causes-attraction hypothesis would be supported if the subjects whose attitudes meshed with what they thought the confederate believed ended up liking that person better than did those who thought they were quite different from the confederate.[8]

Surveys. Whether using questionnaires or structured interviews, survey researchers rely on self-reported data to discover people's past behavior and what they now think, feel, or intend to do. For example, media-effects researchers have used survey methodology to answer the research question, *Do people who watch a high amount of dramatic violence on television hold an exaggerated belief that the world is a mean and scary place?* They asked the number of hours a day the respondents watched TV and then gave a series of forced-choice options that tapped into respondents' perceived odds of becoming a victim of violence. The researchers discovered a positive relationship between the amount of viewing and the amount of fear.[9]

Although the presence of a correlation doesn't necessarily imply a causal relationship, it keeps that possibility alive. It's also the case that if a survey shows two variables *aren't* correlated, that's a powerful clue that one of the variables *isn't* a cause of the other. A survey can save valuable time that would otherwise be needed to establish cause-and-effect by conducting an experiment. In addition to the clues they provide about causal relationships, surveys are often the most convenient way to discover what people are thinking, feeling, and intending to do—the key components of our attitudes.

✕ WHAT MAKES AN INTERPRETIVE THEORY GOOD?

Unlike scientists, interpretive scholars don't have an agreed-on, six-point set of criteria for evaluating their theories. But, even though there is no universally approved model, rhetoricians, critical theorists, and other interpreters repeatedly urge that interpretive theories should accomplish some or all of the following functions: *identify values, create understanding, inspire aesthetic appreciation, stimulate agreement, reform society,* and *conduct qualitative research.* The rest of this chapter examines these oft-mentioned ideals.

Interpretive Standard 1: Clarification of Values

A good interpretive theory brings people's values into the open. The theorist actively seeks to acknowledge, identify, or unmask the ideology behind the message under scrutiny.

Interpretive theorists should also be willing to reveal their own ethical commitments. As Webster University dean of communication Eric Rothenbuhler states, "Theoretical positions have moral implications, and when we teach them, advocate their use by others, or promote policies based upon them they have moral consequences."[10] Of course, not all interpretive scholars occupy the same moral ground, but there are core values most of them share. For example, humanists usually place a premium on individual liberty. Klaus Krippendorff of the Annenberg School for Communication at the University of Pennsylvania wants to make sure that scholars' drive for personal freedom extends to the people they study. His *ethical imperative* directs the theorist to "grant others that occur in your construction the same autonomy you practice constructing them."[11] When theorists follow this rule, scholarly monologue gives way to collegial dialogue. In this way people have a say in what's said about them. This kind of communal assessment requires reporting multiple voices rather than relying on one or two informants.

Ethical imperative
Grant others that occur in your construction the same autonomy you practice constructing them.

Some interpretive scholars value equality as highly as they do freedom. This commitment leads to continual examination of the power relationships inherent in all communication. Critical theorists, in particular, insist that scholars can no longer remain ethically detached from the people they are studying or from the political and economic implications of their work. For critical theorists, "There is no safe harbor in which researchers can avoid the power structure."[12]

Interpretive Standard 2: New Understanding of People

Interpretive scholarship is good when it offers fresh insight into the human condition. Rhetorical critics, ethnographers, and other humanistic researchers seek to gain new understanding by analyzing the activity that they regard as uniquely human—symbolic interaction. As opposed to social science theorists who attempt to identify communication patterns common to all people, an interpretive scholar typically examines a one-of-a-kind speech community that exhibits a specific language style. By analyzing this group's communication practice, the researcher hopes to develop an understanding of local knowledge or members' unique rules for interaction. Interpretive theories are tools to aid this search for situated meaning.

Some critics fear that by relying on rhetorical theory, we will read our preconceived ideas into the text rather than letting the words speak for themselves. They suggest that there are times when we should "just say no" to theory. But University of Minnesota communication theorist Ernest Bormann noted that rhetorical theory works best when it suggests universal patterns of symbol-using: "A powerful explanatory structure is what makes a work of humanistic scholarship live on through time."[13]

Bormann's claim is akin to the behavioral scientist's insistence that theory explains why people do what they do. But the two notions are somewhat different. Science wants an objective explanation; humanism desires subjective understanding. Krippendorff urges us to recognize that we, as theorists, are both the cause and the consequence of what we observe. His *self-referential imperative* for building theory states, "Include yourself as a constituent of your own construction."[14]

> **Self-referential imperative**
> Include yourself as a constituent of your own construction.

Interpretive Standard 3: Aesthetic Appeal

The way a theorist presents ideas can capture the imagination of a reader just as much as the wisdom and originality of the theory he or she has created. As with any type of communication, both content and style make a difference. Objective theorists are constrained by the standard format for acceptable scientific writing—propositions, hypotheses, operationalized constructs, and the like. But interpretive theorists have more room for creativity, so aesthetic appeal becomes an issue. Although the elegance of a theory is in the eye of the beholder, clarity and artistry seem to be the two qualities needed to satisfy this aesthetic requirement.

No matter how great the insights the theory contains, if the essay describing them is disorganized, overwritten, or opaque, the theorist's ideas will come across murky rather than clear. A student of mine who fought through a theorist's monograph filled with esoteric jargon likened the experience to "scuba diving in fudge."

According to University of Pittsburgh professor Barbara Warnick, a rhetorical critic can fill one or more of four roles—artist, analyst, audience, and advocate.[15] As an artist, the critic's job is to spark appreciation. Along with clarity, it's another way to construct an interpretive theory with aesthetic appeal. By artfully incorporating imagery, metaphor, illustration, and story into the core of the theory, the theorist can make his or her creation come alive for others. We can't illustrate all of these artful devices in a single paragraph, but many students of rhetoric are moved by the way University of Wisconsin rhetorical critic Edwin Black summed up his analysis of Lincoln's Gettysburg address:

> The Gettysburg Address is, finally and inevitably, a projection of Lincoln himself, of his discretion, of his modesty on an occasion which invited him to don the mantle of the prophet, of his meticulous measure of how far he ought to go, of the assurance of his self-knowledge: his impeccable discernment of his own competence, his flawless sense of its depth and its limits. As an actor in history and a force in the world, Lincoln does not hesitate to comprehend history and the

world. But he never presumes to cast his mind beyond human dimensions. He does not recite divine intentions; he does not issue cosmic judgments. He knows, to the bottom, what he knows. Of the rest, he is silent.[16]

Interpretive Standard 4: Community of Agreement

We can identify a good interpretive theory by the amount of support it generates within a community of scholars who are interested and knowledgeable about the same type of communication. Interpretation of meaning is subjective, but whether the interpreter's case is reasonable or totally off the wall is ultimately decided by others in the field. Their acceptance or rejection is an objective fact that helps verify or vilify a theorist's ideas.

Sometimes interpretive theorists present a controversial thesis to an audience restricted to true believers—those who already agree with the author's position. But an interpretive theory can't meet the community of agreement standard unless it becomes the subject of widespread analysis. For example, former National Communication Association president David Zarefsky warns that rhetorical validity can be established only when a work is debated in the broad marketplace of ideas. For this Northwestern University rhetorical critic, sound arguments differ from unsound ones in that "sound arguments are addressed to the general audience of critical readers, not just to the adherents of a particular 'school' or perspective. . . . They open their own reasoning process to scrutiny."[17]

John Stewart is the editor of *Bridges, Not Walls*, a collection of humanistic articles on interpersonal communication. As the book has progressed through 11 editions, Stewart's judgment to keep, drop, or add a theoretical work has been made possible by the fact that interpretive scholarship is "not a solitary enterprise carried out in a vacuum." It is instead, he says, "the effort of a community of scholars who routinely subject their findings to the scrutiny of editors, referees, and readers."[18]

Interpretive Standard 5: Reform of Society

A good interpretive theory often generates change. Some interpretive scholars, but by no means all, aren't content merely to interpret the intended meanings of a text. Contrary to the notion that we can dismiss calls for social justice or emancipation as *mere rhetoric*, critical interpreters are reformers who can have an impact on society. They want to expose and publicly resist the ideology that permeates the accepted wisdom of a culture. Kenneth Gergen, a Swarthmore College social psychologist, states that theory has the capacity to challenge the guiding assumptions of the culture, to raise fundamental questions regarding contemporary social life, to foster reconsideration of that which is "taken for granted," and thereby to generate fresh alternatives for social action.[19]

Along with many interpretive scholars, *critical theorists* tend to reject any notion of permanent truth or meaning. They see society's economic, political, social, religious, and educational institutions as socially constructed by unjust communication practices that create or perpetuate gross imbalances of power. The aim of their scholarship is to unmask these communication practices in an

Critical theorists
Scholars who use theory to reveal unjust communication practices that create or perpetuate an imbalance of power.

attempt to stimulate change. To traditional thinkers, their activity looks like a few angry children in kindergarten knocking over other kids' blocks, but they are intentionally using theory to carve out a space where people without power can be heard. For example, a critical theorist working from a Marxist, feminist, or postmodern perspective might craft a theory to support an alternative interpretation of the Golden Rule, namely, *He who has the gold, rules.* The theorist would then apply this reinterpretation to a specific practice, perhaps the publishing and pricing of required textbooks such as the one you're reading. To the extent that the theory stimulates students to rethink, respond, and react to this "free-market" process, it is a good interpretive theory.

Interpretive Standard 6: Qualitative Research

While scientists use *numbers* to support their theories, interpretive scholars use *words.* That's the basic difference between quantitative and qualitative research. As the editors of the *Handbook of Qualitative Research* describe the process, "Qualitative researchers study things in their natural settings, attempting to make sense of, or to interpret, phenomena in terms of the meaning people bring to them."[20] A focus on meaning and significance is consistent with the maxim that once hung on the wall of Einstein's Princeton University office:[21]

> Not everything that can be counted counts, and
> not everything that counts can be counted.

The interpretive scholar's qualitative tools include open-ended interviews, focus groups, visual texts, artifacts, and introspection. But *textual analysis* and *ethnography* are the two methods most often used to study how humans use signs and symbols to create and infer meaning.

Textual Analysis.   The aim of *textual analysis* is to describe and interpret the characteristics of a message. Communication theorists use this term to refer to the intensive study of a single message grounded in a humanistic perspective.

Textual analysis
A research method that describes and interprets the characteristics of any text.

Rhetorical criticism is the most common form of textual research in the communication discipline. For example, rhetorical critics have asked, *What does Martin Luther King's choice of language in his "I Have a Dream" speech on the Washington mall reveal about his strategic intent?* They've then undertaken a close reading of the text and context of that famous speech and concluded that King was trying to simultaneously appeal to multiple audiences without alienating any of them.[22]

Ethnography.   The late Princeton anthropologist Clifford Geertz said that *ethnography* is "not an experimental science in search of law, but an interpretive [approach] in search of meaning."[23] As a sensitive observer of the human scene, Geertz was loath to impose his way of thinking onto a society's construction of reality. He wanted his theory of communication grounded in the meanings that people within a culture share. Getting it right means seeing it from their point of view.

Ethnography
A method of participant observation designed to help a researcher experience a culture's complex web of meaning.

When Stan Musial—one of the greatest baseball players in history—passed away in January 2013 at the age of 92, his many admirers took the opportunity to share their memories. One story that circulated revealed that Musial was an amateur ethnographer. After baseball was desegregated in 1945, Musial noticed a group of black players on his all-star team congregating in the back corner of the dugout to play poker. In an effort to start dialogue, foster team spirit, and begin friendships, Musial cautiously approached the table and sat down. He felt like he had entered another world. In order to befriend his black teammates, he had to learn their group rituals, linguistic expressions, and cultural experiences that were all unfamiliar to him. His task was even more difficult because he didn't know the first thing about poker. Gradually, through listening and making careful mental notes, Musial began to understand his teammates and see the game of baseball through their eyes instead of his. That's ethnography.[24]

CONTESTED TURF AND COMMON GROUND AMONG THEORISTS

Throughout this chapter we have urged using separate measures for weighing the merits of objective and interpretive theories. That's because the two sets of criteria reflect the divergent mindsets of scientists and interpretive scholars as outlined in Chapter 2. Perhaps the field of personality assessment offers a way to understand how deeply these differences run. Some of you have taken the Myers-Briggs Type Indicator, a test that measures individual preferences on four bipolar scales. The *sensing–intuition* scale shows how people perceive or acquire information—how they seek to find out about things. As you read through the descriptions of *sensing* and *intuition* below, consider how closely they reflect the contrast of objective and interpretive epistemology—different ways of knowing.[25]

Sensing.   One way to "find out" is to use your sensing function. Your eyes, ears, and other senses tell you what is actually there and actually happening, both inside and outside of yourself. Sensing is especially useful for appreciating the realities of a situation.

Intuition.   The other way to "find out" is through intuition, which reveals the meanings, relationships, and possibilities that go beyond the information from your senses. Intuition looks at the big picture and tries to grasp the essential patterns.

These are differences that make a difference. It's hard to imagine two theorists becoming intellectual soul mates if each discounts or disdains the other's starting point, method, and conclusion. Does that mean they can't be friends? Not necessarily. There are at least three reasons for guarded optimism.

A firm foundation for their friendship would be a mutual respect for each other's curiosity about the communication process and a recognition that they are both bringing the very best of their intellect to bear on what they study. A second basis for mutual appreciation would be an understanding that the strong point of science is a rigorous comparison of multiple messages or groups, while the forte of humanism is its imaginative, in-depth analysis of a single message or group. Anthropologist Gregory Bateson described *rigor* and *imagination* as the two great contraries of the mind. He wrote that either "by itself is lethal. Rigor alone is paralytic death, but imagination alone is insanity."[26]

A third reason for mutual appreciation can be seen in a side-by-side comparison of the two sets of criteria in Figure 3–1. The chart suggests that the standards set by scientists and the evaluative criteria used by interpretive theorists

Scientific Theory	Interpretive Theory
Prediction of Future	Clarification of Values
Explanation of Data	Understanding of People
Relative Simplicity	Aesthetic Appeal
Testable Hypothesis	Community of Agreement
Practical Utility	Reform of Society
Quantitative Research	Qualitative Research

FIGURE 3–1   Summary of Criteria for Evaluating Communication Theory

share some similarities. Work down through the chart line-by-line and note a bit of overlap for each pair of terms. Here are the points of contact we see:

1. Both *prediction* and *value clarification* look to the future. The first suggests what *will* happen, the second, what *ought* to happen.

2. An *explanation* of communication behavior can lead to further *understanding* of people's motivation.

3. For many students of theory, *simplicity* has an *aesthetic appeal.*

4. *Testing hypotheses* is a way of achieving a *community of agreement.*

5. What could be more *practical* than a theory that *reforms* unjust practices?

6. Both *quantitative research* and *qualitative research* reflect a commitment to learn more about communication.

Identifying reasons for mutual appreciation doesn't guarantee respect. Republicans and Democrats have a common goal to bring about a more perfect union, but it's often impossible to see anything more than political gridlock when members of the two parties get together. Similarly, when objective and interpretive theorists work in the same academic department, tensions can run high. At the very least, the two scholarly communities should have a familiarity with each other's work. That's one reason we've elected to present objective as well as interpretive theories in this book.

You'll find that we often refer to these requirements for good theory in the critique sections at the end of each chapter. As you might expect, the 32 theories stack up rather well—otherwise we wouldn't have picked them in the first place. But constructing theory is difficult, and most theories have an Achilles' heel that makes them vulnerable to criticism. All of the theorists readily admit a need for fine-tuning their work, and some even call for major overhauls. We encourage you to weigh their words by the standards you think are important before reading the critique at the end of each chapter.

QUESTIONS TO SHARPEN YOUR FOCUS

1. How can we call a scientific theory good if it is *capable of being proved wrong?*

2. How can we decide when a *rhetorical critic* provides a *reasonable interpretation?*

36 *OVERVIEW*

3. All theories involve trade-offs; no theory can meet every standard of quality equally well. Of the 12 *criteria* discussed, which two or three are most important to you? Which one is least important?

4. Do you think objective scholars have any room in their approach for *intuition?* If so, how might that work? Do interpretive scholars have any space for *sensing?*

A SECOND LOOK

Scientific evaluation: Steven Chaffee, "Thinking About Theory," in *An Integrated Approach to Communication Theory and Research,* 2nd ed., Don Stacks and Michael Salwen (eds.), Routledge, NY, 2009, pp. 13–29.

Interpretive evaluation: Klaus Krippendorff, "On the Ethics of Constructing Communication," in *Rethinking Communication: Vol. 1,* Brenda Dervin, Lawrence Grossberg, Barbara O'Keefe, and Ellen Wartella (eds.), Sage, Newbury Park, CA, 1989, pp. 66–96.

Progress in scientific research: Franklin Boster, "On Making Progress in Communication," *Human Communication Research,* Vol. 28, 2002, pp. 473–490.

Quantitative theory: Michael Beatty, "Thinking Quantitatively," in Stacks and Salwen, pp. 30–39.

Qualitative theory: James A. Anderson, "Thinking Qualitatively," in Stacks and Salwen, pp. 40–58.

Quantitative methods: Franklin Boster and John Sherry, "Alternative Methodological Approaches to Communication Science," in *The Handbook of Communication Science,* 2nd ed., Charles Berger, Michael Roloff, and David Roskos-Ewoldsen (eds.), Sage, Los Angeles, CA, 2010, pp. 55–71.

Qualitative methods: Norman Denzin and Yvonna Lincoln, *Collecting and Interpreting Qualitative Materials,* Sage, Thousand Oaks, CA, 1998.

To view a chapter-by-chapter list of changes from the previous edition, click on Changes under Theory Resources at *www.afirstlook.com.*

CHAPTER 4

Mapping the Territory
(Seven Traditions in the Field of Communication Theory)

In Chapter 1, we presented working definitions for the concepts of *communication* and *theory*. In Chapters 2 and 3, we outlined the basic differences between objective and interpretive communication theories. These distinctions should help bring order out of chaos when your study of theory seems confusing. And it may seem confusing. University of Colorado communication professor Robert Craig describes the field of communication theory as awash with hundreds of unrelated theories that differ in starting point, method, and conclusion. He suggests that our field of study resembles "a pest control device called the Roach Motel that used to be advertised on TV: Theories check in, but they never check out."[1]

My mind conjures up a different image when I try to make sense of the often baffling landscape of communication theory. I picture a scene from the film *Harry Potter and the Chamber of Secrets* in which the boy wizard ventures into the Forbidden Forest. Inside, he finds it teeming with all kinds of spiders. Some are big, others small, but all look like they might want to eat him for lunch. He's overwhelmed at the sight of them—perhaps not unlike how you felt when you first saw the table of contents for this book. Harry discovers that the spiders momentarily retreat from the bright light of his wand, letting him secure a safe place to stand. It's my hope that the core ideas of Chapters 1–3 will provide you with that kind of space. The fantasy nature of the film is such that I could even imagine Harry emerging from the forest with all the spiders bound together in two sticky webs—the objective batch in his right hand and the interpretive batch in his left. But that's an overly simplistic fantasy. Craig offers a more sophisticated solution.

Craig agrees that the terrain is confusing if we insist on looking for some kind of grand theoretical overview that brings all communication study into focus—a top-down, satellite picture of the communication theory landscape. He suggests, however, that communication theory is a coherent field when we understand communication as a practical discipline.[2] He's convinced that our search for different types of theory should be grounded where real people grapple with everyday problems and practices of communication. Craig explains that "all communication theories are relevant to a common practical lifeworld in which *communication* is already a richly meaningful term."[3] Communication theory is the systematic and thoughtful response of communication scholars to questions posed as humans interact with one another—the best thinking within a practical discipline.

Craig thinks it's reasonable to talk about a *field of communication theory* if we take a collective look at the actual approaches researchers have used to study communication problems and practices. He identifies seven established traditions of communication theory that include most, if not all, of what theorists have done. These already established traditions offer "distinct, alternative vocabularies" that describe different "ways of conceptualizing communication problems and practices."[4] This means that scholars within a given tradition talk comfortably with one another but often take potshots at those who work in other camps. As Craig suggests, we shouldn't try to smooth over these between-group battles. Theorists argue because they have something important to argue about.

In the rest of the chapter I'll outline the seven traditions Craig describes. Taken together, they reveal the breadth and diversity that span the field of communication theory. The classifications will also help you understand why some theories share common ground, while others are effectively fenced off from each other by conflicting goals and assumptions. As I introduce each tradition, I'll highlight how its advocates tend to define communication, suggest a practical communication problem that this kind of theory addresses, and provide an example of research that the tradition has inspired.[5] Since I find that the topic of friendship is of great interest to most college students, the seven research studies I describe will show how each tradition approaches this type of close relationship.

THE SOCIO-PSYCHOLOGICAL TRADITION

Communication as Interpersonal Interaction and Influence

The socio-psychological tradition epitomizes the scientific or objective perspective described in Chapter 2. Scholars in this tradition believe there are communication truths that can be discovered by careful, systematic observation. They look for cause-and-effect relationships that will predict the results when people communicate. When they find causal links, they are well on the way to answering the ever-present question that relationship and persuasion practitioners ask: *How can I get others to change?* In terms of generating theory, the socio-psychological tradition is by far the most prolific of the seven that Craig names. This disciplinary fact of life is reflected in the many theories of this type that we present in the book.

When researchers search for universal laws of communication, they try to focus on what *is* without being biased by their personal view of what *ought to be*. As social scientists, they heed the warning of the skeptical newspaper editor: "You think your mother loves you? Check it out—at least two sources." For communication theorists in the socio-psychological tradition, checking it out usually means designing a series of surveys or controlled experiments. That's been our approach.

Teaching at a small liberal arts college where I've had the opportunity to be personally involved in the lives of my students, I've always wondered if there's a way to predict which college friendships will survive and thrive after graduation. As someone trained in the socio-psychological tradition, I began a longitudinal study spanning two decades to find out the answer.[6] I asked 45 pairs of best friends to respond to questions about (1) when they became close friends; (2) the similarity of their academic majors; (3) their range of mutual-touch behavior;

(4) their perceived status difference; and (5) the extent to which they avoided discussing awkward topics. I also (6) assessed their self-disclosure to each other and (7) measured their communication efficiency by watching them play two rounds of the cooperative word game *Password.* Would any of these measures forecast who would be friends forever?

In order to determine the answer, I needed a reliable and valid measure of relational closeness. Based on social psychologist Harold Kelley's interactional theory, which suggests that close relationships are characterized by "strength, frequency, diversity, and duration," Glenn and I developed a composite measure that assessed these properties.[7] For example, we gauged *relative strength* by asking the pair how many friends they now have to whom they feel closer than their college best friend. And we assessed *frequency of contact* by counting the number of times over the last year that the pair communicated face-to-face, over the phone, by letter, and through email.

Nineteen years after the initial study, Andrew helped me locate the study participants and asked them to respond to the measures of relational closeness mentioned above. We weren't surprised that participants with a longer history as best friends when they came to the study were most likely to remain close two decades later. Past behavior tends to be a good predictor of future behavior. Of more interest to us as communication scholars was the fact that those with similar academic majors and those with better scores on the *Password* game also remained close.[8] Remember that participants' choice of major and the *Password* game occurred about two decades earlier, yet these factors still predicted friendship long after college. It appears that communicating on the same wavelength and sharing common academic interests is a boon to long-lasting friendship. Maybe it's no surprise, then, that working together on this research project solidified our friendship with each other. Eventually, that friendship led to the three of us joining together to write the book you're reading now.

Theorists and researchers working within the socio-psychological tradition often call for longitudinal empirical studies. Only by using this type of research design could we predict which pairs were likely to be friends forever.

THE CYBERNETIC TRADITION

Communication as a System of Information Processing

MIT scientist Norbert Wiener coined the word *cybernetics* to describe the field of artificial intelligence.[9] The term is a transliteration of the Greek word for "steersman" or "governor," and it illustrates the way feedback makes information processing possible in our heads and on our laptops. During World War II, Wiener developed an anti-aircraft firing system that adjusted future trajectory by taking into account the results of past performance. His concept of feedback anchored the cybernetic tradition, which regards communication as the link connecting the separate parts of any system, such as a computer system, a family system, a media system, or a system of social support. Theorists in the cybernetic tradition seek to answer such questions as *How does the system work? What could change it?* and *How can we get the bugs out?*

Cybernetics
The study of information processing, feedback, and control in communication systems.

University of Washington communication professor Malcolm Parks studies personal relationships by asking both partners to describe their social network. In one major study of college students' same-sex friendships, he separately asked

40   *OVERVIEW*

each partner to prepare a list of his or her closest relationships, including four family members and eight non-family ties.[10] In almost all cases, the eight people who weren't family were other friends or romantic partners rather than co-workers, coaches, or teachers. Parks then had the two friends trade their lists and asked them questions that probed their relationship with the key people in their *friend's* social network. These included:

1. Prior contact: Which people did you know before you met your friend?
2. Range of contact: How many of them have you now met face-to-face?
3. Communication: How often do you communicate with each of them?
4. Liking: How much do you like or dislike each of the ones you know?
5. Support: To what extent does each of them support your friendship?
6. Support: To what extent does *your own* network support your friendship?

Note that the first four questions establish the links within and between the friends' social networks. Both support questions reveal the feedback friends receive from these support systems.

Using a number of traditional measures that assess personal relationships, Parks measured the amount of *communication* between the friends, the *closeness* of their relationship, and their *commitment* to see it continue. When he compared these three measures to the quantity and quality of links to their friend's social network, the results were striking. Friends who had multiple and positive interactions with their partner's social networks had more communication with, closeness to, and commitment toward their partner than friends who had little involvement and felt little support from these folks. Friendships don't exist in a vacuum; they are embedded in a network that processes social information.

THE RHETORICAL TRADITION

Communication as Artful Public Address

Rhetoric
The art of using all available means of persuasion, focusing on lines of argument, organization of ideas, language use, and delivery in public speaking.

Whether speaking to a crowd, congregation, legislative assembly, or jury, public speakers have sought practical advice on how to best present their case. Well into the twentieth century, the rhetorical theory and advice from Plato, Aristotle, Cicero, Quintilian, and other Greco-Roman rhetors served as the main source of wisdom about public speaking. There are a half-dozen features that characterize this influential tradition of rhetorical communication:

- A conviction that speech distinguishes humans from other animals. Cicero suggested that only oral communication had the power to lead humanity out of its brutish existence and establish communities with rights of citizenship.[11]

- A confidence that public address delivered in a democratic forum is a more effective way to solve political problems than rule by decree or resorting to force. Within this tradition, the phrase *mere rhetoric* is a contradiction in terms.

- A setting in which a single speaker attempts to influence multiple listeners through persuasive discourse. Effective communication requires audience adaptation.

- Oratorical training as the cornerstone of a leader's education. Speakers learn to deliver strong arguments in powerful voices that carry to the edge of a crowd.

- An emphasis on the power and beauty of language to move people emotionally and stir them to action. Rhetoric is more art than science.

- Oral public persuasion as the province of males. A key feature of the women's movement has been the struggle for the right to speak in public.

Readers of Aristotle's *The Rhetoric* may be surprised to find a systematic analysis of friendship. He defines a friend as "one who loves and is loved in return."[12] The Greek word for this kind of love is *philia*, as in Philadelphia (the city of brotherly love). Based on this mutual love, Aristotle says a friend takes pleasure when good things happen to the other and feels distress when the other goes through bad times—emotions experienced for no other reason than the fact that they are friends. Aristotle then catalogs more than 20 personal qualities that make people attractive to us as friends. For example, we have friendly feelings toward those who are pleasant to deal with, share our interests, aren't critical of others, are willing to make or take a joke, and show that they "are very fond of their friends and not inclined to leave them in the lurch."[13] Although Aristotle wrote 2,500 years ago, this last quality resonates with Bill Withers' classic song "Lean On Me," recently covered by the cast of the hit Fox comedy *Glee*. A good friend helps you make it through tough times.[14]

You might have trouble seeing the link between the main features of the rhetorical tradition and Aristotle's comments on friendship. After an in-depth study on Aristotle's entire body of work—not just *The Rhetoric*—St. John's University philosopher Eugene Garver concluded that Aristotle didn't analyze friendship as a way to help Greek citizens develop close relationships.[15] Rather, he was instructing orators on how to make their case seem more probable by creating a feeling of goodwill among the audience. If by word and deed a speaker appears friendly, listeners will be more open to the message.

Twenty-five years ago I wrote a book on friendship and suggested the title *Making Friends*. The publisher liked my proposal, but at the last minute added a phrase. I was startled when the book came out entitled *Making Friends (and Making Them Count)*.[16] I'm uncomfortable with the idea of using friends as a means to achieve other goals. According to Garver, Aristotle had no such qualms. Rhetoric is the discovery of all available means of persuasion.

THE SEMIOTIC TRADITION

Communication as the Process of Sharing Meaning Through Signs

Semiotics
The study of verbal and nonverbal signs that can stand for something else, and how their interpretation impacts society.

Symbols
Arbitrary words and nonverbal signs that bear no natural connection with the things they describe; their meaning is learned within a given culture.

Semiotics is the study of signs. A *sign* is anything that can stand for something else. High body temperature is a <u>sign</u> of infection. Birds flying south <u>signal</u> the coming of winter. A white cane <u>signi</u>fies blindness. An arrow de<u>sign</u>ates which direction to go.

Words are also signs, but of a special kind. They are *symbols*. Unlike the examples I've just cited, words are arbitrary symbols that have no inherent meaning, no natural connection with the things they describe. For example, there's nothing in the sound of the word *share* or anything visual in the letters *h-u-g* that signifies a good friendship. One could just as easily coin the term *snarf* or *clag* to symbolize a close relationship between friends. The same thing is true for nonverbal symbols like *winks* or *waves*.

Cambridge University literary critic I. A. Richards railed against the semantic trap that he labeled "the proper meaning superstition"—the mistaken belief

42   *OVERVIEW*

that words have a precise definition. For Richards and other semiologists, meaning doesn't reside in words or other symbols; meaning resides in people. Most theorists grounded in the semiotic tradition are trying to explain and reduce the misunderstanding created by the use of ambiguous symbols.

Communication professor Michael Monsour (Metropolitan State University of Denver) recognized that the word *intimacy* used in the context of friendship might mean different things to different people, and the disparity could lead to confusion or misunderstanding. So he asked 164 communication students what they meant by intimacy when used in reference to their same-sex and their opposite-sex friends. Roughly two-thirds of the respondents were female, two-thirds were single, and two-thirds were under the age of 30. Participants offered 27 distinct interpretations of intimacy between friends, and the number of meanings suggested by each respondent ranged from 1–5, with an average of two different meanings per person.[17]

Seven meanings were mentioned often enough to include them in the final analysis. Self-disclosure was by far the meaning of intimacy mentioned most. In rank-order of frequency, the seven interpretations were:

1. Self-disclosure: Revelations about self that the friend didn't know

2. Emotional expressiveness: Closeness, warmth, affection, and caring

3. Physical contact: Nonsexual touch

4. Trust: Confidence that the other is reliable

5. Unconditional support: Being there for the other in good times and bad

6. Sexual contact: Overt sexual activity

7. Activities: Doing things together of a nonsexual nature

The content and order of the top five interpretations of intimacy held relatively constant for both opposite-sex and same-sex friendships, whether the respondent was a man or a woman. The notable deviations were that a few more men in opposite-sex friendships thought of intimacy as sexual contact, but in same-sex relationships characterized intimacy as activities together. For Monsour, the major contribution of this study is that for friends in both kinds of relationships, the word *intimacy* is multidimensional—a polysemic linguistic sign. A symbol like this can easily be misunderstood. Yet if two of the students in Monsour's study referred to intimacy in a conversation, with a few exceptions, it's likely that they'd understand what the other was talking about.

THE SOCIO-CULTURAL TRADITION

Communication as the Creation and Enactment of Social Reality

The socio-cultural tradition is based on the premise that as people talk, they produce and reproduce culture. Most of us assume that words reflect what actually exists. However, theorists in this tradition suggest that the process often works the other way around. Our view of reality is strongly shaped by the language we've used since we were infants.

University of Chicago linguist Edward Sapir and his student Benjamin Lee Whorf were pioneers in the socio-cultural tradition. The Sapir–Whorf hypothesis of linguistic relativity states that the structure of a culture's language shapes what people think and do.[18] "The 'real world' is to a large extent unconsciously built upon the language habits of the group."[19] Their theory of linguistic relativity counters the assumption that words merely act as neutral vehicles to carry meaning. Language actually structures our perception of reality.

Sapir–Whorf hypothesis of linguistic relativity
The claim that the structure of a language shapes what people think and do; the social construction of reality.

Contemporary socio-cultural theorists grant even more power to language. They claim that it is through the process of communication that "reality is produced, maintained, repaired, and transformed."[20] Or, stated in the active voice, *persons-in-conversation co-construct their own social worlds.*[21] When these worlds collide, the socio-cultural tradition offers help in bridging the culture gap that exists between "us" and "them."

Patricia Sias, a communication professor at the University of Arizona, takes a socio-cultural approach when studying friendships that form and dissolve in organizational settings. She writes that "relationships are not entities external to the relationship partners, but are mental creations that depend on communication for their existence and form. . . . If relationships are constituted in communication they are also *changed* through communication."[22] Sias uses a social construction lens through which to view deteriorating friendships in the workplace.

Sias located 25 people in a variety of jobs who were willing to talk about their failing workplace friendships. Some relationships were between peer co-workers, others between a supervisor and a subordinate. All the workers spontaneously told stories about their deteriorating friendship that revealed how communication between the two co-workers had changed. Although the friendships went sour for a variety of reasons—personality problems, distracting life events, conflicting expectations, betrayal, and promotion—the *way* the friendships dissolved was remarkably similar. Almost all workers told stories of using indirect communication to change the relationship.

While their friendships were deteriorating, the former friends still had to talk with each other in order to accomplish their work. But these co-workers stopped eating lunch together and spending time together outside the office. While on the job they avoided personal topics and almost never talked about the declining state of their relationship. Even seemingly safe topics such as sports or movies were no longer discussed; small talk and watercooler chitchat disappeared.

Although linguistic connection was sparse, nonverbal communication spoke loudly. The workers who talked with Sias recalled the lack of eye contact, snappy or condescending tones of voice, and physically backing away from the other. Ideally, social construction research in the office would capture the real-time communication of co-workers, but that would require a video-recorded account of office conversations when the friendship was in the process of deteriorating—a high hurdle for Sias to clear. As for contrasting narratives, she notes that "the damaged nature of the relationships made it difficult to recruit both partners in each friendship."[23] Yet without the actual dialogue of both conversational partners to examine, any statement about their co-creation of social reality must remain tentative.

THE CRITICAL TRADITION

Communication as a Reflective Challenge to Unjust Discourse

The term *critical theory* comes from the work of a group of German scholars known as the "Frankfurt School" because they were part of the independent Institute for Social Research at Frankfurt University. Originally set up to test the ideas of Karl Marx, the Frankfurt School rejected the economic determinism of orthodox Marxism yet carried on the Marxist tradition of critiquing society.

What types of communication practice and research are critical theorists *against*? Although there is no single set of abuses that all of them denounce, critical theorists consistently challenge three features of contemporary society:

1. *The control of language to perpetuate power imbalances.* Critical theorists condemn any use of words that inhibits emancipation.

2. *The role of mass media in dulling sensitivity to repression.* Critical theorists see the "culture industries" of television, film, music, and print media as reproducing the dominant ideology of a culture and distracting people from recognizing the unjust distribution of power within society.

3. *Blind reliance on the scientific method and uncritical acceptance of empirical findings.* Critical theorists are suspicious of empirical work that scientists say is ideologically free, because science is not the value-free pursuit of knowledge that it claims to be.

Culture industries
Entertainment businesses that reproduce the dominant ideology of a culture and distract people from recognizing unjust distribution of power within society; e.g., film, television, music, and advertising.

University of Louisville communication professor Kathy Werking agrees that personal relationship research decisions aren't neutral. In a chapter titled "Cross-Sex Friendship Research as Ideological Practice," Werking acknowledges that the reigning cultural model of relationships between women and men is one of romance. Yet she is critical of scholars for continually reproducing this heterosexual ideology to the point where it seems natural or just common sense to assume that all close male–female relationships are about sex and romance.[24]

In support of her ideological critique, Werking notes that academic journals devoted to the study of personal relationships publish vastly more articles on dating, courtship, and marriage than they do on opposite-sex friendships. Even when a rare study of opposite-sex friendship is reported, the author usually compares this type of relationship unfavorably with romantic ties that "may or may not include equality, are passionate, and have the goal of marriage."[25] Friendship, Werking claims, is best "based on equality, affection, communion, and is an end in itself."[26] This disconnect puts opposite-sex friends in a bind. They have no language that adequately describes or legitimizes their relationship. The term *just friends* downplays its importance, *platonic friends* has an archaic connotation, and if they use the word *love*, it must be qualified so that no one gets the wrong idea.

Werking also criticizes Western scholars for the individualistic ideology that permeates their opposite-sex research. She says they equate biological sex characteristics with gender identity—an assumption that precludes the possibility that masculine and feminine orientations are socially created and can change over time. They also assume that the perceptions of one friend adequately represent the complexity of what's going on in the relationship. And rather than observe friends' actual interactions over time, they naively rely on freeze-frame responses on a structured survey to provide sufficient information to understand a relationship. Werking claims that all of these research practices do an injustice to men and women in opposite-sex relationships.

THE PHENOMENOLOGICAL TRADITION

Communication as the Experience of Self and Others Through Dialogue

Phenomenology
Intentional analysis of everyday experience from the standpoint of the person who is living it; explores the possibility of understanding the experience of self and others.

Although *phenomenology* is an imposing philosophical term, it basically refers to the intentional analysis of everyday life from the standpoint of the person who is living it. Thus, the phenomenological tradition places great emphasis on people's perception and their interpretation of their own experience. For the phenomenologist, an individual's story is more important, and more authoritative, than any research hypothesis or communication axiom. As psychologist Carl Rogers asserted, "Neither the Bible nor the prophets—neither Freud nor research—neither the revelations of God nor man—can take precedence over my own direct experience."[27]

The problem, of course, is that no two people have the same life story. Since we cannot experience another person's experience, we tend to talk past each other and then lament, "Nobody understands what it's like to be me." Thus, theorists who work within the phenomenological tradition seek to answer two questions: *Why is it so hard to establish and sustain authentic human relationships?* and *How can this problem be overcome?*

Communication professor Bill Rawlins (Ohio University) works within this tradition as he studies friendship by taking an in-depth look at the actual conversations between friends. In his book *The Compass of Friendship: Narratives, Identities, and Dialogues,* he devotes an entire chapter to a 90-minute recorded conversation between Chris and Karen, two women who agree they've been friends for "30 years and counting."[28] Rawlins provided no guidelines or instructions. The women only know that he is interested in their friendship. After an hour of recounting stories about shared experiences, Chris brings up Karen's slow retreat into silence the past winter. Obviously bothered by losing contact, Chris continues . . .

> CHRIS: And I thought, "Well that's okay; everybody has these times when they feel this way." But I feel like you should *alert* people that *care* about you [laughs] to the fact that this is what is goin' on—
>
> KAREN: [laughs] Yeah . . .
>
> CHRIS: "I'm going into my cave. See ya in the spring," or whatever. Or "I don't wish to have anything, writing or any communications for a while. Not to worry. Adios. Bye to everybody. Hasta la vista or whatever."
>
> KAREN: Yeah.
>
> CHRIS: Or something, because I [pause], I [pause], I . . .
>
> KAREN: You were worried.[29]

The dialogue above is less than a minute of the women's conversation, yet it provides a rich resource for Rawlins' insight into their friendship. Chris says to herself at the time that such feelings are commonplace and "OK." Even so, she believes that Karen "should *alert* people that *care* about you to the fact that this is going on. . . ." They both laugh at this paradoxical recommendation that Karen communicate to significant others that she does not intend to communicate with them. Chris rehearses two voices for Karen here: a humorous one that trades on a hibernation metaphor, and then a more serious, explicit statement with Spanish flourishes at the end that seem to add a comical flavor. As Karen affirms this idea, however, Chris surrenders her comic tone and makes the frank request, "Or something," haltingly trying to offer her reasons, "I [pause], I [pause], I . . . ," which Karen completes for her: "You were worried." In short, Karen again recognizes the emotional basis of Chris' concerns and legitimates Chris' suggested policy for communicating social withdrawal.[30]

Rawlins' reconstruction of this segment reveals how *he* experiences the women's friendship. After reading his interpretation of the entire conversation, the women independently tell him that he was "right on" and had "nailed it."[31] That's because he paid attention to *their* interpretation of their experience.

FENCING THE FIELD OF COMMUNICATION THEORY

The seven traditions I've described have deep roots in the field of communication theory. Team loyalties run strong, so theorists, researchers, and practitioners working within one tradition often hear criticism from those in other traditions that their particular approach has no legitimacy. In addition to whatever arguments each group might muster to defend their choice, they can also claim "squatters' rights" because scholars who went before had already established the right to occupy that portion of land. Taking the real estate metaphor seriously, in Figure 4–1, I've charted the seven traditions as equal-area parcels of land that collectively make up the larger field of study. A few explanations are in order.

First, it's important to realize that the location of each tradition on the map is far from random. My rationale for placing them where they are is based on the distinction between objective and interpretive theories outlined in Chapter 2. According to the scientific assumptions presented in that chapter, the socio-psychological tradition is the most objective, and so it occupies the far left position on the map—solidly rooted in objective territory. Moving across the map from left to right, the traditions become more interpretive and less objective. Some students wonder why rhetoric is rated more objective than semiotics. It's because rhetoricians have traditionally regarded what language refers to as "real," whereas semiologists perceive the relationship between a word and its referent as more tenuous. I see the phenomenological tradition as the most subjective of the seven traditions, and so it occupies the position farthest to the right—firmly grounded in interpretive territory. The order of presentation in this chapter followed the same progression—a gradual shift from objective to interpretive concerns. Scholars working in adjacent traditions usually have an easier time appreciating each other's work. On the map they share a common border. Professionally, they are closer together in their basic assumptions.

Second, hybrids are possible across traditions. You've seen throughout this chapter that each tradition has its own way of defining communication and its own distinct vocabulary. Thus, it's fair to think of the dividing lines on the map as fences built to keep out strange ideas. Scholars, however, are an independent bunch. They climb fences, read journals, and fly to faraway conferences. This cross-pollination sometimes results in theory grounded in two or three traditions.

Finally, the seven charted traditions might not cover every approach to communication theory. Craig recently suggested the possibility of a *pragmatist tradition*—a pluralistic land where different perspectives on truth could all be

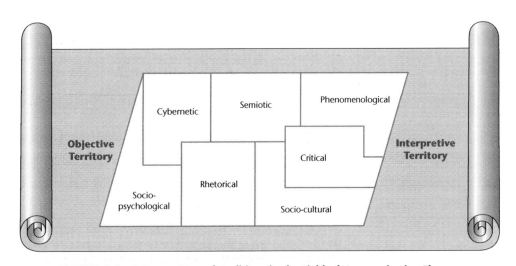

FIGURE 4–1 A Survey Map of Traditions in the Field of Communication Theory

48   *OVERVIEW*

Pragmatism
An applied approach to knowledge; the philosophy that true understanding of an idea or situation has practical implications for action.

legitimate in different ways. He pictures it as a tradition that "orients to practical problems, and evaluates ideas according to their usefulness rather than by an absolute standard of truth."[32] It would be a location where he sees his own work fitting in well. Craig's openness to considering new territories leads us to offer a quite different stream of theory running through the field of communication. Our candidate is an *ethical tradition*.

THE ETHICAL TRADITION

Communication as People of Character Interacting in Just and Beneficial Ways

More than many academic disciplines, the field of communication has been concerned with ethical responsibility. Since the time of Plato and Aristotle, communication scholars have grappled with the obligations that go along with the opportunities we have to communicate. Contemporary discussions of morality are increasingly beleaguered by the rise of ethical relativism.[33] Yet despite the postmodern challenge to all claims of Truth, at the turn of the century, the National Communication Association (NCA) adopted a "Credo for Ethical Communication" (see Appendix C).[34] Like most attempts to deal with communication ethics, it addresses the problem of what is ethical and starts with the issue of honesty versus lying. I'll cite three of the creed's nine principles in order to illustrate the major streams of thought within the ethical tradition:[35]

1. *We advocate truthfulness, accuracy, honesty, and reason as essential to the integrity of communication.* This principle centers on the *rightness* or *wrongness* of a communication act regardless of whether it benefits the people involved. It speaks to the question of *obligation*. Is it always our *duty* to be honest?

2. *We accept responsibility for the short- and long-term consequences of our own communication and expect the same of others.* This principle is concerned with the *harm* or *benefit* that results from our words. It raises the question of *outcomes*. Will a lie promote *well-being* or prevent *injury*?

3. *We strive to understand and respect other communicators before evaluating and responding to their messages.* This principle focuses on the *character* of the communicator rather than the act of communication. It bids us to look at our *motives* and *attitudes*. Do I seek to be a person of *integrity* and *virtue*?

These are difficult questions to answer, and some readers might suggest that they have no place in a communication theory text. But to deal with human intercourse as a mechanical process separate from values would be like discussing sexual intercourse under ground rules that prohibit any reference to love. And within the ethical tradition, communication theorists do offer answers to these questions.

Many ethical theorists come out of interpretive traditions. For example, the final chapter of Bill Rawlins' book *The Compass of Friendship* suggests what a friendship aligned with a moral compass looks like. The friends negotiate their relationship voluntarily, care about each other's well-being, respect each other as equals, and engage in ongoing learning about each other.[36] But some objective scholars care about ethical communication, too. Andrew's TCU friend and colleague Paul Witt is steeped in the socio-psychological tradition. He also teaches "Communication and Character," a course that examines honesty, compassion, courage, patience, and humility—important ingredients for ethical friendships. Thus, we won't try to locate the ethical tradition in any single spot on the objective–interpretive landscape in Figure 4–1. We have, however, encapsuled the thoughts of some influential ethical theorists into 13 summary statements. Each of these *ethical reflections* appears in this book alongside a theory with which it naturally resonates.

With or without our addition of an ethical tradition, Craig's framework can help make sense of the great diversity in the field of communication theory. As you read about a theory in the section on media effects, remember that it may have the same ancestry as a theory you studied earlier in the section on relationship development. On the first page of each of the next 32 chapters, we'll tie each theory to one or more traditions. Hopefully this label will make it easier for you to understand why the theorist has made certain choices. The labels are signposts that will help you navigate the world of communication theory.

QUESTIONS TO SHARPEN YOUR FOCUS

1. Considering the differences between *objective* and *interpretive* theory, can you make a case that the *rhetorical* tradition is less objective than the *semiotic* one or that the *socio-cultural* tradition is more interpretive than the *critical* one?

2. Suppose you and your best friend have recently been on an emotional roller coaster. Which of the seven highlighted *definitions of communication* offers the most promise of helping you achieve a stable relationship? Why?

3. Communication departments rarely have a faculty representing all seven traditions. In order to create specialties and minimize conflict, some recruit from just one or two. What tradition(s) seems well-represented in your department?

4. The map in Figure 4–1 represents seven traditions in the field of communication theory. In which region do you feel most at home? What other areas would you like to explore? Where would you be uncomfortable? Why?

A SECOND LOOK

Recommended resource: Robert T. Craig, "Communication Theory as a Field," *Communication Theory,* Vol. 9, 1999, pp. 119–161.

Communication as a practical discipline: Robert T. Craig, "Communication as a Practical Discipline," in *Rethinking Communication: Vol. 1,* Brenda Dervin, Lawrence Grossberg, Barbara O'Keefe, and Ellen Wartella (eds.), Sage, Newbury Park, CA, 1989, pp. 97–122.

Anthology of primary resources for each tradition: Heidi L. Muller and Robert T. Craig (eds.), *Theorizing Communication: Readings Across Traditions,* Sage, Los Angeles, CA, 2007.

Socio-psychological tradition: Carl Hovland, Irving Janis, and Harold Kelley, *Communication and Persuasion,* Yale University, New Haven, CT, 1953, pp. 1–55.

Cybernetic tradition: Norbert Wiener, *The Human Use of Human Beings,* Avon, New York, 1967, pp. 23–100.

Rhetorical tradition: Thomas M. Conley, *Rhetoric in the European Tradition,* Longman, New York, 1990, pp. 1–52.

Semiotic tradition: C. K. Ogden and I. A. Richards, *The Meaning of Meaning,* Harcourt, Brace & World, New York, 1946, pp. 1–23.

Phenomenological tradition: Carl Rogers, "The Characteristics of a Helping Relationship," in *On Becoming a Person,* Houghton Mifflin, Boston, MA, 1961, pp. 39–58.

50   *OVERVIEW*

Socio-cultural tradition: Benjamin Lee Whorf, "The Relation of Habitual Thought and Behaviour to Language," in *Language, Culture, and Personality: Essays in Memory of Edward Sapir,* University of Utah, Salt Lake City, UT, 1941, pp. 123–149.

Critical tradition: Raymond Morrow with David Brown, *Critical Theory and Methodology,* Sage, Thousand Oaks, CA, 1994, pp. 3–34, 85–112.

Ethical tradition: Richard L. Johannesen, "Communication Ethics: Centrality, Trends, and Controversies," in *Communication Yearbook 25,* William B. Gudykunst (ed.), Lawrence Erlbaum, Mahwah, NJ, 2001, pp. 201–235.

Pragmatic tradition: Robert T. Craig, "Pragmatism in the Field of Communication Theory," *Communication Theory,* Vol. 17, 2007, pp. 125–145.

Critique of Craig's model and his response: David Myers, "A Pox on All Compromises: Reply to Craig (1999)," and Robert T. Craig, "Minding My Metamodel, Mending Myers," *Communication Theory,* Vol. 11, 2001, pp. 218–230, 231–240.

To access three-level sentence outlines for all 37 chapters,
click on Outline under Theory Resources at
www.afirstlook.com.

DIVISION TWO

Interpersonal Communication

Interpersonal   Messages

Communication theorists often use the image of a game to describe interpersonal communication. Various scholars refer to *language games, rules of the game, gamelike behavior,* and even *game theory.* I'll use three specific game metaphors to illustrate what interpersonal communication *is,* and what it *is not.*[1]

Communication as Bowling   The bowling model of message delivery is likely the most widely held view of communication. I think that's unfortunate.

This model sees the bowler as the sender, who delivers the ball, which is the message. As it rolls down the lane (the channel), clutter on the boards (noise) may deflect the ball (the message). Yet if it is aimed well, the ball strikes the passive pins (the target audience) with a predictable effect.

In this one-way model of communication, the speaker (bowler) must take care to select a precisely crafted message (ball) and practice diligently to deliver it the same way every time. Of course, that makes sense only if target listeners are static, interchangeable pins waiting to be bowled over by our words—which they aren't. Communication theory that emphasizes message content to the neglect of relational factors simply isn't realistic. Real-life interpersonal communication is sometimes confusing, often unpredictable, and always involves more than just the speaker's action. This realization has led some observers to propose an interactive model for interpersonal communication.

Communication as Ping-Pong   Unlike bowling, Ping-Pong is not a solo game. This fact alone makes it a better analogy for interpersonal communication. One party puts the conversational ball in play, and the other gets into position to receive. It takes more concentration and skill to receive than to serve because while the speaker (server) knows where the message is going, the listener (receiver) doesn't. Like a verbal or nonverbal message, the ball may appear straightforward yet have a deceptive spin.

Ping-Pong is a back-and-forth game; players switch roles continuously. One moment the person holding the paddle is an initiator; the next second the same player is a responder, gauging the effectiveness of his or her shot by the way the ball comes back. The repeated adjustment essential for good play closely parallels the feedback process described in a number of interpersonal communication theories. There are, however, two inherent flaws in the table-tennis analogy.

The first defect is that the game is played with one ball, which at any point in time is headed in a single direction. A true model of interpersonal encounters would have people sending and receiving multiple balls at the same time. The other problem is that table tennis is a competitive game—there's a winner and a loser. In successful dialogue, both people win.

Communication as Charades   The game of charades best captures the simultaneous and collaborative nature of interpersonal communication. A charade is neither an action, like bowling a strike, nor an interaction, like a rally in Ping-Pong. It's a *transaction.*

Charades is a mutual game; the actual play is cooperative. One member draws a title or slogan from a batch of possibilities and then tries to act it out visually for teammates in a silent minidrama. The goal is to get at least one partner to say the exact words that are on the slip of paper. Of course, the actor is prohibited from talking out loud.

Suppose you drew the saying "God helps those who help themselves." For *God* you might try folding your hands and gazing upward. For *helps* you could act out offering a helping hand or giving a leg-up boost over a fence. By pointing at a number of real or imaginary people you may elicit a response of *them,* and by this point a partner may shout out, "God helps those who help themselves." Success.

Like charades, interpersonal communication is a mutual, ongoing process of sending, receiving, and adapting verbal and nonverbal messages with another person to create and alter the images in both our minds. Communication between us begins when there is some overlap between two images, and is effective to the extent that overlap increases. But even if our mental pictures are congruent, communication will be partial as long as we interpret them differently. The idea that "God helps those who help themselves" could strike one person as a hollow promise, while the other might regard it as a divine stamp of approval for hard work.

The three theories in this section reject a simplistic, one-way bowling analogy and an interactive Ping-Pong model of interpersonal communication. Instead, they view interpersonal communication in a way more akin to charades—a complex transaction in which overlapping messages simultaneously affect and are affected by the other person and multiple other factors.

CHAPTER 6

Objective   Interpretive

Socio-cultural tradition
Phenomenological tradition

Coordinated Management of Meaning (CMM)

of W. Barnett Pearce & Vernon Cronen

Transmission model
Picturing communication as a transfer of meaning by a source sending a message through a channel to a receiver.

Barnett Pearce and Vernon Cronen bemoan the fact that most communication theorists and practitioners hold to a *transmission model* of communication. This model depicts a source that sends a message through a channel to one or more receivers.

Source ➔ Message ➔ Channel ➔ Receiver

In this model, communication is considered successful to the extent that a high-fidelity version of the message gets through the channel and the receiver's interpretation of it closely matches what the sender meant. People who picture communication this way tend to focus either on the message content or on what each party is thinking, but CMM says that they lose sight of the pattern of communication and what that pattern creates.

Pearce, a communication professor at the Fielding Graduate Institute before he died in 2010, and Cronen (University of North Carolina Wilmington) would undoubtedly extend their critique to the definition of communication we offer in Chapter 1. We suggested that *communication is the relational process of creating and interpreting messages that elicit a response.* What's wrong with this description? Although the two theorists would appreciate our concern for relationship and response, they would note that our definition continues to treat communication as merely a means of exchanging ideas. They'd say that our definition looks *through* communication rather than directly *at* it. It renders the ongoing process invisible.

In contrast, Pearce and Cronen offer the *coordinated management of meaning* (CMM) as a theory that looks directly at the communication process and what it's doing. Because that process is complicated, the theory offers multiple insights into what communication is creating and a number of tools for changing our communication patterns. This way, we can grasp the essentials of the theory without being overwhelmed. Kimberly Pearce, Barnett's wife and president of the CMM Institute for Personal and Social Evolution, boils down CMM into four claims about communication.

FIRST CLAIM: OUR COMMUNICATION CREATES OUR SOCIAL WORLDS

Communication perspective
An ongoing focus on how communication makes our social worlds.

Kim Pearce starts with what we've just covered and then adds what communication does: "Communication is not just a tool for exchanging ideas and information. . . . It 'makes' selves, relationships, organizations, communities, cultures, etc. This is what I've referred to as taking the *communication perspective.*"[1]

Selves, relationships, organizations, communities, and cultures are the "stuff" that makes up our social worlds. For CMM theorists, our social worlds are not something we find or discover. Instead, we create them. For most of his professional life, Barnett Pearce summed up this core concept of the theory by asserting that *persons-in-conversation co-construct their own social realities and are simultaneously shaped by the worlds they create.*[2] Figure 6–1 presents artist M. C. Escher's 1955 lithograph *Bond of Union,* which strikingly illustrates a number of CMM's notions of how persons-in-conversation are making the social worlds of which they are a part. I see three parallels between the picture and the theory.

First, Escher's art foregrounds interpersonal communication as the primary activity that's going on in the social universe. This squares with CMM's claim that *the experience of persons-in-conversation is the primary social process of human life.*[3] Barnett Pearce said this idea runs counter to the prevailing intellectual view of "communication as an odorless, colorless vehicle of thought that is interesting or important only when it is done poorly or breaks down."[4] He saw the ribbon in Escher's drawing as representing patterns of communication that literally form who the persons-in-conversation are and create their relationship. Their conversation does something to them quite apart from the issue they're discussing.

FIGURE 6–1   M. C. Escher's *Bond of Union*

Second, the figures in the lithograph are bound together regardless of what they are talking about. This reflects Barnett Pearce's belief that the way people communicate is often more important than the content of what they say. The mood and manner that persons-in-conversation adopt play a large role in the process of social construction. He pointed out that the faces in *Bond of Union* have no substance; they consist in the twists and turns of the spiraling ribbon:

> Were the ribbon straightened or tied in another shape, there would be no loss of matter, but the faces would no longer exist. This image works for us as a model of the way the process of communication (the ribbon) creates the events and objects of our social worlds (the faces), not by its substance but by its form.[5]

Third, the endless ribbon in *Bond of Union* loops back to *re*form both persons-in-conversation. If Escher's figures were in conflict, each person would be wise to ask, "If I win this argument, what kind of person will I become?" Barnett Pearce said it's the same for us. Our actions are reflexively reproduced as the interaction continues; any action we take will bounce back and affect us. That's also true with the social worlds we create. Pearce wrote, "When we communicate, we are not just talking about the world, we are literally participating in the creation of the social universe."[6] And, like the figures in the lithograph, we then have to live in it.

Social constructionists
Curious participants in a pluralistic world who believe that persons-in-conversation co-construct their own social realities and are simultaneously shaped by the worlds they create.

These ideas identify CMM theorists and practitioners as *social constructionists*— curious participants in a pluralistic world. Barnett Pearce said they are *curious* because they think it's folly to profess certainty when dealing with individuals acting out their lives under ever-changing conditions. They are *participants* rather than spectators because they seek to be actively involved in what they study. They live in a *pluralistic world* because they assume that people make multiple truths rather than find a singular Truth.[7] So Escher's *Bond of Union* is an apt representation of persons-in-conversation even when one or both of the parties are CMM advocates.

SECOND CLAIM: THE STORIES WE TELL DIFFER FROM THE STORIES WE LIVE

CMM uses the term *story* to refer to much of what we say when we talk with others about our social worlds—ourselves, others, relationships, organizations, or the larger community. Pearce and Cronen claim that communication is a two-sided process of *stories told* and *stories lived*.[8] Stories told are tales we tell to make sense of the world and tame the terrors that go bump in the night. CMM calls this *making and managing meaning*. Stories lived are the ongoing patterns of interaction we enact as we seek to mesh our lives with others around us. CMM calls this effort *coordinating our actions together*. Pearce and Cronen labeled their theory *coordinated management of meaning* to encompass both types of stories.

Stories Told: Making and Managing Meaning

The stories we tell or hear are never as simple as they seem. Take, for example, the story that appeared in my inbox a month before my high school reunion. Decades earlier, the writer (Bea) and I had been in the same 7th and 8th grade class where we engaged in what I would describe as mild flirtation. Here's what I read:

> I'm writing because I still think about the mystery of you not speaking to me all the way through high school. You may not even remember that you ignored me,

but I do. What did I do to make you so angry? My mother always wondered if someone had said something to you about me that wasn't true. I just never knew. I would feel better if we could say "hello" at least at the gathering.

This seems to be a rather straightforward tale of a young girl who felt bad when a guy ignored her. If so, you might expect a *that-was-years-ago* reaction, a *get-a-life* response, or a quick mouse click on *delete.* Pearce and Cronen suggest, however, that there's always much more to stories told that could enrich or alter their meaning. Emphasizing that CMM is a practical theory, they offer a number of analytical tools to help the listener consider alternative or additional interpretations. When I got this message from Bea, I used their LUUUUTT model pictured in Figure 6–2 to help me expand the story and possibly narrow the disparity between her account of me in the distant past and the stories each of us might want to live now.

LUUUUTT is an acronym to label the seven types of stories identified in the model.[9] The focus of the model depicts the tension between our stories lived and our stories told. That tension can be increased or decreased by the manner in which the stories are presented. The four descriptions of non-obvious stories radiating toward the corners remind us there's always more to the situation that we haven't seen or heard. Barnett and Kim Pearce use the term *mystery* to cover everything relevant that is not, or cannot, be said. As I reread Bea's message, I tried to imagine what each of those seven interrelated stories in the LUUUUTT model might be.

1. **L**ived stories—*what we actually did or are doing.* I have no reason to doubt Bea's claim. Although I can't recall intentionally avoiding conversation with her in high school, neither do I have a mental image of us talking together, even though we were both cast members in the school play. In contrast, I know we chatted in junior high.

2. **U**nknown stories—*information that's missing.* Bea's mother suggested that I was turned off by lies I heard about her daughter. Not so. But the multiple possibilities that Bea imagined and couldn't discount would surely be distressing.

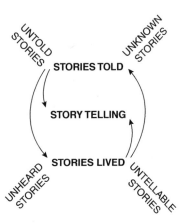

FIGURE 6–2 CMM's LUUUUTT Model

3. Untold stories—*what we choose not to say.* There was nothing in Bea's message about the attention I paid to her in junior high or anger she might have felt at the abrupt change in my behavior. Nor did she say anything about her current life.

4. Unheard stories—*what we say that isn't heard or acknowledged.* Did Bea try to reach out to me during those four years of silence and, if so, did I snub her? To ignore her email message now would add insult to injury.

5. Untellable stories—*stories that are forbidden or too painful for us to tell.* It would be the height of arrogance on my part to think that I had the power to ruin Bea's life back then. Yet I did wonder what she couldn't say.

6. Story Telling—*the manner in which we communicate.* "Why" questions often impute blame, but the tone of Bea's message struck me as a mix of curiosity, sadness, courage, and an honest effort to clear the air before the class reunion.

7. Stories Told—*what we say we are doing.* With Bea's permission, I've already cited the story she told in her email. The additional six stories that the LUUUUTT model generated don't negate what she expressed. As Kim Pearce explains,

> The point of the LUUUUTT model is not to "find the correct story" or "the correct interpretation" as much as enlarging your awareness of how complex our social worlds are. The more aware we are of the complexity of our social worlds, the greater our capacity for holding frustrating situations and people more compassionately.[10]

I'll revisit these stories told and my response to Bea when we examine the third claim of CMM.

Stories Lived: Coordinating Our Patterns of Interaction

There's almost always a difference or tension between our stories told and stories lived. That's because we can craft the stories we tell to be coherent and consistent, but the stories we live intersect with the actions and reactions of others. That makes them messy.

As communication scholars, Pearce and Cronen were particularly concerned with the patterns of communication we create with others. They offered the *serpentine model* shown in Figure 6–3 as a tool to capture what's taking place between persons-in-conversation. Without such a tool, we may miss the repetitive patterns that either benefit or pollute the social environment. Pearce wrote that the model is called serpentine because it "looks like a snake crawling from one person or group to another and back again. This model directs our attention to the 'back and forth-ness' of social interaction. Every aspect of our social worlds is made by the collaborative action of multiple people."[11] Note that the model almost seems to be a schematic drawing of Escher's *Bond of Union*, which is utterly different from the standard one-way message transmission model of communication.

The serpentine model can analyze any conversation and map out its history. The conversation between Wilson and Larry has only six turns and clearly reveals the deterioration of their stories lived. Turns 1 and 2 show an honest difference of opinion, each stated vehemently. In turn 3, Wilson's comment about the film director expands on his enthusiasm. But he also shows disdain for anyone who doesn't agree with him, lumping Larry with a class of people who are mentally

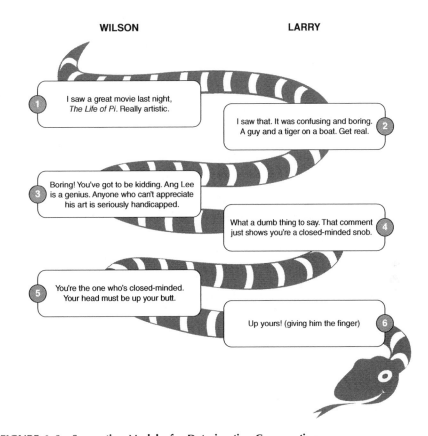

FIGURE 6–3   Serpentine Model of a Deteriorating Conversation

handicapped. Larry then goes on the attack—no surprise. Note that in just four turns the guys have moved into an escalating pattern in which both are competing to see who can say the most hurtful things to the other. The original topic of conversation has become irrelevant. Trapped in a sense of oughtness that has them in its grip, they can continue this feud forever, fueled only by the *logical force* of the interaction.[12]

Logical force
The moral pressure or sense of obligation a person feels to respond in a given way to what someone else has just said or done—"I had no choice."

CMM describes this type of conversational sequence as an *unwanted repetitive pattern (URP).*[13] It's likely that neither party wants it, yet both seem compelled to relive it over and over. Those who've seen Bill Murray's classic film *Groundhog Day* will appreciate the irony. And all Americans have seen this URP reenacted in the reciprocated diatribe between Republicans and Democrats.[14] Yet Pearce and Cronen maintained that it's possible for people to mesh their stories lived without agreeing on the meaning of their stories told. That's the coordination part of CMM.

Coordination
People collaborating in an attempt to bring into being their vision of what is necessary, noble, and good, and to preclude the enactment of what they fear, hate, or despise.

According to Barnett Pearce, *coordination* refers to the "process by which persons collaborate in an attempt to bring into being their vision of what is necessary, noble, and good, and to preclude the enactment of what they fear, hate, or despise."[15] This intentional meshing of stories lived doesn't require people to reach agreement on the meaning of their joint action. They can decide to coordinate their behavior without sharing a common interpretation of the event. For example, conservative activists and staunch feminists could temporarily join forces to protest the public showing of a hardcore pornographic movie. Although

72   *INTERPERSONAL COMMUNICATION*

they have discrepant views of social justice and different reasons for condemning the film, they might agree on a unified course of action.

Pearce used the phrase *coordination without coherence* to refer to people cooperating for quite different reasons. Sarah's application log for CMM provides a striking example:

> CMM suggests that people may synchronize their actions even if they don't share the other's motives. This was the case with my core group of friends in high school. Our group consisted of Colin—a gay atheist, Stephany—a non-practicing Jewish girl, Aliza—a devout Jewish girl, and me—a Christian. We all abstained from drinking, drugs, and sex, but the reasons for our behavior were extremely different.

In light of the way real groups of people coordinate their actions without a great amount of mutual understanding, Calvin and Hobbes' game of "Calvinball" on page 72 doesn't seem that strange.

THIRD CLAIM: WE GET WHAT WE MAKE

Since CMM claims we create our social worlds through our patterns of communication, it follows that we get what we make. Kim Pearce explains, "If your patterns of interaction contain destructive accusations and reactive anger, you will most likely make a defensive relationship; if your patterns contain genuine questions and curiosity, you will have a better chance of making a more open relationship."[16]

In the last major article he wrote before his death, Barnett Pearce urged that we ask three questions when we reflect on past interactions, are in the midst of a current conversation, or contemplate what we might say in the future:[17]

> *How did that get made?*
> *What are we making?*
> *What can we do to make better social worlds?*

These questions motivated me to do the LUUUUTT analysis of Bea's email message that I outlined in the "Stories Told" section. The *How did that get made?* question is easy to figure out, although I don't like the answer. Bea's angst seemed to be the product of my total disregard over a four-year period. My behavior may not have been the sole cause of the confusion and hurt she felt, but after reading the story she told I wished I had lived a story back then that created something positive.

The second question was more pressing. What were Bea and I making through the pattern of our email exchange? You've already read Bea's query and request expressed below in turn 3. But CMM theorists believe you can only come to understand what we were creating by looking at the twists and turns of the whole serpentine flow.

A Digital Conversation between Bea and Em

#1 BEA: Hi Emory. Are you the Emory Griffin that went to Morgan Park High School? If so, I saw your name on the list as coming to the reunion.

#2 EM: Hi Bea. That's me. I look forward to seeing you and everyone else next month.

#3 BEA: I'm writing because I still think about the mystery of you not speaking to me all the way through high school. You may not even remember that you ignored me, but I do. What did I do to make you so angry? My mother always wondered if someone had said something to you about me that wasn't true. I just never knew. I would feel better if we could say "hello" at least at the gathering.

#4 EM: Wow, I am so sorry. Please forgive me for this hurtful behavior, and even more so that I'm not even conscious that I didn't speak. Thank you for having the courage to raise the issue. I feel bad that on the basis of my stupid behavior, for decades you've thought there was something wrong with you. Obviously the problem was in me. Was I too conceited, insecure, insensitive, or oblivious? Probably all of the above.

No, you didn't say or do anything to make me angry and I never heard anything derogatory about you from others. So why didn't I talk to you? I honestly don't know. And I feel bad that I wasn't approachable enough that you could say something back then. ("Excuse me, Em. Why aren't you talking to me?") Not likely I guess. I'd like to spend some time together at the reunion catching up, if you're willing. But I'd understand if "Hello" is all you want. Again, thanks so much for writing.

#5 BEA: Was that ever nice! I've been doing computer stuff all day and receiving your email was the best part. Thanks for your response, it felt so good. Yes, I'll enjoy catching up at the reunion. What is it that you teach?

#6 EM: You'll laugh! I teach communication. I'm even supposed to be an expert.

An additional four turns set up where and when we'd meet at the reunion. We ate dinner together with other friends at the table and swapped stories and pictures. That night our stories told and our stories lived seemed to mesh well. I had the rest of the night and breakfast in the morning to enjoy the company of old friends.

A CMM Interpretation

Turns 1 and 2 are noteworthy for their guarded tone. Bea is checking to see if I'm the right guy—a reasonable caution because it was only in high school that friends started to call me Em. I respond that it's me, but my "looking forward" statement covers all who come to the party. I've expressed no special encouragement or excitement to Bea. If the pattern continued in that noncommittal tone, Barnett Pearce would have called it a "dead snake."

Bea then shares her bewilderment, desire for online clarity, and a request for face-to-face civility at the reunion. Given my lack of responsiveness throughout high school, it struck me as a gutsy move. After reading this message I sat back and mulled over how I wanted to respond. This is when I did the LUUUUTT analysis described earlier. We were at the crucial place in our email exchange that Barnett and Kim Pearce called a *bifurcation point*. They said it's the turn "in a conversation where what happens next will affect the unfolding pattern of interaction and take it in a different direction."[18]

Bifurcation point
A critical point in a conversation where what one says next will affect the unfolding pattern of interaction and potentially take it in a different direction.

I was at a fork in the road. I could deny that I had ignored Bea, stonewall her query, or casually reply that I would "of course say hello" when we met. That kind of response would likely have created more tension, hurt, anger, guilt, fear, and all the other yucky stuff that pollutes the social environment. And for sure it would take away any desire to attend the class reunion. Instead, I chose the route shown in turn 4. As Bea's and my comments in turns 5 and 6 reveal, we created a social world more to our liking—one that may have even benefitted others at the reunion.

I was fortunate that Bea raised these issues through email rather than confronting me with the same words face-to-face at the reunion. The time lag possible in computer-mediated communication offered me an opportunity to do the LUUUUTT analysis, which got me in touch with the depth and complexity of the story Bea told. That gap gave me a chance to craft what I hoped would be a thoughtful and caring response. The privacy also made it possible for me to convey my apology without a bunch of onlookers weighing in or taking sides. But it was Barnett Pearce's hope that every student majoring in communication would become adept at spotting the bifurcation points in the midst of tough discussions and have the desire and skill to craft a response on the fly that would make better social worlds. If the current crop of more than 400,000 undergraduate communication majors developed that mindset and ability, he was convinced we could make a radically different social world.[19]

FOURTH CLAIM: GET THE PATTERN RIGHT, CREATE BETTER OUTCOMES

What do the best social worlds look like? Barnett Pearce admitted he couldn't be specific, because each situation is different. He also feared that those who have a precise image of what the ideal social world should be will try to compel others to live within their vision and end up making things worse.[20] But throughout their most recent publications on CMM, Barnett and Kim Pearce described better social worlds as replete with *caring, compassion, love,* and *grace* among its inhabitants—not the stated goal of most communication theories.[21] And Kim stresses that these are not just internal emotional experiences. Rather, they are "a way of being with others that makes a space for something new to emerge."[22]

This interpersonal goal of CMM raises a serious question for students of communication. What personal characteristics or abilities does it take for a person to create conversational patterns that will change the social world for the better? The theorists' answer is that one does not need to be a saint, a genius, or an orator. The communicator, however, must be *mindful.*[23]

Mindfulness
The presence or awareness of what participants are making in the midst of their own conversation.

Mindfulness is a presence or awareness of what participants are making in the midst of a difficult conversation. It's paying less attention to what they are talking about and focusing on what they are *doing.* Mindful participants don't speak on mental automatic pilot or cognitive cruise control. They are participant observers willing to step back and look for places in the conversational flow where they can say or do something that will make the situation better for everyone involved. For example, are you willing and able to be mindful when

. . . talking to your roommate about the mess in your apartment?
. . . replying to your mom's phone plea to spend spring break at home?
. . . listening to your teammates complain about the coach?
. . . responding to a sarcastic comment posted on Facebook?
. . . dealing with a demanding customer at your minimum-wage McJob?
. . . fending off unwelcome advances during a Friday night pub crawl?

To the extent that your answer is *yes,* CMM claims you have the capacity to make better social worlds.

Once the mindful communicator spots a bifurcation point in a pattern of communication that's deteriorating, what should he or she say? Barnett Pearce found it helpful to respond to challenging or boorish statements with phrases that showed curiosity rather than offense.[24] *Tell me more about that. What else was going on at the time? What experiences have led you to that position? Why don't people understand?* Those familiar with Hebrew wisdom literature will recognize the parallel with Proverbs 15:1, "A gentle answer turns away wrath."

Even a single word like *yes* can change the direction of the conversational pattern. In her autobiography, *Bossypants*, actress, comedian, writer, and producer Tina Fey offers "The Rules of Improvisation That Will Change Your Life . . ."

> The first rule of improvisation is **AGREE**. Always agree and SAY YES. When you're improvising, this means you are required to agree with whatever your partner has created. So if we're improvising and I say, "Freeze, I have a gun," and you say, "That's not a gun. It's your finger. You're pointing your finger at me," our improvised scene has ground to a halt. But if I say, "Freeze, I have a gun!" and you say, "The gun I gave you for Christmas. You bastard!" then we have started a scene because we have AGREED that my finger is in fact a Christmas gun.
>
> Now, obviously in real life you're not always going to agree with everything everyone says. But the Rule of Agreement reminds you to respect what your partner has created and to at least start from an open-minded place. Start with a YES and see where it takes you.
>
> As an improviser, I always find it jarring when I meet someone in real life whose first answer is no. "No we can't do that." "No that's not in the budget . . ." What kind of way is that to live?[25]

For an overall remedy to unsatisfactory or destructive patterns of interaction, CMM theorists advocate *dialogue,* a specific form of communication that they believe will create a social world where we can live with dignity, honor, joy, and love.[26] Although the term is used in multiple ways within our discipline, Barnett and Kim Pearce have adopted the perspective of Jewish philosopher Martin Buber.

Dialogic communication Conversation in which parties remain in the tension between holding their own perspective while being profoundly open to the other.

For Buber, dialogue "involves remaining in the tension between holding our own perspective while being profoundly open to the other."[27] This of course takes "courage because it means giving up a person-position of clarity, certainty, or moral/intellectual superiority."[28] We might actually learn something new that will change what we think, or even who we are.[29] The following ethical reflection expands on Buber's concept of dialogue.

ETHICAL REFLECTION: MARTIN BUBER'S DIALOGIC ETHICS

Martin Buber was a German Jewish philosopher and theologian who immigrated to Palestine before World War II and died in 1965. His ethical approach focuses on relationships between people rather than on moral codes of conduct. "In the beginning is the relation," Buber wrote. "The relation is the cradle of actual life."[30]

Buber contrasted two types of relationships—*I-It* versus *I-Thou.* In an I-It relationship we treat the other person as a thing to be used, an object to be manipulated. Created by monologue, an I-It relationship lacks mutuality. Parties come together as individuals intent on creating only an impression. Deceit is a way to maintain appearances.

In an I-Thou relationship we regard our partner as the very one we are. We see the other as created in the image of God and resolve to treat him or her as a valued end rather than a means to our own end. This implies that we will seek to experience the relationship as it appears to the other person. Buber said we can do this only through dialogue.

For Buber, *dialogue* was a synonym for ethical communication. Dialogue is mutuality in conversation that creates the *Between,* through which we help each other to be more human. Dialogue is not only a morally appropriate act, but it is also a way to discover what is ethical in our relationship. It thus requires self-disclosure to, confirmation of, and vulnerability with the other person.

Buber used the image of the *narrow ridge* to illustrate the tension of dialogic living. On one side of the moral path is the gulf of relativism, where there are no standards. On the other side is the plateau of absolutism, where rules are etched in stone:

> On the far side of the subjective, on this side of the objective, on the narrow ridge, where I and Thou meet, there is the realm of the Between.[31]

Narrow ridge
A metaphor of I-Thou living in the dialogic tension between ethical relativism and rigid absolutism.

Duquesne University communication ethicist Ron Arnett notes that "living the narrow-ridge philosophy requires a life of personal and interpersonal concern, which is likely to generate a more complicated existence than that of the egoist or the selfless martyr."[32] Despite that tension, many interpersonal theorists and practitioners have carved out ethical positions similar to Buber's philosophy. Consistent with CMM's foundational belief that persons-in-conversation co-construct their own social realities, Barnett and Kim Pearce were attracted to Buber's core belief that dialogue is a joint achievement that cannot be produced on demand, but occurs among people who seek it and are prepared for it.

CRITIQUE: HIGHLY PRACTICAL AS IT MOVES FROM CONFUSION TO CLARITY

Because CMM is an interpretive theory, I'll apply the six criteria suggested in Chapter 3 as I did when evaluating Mead's theory of *symbolic interactionism* in the previous chapter.

New understanding of people. By offering such diagnostic tools as the serpentine and LUUUUTT models of communication, CMM promotes a deeper *understanding of people* and of the social worlds they create through their conversation. Those models are just two of the tools the theorists offer. Students who take a further look at the theory will find the daisy model, the hierarchical model, and strange loops equally helpful.

Clarification of values. For interpretive scholars, CMM leaves no doubt as to the commitments and practices that make better social worlds. Barnett and Kim Pearce are clearly on record as valuing curiosity, caring, compassion, mindfulness, gratitude, grace, and love. They have invited us to join them in an ongoing effort to enact these qualities in our stories lived. Some objective theorists may personally share these values, but believe a communication theory holding out the promise of making *better social worlds* should describe that goal in terms of specific behaviors and outcomes.

Community of agreement.   Although many objectivist theorists dismiss CMM because of its social constructionist assumptions, CMM has generated widespread interest and *acceptance within the community* of interpretive communication scholars. For example, when Robert Craig proposed that a pragmatic tradition be added to his original list of seven traditions of communication theory (see Chapter 4), he cited CMM as the exemplar of a practical theory.[33]

Reform of society.   If changing destructive patterns of communication in whole communities strikes you as a bit of a stretch, you should know that pursuit of this goal is why Barnett and Kim Pearce founded the Public Dialogue Consortium and the CMM Institute.[34] Not only have many associates signed on to the cause, but these groups have also demonstrated that a dialogic form of communication is "learnable, teachable, and contagious."[35]

Qualitative research.   CMM scholars and practitioners use a wide range of qualitative research methods—textual and narrative analyses, case studies, interviews, participant observation, ethnography, and collaborative action research.[36] It's not clear that this research has spawned new theoretical development,[37] but these studies have definitely helped refine the models of communication that practitioners use in their training and consulting.

Aesthetic appeal.   Despite meeting the previous five criteria with ease, lack of clarity has seriously limited CMM's wider use. The theory has a reputation of being a confusing mix of ideas that are hard to pin down because they're expressed in convoluted language. In 2001, when Pearce asked those who use CMM in their teaching, training, counseling, and consulting what changes or additions they thought should be made to the theory, the most frequent plea was for user-friendly explanations expressed in easy-to-understand terms. The following story from the field underscores why this call for clarity is so crucial:

> My counseling trainees often find CMM ideas exciting, but its language daunting or too full of jargon. Some trainees connect with the ideas but most feel intimidated by the language and the concepts—diminished in some way or excluded! One trainee sat in a posture of physically cringing because she did not understand. This was a competent woman who had successfully completed counselor training three years ago and was doing a "refresher" with us. I don't think she found it too refreshing at that moment. CMM ideas would be more useful if they were available in everyday language—perhaps via examples and storytelling.[38]

I've tried to heed this advice while writing about CMM. Hopefully, you haven't cringed. But in order to reduce the wince factor, I've had to leave out many of the valued terms, tools, and models that are the working vocabulary of this complex theory. I've been guided by Kim Pearce's new book, *Compassionate Communicating Because Moments Matter,* where she lays out the essentials of CMM in the way the advocate requested.[39] This little volume, which is my recommended resource, is a clear statement of CMM's four core claims. In user-friendly language, Kim illustrates them with stories from her work and life together with her husband, Barnett. CMM's aesthetic appeal is on the rise.

QUESTIONS TO SHARPEN YOUR FOCUS

1. *Social constructionists* see themselves as curious participants in a pluralistic world. Are you willing to accept uncertainty, abandon a detached perspective, and not insist on a singular view of Truth so that you can join them?

2. Can you provide a rationale for placing this chapter on CMM immediately after the chapter on *symbolic interactionism?*

3. CMM suggests that we can take part in joint action without a common understanding—*coordination* without *shared meaning.* Can you think of examples from your own life?

4. Can you recall an important conversation in which you were *mindful* of what you were making and you spotted a *bifurcation point* where you could change the *pattern of conversation* so as to create a *better social world?*

CONVERSATIONS

View this segment online at www.mhhe.com/griffin9e or www.afirstlook.com.

As you watch my conversation with Barnett Pearce, you might think of us as the persons-in-conversation pictured in Escher's *Bond of Union.* What kind of social world do you see us creating as we talk? I like to think that our conversation displays a few examples of dialogic communication. If so, was Pearce right in thinking that you'll find this kind of talk contagious? At one point I repeat my "Questions to Sharpen Your Focus" query about how social constructionists must give up claims of certainty, objectivity, and Truth. I then ask if that's a fair question. See if you agree with Pearce's response and the reason he gave.

A SECOND LOOK

Recommended resource: Kimberly Pearce, *Compassionate Communicating Because Moments Matter: Poetry, Prose, and Practices,* Lulu, 2012. www.lulu.com

Brief overview: W. Barnett Pearce, "The Coordinated Management of Meaning (CMM)," in *Theorizing About Intercultural Communication,* William Gudykunst (ed.), Sage, Thousand Oaks, CA, 2004, pp. 35–54.

Comprehensive statement: W. Barnett Pearce, *Making Social Worlds: A Communication Perspective,* Blackwell, Malden, MA, 2008.

Original statement: W. Barnett Pearce and Vernon E. Cronen, *Communication, Action, and Meaning: The Creation of Social Realities,* Praeger, New York, 1980; also www.cios.org/www/opentext.htm.

Evolution of the theory: W. Barnett Pearce, "Evolution and Transformation: A Brief History of CMM and a Meditation on What Using It Does to Us," in *The Reflective, Facilitative, and Interpretative Practice of the Coordinated Management of Meaning: Making Lives, Making Meaning,* Catherine Creede, Beth Fisher-Yoshida, and Placida Gallegos (eds.), Fairleigh Dickinson, Madison, NJ, 2012, pp. 1–21.

Social construction: W. Barnett Pearce, "Communication as Social Construction: Reclaiming Our Birthright," in *Socially Constructing Communication,* Gloria J. Galanes and Wendy Leeds-Hurwitz (eds.), Hampton, Cresskill, NJ, 2009, pp. 33–56.

Making meaning and coordinating actions: W. Barnett Pearce, *Communication and the Human Condition,* Southern Illinois University, Carbondale, IL, 1989, pp. 32–87.

Intellectual heritage: Vernon E. Cronen, "Coordinated Management of Meaning: The Consequentiality of Communication and the Recapturing of Experience," in *The Consequentiality of Communication,* Stuart Sigman (ed.), Lawrence Erlbaum, Hillsdale, NJ, 1995, pp. 17–65.

80   *INTERPERSONAL COMMUNICATION*

Peacemaking: W. Barnett Pearce and Stephen W. Littlejohn, *Moral Conflict: When Social Worlds Collide*, Sage, Thousand Oaks, CA, 1997.

Dialogic communication: W. Barnett Pearce and Kimberly A. Pearce, "Combining Passions and Abilities: Toward Dialogic Virtuosity," *Southern Communication Journal*, Vol. 65, 2000, pp. 161–175.

Buber's dialogic ethics: Martin Buber, *I and Thou*, 2nd ed., R. G. Smith (trans.), Scribner, New York, 1958.

Research review of CMM: J. Kevin Barge and W. Barnett Pearce, "A Reconnaissance of CMM Research," *Human Systems*, Vol. 15, 2004, pp. 13–32.

CMM as a practical theory: J. Kevin Barge, "Articulating CMM as a Practical Theory," *Human Systems*, Vol. 15, 2004, pp. 193–204.

To access scenes from feature films that illustrate CMM and other theories, click on Suggested Movie Clips under Theory Resources at *www.afirstlook.com*.

CHAPTER **7**

Expectancy Violations Theory

of Judee Burgoon

Early in my teaching career, I was walking back to my office, puzzling over classroom conversations with four students. All four had made requests. Why, I wondered, had I readily agreed to two requests but just as quickly turned down two others? Each of the four students had spoken to me individually during the class break. Andre wanted my endorsement for a graduate scholarship, and Dawn invited me to eat lunch with her the next day. I said yes to both of them. Belinda asked me to help her on a term paper for a class with another professor, and Charlie encouraged me to play water polo that night with guys from his house, something I had done before. I said no to those requests.

Sitting down at my desk, I idly flipped through the pages of *Human Communication Research (HCR)*, a relatively new behavioral science journal that had arrived in the morning mail. I was still mulling over my uneven response to the students when my eyes zeroed in on an article entitled "A Communication Model of Personal Space Violations."[1] "That's it," I blurted out to our surprised department secretary. I suddenly realized that in each case my response to the student may have been influenced by the conversational distance between us.

I mentally pictured the four students making their requests—each from a distance that struck me as inappropriate in one way or another. Andre was literally in my face, less than a foot away. Belinda's 2-foot interval invaded my personal space, but not as much. Charlie stood about 7 feet away—just outside the range I would have expected for a let's-get-together-and-have-some-fun-that-has-nothing-to-do-with-school type of conversation. Dawn offered her luncheon invitation from across the room. At the time, each of these interactions had seemed somewhat strange. Now I realized that all four students had violated my expectation of an appropriate interpersonal distance.

Because I describe my impressions and reactions to these students, I've changed their names, and replaced them with names that start with the letters *A, B, C,* and *D* to represent the increasing distance between us when we spoke. (Andre was the closest; Dawn, the farthest away.) Figure 7–1 plots the intervals relative to my expectations.

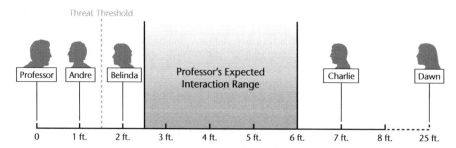

FIGURE 7–1   Expectancy Violations in a Classroom Setting

Judee Burgoon, a communication scholar at the University of Arizona, wrote the journal article that stimulated my thinking. The article was a follow-up piece on the *nonverbal expectancy violations model* that she had introduced in *HCR* two years earlier. Since my own dissertation research focused on interpersonal distance, I knew firsthand how little social science theory existed to guide researchers studying nonverbal communication. I was therefore excited to see Burgoon offering a sophisticated theory of personal space. The fact that she was teaching in a communication department and had published her work in a communication journal was value added. I eagerly read Burgoon's description of her nonverbal expectancy violations model to see whether it could account for my mixed response to the various conversational distances chosen by the four students.

PERSONAL SPACE EXPECTATIONS: CONFORM OR DEVIATE?

Personal space
The invisible, variable volume of space surrounding an individual that defines that individual's preferred distance from others.

Burgoon defined *personal space* as the "invisible, variable volume of space surrounding an individual that defines that individual's preferred distance from others."[2] She claimed that the size and shape of our personal space depend on our cultural norms and individual preferences, but our space always reflects a compromise between the conflicting approach–avoidance needs that we as humans have for affiliation and privacy.

Proxemics
The study of people's use of space as a special elaboration of culture.

The idea of personal space wasn't original with Burgoon. In the 1960s, Illinois Institute of Technology anthropologist Edward Hall coined the term *proxemics* to refer to the study of people's use of space as a special elaboration of culture.[3] He entitled his book *The Hidden Dimension* because he was convinced that most spatial interpretation is outside our awareness. He claimed that Americans have four proxemic zones, which nicely correspond with the four interpersonal distances selected by my students:

1. Intimate distance: 0 to 18 inches (Andre)
2. Personal distance: 18 inches to 4 feet (Belinda)
3. Social distance: 4 to 12 feet (Charlie)
4. Public distance: 12 to 25 feet (Dawn)

Hall's book is filled with examples of "ugly Americans" who were insensitive to the spatial customs of other cultures. He strongly recommended that in order to be effective, we learn to adjust our nonverbal behavior to conform to the communication rules of our partner. We shouldn't cross a distance boundary uninvited.

Cartoon by Peter Steiner. Reprinted with permission.

In his poem "Prologue: The Birth of Architecture," poet W. H. Auden echoes Hall's analysis and puts us on notice that we violate his personal space at our peril:

> Some thirty inches from my nose
> The frontier of my Person goes,
> And all the untilled air between
> Is private pagus or demesne.
> Stranger, unless with bedroom eyes
> I beckon you to fraternize,
> Beware of rudely crossing it:
> I have no gun, but I can spit.[4]

Burgoon's nonverbal expectancy violations model offered a counterpoint to Hall's and Auden's advice. She didn't argue with the idea that people have definite expectations about how close others should come. In fact, she would explain Auden's 30-inch rule as based on well-established American norms, plus the poet's own idiosyncrasies. But contrary to popular go-along-to-get-along wisdom, Burgoon suggested that there are times when it's best to break the rules. She believed that under some circumstances, violating social norms and personal expectations is "a superior strategy to conformity."[5]

AN APPLIED TEST OF THE ORIGINAL MODEL

Whether knowingly or not, each of the four students making a request deviated from my proxemic expectation. How well did Burgoon's initial model predict my responses to these four different violations? Not very well. To help you capture the flavor of Burgoon's early speculation and recognize how far her current theory has come, I'll outline what the model predicted my responses would be and, in each case, compare that forecast to what I actually did.

Threat threshold
The hypothetical outer boundary of intimate space; a breach by an uninvited other occasions fight or flight.

Andre.   According to Burgoon's early model, Andre made a mistake when he crossed my invisible *threat threshold* and spoke with me at an intimate eyeball-to-eyeball distance. The physical and psychological discomfort I'd feel would hurt his cause. But the model missed on that prediction, since I wrote the recommendation later that day.

Belinda.   In the follow-up article I read that day, Burgoon suggested that noticeable deviations from what we expect cause us to experience a heightened state of arousal. She wasn't necessarily referring to the heart-pounding, sweaty-palms reaction that drives us to fight or flight. Instead, she pictured violations stimulating us to mentally review the nature of our relationship with the person who acted in a curious way. That would be good news for Belinda if I thought of her as a highly rewarding person. But every comment she made in class seemed to me a direct challenge, dripping with sarcasm. Just as Burgoon predicted, the narrow, 2-foot gap Belinda chose focused my attention on our rocky relationship, and I declined her request for help in another course. Score one for the nonverbal expectancy violations model.

Charlie.   Charlie was a nice guy who cared more about having a good time than he did about studies. He knew I'd played water polo in college, but he may not have realized that his casual attitude toward the class was a constant reminder that I wasn't as good a teacher as I wanted to be. In her 1978 *HRC* article, Burgoon wrote that a person with "punishing power" (like Charlie) would do best to observe proxemic conventions or, better yet, stand slightly farther away than expected. Without ever hearing Burgoon's advice, Charlie did it right. He backed off to a distance of 7 feet—just outside the range of interaction I anticipated. Even so, I declined his offer to swim with the guys.

Dawn.   According to this nonverbal expectancy violations model, Dawn blew it. Because she was an attractive communicator, a warm, close approach would have been a pleasant surprise. Her decision to issue an invitation from across the room, however, would seem to guarantee a poor response. The farther she backed off, the worse the effect would be. There's only one problem with this analysis: Dawn and I had lunch together in the student union the following day.

Obviously, my attempt to apply Burgoon's original model to conversational distance between me and my students didn't meet with much success. The theoretical scoreboard read:

> Nonverbal expectancy violations model: **1**
> Unpredicted random behavior: **3**

Burgoon's first controlled experiments didn't fare much better. But where I was ready to dismiss the whole model as flawed, she was unwilling to abandon *expectancy violation* as a key concept in human interaction. At the end of her journal article she hinted that some of her basic assumptions might need to be tested and reevaluated.

Of course, that was then; this is now. For more than three decades, Judee Burgoon and her students have crafted a series of sophisticated laboratory experiments and field studies to discover and explain the effects of expectancy violations. One of the reasons I chose to write about her theory is that the current version is an excellent example of ideas continually revised as a result of empirical disconfirmation. As she has demonstrated, in science, failure can lead to success.

A CONVOLUTED MODEL BECOMES AN ELEGANT THEORY

When applied to theories, the term *elegant* suggests "gracefully concise and simple; admirably succinct."[6] That's what expectancy violations theory has become. Burgoon has dropped concepts that were central in earlier versions but never panned out. Early on, for example, she abandoned the idea of a "threat threshold." Even though that hypothetical boundary made intuitive sense, repeated experimentation failed to confirm its existence.

Burgoon's retreat from *arousal* as an explanatory mechanism has been more gradual. She originally stated that people felt physiologically aroused when their proxemic expectations were violated. Later she softened the concept to "an orienting response" or a mental "alertness" that focuses attention on the violator. She now views arousal as a side effect of a partner's deviation and no longer considers it a necessary link between expectancy violation and communication outcomes such as attraction, credibility, persuasion, and involvement.

Arousal, relational
A heightened state of awareness, orienting response, or mental alertness that stimulates a review of the relationship.

By removing extraneous features, Burgoon has streamlined her model. By extending its scope, she has produced a complete theory. Her original nonverbal expectancy violations model was concerned only with spatial violations—a rather narrow focus. But by the mid-1980s, Burgoon concluded that proxemic behavior is part of an interconnected system of nonlinguistic cues. It no longer made sense to study interpersonal distance in isolation. She began to apply the model to a host of other nonverbal variables—facial expression, eye contact, touch, and body lean, for example. Burgoon continues to expand the range of expectancy violations. While not losing interest in nonverbal communication, she now applies the theory to what's said in emotional, marital, and intercultural communication as well. Consistent with this broad sweep, she has dropped the *nonverbal* qualifier and refers to her theory as "expectancy violations theory," or EVT. From this point on, so will I.

What does EVT predict? Burgoon sums up her empirically driven conclusions in a single paragraph. I hope that my long narrative of the theory's development will help you appreciate the 30 years of work that lie behind these simple lines.

> Expectancies exert significant influence on people's interaction patterns, on their impressions of one another, and on the outcomes of their interactions. Violations of expectations in turn may arouse and distract their recipients, shifting greater attention to the violator and the meaning of the violation itself. People who can assume that they are well regarded by their audience are safer engaging in violations and more likely to profit from doing so than are those who are poorly regarded. When the violation act is one that is likely to be ambiguous in its meaning or to carry multiple interpretations that are not uniformly positive or negative, then the reward valence of the communicator can be especially significant in moderating interpretations, evaluations, and subsequent outcomes. . . . In other cases, violations

have relatively consensual meanings and valences associated with them, so that engaging in them produces similar effects for positive- and negative-valenced communicators.[7]

CORE CONCEPTS OF EVT

A close reading of Burgoon's summary suggests that EVT offers a "soft determinism" rather than hard-core universal laws (see Chapter 2). The qualifying terms *may, more likely, can be,* and *relatively* reflect her belief that too many factors affect communication to ever allow us to discover simple cause-and-effect relationships. She does, however, hope to show a link among surprising interpersonal behavior and attraction, credibility, influence, and involvement. These are the potential outcomes of expectancy violation that Burgoon and her students explore. In order for us to appreciate the connection, we need to understand three core concepts of EVT: *expectancy, violation valence,* and *communicator reward valence.* I'll illustrate these three variables by referring back to my students' proxemic behavior and to another form of nonverbal communication—touch.

Expectancy

When I was a kid, my mother frequently gave notice that she *expected* me to be on my best behavior. I considered her words to be a wish or a warning rather than a forecast of my future actions. That's not how Burgoon uses the word. She and her colleagues "prefer to reserve the term *expectancy* for what is predicted to occur rather than what is desired."[8] Figure 7–1 shows that I anticipated conversations with students to take place at a distance of 2½ to 6 feet. How did this expectation arise? Burgoon suggests that I processed the context, type of relationship, and characteristics of the others automatically in my mind so that I could gauge what they might do.

Expectancy
What people predict will happen, rather than what they desire.

Context begins with cultural norms. Three feet is too close in England or Germany yet too far removed in Saudi Arabia, where you can't trust people who won't let you smell their breath. Context also includes the setting of the conversation. A classroom environment dictates a greater speaking distance than would be appropriate for a private chat in my office.

Relationship factors include similarity, familiarity, liking, and relative status. In one study, Burgoon discovered that people of all ages and stations in life anticipate that lower-status people will keep their distance. Because of our age difference and teacher–student relationship, I was more surprised by Andre's and Belinda's invasion of my personal space than I was by Charlie's and Dawn's remote location.

Communicator characteristics include all of the age/sex/place-of-birth demographic facts requested on applications, but they also include personal features that may affect expectation even more—physical appearance, personality, and communication style. Dawn's warm smile was a counterpoint to Belinda's caustic comments. Given this difference, I would have assumed that Dawn would be the one to draw close and Belinda the one to keep her distance. That's why I was especially curious when each woman's spatial "transgression" was the opposite of what I would have predicted.

We can do a similar analysis of my expectation for touch in that classroom situation. Edward Hall claimed that the United States is a "noncontact culture," so I wouldn't anticipate touch during the course of normal conversation.[9] Does this mean that Latin American or Southern European "contact cultures" wouldn't have tight expectations for nonverbal interaction? By no means; Burgoon is convinced that all cultures have a similar *structure* of expected communication behavior, but that the *content* of those expectations can differ markedly from culture to culture. Touch is fraught with meaning in every society, but the who, when, where, and how of touching are a matter of culture-specific standards and customs.

As a male in a role relationship, it never occurred to me that students might make physical contact while voicing their requests. If it had, Dawn would have been the likely candidate. But at her chosen distance of 25 feet, she'd need to be a bionic woman to reach me. As it was, I would have been shocked if she'd violated my expectation and walked over to give me a hug. (As a lead-in to the next two sections, note that I didn't say I would have been disturbed, distressed, or disgusted.)

Violation Valence

Violation valence

The perceived positive or negative value assigned to a breach of expectations, regardless of who the violator is.

The term *violation valence* refers to the positive or negative value we place on a specific unexpected behavior, regardless of who does it. Do we find the act itself pleasing or distressing, and to what extent? With her commitment to the scientific method, Burgoon may have borrowed the concept of valence from chemistry, where the valence of a substance is indicated by a number and its sign ($+3$ or -2, for example). The term *net worth* from the field of accounting seems to capture the same idea.

We usually give others a bit of wiggle room to deviate from what we regard as standard operating procedure. But once we deal with someone who acts outside the range of expected behavior, we switch into evaluation mode. According to Burgoon, we first try to interpret the meaning of the violation, and then figure out whether we like it.

The meaning of some violations is easy to spot. As a case in point, no one would agonize over how to interpret a purposeful poke in the eye with a sharp stick. It's a hostile act, and if it happened to us, we'd be livid. Many nonverbal behaviors are that straightforward. For example, moderate to prolonged eye contact in Western cultures usually communicates awareness, interest, affection, and trust. A level gaze is welcome; shifty eyes are not. With the exception of a riveting stare, we value eye contact. Even Emerson, a man of letters, wrote, "The eyes of men converse as much as their tongues, with the advantage that the ocular dialect needs no dictionary. . . ."[10]

When a behavior has a socially recognized meaning, communicators can usually figure out whether to go beyond what others expect. If the valence is negative, do less than expected. If the valence is positive, go further. Burgoon validated this advice when she studied the effect of expectancy on marital satisfaction.[11] She questioned people about how much intimate communication they expected from their partner compared to how much focused conversation they actually got. Not surprisingly, intimacy was ranked as positive. Partners who received about as much intimacy as they expected were moderately satisfied with their marriages. But people were highly satisfied with their marriages when they had more good talks with their husbands or wives than they originally thought they would.

On the other hand, many expectancy violations are ambiguous and open to multiple interpretations. For example, the meaning of unexpected touch can be puzzling. Is it a mark of total involvement in the conversation, a sign of warmth and affection, a display of dominance, or a sexual move? Distance violations can also be confusing. Andre isn't from the Middle East, so why was he standing so close? I don't bark or bite, so why did Dawn issue her invitation from across the room? According to EVT, it's at times like these that we consider the reward valence of the communicator as well as the valence of the violation.

Before we look at the way communicator reward valence fits into the theory, you should know that Burgoon has found few nonverbal behaviors that are ambiguous when seen in a larger context. A touch on the arm might be enigmatic in isolation, but when experienced along with close proximity, forward body lean, a direct gaze, facial animation, and verbal fluency, almost everyone interprets the physical contact as a sign of high involvement in the conversation.[12] Or consider actor Eric Idle's words and nonverbal manner in a *Monty Python* sketch. He punctuates his question about Terry Gilliam's wife with a burlesque wink, a leering tone of voice, and gestures to accompany his words: "Nudge nudge. Know what I mean? Say no more . . . know what I mean?"[13] Taken alone, an exaggerated wink or a dig with the elbow might have many possible meanings, but as part of a coordinated routine, both gestures clearly transform a questionable remark into a lewd comment.

There are times, however, when nonverbal expectancy violations are truly equivocal. The personal space deviations of my students are cases in point. Perhaps I just wasn't sensitive enough to pick up the cues that would help me make sense of their proxemic violations. But when the meaning of an action is unclear, EVT says that we interpret the violation in light of how the violator can affect our lives.

Communicator Reward Valence

EVT is not the only theory that describes the tendency to size up other people in terms of the potential rewards they have to offer. *Social penetration theory* suggests that we live in an interpersonal economy in which we all "take stock" of the relational value of others we meet (see Chapter 8). The questions *What can you do for me?* and *What can you do to me?* often cross our minds. Burgoon is not a cynic, but she thinks the issue of reward potential moves from the background to the foreground of our minds when someone violates our expectation and there's no social consensus on the meaning of the act. She uses the term *communicator reward valence* to label the results of our mental audit of likely gains and losses.

The reward valence of a communicator is the sum of the positive and negative attributes the person brings to the encounter plus the potential he or she has to reward or punish in the future. The resulting perception is usually a mix of good and bad and falls somewhere on a scale between those two poles. I'll illustrate communicator characteristics that Burgoon frequently mentions by reviewing one feature of each student that I thought about immediately after their perplexing spatial violations.

Communicator reward valence
The sum of positive and negative attributes brought to the encounter plus the potential to reward or punish in the future.

Andre was a brilliant student. Although writing recommendations is low on my list of fun things to do, I would bask in reflected glory if he were accepted into a top graduate program.

Belinda had a razor-sharp mind and a tongue to match. I'd already felt the sting of her verbal barbs and thought that thinly veiled criticism in the future was a distinct possibility.

Charlie was the classic goof-off—seldom in class and never prepared. I try to be evenhanded with everyone who signs up for my classes, but in Charlie's case I had to struggle not to take his casual attitude toward the course as a personal snub.

Dawn was a beautiful young woman with a warm smile. I felt great pleasure when she openly announced that I was her favorite teacher.

My views of Andre, Belinda, Charlie, and Dawn probably say more about me than they do about the four students. I'm not particularly proud of my stereotyped assessments, but apparently I have plenty of company in the criteria I used. Burgoon notes that the features that impressed me also weigh heavily with others when they compute a reward valence for someone who is violating their expectations. Status, ability, and good looks are standard "goodies" that enhance the other person's reward potential. The thrust of the conversation is even more important. Most of us value words that communicate acceptance, liking, appreciation, and trust. We're turned off by talk that conveys disinterest, disapproval, distrust, and rejection.

Why does Burgoon think that the expectancy violator's power to reward or punish is so crucial? Because puzzling violations force victims to search the social context for clues to their meaning.[14] Thus, an ambiguous violation embedded in a host of relationally warm signals takes on a positive cast. An equivocal violation from a punishing communicator stiffens our resistance.

Now that I've outlined EVT's core concepts of expectancy, violation valence, and communicator reward valence, you can better understand the bottom-line advice that Burgoon's theory offers. Should you communicate in a totally unexpected way? If you're certain that the novelty will be a pleasant surprise, the answer is yes. But if you know that your outlandish behavior will offend, don't do it.

When you aren't sure how others will interpret your far-out behavior, let their overall attitude toward you dictate your verbal and nonverbal actions. So if, like Belinda and Charlie, you have reason to suspect a strained relationship, and the meaning of a violation might be unclear, stifle your deviant tendencies and do your best to conform to expectations. But when you know you've already created a positive personal impression (like Andre or Dawn), a surprise move is not only safe, it will probably enhance the positive effect of your message.

INTERACTION ADAPTATION—ADJUSTING EXPECTATIONS

As evidence of its predictive power, EVT has been used to explain and predict attitudes and behaviors in a wide variety of communication contexts. These include students' perceptions of their instructors, patients' responses to health care providers, and individuals' actions in romantic relationships. For example, Arizona State University communication professor Paul Mongeau has studied men's and women's expectations for first dates and compared those expectations with their actual experiences.[15] He discovered that men are pleasantly surprised when a woman initiates a first date, and that they usually interpret such a request as a sign that she's interested in sexual activity. But there's a second surprise in store for most of these guys when it turns out that they have less physical intimacy than they do on the traditional male-initiated first date. We might expect that the men's disappointment would put a damper on future dates together but, surprisingly, it doesn't.

For Mongeau, EVT explains how dating partners' expectations are affected by who asks out whom. Yet unlike early tests of EVT, Mongeau's work considers how one person's actions might reshape a dating partner's perceptions after their time together—a morning-after-the-night-before adjustment of expectations. In the same way, Burgoon has reassessed EVT's single-sided view and now favors a dyadic model of adaptation. That's because she regards conversations as more akin to duets than solos. Interpersonal interactions involve synchronized actions rather than unilateral moves. Along with her former students Lesa Stern and Leesa Dillman, Burgoon has crafted *interaction adaptation theory (IAT)* as an extension and expansion of EVT.[16]

Interaction adaptation theory

A systematic analysis of how people adjust their approach when another's behavior doesn't mesh with what's needed, anticipated, or preferred.

Burgoon states that human beings are predisposed to adapt to each other. That's often necessary, she says, because another person's actions may not square with the thoughts and feelings we bring to the interaction. She sees this initial *interaction position* as made up of three factors: requirements, expectations, and desires. *Requirements (R)* are the outcomes that fulfill our basic needs to survive, be safe, belong, and have a sense of self-worth. These are the panhuman motivations that Abraham Maslow outlined in his famous hierarchy of needs.[17] As opposed to requirements that represent what we need to happen, *expectations (E)* as defined in EVT are what we think really will happen. Finally, *desires (D)* are what we personally would like to see happen. These RED factors coalesce or meld into our interaction position of what's needed, anticipated, and preferred. I'll continue to use touch behavior to show how Burgoon uses this composite mindset to predict how we adjust to another person's behavior.

Interaction position

A person's initial stance toward an interaction as determined by a blend of personal requirements, expectations, and desires (RED).

In her course application log, Lindi briefly describes a roommate's unanticipated interaction with a casual friend:

> At the end of last year my roommate was hanging out with a bunch of our friends late at night and one of the guys started playing with her hair and continued to do so for the rest of the night. This unexpected violation of her personal space surprised her, but turned out to be a very pleasant experience. She was forced then to reevaluate their relationship. Even though they didn't develop a romantic relationship, this violation brought them closer together and helped them redefine their friendship.

Although details are sparse, it's possible to approximate the roommate's interactional position at the start of the evening. Her willingness to spend the night hanging around with a group of friends suggests that she has a high need or requirement for affiliation and belongingness (R). Given her surprise at the fellow fiddling with her hair, we can assume that this ongoing touch was definitely not the behavioral norm of the group, nor what she expected based on the guy's past behavior (E). Yet her pleasure with this fellow's continual touch indicates that she had a strong desire for this kind of personal attention from him (D). Her initial interaction position would therefore be an amalgam of what she needed, expected, and preferred.

With the help of hindsight, we can see that the valence of the guy playing with her hair was more positive than her interaction position. According to IAT, the pattern of response would therefore be one of reciprocity or convergence. Reciprocity would mean that she then ran her fingers through his hair. There's no hint that this happened. Yet since the whole group of friends could monitor her response, it's unlikely he would have continued with this form of touch unless she encouraged him with a smile or words indicating pleasure. That would be convergence. If, on the other hand, the valence she assigned to him messing with her hair was more negative than her interaction position, Burgoon predicts some form of compensation or divergent behavior. She might lean away from him, excuse herself to comb her hair, or simply look at him and say, "Cut it out." Unlike EVT, IAT addresses how people adjust their behavior when others violate their expectations.

Burgoon outlined two shortcomings of expectancy violations theory that she found particularly troubling:

Reciprocity
A strong human tendency to respond to another's action with similar behavior.

> First, EVT does not fully account for the overwhelming prevalence of reciprocity that has been found in interpersonal interactions. Second, it is silent on whether communicator reward valence supersedes behavior valence or vice versa when the two are incongruent (such as when a disliked partner engages in a positive violation).[18]

Interaction adaptation theory is Burgoon's attempt to address these problems within the broader framework of ongoing behavioral adjustments. There's obviously more to the theory than I've been able to present, but hopefully this brief sketch lets you see that for Burgoon, one theory leads to another.

CRITIQUE: A WELL-REGARDED WORK IN PROGRESS

I have a friend who fixes my all-terrain cycle whenever I bend it or break it. "What do you think?" I ask Bill. "Can it be repaired?" His response is always the same: "Man made it. Man can fix it!"

Judee Burgoon shows the same resolve as she seeks to adjust and redesign an expectancy violations model that never quite works as well in practice as its theoretical blueprint says it should. Almost every empirical test she runs seems to yield mixed results. For example, her early work on physical contact suggested that touch violations were often ambiguous. However, a sophisticated experiment she ran in 1992 showed that unexpected touch in a problem-solving situation was almost always welcomed as a positive violation, regardless of the status, gender, or attractiveness of the violator.

Do repeated failures to predict outcomes when a person stands far away, moves in too close, or reaches out to touch someone imply that Burgoon ought to trade in her expectancy violations theory for a new model? Does IAT render EVT obsolete? From my perspective, the answer is no.

Taken as a whole, Burgoon's expectancy violations theory continues to meet five of the six criteria of a good scientific theory as presented in Chapter 3. Her theory advances a reasonable *explanation* for the effects of expectancy violations during communication. The explanation she offers is *relatively simple* and has actually become less complex over time. The theory has *testable hypotheses* that the theorist is willing to adjust when her *quantitative research* doesn't support the prediction. Finally, the model offers *practical advice* on how to better achieve important communication goals of increased credibility, influence, and attraction. Could we ask for anything more? Of course.

We could wish for *predictions* that prove more reliable than the *Farmer's Almanac* long-range forecast of weather trends. A review of expectancy violations research suggests that EVT may have reached that point. For example, a comparative empirical study tested how well three leading theories predict interpersonal responses to nonverbal immediacy—close proximity, touch, direct gaze, direct body orientation, and forward lean.[19] None of the theories proved to be right all of the time, but EVT did better than the other two. And based on what a revised EVT now predicts, the scoreboard for my responses to the proxemic violations of Andre, Belinda, Charlie, and Dawn shows four hits and no misses.

ETHICAL REFLECTION: KANT'S CATEGORICAL IMPERATIVE

EVT focuses on what's *effective.* But, according to German philosopher Immanuel Kant, before we knowingly violate another's expectation we should consider what's *ethical.* Kant believed that any time we speak or act, we have a moral obligation to be truthful. He wrote that "truthfulness in statements which cannot be avoided is the formal duty of an individual to everyone, however great may be the disadvantage accruing to himself or another."[20] Others might wink at white lies, justify deception for the other's own good, or warn of the dire consequences that can result from total honesty. But from Kant's perspective, there are no mitigating circumstances. Lying is wrong—always. So is breaking a promise. He'd regard nonverbal deception the same way.

Categorical imperative
Duty without exception; act only on that maxim which you can will to become a universal law.

Kant came to this absolutist position through the logic of his *categorical imperative,* a term that means duty without exception. He stated the categorical imperative as an ethical absolute: "Act only on that maxim which you can will to become a universal law."[21] In terms of EVT, Kant would have us look at the violation we are considering and ask, *What if everybody did that all the time?* If we don't like the answer, we have a solemn duty not to do the deed.

The categorical imperative is a method of determining right from wrong by thinking through the ethical valence of an act, regardless of motive. Suppose we're thinking about touching someone in a way he or she doesn't expect and hasn't clearly let us know is welcome. Perhaps the other person, like Lindi's roommate, might be pleasantly surprised. But unless we can embrace the idea of everyone—no matter what their communication reward valence—having that kind of unbidden access to everybody, the categorical imperative says don't do it. No exceptions. In the words of a sports-minded colleague who teaches ethics, "Kant plays ethical hardball without a mitt." If we say, *I "Kant" play in that league,* what ethical scorecard will we use in place of his categorical imperative?

QUESTIONS TO SHARPEN YOUR FOCUS

1. What *proxemic* advice would you give to communicators who believe they are seen as *unrewarding?*

2. EVT suggests that *violation valence* is especially important when it's clearly positive or negative. What verbal or nonverbal expectancy violations would be confusing to you even when experienced in context?

3. Using the concepts of *expectancy, violation valence,* and *communicator reward valence,* can you explain how the final version of EVT accurately predicts Em's response to the four requests made by Andre, Belinda, Charlie, and Dawn?

4. EVT and coordinated management of meaning (see Chapter 6) hold divergent views about the nature of *ways of knowing, human nature,* and *communication research.* Can you spot the different assumptions?

CONVERSATIONS

View this segment online at
www.mhhe.com/griffin9e or
www.afirstlook.com.

A few minutes into my discussion with Judee Burgoon, you'll notice that one of us violates a communication expectation of the other. See if you think the violation is accidental or strategic. How does this event affect the rest of the conversation? Burgoon's love of theory is apparent throughout the segment. Do you think her enthusiasm is bolstered by a view of theories as systematic hunches rather than timeless principles chiseled in stone? As a scientist, Burgoon believes that much of human behavior is genetically programmed, yet she insists that communication is also a choice-driven, strategic behavior. As you watch, decide whether you think these beliefs are compatible.

A SECOND LOOK

Recommended resource: Judee K. Burgoon and Jerold Hale, "Nonverbal Expectancy Violations: Model Elaboration and Application to Immediacy Behaviors," *Communication Monographs,* Vol. 55, 1988, pp. 58–79.

Original model: Judee K. Burgoon, "A Communication Model of Personal Space Violations: Explication and an Initial Test," *Human Communication Research,* Vol. 4, 1978, pp. 129–142.

Expectancy: Judee K. Burgoon and Beth A. LePoire, "Effects of Communication Expectancies, Actual Communication, and Expectancy Disconfirmation on Evaluations of Communicators and Their Communication Behavior," *Human Communication Research,* Vol. 20, 1993, pp. 67–96.

Communicator reward valence: Judee K. Burgoon, "Relational Message Interpretations of Touch, Conversational Distance, and Posture," *Journal of Nonverbal Behavior,* Vol. 15, 1991, pp. 233–259.

Extension of the theory: Walid A. Afifi and Judee K. Burgoon, "The Impact of Violations on Uncertainty and the Consequences for Attractiveness," *Human Communication Research,* Vol. 26, 2000, pp. 203–233.

Cultural violations: Judee K. Burgoon and Amy Ebesu Hubbard, "Cross-Cultural and Intercultural Applications of Expectancy Violations Theory and Interaction Adaptation Theory," in *Theorizing About Intercultural Communication,* William B. Gudykunst (ed.), Sage, Thousand Oaks, CA, 2004, pp. 149–171.

Interaction adaptation theory: Judee K. Burgoon, Lesa Stern, and Leesa Dillman, *Interpersonal Adaptation: Dyadic Interaction Patterns,* Cambridge University, Cambridge, 1995.

Interaction adaptation theory application: Keri K. Stephens, Marian L. Houser, and Renee L. Cowan, "R U Able to Meat Me: The Impact of Students' Overly Casual Email Messages to Instructors," *Communication Education,* Vol. 58, 2009, pp. 303–326.

Explanation and comparison of EVT and IAT: Cindy H. White, "Expectancy Violations Theory and Interaction Adaptation Theory: From Expectations to Adaptation," in *Engaging Theories in Interpersonal Communication: Multiple Perspectives,* Leslie A. Baxter and Dawn O. Braithwaite (eds.), Sage, Thousand Oaks, CA, 2008, pp. 189–202.

Kant's categorical imperative: Immanuel Kant, *Groundwork of the Metaphysics of Morals,* H. J. Paton (trans.), Harper Torchbooks, New York, 1964, pp. 60–88.

Critique: Peter A. Andersen, Laura K. Guerrero, David B. Buller, and Peter F. Jorgensen, "An Empirical Comparison of Three Theories of Nonverbal Immediacy Exchange," *Human Communication Research,* Vol. 24, 1998, pp. 501–535.

Relationship Development

Think about your closest personal relationship. Is it one of "strong, frequent and diverse interdependence that lasts over a considerable period of time?"[1] That's how UCLA psychologist Harold Kelley and eight co-authors defined the concept of close relationship. Though their definition could apply to parties who don't even like each other, most theorists reserve the term *close* for relationships that include a positive bond—usually romantic, friend, and family. All three types of intimacy can provide enjoyment, trust, sharing of confidences, respect, mutual assistance, and spontaneity.[2] The question is, *How do we develop a close relationship?*

Two distinct approaches have dominated the theory and practice of relational development. One *experiential approach* is typified by humanistic psychologist Carl Rogers. Based upon his years of nondirective counseling, Rogers described three necessary and sufficient conditions for relationship growth. When partners perceived (1) congruence; (2) unconditional positive regard; and (3) empathic understanding of each other, they could and would draw closer.[3]

Congruence is the match or fit between an individual's inner feelings and outer display. The congruent person is genuine, real, integrated, whole, transparent. The noncongruent person tries to impress, plays a role, puts up a front, hides behind a facade. "In my relationship with persons," Rogers wrote, "I've found that it does not help, in the long run, to act as though I was something I was not."[4]

Unconditional positive regard is an attitude of acceptance that isn't contingent upon performance. Rogers asked, "Can I let myself experience positive attitudes toward this other person—attitudes of warmth, caring, liking, interest, and respect?"[5] When the answer was *yes,* both he and his clients matured as human beings. They also liked each other.

Empathic understanding is the caring skill of temporarily laying aside our views and values and entering into another's world without prejudice. It is an active process of seeking to hear the other's thoughts, feelings, tones, and meanings as if they were our own. Rogers thought it was a waste of time to be suspicious or to wonder, *What does she really mean?* He believed that we help people most when we accept what they say at face value. We should assume that they describe their world as it really appears to them.

Rogerian ideas have permeated the textbooks and teaching of interpersonal communication.[6] The topics of self-disclosure, nonverbal warmth, empathic listening, and trust are mainstays of an introductory course.

The other approach assumes that relationship behavior is shaped by the *rewards and costs of interaction.* In 1992, University of Chicago economist Gary Becker won the Nobel Prize in economics on the basis of his application of supply-and-demand market models to predict the behavior of everyday living, including love and marriage.[7] News commentators expressed skepticism that matters of the heart could be reduced to cold numbers, but the economic metaphor has dominated social science discussions of interpersonal attraction and behavior for the last five decades. It's also the approach of popular dating websites like eHarmony, where customers complete a questionnaire that matches them to "singles who have been prescreened on 29 Dimensions of Compatibility:

scientific predictors of long-term relationship success."[8] Like such dating services, the basic assumption of many relational theorists is that people interact with others in a way that maximizes their personal benefits and minimizes their personal costs.

Numerous parallels exist between the stock market and relationship market:

Law of supply and demand. A rare, desirable characteristic commands higher value on the exchange.

Courting a buyer. Most parties in the market prepare a prospectus that highlights their assets and downplays their liabilities.

Laissez-faire rules. Let the buyer beware. All's fair in love and war. It's a jungle out there.

Investors and traders. Investors commit for the long haul; traders try to make an overnight killing.

Even from these brief summaries, you can tell that a humanistic model of relational development is quite different from an economic model of social exchange. Yet both models affect each of the theories presented in this section.

All three theories regard communication as the means by which people can draw close to one another. Each considers instant intimacy a myth; relationships take time to develop and they don't always proceed on a straight-line trajectory toward that goal. In fact, most relationships never even get close. Yet some people do have deep, satisfying, long-lasting relationships. Why do they develop close ties when others don't? Each of the theories in this section offers an answer.

"I've done the numbers, and I will marry you."

© William Hamilton/The New Yorker Collection/www.cartoonbank.com

CHAPTER 8

Social Penetration Theory

of Irwin Altman & Dalmas Taylor

A friend in need is a friend indeed.
Neither a borrower nor a lender be.

A soft answer turns away wrath.
Don't get mad, get even.

To know him is to love him.
Familiarity breeds contempt.

Proverbs are the wisdom of the ages boiled down into short, easy-to-remember phrases. There are probably more maxims about interpersonal relationships than about any other topic. But are these truisms dependable? As we can see in the pairings above, the advice they give often seems contradictory.

Consider the plight of Pete, a freshman at a residential college, as he enters the dorm to meet his roommate face-to-face for the first time. Pete has just waved good-bye to his folks and already feels pangs of loneliness as he thinks of his girlfriend back home. He worries how she'll feel about him when he goes home at Thanksgiving. Will she illustrate the reliability of the old adage "absence makes the heart grow fonder," or will "out of sight, out of mind" be a better way to describe the next few months?

Pete finds his room and immediately spots the familiar shape of a lacrosse stick. He's initially encouraged by what appears to be a common interest, but he also can't forget that his roommate's Facebook profile expressed enthusiasm for several candidates on the opposite end of the political spectrum from Pete. Will "birds of a feather flock together" hold true in their relationship, or will "opposites attract" better describe their interaction?

Just then Jon, his roommate, comes in. For a few minutes they trade the stock phrases that give them a chance to size up each other. Something in Pete makes him want to tell Jon how much he misses his girlfriend, but a deeper sense of what is an appropriate topic of conversation when first meeting someone prevents him from sharing his feelings. On a subconscious level, perhaps even a conscious one, Pete is torn between acting on the old adage "misery loves company" or on the more macho "big boys don't cry."

Social penetration
The process of developing deeper intimacy with another person through mutual self-disclosure and other forms of vulnerability.

Pete obviously needs something more than pithy proverbs to help him understand relational dynamics. More than two decades before Pete was born, social psychologists Irwin Altman and Dalmas Taylor proposed a *social penetration process* that explains how relational closeness develops. Altman is distinguished professor emeritus of psychology at the University of Utah, and Taylor, now deceased, was provost and professor of psychology at Lincoln University in Pennsylvania. They predicted that Pete and Jon would end up best friends only if they proceeded in a "gradual and orderly fashion from superficial to intimate levels of exchange as a function of both immediate and forecast outcomes."[1] In order to capture the process, we first have to understand the complexity of people.

PERSONALITY STRUCTURE: A MULTILAYERED ONION

Personality structure
Onion-like layers of beliefs and feelings about self, others, and the world; deeper layers are more vulnerable, protected, and central to self-image.

Altman and Taylor compared people to onions. This isn't a commentary on the human capacity to offend. Like the self-description that the ogre in *Shrek* shares with his donkey sidekick in the original film, it is a depiction of the multilayered *structure* of personality. Peel the outer skin from an onion, and you'll find another beneath it. Remove that layer and you'll expose a third, and so on. Pete's outer layer is his public self that's accessible to anyone who cares to look. The outer layer includes a myriad of details that certainly help describe who he is but are held in common with others at the school. On the surface, people see a tall, 18-year-old male business major from Michigan who lifts weights and gets lots of Facebook posts from friends back home. If Jon can look beneath the surface, he'll discover the semiprivate attitudes that Pete reveals only to some people. Pete is sympathetic to liberal social causes, deeply religious, and prejudiced against overweight people.

Pete's inner core is made up of his values, self-concept, unresolved conflicts, and deeply felt emotions—things he'd never dream of posting on Facebook. This is his unique private domain, which is invisible to the world but has a significant impact on the areas of his life that are closer to the surface. Perhaps not even his girlfriend or parents know his most closely guarded secrets about himself.

CLOSENESS THROUGH SELF-DISCLOSURE

Self-disclosure
The voluntary sharing of personal history, preferences, attitudes, feelings, values, secrets, etc., with another person; transparency.

Pete becomes accessible to others as he relaxes the tight boundaries that protect him and makes himself vulnerable. This can be a scary process, but Altman and Taylor believed it's only by allowing Jon to penetrate well below the surface that Pete can truly draw close to his roommate. Nonverbal paths to closeness include mock roughhousing, eye contact, and smiling. But the main route to deep social penetration is through verbal *self-disclosure.*

Figure 8–1 illustrates a wedge being pulled into an onion. It's as if a strong magnetic force were drawing it toward the center. The depth of penetration represents the degree of personal disclosure. To get to the center, the wedge must first separate the outer layers. Altman and Taylor claimed that on the surface level this kind of biographical information exchange takes place easily, perhaps at the first meeting. But they pictured the layers of onion skin tougher and more tightly wrapped as the wedge nears the center.

Recall that Pete is hesitant to share his longing for his girlfriend with Jon. If he admits these feelings, he's opening himself up for some heavy-handed

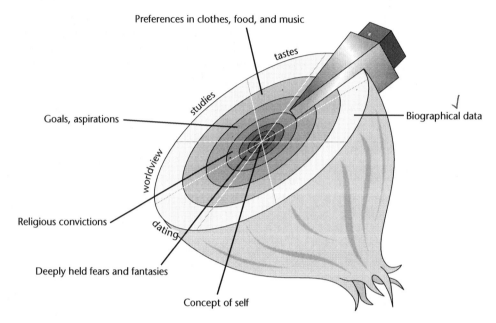

Preferences in clothes, food, and music

tastes

studies

Goals, aspirations

worldview

Biographical data

Religious convictions

dating

Deeply held fears and fantasies

Concept of self

FIGURE 8–1   Penetration of Pete's Personality Structure

kidding or emotional blackmail. In addition, once the wedge has penetrated deeply, it will have cut a passage through which it can return again and again with little resistance. Future privacy will be difficult. Realizing both of these factors, Pete may be extra cautious about exposing his true feelings. Perhaps he'll fence off this part of his life for the whole school term. According to social penetration theory, a permanent guard will limit the closeness these two young men can achieve.

THE DEPTH AND BREADTH OF SELF-DISCLOSURE

Depth of penetration
The degree of disclosure in a specific area of an individual's life.

The *depth of penetration* is the degree of intimacy. Although Altman and Taylor's penetration analogy strikes some readers as sexual, this was not their intent. The analogy applies equally to intimacy in friendship and romance. Figure 8–1 diagrams the closeness Jon gains if he and Pete become friends during the year. In their framework of social penetration theory, Altman and Taylor outlined four observations about the process that will bring Pete and Jon to this point:

1. *Peripheral items are exchanged sooner and more frequently than private information.* When the sharp edge of the wedge has barely reached the intimate area, the thicker part has cut a wide path through the outer rings. The relationship is still at a relatively impersonal level ("big boys don't cry"). University of Connecticut communication professor Arthur VanLear analyzed the content of conversations in developing relationships. His study showed that 14 percent of talk revealed nothing about the speaker, 65 percent dwelled on public items, 19 percent shared semiprivate details, and only 2 percent disclosed intimate confidences.[2] Further penetration will bring Pete to the point where he can share deeper feelings ("misery loves company").

2. *Self-disclosure is reciprocal, especially in the early stages of relationship development.* The theory predicts that new acquaintances like Pete and Jon will reach roughly equal levels of openness, but it doesn't explain why. Pete's vulnerability could make him seem more trustworthy, or perhaps his initial openness makes transparency seem more attractive. The young men might also feel a need for emotional equity, so a disclosure by Pete leaves Jon feeling uneasy until he's balanced the account with his own payment—a give-and-take exchange in which each party is sharing deeper levels of feeling with the other. Whatever the reason, social penetration theory asserts a *law of reciprocity.*

Law of reciprocity
A paced and orderly process in which openness in one person leads to openness in the other; "You tell me your dream; I'll tell you mine."

3. *Penetration is rapid at the start but slows down quickly as the tightly wrapped inner layers are reached.* Instant intimacy is a myth. Not only is there internal resistance to quick forays into the soul, but there are societal norms against telling too much too fast. Most relationships stall before a stable intimate exchange is established. For this reason, these relationships fade or die easily after a separation or a slight strain. A comfortable sharing of positive and negative reactions is rare. When it is achieved, relationships become more important to both parties, more meaningful, and more enduring.

4. *Depenetration is a gradual process of layer-by-layer withdrawal.* A warm friendship between Pete and Jon will deteriorate if they begin to close off areas of their lives that had previously been opened. Relational retreat is a sort of taking back of what has already been exchanged in the building of a relationship. Altman and Taylor compared the process to a movie shown in reverse. Surface talk still goes on long after deep disclosure is avoided. Relationships are likely to terminate not in an explosive flash of anger but in a gradual cooling off of enjoyment and care.

While depth is crucial to the process of social penetration, *breadth* is equally important. Note that in Figure 8–1 I have segmented the onion much like an orange to represent how Pete's life is cut into different areas—dating, studies, and so forth. It's quite possible for Pete to be candid about every intimate detail of his romance yet remain secretive about his father's alcoholism or his own minor dyslexia. Because only one area is accessed, the relationship depicted in the onion drawing is typical of a summer romance—depth without breadth. Of course, breadth without depth describes the typical "Hi, how are you?" casual friendship. A model of true intimacy would show multiple wedges inserted deeply into every area.

Breadth of penetration
The range of areas in an individual's life over which disclosure takes place.

REGULATING CLOSENESS ON THE BASIS OF REWARDS AND COSTS

Will Pete and Jon become good friends? To answer that question, Altman and Taylor borrowed ideas from another theory called *social exchange theory,* developed by psychologists John Thibaut (University of North Carolina at Chapel Hill) and Harold Kelley (University of California, Los Angeles).[3] If you want to know more about social exchange theory, I encourage you to visit www.afirstlook.com to read a chapter on the theory from a previous edition of this book. Here, I'll focus on the ideas from the theory that Altman and Taylor thought are useful for understanding the process of self-disclosure.

Investors choose where to put their money in the stock market. College freshmen like Pete and Jon choose where to put their time in friendships. Social exchange theory claims we make both decisions in similar ways. Whether finance or friendship, we want a good return on our investment, so we do a cost-benefit analysis beforehand. For the financial investor, that might involve combing the pages of *The Wall Street Journal* for tips about which stocks might increase in value. Pete and Jon don't have a newspaper with that kind of expert interpersonal advice[so instead they'll think about whether they'll enjoy interacting in the future. Right after their first encounter, Pete will sort out the pluses and minuses of friendship with Jon, computing a bottom-line index of relational satisfaction. Jon will do the same regarding Pete. If the perceived mutual benefits outweigh the costs of greater vulnerability, the process of social penetration will proceed.

Social exchange theory identifies three key components of this mental calculation: relational outcome, relational satisfaction, and relational stability. Altman and Taylor agreed these factors are important, and therefore included them in social penetration theory. I'll describe each of the three concepts below.

Social exchange
Relationship behavior and status regulated by both parties' evaluations of perceived rewards and costs of interaction with each other.

Relational Outcome: Rewards Minus Costs

Thibaut and Kelley suggested that people try to predict the *outcome* of an interaction before it takes place. Thus, when Pete first meets his roommate, he mentally gauges the potential rewards and costs of friendship with Jon. He perceives a number of benefits. As a newcomer to campus, Pete strongly desires someone to talk to, eat with, and just hang out with when he's not in class or studying. His roommate's interest in lacrosse, easy laugh, and laid-back style make Jon an attractive candidate.

Pete is also aware that there's a potential downside to getting to know each other better. If he reveals some of his inner life, his roommate may scoff at his faith in God or ridicule his liberal "do-gooder" values. Pete isn't ashamed of his convictions, but he hates to argue, and he regards the risk of conflict as real. Factoring in all the likely pluses and minuses, reaching out in friendship to Jon strikes Pete as net positive, so he makes the first move.

The idea of totaling potential benefits and losses to determine behavior isn't new. Since the nineteenth century, when philosopher John Stuart Mill first stated his principle of utility,[4] there's been a compelling logic to the *minimax principle of human behavior*. The minimax principle claims that people seek to maximize their benefits and minimize their costs. Thus, the higher we rate a relational outcome, the more attractive we find the behavior that might make it happen.

Social exchange theorists assume that we can accurately gauge the payoffs of a variety of interactions and that we have the good sense to choose the action that will provide the best result. Altman and Taylor weren't sure that we always base such decisions on reliable information, but that's not the issue. What mattered to them is that we decide to open up with another person using the perceived benefit-minus-cost outcome.

Lee, a former student of Em's, shared how he calculated cost–benefit ratios in one of his friendships. For him, self-disclosure has a higher emotional cost than it does for the average person:

Outcome
The perceived rewards minus the costs of interpersonal interaction.

Minimax principle of human behavior
People seek to maximize their benefits and minimize their costs.

> Self-disclosure makes me uncomfortable. However, the medium of music makes me a bit more comfortable and my desire to write a good song forces me to open up in ways I wouldn't otherwise. For example, I wrote a song for my friend John's birthday party where I put together a series of verses that commemorated all the

things in the last year that John and I shared or thought were funny. John and I still had a relatively superficial relationship at that point, but I think by showing that I cared through the song, another layer of the onion was peeled away.

Early in a relationship, we tend to see physical appearance, similar backgrounds, and mutual agreement as benefits ("birds of a feather flock together"). Disagreement and deviance from the norm are negatives. But as the relationship changes, so does the nature of interaction that friends find rewarding. Deeper friendships thrive on common values and spoken appreciation, and we can even enjoy surface diversity ("opposites attract").

If Pete sees much more benefit than cost in a relationship with Jon, he'll start to reveal more of who he is. If the negatives outweigh the positives, he'll try to avoid contact with Jon as much as possible. Even though they're stuck together physically in the same dorm room, a negative assessment could cause him to hold back emotionally for the rest of the year.

Gauging Relational Satisfaction—The Comparison Level (CL)

Evaluating outcomes is a tricky business. Even if we mentally convert intangible benefits and costs into a bottom-line measure of overall effect, its psychological impact upon us may vary. A relational result has meaning only when we contrast

it with other real or imagined outcomes. Social exchange theory offers two standards of comparison that Pete and others use to evaluate their interpersonal outcomes. The first point of reference deals with relative *satisfaction*—how happy or sad an interpersonal outcome makes a participant feel. Thibaut and Kelley called this the *comparison level*.

Comparison level (CL)
The threshold above which an interpersonal outcome seems attractive; a standard for relational satisfaction.

A person's comparison level (CL) is the threshold above which an outcome seems attractive. Suppose, for example, that Pete is looking forward to his regular Sunday night phone call with his girlfriend. Since they usually talk for about a half hour, 30 minutes is Pete's comparison level for what makes a pleasing conversation. If he's not in a hurry, a 45-minute call will seem especially gratifying, while a 15-minute chat would be quite disappointing. Of course, the length of the call is only one factor that affects Pete's positive or negative feelings when he hangs up the phone. He has also developed expectations for the topics they'll discuss, his girlfriend's tone of voice, and the warmth of her words when she says good-bye. These are benchmarks that Pete uses to gauge his relative satisfaction with the interaction.

To a big extent, our relational history establishes our CLs for friendship, romance, and family ties. We judge the value of a relationship by comparing it to the baseline of past experience. If Pete had little history of close friendship in high school, a relationship with Jon would look quite attractive. If, on the other hand, he's accustomed to being part of a close-knit group of intimate friends, hanging out with Jon could pale by comparison.

Sequence plays a large part in evaluating a relationship. The result from each interaction is stored in the individual's memory. Experiences that take place early in a relationship can have a huge impact because they make up a large proportion of the total relational history. One unpleasant experience out of 10 is merely troublesome, but 1 out of 2 can end a relationship before it really begins. Trends are also important. If Pete first senses coolness from Jon yet later feels warmth and approval, the shift will raise Jon's attractiveness to a level higher than it would be if Pete had perceived positive vibes from the very beginning.

Gauging Relational Stability—The Comparison Level of Alternatives (CL$_{alt}$)

Thibaut and Kelley suggested that there is a second standard by which we evaluate the outcomes we receive. They called it the *comparison level of alternatives (CL$_{alt}$)*. Don't let the similarity of the names confuse you—CL and CL$_{alt}$ are two entirely different concepts. CL is your overall standard for a specific type of relationship, and it remains fairly stable over time. In contrast, CL$_{alt}$ represents your evaluation of other relational options at the moment. For Pete, it's the result of thinking about his interactions with other people in his dorm. As he considers whether to invest his limited time in getting to know Jon, he'll ask, *Would my relational payoffs be better with another person?* His CL$_{alt}$ is his *best available alternative* to a friendship with Jon. If CL$_{alt}$ is less than Pete's current outcomes, his friendship with Jon will be *stable*. But if more attractive friendship possibilities become available, or roommate squabbles drive his outcomes below the established CL$_{alt}$, the instability of their friendship will increase.

Comparison level of alternatives (CL$_{alt}$)
The best outcome available in other relationships; a standard for relational stability.

Taken together, CL and CL$_{alt}$ explain why some people remain in relationships that aren't satisfying. For example, social workers describe the plight of a physically abused wife as "high cost, low reward." Despite her anguish, the woman feels trapped in the distressing situation because being alone in the world appears even worse. As dreadful as her outcomes are, she can't imagine a better alternative. She won't leave until she perceives an outside alternative that promises a better life. Her relationship is very unsatisfying because her outcomes are far below her CL, but also quite stable because her outcomes are above her CL_{alt}.

The relative values of outcome, CL, and CL_{alt} go a long way in determining whether a person is willing to become vulnerable in order to have a deeper relationship. The optimum situation is when both parties find

$$Outcome > CL_{alt} > CL$$

Using Pete as an example, this notation shows that he forecasts a friendship with Jon that will be more than *satisfying*. The tie with Jon will be *stable* because there's no other relationship on campus that is more attractive. Yet Pete won't feel trapped, because he has other satisfying options available should this one turn sour. We see, therefore, that social exchange theory explains why Pete is primed for social penetration. If Jon's calculations are similar, the roommates will begin the process of mutual vulnerability that Altman and Taylor described, and reciprocal self-disclosure will draw them close.

ETHICAL REFLECTION: EPICURUS' ETHICAL EGOISM

The minimax principle that undergirds social exchange theory—and therefore social penetration theory as well—is also referred to as *psychological egoism*. The term reflects many social scientists' conviction that all of us are motivated by self-interest. Unlike most social scientists who limit their study to what *is* rather than what *ought* to be, *ethical egoists* claim we *should* act selfishly. It's right and it's good for us to look out for number one.

Epicurus, a Greek philosopher who wrote a few years after Aristotle's death, defined the good life as getting as much pleasure as possible: "I spit on the noble and its idle admirers when it contains no element of pleasure."[5] Although his position is often associated with the adage "Eat, drink, and be merry," Epicurus actually emphasized the passive pleasures of friendship and good digestion, and above all, the absence of pain. He cautioned that "no pleasure is in itself evil, but the things which produce certain pleasures entail annoyances many times greater than the pleasures themselves."[6] The Greek philosopher put lying in that category. He said that the wise person is prepared to lie if there is no risk of detection, but since we can never be certain our falsehoods won't be discovered, he didn't recommend deception.

Ethical egoism
The belief that individuals should live their lives so as to maximize their own pleasure and minimize their own pain.

A few other philosophers have echoed the Epicurean call for selfish concern. Thomas Hobbes described life as "nasty, brutish and short" and advocated political trade-offs that would gain a measure of security. Adam Smith, the spiritual father of capitalism, advised every person to seek his or her own profit. Friedrich Nietzsche announced the death of God and stated that the noble soul has reverence for itself. Egoist writer Ayn Rand dedicated her novel *The Fountainhead* to "the exultation of man's self-esteem and the sacredness of his happiness on earth."[7] Of course, the moral advice of Epicurus, Hobbes, Nietzsche, and Rand may be suspect. If their counsel consistently reflects their beliefs, their words are spoken for their own benefit, not ours.

Most ethical and religious thinkers denounce the selfishness of egoism as morally repugnant. How can one embrace a philosophy that advocates terrorism

104   *INTERPERSONAL COMMUNICATION*

as long as it brings joy to the terrorist? When the egoistic pleasure principle is compared to a life lived to reduce the suffering of others, as with the late Mother Teresa, ethical egoism seems to be no ethic at all. Yet the egoist would claim that the Nobel Peace Prize winner was leading a sacrificial life because she took pleasure in serving the poor. If charity becomes a burden, she should stop.

DIALECTICS AND THE ENVIRONMENT

Viewing increased self-disclosure as the path to intimacy is a simple idea—one that's easily portrayed in the onion model of Figure 8–1. It can also be summarized in less than 40 words:

Interpersonal closeness proceeds in a gradual and orderly fashion from superficial to intimate levels of exchange, motivated by current and projected future outcomes. Lasting intimacy requires continual and mutual vulnerability through breadth and depth of self-disclosure.

But Altman later had second thoughts about his basic assumption that openness is the predominant quality of relationship development. He began to speculate that the desire for privacy may counteract what he first thought was a unidirectional quest for intimacy. He now proposes a *dialectical model*, which assumes that "human social relationships are characterized by openness or contact and closedness or separateness between participants."[8] He believes that the tension between openness and closedness results in cycles of disclosure or withdrawal.

Altman also identifies the *environment* as a factor in social penetration.[9] Sometimes the environment guides our decision to disclose—a quiet, dimly lit sit-down restaurant might make us more willing to open up than when sitting on stools under the harsh lights of a noisy fast food joint. Other times we actively manipulate our environment to meet our privacy and disclosure goals. Thus, we might choose a quiet booth in the corner if we don't want others to overhear a sensitive conversation.

Dialectical model
The assumption that people want both privacy and intimacy in their social relationships; they experience a tension between disclosure and withdrawal.

Pete and Jon face choices about how to manage their room's environment. For Altman, this is more than just deciding whether to put a mini-fridge under the desk or next to the bed. He believes the way the two manage their dorm room says a lot about their relationship with each other and with their peers. Will they keep the door open on weeknights? Will they lock the room when they're away? Will they split the room down the middle, or will their possessions intermingle? Each decision shapes how the roommates manage the ongoing tension between openness and closedness during the year.

Because college freshmen face so many decisions about disclosure, privacy, and their physical environment, Altman studied social penetration in dorm living at the University of Utah.[10] He asked college freshmen how they used their environment to seek out and avoid others. To probe deeper into how students managed their space, he visited their rooms and photographed the wall above their beds. Two years later he examined school records to see if students' choices about their physical space predicted success and satisfaction at college. Overall, Altman found that students were more likely to remain at the university when they honored their need for *territoriality*, the human (and animalistic) tendency to claim a physical location or object as our own. This need shows that the onion of social penetration includes both our mind and our physical space.

Territoriality
The tendency to claim a physical location or object as our own.

Some students in Altman's study crafted a dorm room environment that welcomed others. They kept their doors open, invited others to visit, and even used music to draw people into the room. Their wall decorations promoted mutual self-disclosure by showing multiple facets of their identity, ranging from calendars and schedules to hobbies and photographs of friends. Just like verbal disclosure, environmental disclosure can vary in its breadth. If Pete and Jon decorate their room with several facets of their identities, the law of reciprocity suggests that visitors might feel more comfortable disclosing verbally as well. The students who created this kind of warm atmosphere tended to succeed at college.

The students who later dropped out used wall decorations that didn't reveal a range of interests, like one student who only displayed ballet-related images, or another with only ski posters. Such students tended to shut out potential visitors and play loud music that discouraged discussion. Also, students who eventually left the university didn't honor their need for personal territory. Compared to those who remained, they were less likely to arrange the furniture to create some private spaces or occasionally retreat from the dorm room for time alone. To explain this curious finding, Altman reasoned that "the dormitory environment inherently provides many opportunities for social contact," and therefore "it may be more important to develop effective avoidance techniques in such a setting."[11] Consequently, Pete and Jon would be wise to recognize each other's need for clearly defined territory. Each of them might be unwilling to let the other penetrate his physical space until they've first penetrated each other's psychological space—their onion.

Altman's results demonstrate the importance of both psychological and territorial boundaries in the process of social penetration. Students who were successful at college honored their dialectical needs for both contact and separateness. Sandra Petronio, a communication theorist at Indiana University–Purdue University Indianapolis, was intrigued by Altman's use of territoriality to explain dialectical forces. She later crafted *communication privacy management theory* to further explain the intricate ways people manage boundaries around their personal information. You can read about her insights in Chapter 12.

CRITIQUE: PULLING BACK FROM SOCIAL PENETRATION

Social penetration theory is an established and familiar explanation of how closeness develops in ongoing relationships. Altman and Taylor's image of multiple wedges penetrating deeply into a multilayered onion has proved to be a helpful model of growing intimacy. But just as these theorists described people continually reappraising their relationships in light of new experiences, it makes sense for us to reconsider the basic assumptions and claims of their theory. Social penetration theory has many critics.

As you will read in Chapter 12, Petronio challenges some core assumptions of social penetration theory. She thinks it's simplistic to equate self-disclosure with relational closeness. It can *lead* to intimacy, but a person may reveal private information merely to express oneself, to release tension, or to gain relational control. In these cases the speaker doesn't necessarily desire nor achieve a stronger bond with the confidant. And if the listener is turned off or disgusted by what was said, depenetration can be swift. Petronio also questions Altman and Taylor's view of personality structure. The onion-layer model of social penetration theory posits fixed boundaries that become increasingly thick as one penetrates toward the inner core of personality. In contrast, for Petronio, our privacy boundaries are personally created, often shifting, and frequently permeable.

Other personal relationship scholars are uncomfortable with Altman and Taylor's wholesale use of a reward–cost analysis to explain the differential drive for penetration. Can a complex blend of advantages and disadvantages be reduced to a single numerical index? And assuming that we can forecast the value of relational outcomes, are we so consistently selfish that we always opt for what we calculate is in our own best interest? Julia Wood, a communication theorist associated with standpoint theory (see Chapter 35), is skeptical. She argues, "The focus in exchange theories is one's own gains and outcomes; this focus is incapable of addressing matters such as compassion, caring, altruism, fairness, and other ethical issues that should be central to personal relationships."[12] To her and like-minded scholars, relational life has a human core that pure economic calculus cannot touch.

University of North Dakota psychologist Paul Wright believes Pete and Jon could draw close enough that their relationship would no longer be driven by a self-centered concern for personal gain. When friendships have what Wright calls "an intrinsic, end-in-themselves quality," people regard good things happening to their friends as rewards in themselves.[13] When that happens, Jon would get just as excited if Pete had a successful employment interview as if he himself had been offered the job. This rare kind of selfless love involves a relational transformation, not just more self-disclosure.[14] Altman and Taylor's theory doesn't speak about the transition from *me* to *we*, but that apparently takes place only after an extended process of social penetration.

QUESTIONS TO SHARPEN YOUR FOCUS

1. The onion model in Figure 8–1 is sectioned into eight parts, representing the *breadth* of a person's life. How would you label eight regions of interest in your life?

2. Jesus said, "There is no greater love than this: to lay down one's life for one's friends."[15] Given the *minimax principle* of human behavior used in a *social exchange* analysis, how is such a sacrifice possible?

3. Altman conducted his study of first-year students in the 1970s. How have subsequent technological advances changed the ways students manage contact and privacy in their personal territory?

4. The romantic truism "to know her is to love her" seems to contradict the relational adage "familiarity breeds contempt." Given the principles of social penetration theory, can you think of a way both statements might be true?

A SECOND LOOK

Recommended resource: Irwin Altman and Dalmas Taylor, *Social Penetration: The Development of Interpersonal Relationships*, Holt, New York, 1973.

Altman's reflective research summary: Irwin Altman, "Toward a Transactional Perspective: A Personal Journey," in *Environment and Behavior Studies: Emergence of Intellectual Traditions: Advances in Theory and Research*, Vol. 11, *Human Behavior and Environment, Environment and Behavior Studies*, Irwin Altman and Kathleen Christensen (eds.), Plenum, New York, 1990, pp. 225–255.

Social penetration in intercultural and interracial friendships: Yea-Wen Chen and Masato Nakazawa, "Influences of Culture on Self-Disclosure as Relationally Situated in Intercultural and Interracial Friendships from a Social Penetration Perspective," *Journal of Intercultural Communication Research,* Vol. 38, 2009, pp. 77–98.

Social exchange theory: John W. Thibaut and Harold H. Kelley, *The Social Psychology of Groups,* John Wiley & Sons, New York, 1952.

Dialectic revision: Irwin Altman, Anne Vinsel, and Barbara Brown, "Dialectic Conceptions in Social Psychology: An Application to Social Penetration and Privacy Regulation," in *Advances in Experimental Social Psychology, Vol. 14,* Leonard Berkowitz (ed.), Academic Press, New York, 1981, pp. 107–160.

Cost-benefit analysis: Dalmas Taylor and Irwin Altman, "Self-Disclosure as a Function of Reward–Cost Outcomes," *Sociometry,* Vol. 38, 1975, pp. 18–31.

Online self-disclosure in the United States, Japan, and South Korea: Young-ok Yum and Kazuya Hara, "Computer-Mediated Relationship Development: A Cross-Cultural Comparison," *Journal of Computer-Mediated Communication,* Vol. 11, 2005, pp. 133–152.

Effects of environment on relationship closeness: Carol Werner, Irwin Altman, and Barbara B. Brown, "A Transactional Approach to Interpersonal Relations: Physical Environment, Social Context and Temporal Qualities," *Journal of Social and Personal Relationships,* Vol. 9, 1992, pp. 297–323.

Environmental study of first-year roommates: Anne Vinsel, Barbara B. Brown, Irwin Altman, and Carolyn Foss, "Privacy Regulation, Territorial Displays, and Effectiveness of Individual Functioning," *Journal of Personality and Social Psychology,* Vol. 39, 1980, pp. 1104–1115.

Ethical egoism: Edward Gegis, "What Is Ethical Egoism?" *Ethics,* Vol. 91, 1980, pp. 50–62.

To access a chapter on social exchange driven by rewards and costs, click on Social Exchange Theory in Archive under Theory Resources at *www.afirstlook.com.*

CHAPTER 9

Uncertainty Reduction Theory

of Charles Berger

No matter how close two people eventually become, they always begin as strangers. Let's say you've just taken a job as a driver for a delivery service over the winter break. After talking with the other drivers, you conclude that your income and peace of mind will depend on working out a good relationship with Heather, the radio dispatcher. All you know for sure about Heather is her attachment to Hannah, a 100-pound Labrador retriever that never lets Heather out of her sight. The veteran drivers joke that it's hard to tell the difference between the voices of Heather and Hannah over the radio. With some qualms you make arrangements to meet Heather (and Hannah) over coffee and donuts before your first day of work. You really have no idea what to expect.

Chuck Berger believes it's natural to have doubts about our ability to predict the outcome of initial encounters. Berger, professor emeritus of communication at the University of California, Davis, notes that "the beginnings of personal relationships are fraught with uncertainties."[1] Unlike social penetration theory, which tries to forecast the future of a relationship on the basis of projected rewards and costs (see Chapter 8), Berger's uncertainty reduction theory (URT) focuses on how human communication is used to gain knowledge and create understanding.

> Central to the present theory is the assumption that when strangers meet, their primary concern is one of uncertainty reduction or increasing predictability about the behavior of both themselves and others in the interaction.[2]

Interpersonal ignorance is not bliss; it's frustrating! Berger contends that our drive to reduce uncertainty about new acquaintances gets a boost from any of three prior conditions:[3]

1. *Anticipation of future interaction:* We know we will see them again.
2. *Incentive value:* They have something we want.
3. *Deviance:* They act in a weird way.

Heather hooks you on all three counts. You know you're going to be dealing with her for the next few weeks, she can make or break you financially according to the routes she assigns, and she has this strange attachment to Hannah. According to Berger, when you add these three factors to your natural curiosity, you'll *really* want to solve the puzzle of who she is.

Berger believes that our main purpose in talking to people is to "make sense" of our interpersonal world. That's why you're having breakfast with a stranger and her dog. If you brought your own hound to the meeting, chances are the two dogs would circle and sniff each other, trying to get some idea of what their counterpart was like. Humans are no different; we're just a bit more subtle, using symbols instead of smells to reach our conclusions.

UNCERTAINTY REDUCTION: TO PREDICT AND EXPLAIN

Attribution theory
A systematic explanation of how people draw inferences about the character of others based upon observed behavior.

Berger focuses on predictability, which he sees as the opposite of uncertainty. "As the ability of persons to predict which alternative or alternatives are likely to occur next decreases, uncertainty increases."[4] He owes a debt to Fritz Heider's view of people as intuitive psychologists. Heider, the father of *attribution theory*, believed that we constantly draw inferences about why people do what they do.[5] We need to predict *and* explain. If Heather's going to bark at you on the radio, you want to understand why.

Berger notes that there are at least two kinds of uncertainty you face as you set out for your first meeting with Heather. Because you aren't sure how you

"What say we find another way to say hello?"

© Peter Steiner/The New Yorker Collection/www.cartoonbank.com

should act, one kind of uncertainty deals with *behavioral* questions. Should you shake hands? Who pays for the donuts? Do you pet the dog? Often there are accepted procedural protocols to ease the stress that behavioral uncertainty can cause. Good manners go beyond common sense.

A second kind of uncertainty focuses on *cognitive* questions aimed at discovering who the other person is as a unique individual. What does Heather like about her job? What makes her glad, sad, or mad? Does she have other friends, or does she lavish all her attention on Hannah? When you first meet a person, your mind may conjure up a wild mix of potential traits and characteristics. Reducing cognitive uncertainty means acquiring information that allows you to discard many of these possibilities. That's the kind of uncertainty reduction Berger's theory addresses—cognitive rather than behavioral uncertainty.

Uncertainty reduction
Increased knowledge of what kind of person another is, which provides an improved forecast of how a future interaction will turn out.

AN AXIOMATIC THEORY: CERTAINTY ABOUT UNCERTAINTY

Berger proposes a series of axioms to explain the connection between his central concept of uncertainty and eight key variables of relationship development: *verbal communication, nonverbal warmth, information seeking, self-disclosure, reciprocity, similarity, liking,* and *shared networks.*[6] *Axioms* are traditionally regarded as self-evident truths that require no additional proof. (All people are created equal. The shortest distance between two points is a straight line. What goes up must come down.) Here are Berger's eight truths about initial uncertainty.

Axiom
A self-evident truth that requires no additional proof.

> *Axiom 1, Verbal Communication:* Given the high level of uncertainty present at the onset of the entry phase, as the amount of verbal communication between strangers increases, the level of uncertainty for each interactant in the relationship will decrease. As uncertainty is further reduced, the amount of verbal communication will increase.

When you first sit down with Heather, the conversation will be halting and somewhat stilted. But as words begin to flow, you'll discover things about each other that make you feel more confident in each other's presence. When your comfort level rises, the pace of the conversation will pick up.

> *Axiom 2, Nonverbal Warmth:* As nonverbal affiliative expressiveness increases, uncertainty levels will decrease in an initial interaction situation. In addition, decreases in uncertainty level will cause increases in nonverbal affiliative expressiveness.

When initial stiffness gives way to head nods and tentative smiles, you'll have a better idea of who Heather is. This assurance leads to further signs of warmth, such as prolonged eye contact, forward body lean, and pleasant tone of voice.

> *Axiom 3, Information Seeking:* High levels of uncertainty cause increases in information-seeking behavior. As uncertainty levels decline, information-seeking behavior decreases.

What is it about Heather that prompted the other drivers to warn you not to start off on the wrong foot? You simply have no idea. Like a bug with its antennae twitching, you carefully monitor what she says and how she acts in order to gather clues about her personality. But you become less vigilant after she explains that her pet peeve is drivers who complain about their assignments on the radio. Whether or not you think her irritation is justified, you begin to relax because you have a better idea of how to stay on her good side.

Axiom 4, Self-Disclosure: High levels of uncertainty in a relationship cause decreases in the intimacy level of communication content. Low levels of uncertainty produce high levels of intimacy.

Like Altman and Taylor (see Chapter 8), Berger equates intimacy of communication with depth of self-disclosure. Demographic data revealing that Heather was raised in Toledo and that you are a communication major are relatively nonintimate. They typify the opening gambits of new acquaintances who are still feeling each other out. But Heather's comment that she feels more loyalty from Hannah than from any person she knows is a gutsy admission that raises the intimacy level of the conversation to a new plane. Most people wait to express attitudes, values, and feelings until they have a good idea what the listener's response will be.

Axiom 5, Reciprocity: High levels of uncertainty produce high rates of reciprocity. Low levels of uncertainty produce low levels of reciprocity.

Self-disclosure research confirms the notion that people tend to mete out the personal details of their lives at a rate that closely matches their partner's willingness to share intimate information.[7] Reciprocal vulnerability is especially important in the early stages of a relationship. The issue seems to be one of power. When knowledge of each other is minimal, we're careful not to let the other person one-up us by being the exclusive holder of potentially embarrassing information. But when we already know some of the ups and downs of a person's life, an even flow of information seems less crucial. Berger would not anticipate long monologues at your first get-together with Heather; future meetings might be a different story.

Axiom 6, Similarity: Similarities between persons reduce uncertainty, while dissimilarities produce increases in uncertainty.

The more points of contact you establish with Heather, the more you'll feel you understand her inside and out. If you are a dog lover, the two of you will click. If, however, you are partial to purring kittens, Heather's devotion to this servile beast will cause you to wonder if you'll ever be able to figure out what makes her tick.

Axiom 7, Liking: Increases in uncertainty level produce decreases in liking; decreases in uncertainty produce increases in liking.

This axiom suggests that the more you find out about Heather, the more you'll appreciate who she is. It directly contradicts the cynical opinion that "familiarity breeds contempt" and affirms instead the relational maxim that "to know her is to love her."

Axiom 8, Shared Networks: Shared communication networks reduce uncertainty, while lack of shared networks increases uncertainty.

This axiom was not part of Berger's original theory, but his ideas triggered extensive research by other communication scholars who soon moved uncertainty reduction theory beyond the confines of two strangers meeting for the first time. Berger applauds this extension: "The broadening of the theory's scope suggests the potential usefulness of reconceptualizing and extending the original formulation."[8] For example, Malcolm Parks (University of Washington) and Mara Adelman (Seattle University) discovered that men and women who communicate more often with their romantic partners' family and friends have less uncertainty about the person they love than do those whose relationships exist in relative isolation.[9] Networking couples also tend to stay together. On the basis of these findings, Berger incorporated this axiom into his formal design.

THEOREMS: THE LOGICAL FORCE OF UNCERTAINTY AXIOMS

Theorem
A proposition that logically and necessarily follows from two axioms.

Once we grant the validity of the eight axioms, it makes sense to pair two of them together to produce additional insight into relational dynamics. The combined axioms yield an inevitable conclusion when inserted in the well-known pattern of deductive logic:

$$\text{If } A = B$$
$$\text{and } B = C$$
$$\text{then } A = C$$

Berger does this for all possible combinations, thereby generating 28 theorems—for example:

If similarity reduces uncertainty (axiom 6)
and reduced uncertainty increases liking (axiom 7)
then similarity and liking are positively related (theorem 21)

In this case, the result isn't exactly earthshaking. The connection between similarity and liking is a long-established finding in research on interpersonal attraction.[10] When viewed as a whole, however, these 28 logical extensions sketch out a rather comprehensive theory of interpersonal development—all based on the importance of reducing uncertainty in human interaction.

Instead of listing all 28 theorems, I've plotted the relationships they predict in Figure 9–1. The chart reads like a mileage table you might find in a road atlas.

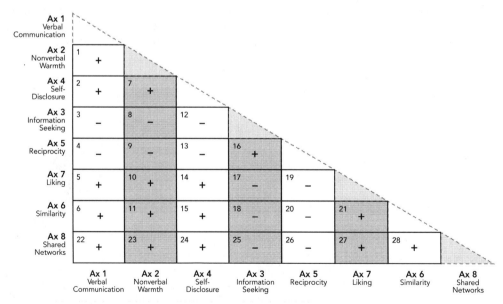

FIGURE 9–1 Theorems of Uncertainty Reduction Theory
Adapted from Berger and Calabrese, "Some Explorations in Initial Interaction and Beyond"

Select one axiom along the bottom and another down the side. The intersection between the two shows the number of Berger's theorem and the type of correlation it asserts. A plus sign (+) shows that the two interpersonal variables rise or fall together. A minus sign (−) indicates that as one increases, the other decreases. Will the warmth of Heather's nonverbal communication increase as the intimacy of her self-disclosure deepens? Theorem 7 says it will. Suppose you grow fond of Heather as a friend. Will you seek to find out more about her? Theorem 17 makes the surprising prediction that you won't (more on this later).

Recall from Malcolm Parks' research that good friends who have overlapping social networks communicate more frequently with each other than those who don't have those connections (see the cybernetic tradition in Chapter 4). You and Heather aren't good friends, but suppose you unexpectedly discover that her parents and your folks attend the same church service and sometimes play cards together. Does URT predict you'll be talking with each other more in the future? Check the intersection between axioms 1 and 8 on the chart for Berger's prediction.

MESSAGE PLANS TO COPE WITH UNCERTAIN RESPONSES

Berger believes most social interaction is goal-driven; we have reasons for saying what we say. So after developing the core axioms and theorems of uncertainty reduction theory, he devoted his attention to explaining *how* we communicate to reduce uncertainty. Berger labeled his work "A Plan-Based Theory of Strategic Communication" because he was convinced we continually construct cognitive plans to guide our communication.[11] According to Berger, *"plans* are mental representations of action sequences that may be used to achieve goals."[12] Figure 9–2 offers a possible example of a strategic plan for your breakfast with Heather.

Your main reason for getting together with the dispatcher is to maximize your income over the holidays. Your overall strategy to reach that goal is to build a good working relationship with Heather, since she assigns the routes. The term *overall* is appropriate because Berger claims that plans are "hierarchi-

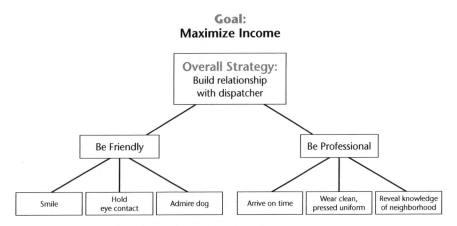

FIGURE 9–2   A Hierarchical Plan of Goal-Directed Communication

cally organized with abstract action representations at the top of the hierarchy and progressively more concrete representations toward the bottom."[13] In order to build that relationship, you intend to converse in a *friendly* and *professional* manner. In this case, friendly means smiling, holding eye contact when she speaks, and admiring her dog. You'll show professionalism by arriving on time; wearing a clean, pressed uniform; and revealing knowledge of the neighborhood.

If you switch strategies at the top—seeking pity for a poor, struggling college student in the midst of a recession, for example—the alteration will cascade down the hierarchy, requiring changes in many of the behaviors below. Thus, a top-down revision of an action plan requires great amounts of cognitive capacity.

Even if you think carefully about your plan, Berger claims you can't be sure you'll reach your goal. You may have a great plan but execute it poorly. Heather may interpret words that you meant one way to mean something else. Or she may have her own goals and plans that will inevitably thwart yours. Berger has come to the conclusion that uncertainty is central to *all* social interaction: "The probability of perfect communication is zero."[14] Thus he asks, "How do individuals cope with the inevitable uncertainties they must face when constructing messages?"[15] The following strategies are some of his answers.

Seeking Information. Uncertainty reduction theorists have outlined four approaches we can use to reduce uncertainty. Using a *passive strategy*, we unobtrusively observe others from a distance. This fly-on-the-wall tactic works best when we spot others reacting to people in informal, or "backstage," settings. (The strategy sounds like normal "scoping" behavior on any college campus.) Unless Heather lives in your neighborhood or hangs out in the same places, you might not have an opportunity to simply observe her behavior.

In an *active strategy*, we ask a third party for information. We realize that our mutual acquaintance will probably give a somewhat slanted view, but most of us have confidence in our ability to filter out the bias and gain valuable information. Regarding Heather, you've already used the active strategy by querying other drivers for their opinions about her.

With an *interactive strategy*, we talk face-to-face with the other person and ask specific questions—just what you're planning to do with Heather. This is the quickest route to reducing uncertainty, but continual probing in social settings begins to take on the feel of a cross-examination or the third degree. Our own self-disclosure offers an alternative way to elicit information from others without seeming to pry. By being transparent, we create a safe atmosphere for others to respond in kind—something the "law of reciprocity" suggests they will do (see Chapter 8).

When I (Andrew) told my 5-year-old daughter I was working on this chapter, I asked what she thought was the best way to find information about someone. Her answer demonstrates she's a child of the 21st century: "Check on Facebook!" Clearly she's already learned the *extractive strategy* of searching for information online. Although this method was not part of Berger's original three uncertainty reduction strategies, Art Ramirez (University of South Florida) believes the Internet creates a new way for us to reduce uncertainty. Sometimes a name is all that's necessary to search for blogs, archived newspaper articles, tweets, and more—an unobtrusive process that is something like

Passive strategy
Impression formation by observing a person interacting with others.

Active strategy
Impression formation by asking a third party about a person.

Interactive strategy
Impression formation through face-to-face discussion with a person.

Extractive strategy
Impression formation by searching the Internet for information about a person.

"conducting a personalized background check."[16] If you discover Heather writes a blog about her dog, you might reduce a lot of uncertainty even before you meet.

Choosing Plan Complexity. The complexity of a message plan is measured in two ways—the level of detail the plan includes and the number of contingency plans prepared in case the original one doesn't work. If it's crucial that you make top dollar in your holiday delivery job, you're likely to draw upon a plan from memory or create a new one far more complex than the sample shown in Figure 9–2. You're also likely to have a fallback plan in case the first one fails. On the other hand, you don't know much about Heather's goals or feelings, and high uncertainty argues for a less complex plan that you can adjust in the moment, once you get a feel for who she is and what she wants. This simpler approach is preferred for another reason. Enacting a complex plan takes so much cognitive effort that there's usually a deterioration in verbal and nonverbal fluency, with a resultant loss in credibility. Jeff, a student athlete, used an interactive strategy that has low complexity:

> I thought of URT this afternoon in the trainer's room where I again made eye contact with a girl I'd never met. We were the only two people in the room and I realized I needed a plan of action. I quickly ran through several strategies to reduce uncertainty. I chose a tried-and-true icebreaker line: "Hi, I know I've seen you around a ton of times, but I don't think I've ever met you. What's your name?" I hoped for the best, but prepared for a negative reaction. My contingency plan was to simply end the attempt at conversation and seem preoccupied with my treatment. Fortunately she responded with a look of relief, her name, and then a smile. Let the conversation begin. As Berger said, "Uncertainty is central to all social interaction." It sure makes life interesting.

Hedging. The possibility of plan failure suggests the wisdom of providing ways for both parties to save face when at least one of them has miscalculated. Berger catalogs a series of planned hedges that allow a somewhat gracious retreat. For instance, you may be quite certain about what you want to accomplish in your meeting with Heather, yet choose words that are *ambiguous* so as not to tip your hand before you find out more about her. You might also choose to be equivocal in order to avoid the embarrassment that would come from her refusing your specific request for preferred treatment in route assignment. *Humor* can provide the same way out. You could blatantly propose to use a portion of the saved time and good tips that come from prime assignments to stop at the butcher shop for a juicy bone for Hannah—but make the offer in a joking tone of voice. If Heather takes offense, you can respond, "Hey, I was just kidding."

The Hierarchy Hypothesis. What happens to action choices when plans are frustrated? Berger's *hierarchy hypothesis* asserts that "when individuals are thwarted in their attempts to achieve goals, their first tendency is to alter lower level elements of their message."[17] For example, when it's obvious the person we're talking to has failed to grasp what we are saying, our inclination is to repeat the same message—but this time louder. The tactic seldom works, but it takes less mental effort than altering strategic features higher up in the action plan. Berger describes people as "cognitive misers" who would rather try a

Plan complexity
A characteristic of a message plan based on the level of detail it provides and the number of contingencies it covers.

Hedging
Use of strategic ambiguity and humor to provide a way for both parties to save face when a message fails to achieve its goal.

Hierarchy hypothesis
The prediction that when people are thwarted in their attempts to achieve goals, their first tendency is to alter lower-level elements of their message.

quick fix than expend the effort to repair faulty plans.[18] There's no doubt that in-the-moment modifications are taxing, but when the issue is important, the chance to be effective makes it worth the effort. An additional hedge against failure is to practice in front of a friend who will critique your action plan before you put it into effect.[19] As a Hebrew proverb warns, "Without counsel, plans go wrong."[20]

THE RELATIONAL TURBULENCE MODEL

Berger developed uncertainty reduction theory to explain first-time encounters. Can uncertainty also wreak havoc in ongoing relationships? Leanne Knobloch at the University of Illinois believes the answer is yes, although the uncertainty differs from what we experience with new acquaintances. After the get-to-know-you phase has passed, we're unlikely to wonder about someone's age, hobbies, or hometown. Instead, uncertainty in close relationships arises from whether we're sure about our own thoughts (*Am I really in love?*), those of the other person (*Does he really enjoy spending time together?*), and the future of the relationship (*Are we headed for a breakup?*).[21] Since Knobloch's work has focused on romantic relationships, I'll describe such *relational uncertainty* in that context, although we can experience uncertainty with friends and family, too.

Relational uncertainty
Doubts about our own thoughts, the thoughts of the other person, or the future of the relationship.

Like the common cold, romantic partners might "catch" relational uncertainty at any time. But just as colds occur more often in cooler weather and enclosed spaces, some life circumstances tend to generate relational uncertainty. Knobloch's initial research focused on romantic couples' transition from casual to serious dating—a time when couples negotiate what the relationship means and whether it's likely to continue.[22] Not only can this phase produce feelings of uncertainty, but couples also experience *partner interference* as they learn to coordinate their individual goals, plans, and activities in ways that don't annoy each other. The learning process isn't always smooth.

Partner interference
Occurs when a relational partner hinders goals, plans, and activities.

Relational turbulence
Negative emotions arising from perceived problems in a close relationship.

Knobloch believes uncertainty leads close partners to experience *relational turbulence*. If you've flown in an airplane, you've probably felt the bumps and lurches caused by turbulent air. Knobloch thinks that's a good metaphor for partners facing uncertainty and interference:

> When an aircraft encounters a dramatic change in weather conditions, passengers feel turbulence as the plane is jostled, jerked, and jolted erratically. Similarly, when a [couple] undergoes a period of transition that alters the climate of the relationship, partners experience turbulence as sudden intense reactions to their circumstances. Just as turbulence during a flight may make passengers [reconsider] their safety, fear a crash, or grip their seat, turbulence in a relationship may make partners ruminate about hurt, cry over jealousy, or scream during conflict.[23]

In times of relational turbulence, we're likely to feel unsettling emotions like anger, sadness, and fear. It's a bumpy emotional ride that makes us more *reactive,* or sensitive, to our partner's actions. Let's say your dating partner asks you to pick up a candy bar while you're at the store. If you forget, your partner might be bothered but probably won't make a big deal about the brief lapse in memory. When couples are already experiencing relational turbulence, however, the same gaffe could ignite a ridiculously big argument. Over time, turbulence leads to even more uncertainty and interference, which then creates more turbulence—a vicious cycle that could threaten the health of the relationship.

Knobloch's research supports her relational turbulence model across many types of romantic relationships, ranging from couples facing clinical depression[24] to military spouses returning from deployment.[25] Throughout these studies, Knobloch has focused more on diagnosing the causes and symptoms of relational uncertainty than prescribing a cure. Like Berger, she suspects direct attempts to reduce uncertainty (such as the interactive strategy) may help resolve relational turbulence. She believes we're most likely to talk directly when the relationship has high intimacy and equal power. The talk still may produce pain, but intimacy and power equality provide stability in the face of relational turbulence.[26]

CRITIQUE: NAGGING DOUBTS ABOUT UNCERTAINTY

Within the communication discipline, Berger's uncertainty reduction theory was an early prototype of what an objective theory should be and it continues to inspire a new generation of scholars today. His theory makes specific testable predictions, and offers the human need to reduce interpersonal uncertainty as the engine that drives its axioms. Although combining the axioms generates a slew of theorems, they are straightforward, logically consistent, and simple to understand. As for practical utility, readers interested in promoting interpersonal ties can regard the linkages the theorems describe as a blueprint for constructing solid relationships. Subsequent survey and experimental research supports most of URT's axioms and has expanded the scope of the theory to cover development of established relationships. There are, however, continuing questions about Berger's reliance on the concept of *uncertainty* and his assumption that we're motivated to reduce it.

A dozen years after publishing the theory, Berger admitted that his original statement contained "some propositions of dubious validity."[27] Critics quickly point to theorem 17, which predicts that the more you like people, the less you'll seek information about them.

> Frankly, it is not clear why information-seeking would decrease as liking increased other than being required by deductive inference from the axiomatic structure of uncertainty reduction theory. In fact, it seems more reasonable to suggest that persons will seek information about and from those they like rather than those they dislike.[28]

That's the blunt assessment of Kathy Kellermann at ComCon consulting, who originally participated in Berger's research program. We might be willing to dismiss this apparent error as only one glitch out of 28 theorems, but the tight logical structure that is the genius of the theory doesn't give us that option. Theorem 17 is dictated by axioms 3 and 7. If the theorem is wrong, one of the axioms is suspect. Kellermann targets the motivational assumption of axiom 3 as the problem.

Axiom 3 assumes that lack of information triggers a search for knowledge. But as Kellermann and Rodney Reynolds at California Lutheran University discovered when they studied motivation to reduce uncertainty in more than a thousand students at 10 universities, "wanting knowledge rather than lacking knowledge is what promotes information-seeking in initial encounters with others."[29] The distinction is illustrated by the story of a teacher who asked a boy, "What's the difference between *ignorance* and *apathy?*" The student replied, "I don't know, and I don't care." (He was right.)

Kellermann and Reynolds also failed to find that anticipated future interaction, incentive value, or deviance gave any motivational kick to information seeking, as Berger claimed they would. Thus, it seems that Berger's suggestion of a universal drive to reduce uncertainty during initial interaction is questionable at best. Yet along with the suspect third axiom, it, too, remains part of the theory.

Another attack on the theory comes from Michael Sunnafrank at the University of Minnesota Duluth. He challenges Berger's claim that uncertainty reduction is the key to understanding early encounters. Consistent with Altman and Taylor's social penetration model (see Chapter 8) is Sunnafrank's insistence that the early course of a relationship is guided by its *predicted outcome value (POV)*.[30] He's convinced that the primary goal of our initial interaction with another is maximizing our relational outcomes rather than finding out who he or she is. If this is true, you'll be more concerned with establishing a smooth working relationship with Heather at your initial meeting than you will be in figuring out why she does what she does.

Who's right—Berger or Sunnafrank? Berger thinks there's no contest. He maintains that any predictions you make about the rewards and costs of working with Heather are only as good as the quality of your current knowledge. To the extent that you are uncertain of how an action will affect the relationship, predicted outcome value has no meaning. Walid Afifi (University of Iowa) thinks *both* theories are too narrow.[31] In his *theory of motivated information management,* he suggests we're most motivated to reduce anxiety rather than uncertainty. So when uncertainty doesn't make us feel anxious, we won't seek to reduce it—like a couple enjoying the mystery of a date planned by one person for the other. As relational dialectics suggests (see Chapter 11), complete certainty is complete boredom.

Even though the validity of Berger's theory is in question, his analysis of initial interaction is a major contribution to communication scholarship. Berger notes that "the field of communication has been suffering and continues to suffer from an intellectual trade deficit with respect to related disciplines; the field imports much more than it exports."[32] Uncertainty reduction theory was an early attempt by a scholar trained within the discipline to reverse that trend. His success at stimulating critical thinking among his peers can be seen in the fact that every scholar cited in this chapter has been a member of a communication faculty.

Although some of Berger's axioms may not perfectly reflect the acquaintance process, his focus on the issue of reducing uncertainty is at the heart of communication inquiry. Appealing for further dialogue and modification rather than wholesale rejection of the theory, Berger asks:

> What could be more basic to the study of communication than the propositions that (1) adaptation is essential for survival, (2) adaptation is only possible through the reduction of uncertainty, and (3) uncertainty can be both reduced and produced by communicative activity?[33]

It's a sound rhetorical question.

Predicted outcome value
A forecast of future benefits and costs of interaction based on limited experience with the other.

QUESTIONS TO SHARPEN YOUR FOCUS

1. An *axiom* is a self-evident truth. Which one of Berger's axioms seems least self-evident to you?

2. Check out *theorem 13* in Figure 9–1. Does the predicted relationship between *self-disclosure* and *reciprocity* match the forecast of social penetration theory?

3. What is your goal for the class period when *uncertainty reduction theory* will be discussed? What is your *hierarchical action plan* to achieve that goal?

4. When are you most likely to feel *relational turbulence* in your close relationships? Does anything other than *partner interference* or *relational uncertainty* help explain why you experience a bumpy emotional ride?

CONVERSATIONS

View this segment online at www.mhhe.com/griffin9e or www.afirstlook.com.

Chuck Berger would not be surprised if you were confused by the mid-chapter switch from axioms of uncertainty reduction to plan-based strategic communication. In his conversation with Em he describes why he originally viewed the two lines of research as separate but now sees them as tightly linked. Many students find this interview especially fascinating because of Berger's strongly stated opinions. For example, he dismisses CMM's idea of co-creation of social reality (see Chapter 6) because it offers a "total amnesia model." He also criticizes social scientists who purposely create ambiguity so that they can never be proved wrong. Berger's explicit and forthright statements show that he's willing to take that risk.

A SECOND LOOK

Recommended resource: Leanne K. Knobloch, "Uncertainty Reduction Theory," in *Engaging Theories in Interpersonal Communication: Multiple Perspectives,* Leslie A. Baxter and Dawn O. Braithwaite (eds.), Sage, Thousand Oaks, CA, 2008, pp. 133–144.

Original statement: Charles R. Berger and Richard Calabrese, "Some Explorations in Initial Interaction and Beyond: Toward a Developmental Theory of Interpersonal Communication," *Human Communication Research,* Vol. 1, 1975, pp. 99–112.

Comparison with other uncertainty theories: Walid A. Afifi, "Uncertainty and Information Management in Interpersonal Contexts," in *New Directions in Interpersonal Communication Research,* Sandi W. Smith and Steven R. Wilson (eds.), Sage, Thousand Oaks, CA, 2010, pp. 94–114.

Uncertainty reduction and online dating: Jennifer L. Gibbs, Nicole B. Ellison, and Chih-Hui Lai, "First Comes Love, Then Comes Google: An Investigation of Uncertainty Reduction Strategies and Self-Disclosure in Online Dating," *Communication Research,* Vol. 38, 2011, pp. 70–100.

Goals and plans in message production: Charles R. Berger, "Message Production Skill in Social Interaction," in *Handbook of Communication and Social Interaction Skills,* John O. Greene and Brant R. Burleson (eds.), Lawrence Erlbaum, Mahwah, NJ, 2003, pp. 257–290.

Uncertainty reduction in close relationships: Leanne K. Knobloch and Denise H. Solomon, "Information Seeking Beyond Initial Interaction: Negotiating Relational Uncertainty Within Close Relationships," *Human Communication Research,* Vol. 28, 2002, pp. 243–257.

Relational turbulence and military couples: Leanne K. Knobloch and Jennifer A. Theiss, "Experiences of U.S. Military Couples During the Post-Deployment Transition: Applying the Relational Turbulence Model," *Journal of Social and Personal Relationships,* Vol. 29, 2012, pp. 423–450.

Critique of axiom 3: Kathy Kellermann and Rodney Reynolds, "When Ignorance Is Bliss: The Role of Motivation to Reduce Uncertainty in Uncertainty Reduction Theory," *Human Communication Research,* Vol. 17, 1990, pp. 5–75.

Predicted outcome value theory: Artemio Ramirez Jr., Michael Sunnafrank, and Ryan Goei, "Predicted Outcome Value Theory in Ongoing Relationships," *Communication Monographs,* Vol. 77, 2010, pp. 27–50.

To access a chapter on reducing uncertainty when communicating across cultures, click on Anxiety/Uncertainty Management Theory in Archive under Theory Resources at
www.afirstlook.com.

Relationship Maintenance

The term *maintenance* may call to mind an auto repair shop where workers with oil-stained coveralls and grease under their fingernails struggle to service or fix a well-worn engine. The work is hard, the conditions are messy, and the repair is best performed by mechanics who have a good idea what they're doing.

This image of rugged work is appropriate when thinking about the ongoing effort required to maintain a close relationship. Forming a relational bond is often easier than sustaining it. The beginning stages of intimacy are typically filled with excitement at discovering another human being who sees the world as we do, with the added touch of wonder that the person we like likes us as well. As the relationship becomes more established, however, irritating habits, conflict, jealousy, and boredom can be the friction that threatens to pull the engine apart. The owner's manual of a new "Intimacy" should warn that periodic maintenance is necessary for friends, romantic partners, and even blood relatives to make it for the long haul.

Of course, personal relationships aren't inanimate machines with interchangeable parts that can be adjusted with a wrench. Expanding the *maintenance* metaphor to living organisms underscores the importance of individualized attention in relational health. Humanist communication writer John Stewart refers to a pair's

"They're a perfect match—she's high-maintenance, and he can fix anything."

© Edward Koren/The New Yorker Collection/www.cartoonbank.com

personal relationship as a "spiritual child," born as the result of their coming together.[1] His analogy stresses that a relationship requires continual care and nurture for sustained growth. Stewart thinks it's impossible to totally kill a relationship as long as one of the "parents" is still alive. Yet when people ignore or abuse the spiritual children they've created, the results are stunted or maimed relationships.

What does a healthy relationship look like? Through an extensive research program on relationship maintenance, Dan Canary (Arizona State University) and Laura Stafford (Bowling Green State University) conclude that long-term satisfying relationships have at least four characteristics—*liking, trust, commitment,* and *control mutuality.*[2] The first three seem like old relational friends. But control mutuality is a less familiar concept. According to Canary and Stafford, it is "the degree to which partners agree about which of them should decide relational goals and behavioral routines."[3] They may have an egalitarian relationship, or perhaps one person regularly defers to the other but is genuinely happy to do so. Either way, they could each embrace the following statement: *Both of us are satisfied with the way we handle decisions.*

Stafford and Canary surveyed 662 people involved in extended romantic relationships to find out what maintenance behaviors promoted liking, trust, commitment, and control mutuality. They discovered five interpersonal actions that contribute to long-term relational satisfaction:[4]

Positivity—Cheerful, courteous talk, avoiding criticism.

Openness—Self-disclosure and frank talk about their relationship.

Assurances—Affirming talk about the future of their relationship.

Networking—Spending time together with mutual friends and family.

Sharing tasks—Working together on routine jobs, chores, and assignments.

Researchers have found that friends and family members use these maintenance behaviors, too.[5] But why do we maintain some relationships and not others? Scholars have suggested two possible answers. First, the *exchange-oriented* perspective appeals to social exchange theory (see Chapter 9). Theorists in this tradition, including Canary and Stafford, believe we maintain relationships when costs and rewards are distributed fairly between partners. In contrast, the *communally oriented* perspective argues that maintenance doesn't involve such economic calculations. Rather, theorists in this tradition believe we maintain relationships when we see the other person as part of who we are—cost/reward ratio doesn't influence that choice.[6]

I (Andrew) recently conducted a study comparing the exchange and communal explanations. The results weren't simple—although communal orientation was the strongest predictor of couples' maintenance communication, cost/reward ratio was a significant predictor as well.[7] How could rewards and costs matter to partners, yet also *not* matter to them? It's a theoretical puzzle that wouldn't surprise the scholars who developed the three theories presented in this section. All three theories claim that the essence of relational maintenance is dialogue about *me, you,* and *we.* Sometimes that dialogue involves contradiction, confusion, and frustration—in other words, balancing relational needs is harder than balancing tires. Although maintaining relationships is tricky, these theorists agree that smooth-running, long-lasting relationships are worth the effort.

CHAPTER 13

The Interactional View
of Paul Watzlawick

The Franklin family is in trouble. A perceptive observer could spot their difficulties despite their successful façade. Sonia Franklin is an accomplished pianist who teaches advanced music theory and keyboard technique in her home. Her husband, Stan, will soon become a partner in a Big Four accounting firm. Their daughter, Laurie, is an honor student, an officer in her high school class, and the number two player on the tennis team. But Laurie's younger brother, Mike, has dropped all pretense of interest in studies, sports, or social life. His only passion is drinking beer and smoking pot.

Each of the Franklins reacts to Mike's substance abuse in different but less than helpful ways. Stan denies that his son has a problem. Boys will be boys, and he's sure Mike will grow out of this phase. The only time he and Mike actually talked about the problem, Stan said, "I want you to cut back on your drinking—not for me and your mother—but for your own sake."

Laurie has always felt responsible for her kid brother and is scared because Mike is getting wasted every few days. She makes him promise he'll quit using, and continues to introduce him to her straightlaced friends in the hope that he'll get in with a good crowd.

Sonia worries that alcohol and drugs will ruin her son's future. One weekday morning when he woke up with a hangover, she wrote a note to the school saying Mike had the flu. She also called a lawyer to help Mike when he was stopped for drunk driving. Although she promised never to tell his father about these incidents, she chides Stan for his lack of concern. The more she nags, the more he withdraws.

Mike feels caught in a vicious circle. Smoking pot helps him relax, but then his family gets more upset, which makes him want to smoke more, which. . . . During a tense dinner-table discussion he lashes out: "You want to know why I use? Go look in a mirror." Although the rest of the family sees Mike as "the problem," psychotherapist Paul Watzlawick would have described the whole family system as disturbed. He formed his theory of social interaction by looking at dysfunctional patterns within families in order to gain insight into healthy communication.

THE FAMILY AS A SYSTEM

Picture a family as a mobile suspended from the ceiling. Each figure is connected to the rest of the structure by a strong thread tied at exactly the right place to keep the system in balance. Tug on any string and the force sends a shock wave throughout the whole network. Sever a thread and the entire system tilts in disequilibrium.

The threads in the mobile analogy represent communication rules that hold the family together. Paul Watzlawick believed that in order to understand the movement of any single figure in the *family system,* one has to examine the communication patterns among all its members. He regarded the communication that family members have among themselves about their relationships as especially important.

Family system
A self-regulating, interdependent network of feedback loops guided by members' rules; the behavior of each person affects and is affected by the behavior of another.

Watzlawick (pronounced VAHT-sla-vick) was a senior research fellow at the Mental Research Institute of Palo Alto, California, and clinical professor of psychiatry at Stanford University. He was one of about 20 scholars and therapists who were inspired by and worked with anthropologist Gregory Bateson. The common denominator that continues to draw the Palo Alto Group together is a commitment to studying interpersonal interaction as part of an entire system. This sets their thinking apart from the widespread conception that communication is a linear process of a source sending a message through a channel to a receiver. In place of that transmission model, they picture communication as akin to an orchestra playing without a conductor.[1] Each person plays a part, affecting and being affected by all the others. It's impossible to isolate what causes what. It's interactional—so Watzlawick and his colleagues referred to their theory as the *interactional view.*

This systems approach suggests that interpersonal relationships are complicated, defying simplistic explanations of why family members do what they do. The Palo Alto Group rejects the notion that individual motives, personality traits, or DNA determines the nature of communication within a family or with others. In fact, these therapists care little about *why* a person acts a certain way, but they have great interest in *how* that behavior affects everyone in the group. For example, some pop psychology books on body language claim that a listener standing in a hands-on-hips position is skeptical about what the speaker is saying. Watzlawick was certainly interested in the reaction others have to this posture, but he didn't think that a particular way of standing should be viewed as part of a cause-and-effect chain of events:

$$a \to b \to c \to d$$

Relationships are not simple, nor are they "things," as suggested by the statement "We have a good relationship." Relationships are complex functions in the same sense that mathematical functions link multiple variables:

$$x = b^2 + \frac{2c}{a} - 5d$$

Just as x will be affected by the value of *a, b, c,* or *d,* so the hands-on-hips stance can be due to a variety of attitudes, emotions, or physical conditions. Maybe the stance does show skepticism. But it also might reflect boredom, a feeling of awkwardness, aching shoulder muscles, or self-consciousness about middle-aged love handles.

Watzlawick used the math metaphor throughout his book *Pragmatics of Human Communication.*[2] Along with co-authors Janet Beavin Bavelas and Don

Jackson, he presented key axioms that describe the "tentative calculus of human communication." These axioms make up the *grammar of conversation*, or, to use another analogy that runs through the book, the *rules of the game*.

There is nothing particularly playful about the game the Franklins are playing. Psychologist Alan Watts said that "life is a game where rule No. 1 is: This is no game, this is serious."[3] Watzlawick defined *games* as sequences of behavior governed by rules. Even though Sonia and Stan are involved in an unhealthy *game without end* of nag-withdrawal-nag-withdrawal, they continue to play because it serves a function for both of them. (Sonia feels superior; Stan avoids hassles with his son.) Neither party may recognize what's going on, but their rules are a something-for-something bargain. Mike's drinking and his family's distress may fit into the same category. (Getting drunk not only relieves tension temporarily, it's also a great excuse for sidestepping the pressure to excel, which is the name of the game in the Franklin family.)

Lest we be tempted to see the Franklins' relationships as typical of all families dealing with addiction, Watzlawick warned that each family plays a one-of-a-kind game with homemade rules. Just as CMM claims that persons-in-conversation co-construct their own social worlds (see Chapter 6), the Palo Alto Group insists that each family system creates its own reality. That conviction shapes its approach to family therapy:

> In the systemic approach, we try to understand as quickly as possible the functioning of this system: What kind of reality has this particular system constructed for itself? Incidentally, this rules out categorizations because one of the basic principles of systems theory is that "every system is its own best explanation."[4]

Games
Sequences of behavior governed by rules.

AXIOMS OF INTERPERSONAL COMMUNICATIONS

As therapists who met with a wide variety of clients, the Palo Alto Group spotted regularly occurring features of communication among family members. Watzlawick stated these interactional trends in the form of axioms—the preferred way to present academic scholarship 50 years ago. He cautioned that these maxims were tentative and open for revision after further study. Despite the preliminary nature of these axioms, their publication played a key role in launching the study of interpersonal communication within our discipline.[5]

One Cannot Not Communicate

You've undoubtedly been caught in situations where you've felt obliged to talk but would rather avoid the commitment to respond that's inherent in all communication. Perhaps you currently need to study but your roommate wants to chat. In an attempt to avoid communication, you could bluntly state that your test tomorrow morning makes studying more important than socializing. But voicing your desire for privacy can stretch the rules of good behavior and result in awkward silence that speaks loudly about the relationship.

Or what if you come home from a date or a party and your mother meets you inside the door and says, "Tell me all about it." You could flood her with a torrent of meaningless words about the evening, merely say it was "fine" as you duck into your room, or plead fatigue, a headache, or a sore throat. Watzlawick called this the *symptom strategy* and said it suggests, "*I* wouldn't mind talking to you, but something stronger than *I*, for which I cannot be blamed, prevents me."

Symptom strategy
Ascribing our silence to something beyond our control that renders communication justifiably impossible—sleepiness, headache, drunkenness, etc.

Whatever you do, however, it would be naïve not to realize that your mother will analyze your behavior for clues about the evening's activities. His face an immobile mask, Mike Franklin may mutely encounter his parents. But he communicates in spite of himself by his facial expression and his silence. Communication is inevitable. Those nonverbal messages will obviously have an impact on the rest of his family. A corollary to the first axiom is that "one cannot *not* influence."[6]

Communication = Content + Relationship

Content
The report part of a message; *what* is said verbally.

The heading is a shorthand version of the formal axiom "Every communication has a content and relationship aspect such that the latter classifies the former and is therefore metacommunication."[7] Watzlawick chose to rename the two aspects of communication that Gregory Bateson had originally called *report* and *command*. Report, or *content*, is *what* is said. Command, or *relationship*, is *how* it's said. Edna Rogers, University of Utah communication professor emerita and early interpreter of the interactional view, illustrates the difference with a two-word message:

> The content level provides information based on what the message is about, while the relational level "gives off" information on how the message is to be interpreted. For example, the content of the comment "You're late" refers to time, but at the relational level the comment typically implies a form of criticism of the other's lack of responsibility or concern.[8]

Relationship
The command part of the message; *how* it's said nonverbally.

Figure 13–1 outlines the content–relationship distinction that is crucial to the interactional model. Yet neither the equation in the heading above nor the terms in the figure quite capture the way relationship surrounds content and provides a context, frame, or atmosphere for interpretation. It's the difference between data fed into a computer and the program that directs how the data should be processed. In written communication, punctuation gives direction as to how the words should be understood. Shifting a question mark to an exclamation point alters the meaning of the message. Right? Right! In spoken communication, however, tone of voice, emphasis on certain words, facial cues, and so forth direct how the message was meant to be interpreted.

Metacommunication
Communication about communication.

Watzlawick referred to the relational aspect of interaction as *metacommunication*. It's communication about communication. Metacommunication says, "This is how I see myself, this is how I see you, this is how I see you seeing me. . . ." According to Watzlawick, relationship messages are always the most important

Content	Relationship
Report	Command
What is said	How it is said
Computer data	Computer program
Words	Punctuation
Verbal channel	Nonverbal channel
Communication	Metacommunication

FIGURE 13–1 The Content and Relationship Levels of Communication

element in any communication—healthy or otherwise. But when a family is in trouble, metacommunication dominates the discussion. Mike Franklin's dinner-table outburst is an example of pathological metacommunication that shakes the entire family system. The Palo Alto Group is convinced it would be a mistake for the Franklins to ignore Mike's attack in the hope that the tension will go away. Sick family relationships get better only when family members are willing to talk with each other about their patterns of communication.

The Nature of a Relationship Depends on How Both Parties Punctuate the Communication Sequence

Watzlawick uses the term *punctuate* to refer to the mental process of interpreting an ongoing sequence of events, labeling one event as the cause and the following event as the response. The fact that participants might view the sequence radically differently is captured in a classic cartoon displayed in many experimental psychology labs. One rat in a cage brags to another, "I've got my experimenter trained. Whenever I push this lever he gives me food."

In human relationships, divergent views of what-causes-what can give rise to great conflict. Consider the contrasting realities reflected in a typical argument between Sonia and Stan.

> SONIA: Talk to Mike. The boy needs a father.
>
> STAN: Mike's going to be OK.
>
> SONIA: Don't be so passive. You'd never do anything if I didn't push you.
>
> STAN: Quit harping on me all the time. It's because you nag that I withdraw.
>
> SONIA: It's because you withdraw that I nag.

An outsider who observes the interaction diagrammed below will spot a reciprocal pattern of nagging and withdrawal that has no beginning or end. But Sonia, who is enmeshed in the system, *punctuates* or cleaves the sequence with *P, R,* or *T* as the starting point. She's convinced that Stan's passivity is the cause of her nagging.

Equally ensnared in the system, Stan punctuates the sequence by designating Sonia's nagging at point *Q* or *S* as the initial event. He's quite sure that her constant scolding is the reason he backs away. Asking either of them *Who started it?* wouldn't help because the question merely feeds into their fruitless struggle for control.

Watzlawick suggested that "what is typical about the sequence and makes it a problem of punctuation is that the individual concerned conceives of him or herself only as reacting to, but not as provoking, these attitudes."[9] Stan sees himself detaching from Sonia and Mike only because of his wife's constant nagging. Sonia feels certain that she wouldn't harp on the issue if Stan would face the problem of Mike's drinking. The couple will be trapped in this vicious circle

Punctuate
Interpreting an ongoing sequence of events by labeling one event as the cause and the following event as the response.

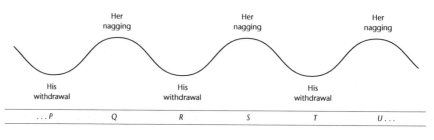

until they engage in a better brand of metacommunication—communication about their communication.

All Communication Is Either Symmetrical or Complementary

This axiom continues to focus on metacommunication. While definitions of relationships include the issues of belongingness, affection, trust, and intimacy, the interactional view pays particular attention to questions of control, status, and power. Remember that Bateson's original label for relationship communication was *command*. According to Watzlawick, *symmetrical* interchange is based on equal power; *complementary* communication is based on differences in power. He makes no attempt to label one type as good and the other as bad. Healthy relationships have both kinds of communication.

In terms of ability, the women in the Franklin family have a *symmetrical* relationship; neither one tries to control the other. Sonia has expertise on the piano; Laurie excels on the tennis court. Each of them performs without the other claiming dominance. Fortunately, their skills are in separate arenas. Too much similarity can set the stage for an anything-you-can-do-I-can-do-better competition.

Sonia's relationship with Mike is *complementary*. Her type of mothering is strong on control. She hides the extent of Mike's drinking from his father, lies to school officials, and hires a lawyer on the sly to bail her son out of trouble with the police. By continuing to treat Mike as a child, she maintains their dominant–submissive relationship. Although complementary relationships aren't always destructive, the status difference between Mike and the rest of the Franklins is stressing the family system.

The interactional view holds that there is no way to label a relationship on the basis of a single verbal statement. Judgments that an interaction is either symmetrical or complementary require a sequence of at least two messages—a statement from one person and a response from the other. While at Michigan State University, communication researchers Edna Rogers and Richard Farace devised a coding scheme to categorize ongoing marital interaction on the crucial issue of who controls the relationship.

One-up communication (↑) is movement to *gain* control of the exchange. A bid for dominance includes messages that instruct, order, interrupt, contradict, change topics, or fail to support what the other person said. *One-down communication* (↓) is movement to *yield* control of the exchange. The bid for submission is evidenced by agreement with what the other person said. Despite Watzlawick's contention that all discourse is either symmetrical or complementary, Rogers and Farace code *one-across communication* (→) as well. They define it as *transitory* communication that moves toward *neutralizing* control.

Figure 13–2 presents the matrix of possible relational transactions. The pairs that are circled show a symmetrical interaction. The pairs in triangles indicate complementary relations. The pairs in squares reveal transitory communication. As Rogers' later research shows, bids for dominance (↑) don't necessarily result in successful control of the interaction (↑↓).[10] Matt, a student in my comm theory class, gained new insight about his relationship with his mother when he read this section:

I'm really pumped on the interactional view. What makes me wide-eyed is how Watzlawick breaks down family communication into symmetrical and

Symmetrical interchange
Interaction based on equal power.

Complementary interchange
Interaction based on accepted differences of power.

One-up communication
A conversational move to gain control of the exchange; attempted domination.

One-down communication
A conversational move to yield control of the exchange; attempted submission.

One-across communication
A conversational move to neutralize or level control within the exchange; when just one party uses it, the interchange is labeled *transitory*.

170 *INTERPERSONAL COMMUNICATION*

Response to Message

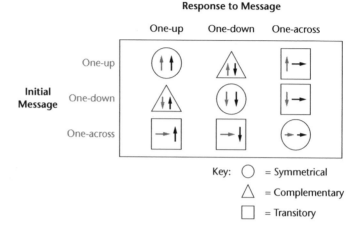

FIGURE 13–2 Matrix of Transactional Types

Adapted from Rogers and Farace, "Analysis of Relational Communication in Dyads: New Measurement Procedures"

complementary. It brings to mind a statement my father would often say: "You and your mother have heated arguments because you are so similar." I usually dismissed this idea as baloney. I'd respond, "What, Mom and I similar? Yeah, right—look how often we disagree!" Looking back through the eyes of Watzlawick, Dad was right. Mom and I were both shooting out one-up messages, thus forming an ongoing symmetrical interaction that wasn't very comfortable.

TRAPPED IN A SYSTEM WITH NO PLACE TO GO

Enabler
Within addiction culture, a person whose nonassertive behavior allows others to continue in their substance abuse.

Double bind
A person trapped under mutually exclusive expectations; specifically, the powerful party in a complementary relationship insists that the low-power party act as if it were symmetrical.

Family systems are highly resistant to change. This inertia is especially apparent in a home where someone has an addiction. Each family member occupies a role that serves the status quo. In the Franklin family, Mike, of course, is the one with "the problem." With the best of intentions, Sonia is the *enabler* who cushions Mike from feeling the pain caused by his chemical abuse. Stan is the "denier," while Laurie is the family "hero" who compensates for her brother's failure. Family therapists note that when one person in a distressed family gets better, another member often gets worse. If Mike stopped drinking and using pot, Laurie might quit the tennis team, ignore her studies, or start smoking marijuana herself. Dysfunctional families confirm the adage "The more things change, the more they stay the same."

Watzlawick saw family members as often caught in the *double bind* of mutually exclusive expectations, which Bateson originally described. Parental messages such as "You ought to love me" or "Be spontaneous" place children in an untenable position. The children are bound to violate some aspect of the injunction no matter how they respond. (Love can only be freely given; spontaneity on demand is impossible.) The paradox of the double bind is that the high-status party in a complementary relationship insists that the low-status person act as if the relationship were symmetrical—which it isn't. Stan's *demand* that his son stay sober for his *own sake* places Mike in a no-win situation. He can't obey his dad and be autonomous at the same time.

REFRAMING: CHANGING THE GAME BY CHANGING THE RULES

How can the members of the Franklin family break out of their never-ending game and experience real change in the way they relate to each other? According to Watzlawick, effective change for the whole family will come about only when members are helped to step outside the system and see the self-defeating nature of the rules under which they're playing. He calls this process *reframing:*

> To reframe . . . means to change the conceptual and/or emotional setting or viewpoint in relation to which a situation is experienced and to place it in another frame which fits the "facts" of the same concrete situation equally well or even better, and thereby changes its entire meaning.[11]

Watzlawick compared reframing to the process of waking up from a bad dream. He pointed out that during a nightmare you may run, hide, fight, scream, jump off a cliff, or try dozens of other things to make the situation better, but nothing really changes. Relief comes only when you step outside the system by waking up. Without the intervention of a timely alarm clock or a caring roommate, relief can be a long time coming.

Reframing
The process of instituting change by stepping outside of a situation and reinterpreting what it means.

Reframing is the sudden "aha" of looking at things in a new light. Suppose you could talk with Watzlawick about your struggles to keep up with the assignments for your comm theory class. You've chosen to be a communication major, so you believe you ought to *like* studying the material. Since you don't, you think there's something wrong with you. You also know that your family is making a financial sacrifice for you to be in college, so you feel guilty that you aren't getting good grades or experiencing deep gratitude for their help. In fact, you resent having to be grateful.

If you described these dilemmas to Watzlawick, he would want you to reframe your attitudes as *unrealistic* and *immature*—nightmarish interpretations for most college students. Even under the best of circumstances, he'd explain, studying is an unpleasant necessity and to believe that it should be fun is ridiculous. As far as your folks are concerned, they have a right to your gratitude, but that doesn't mean you have to *enjoy* being thankful. So it's up to you. You can "continue in these immature outlooks or have the adult courage to reject them and to begin to look at life as a mixture of pleasant and unpleasant things."[12] The *facts* haven't changed, but he's given you a new way to *interpret* them. If you accept Watzlawick's frame, you'll probably cope better and feel less pain.

For the Franklins, reframing means they must radically change their perspective. One way to do this is by adopting the view of Alcoholics Anonymous (AA) that Mike's addiction is a disease over which he has no control. His drinking is not a sign of moral weakness or an intentional rebuff of his family's values—he drinks because he's an alcoholic. The AA interpretation would imply that the Franklins need to abandon their fruitless search for someone to blame. Despite Mike's look-in-the-mirror accusation, the members of his family aren't responsible for his addiction. They didn't cause it, they can't cure it, and they can't control it. It's a disease. Does that mean Mike's not responsible for being chemically dependent? Right . . . but he *is* responsible for putting all of his energy into getting well.

Accepting a new frame implies rejecting the old one. The Franklins must admit that their so-called solutions are as much a problem as their son's drinking.

"Instead of 'It sucks' you could say, 'It doesn't speak to me.'"

© Mike Twohy/The New Yorker Collection/www.cartoonbank.com

Mike will never seek treatment for his illness as long as his family continues to shield him from the consequences of his behavior. Reframing will help Sonia see that writing excuses and hiring lawyers may be less caring than letting her son get kicked out of school or allowing his driver's license to be suspended.

Adopting a tough-love perspective or any new interpretive frame is usually accomplished only with outside help. For Watzlawick, that meant therapy. As a social constructionist, he wouldn't try to discover the "real" reason Mike drinks or worry if it's "true" that some people are genetically predisposed to addiction. In his view, the main goal of therapy is to reduce pain. He would regard the disease model of addiction as an alternative construction—a fiction, perhaps, but for the Franklin family a useful and less painful one.[13]

CRITIQUE: ADJUSTMENTS NEEDED WITHIN THE SYSTEM

Janet Beavin Bavelas co-authored *Pragmatics of Human Communication* with Watzlawick in 1967. Twenty-five years later, she reviewed the status of the axioms that are the central focus of the interactional view.[14] (Recall they were labeled as tentative.) Based on the research program she conducted at the University of Victoria in Canada, Bavelas recommends modifying some axioms of the theory. Her proposal serves as an informed critique of the original theory.

The first axiom claims that *we cannot not communicate*. Perhaps because of the catchy way it's stated, this axiom has been both challenged and defended more than the others. Although Bavelas is fascinated by the way people avoid eye contact or physically position themselves to communicate that they don't want to communicate, she now concedes that not all nonverbal behavior is communication. Observers may draw inferences from what they see, but in the absence of a sender–receiver relationship and the intentional use of a shared code, Bavelas would describe nonverbal behavior as *informative* rather than *communicative*.

As Figure 13–1 shows, the Palo Alto Group treated the verbal and nonverbal channels as providing different kinds of information. Bavelas now thinks that the notion of functionally separate channels dedicated to different uses is wrong. She suggests a *whole-message model* that treats verbal and nonverbal acts as completely integrated and often interchangeable. In effect, she has erased the broken vertical line that divides Figure 13–1 down the middle—a major shift in thinking.

Whole-message model
Regards verbal and nonverbal components of a message as completely integrated and often interchangeable.

The content/relationship distinction of another axiom is still viable for Bavelas. As did Watzlawick, she continues to believe that the content of communication is always embedded in the relationship environment. Looking back, however, she thinks they confused readers by sometimes equating the term *metacommunication* with all communication about a relationship. She now wants to reserve the word for explicit communication about the *process of communicating*. Examples of metacommunication narrowly defined would be Laurie Franklin telling her brother, "Don't talk to me like a kid," and Mike's response, "What do you mean by that?" Laurie's raised eyebrows and Mike's angry tone of voice would also be part of their tightly integrated packages of meaning.

Despite Bavelas' second thoughts, I'm impressed with the lasting impact that Watzlawick and his associates have had on the field of interpersonal communication. The publication of *Pragmatics of Human Communication* marked the beginning of widespread study of the way communication patterns sustain or destroy relationships. The interactional view has also encouraged communication scholars to go beyond narrow cause-and-effect assumptions. The entanglements Watzlawick described reflect the complexities of real-life relationships that most of us know. In that way, the interactional view is similar to the other two interpretive theories covered in this section on relationship maintenance. All of them major in description of communication rather than prediction.

QUESTIONS TO SHARPEN YOUR FOCUS

1. *Systems theorists* compare the family system to a mobile. What part of the mobile represents *metacommunication?* If you were constructing a mobile to model your family, how would you depict *symmetrical* and *complementary* relationships?

2. For decades, the United States and the former Soviet Union were engaged in a nuclear arms race. How does Watzlawick's axiom about the *punctuation of communication sequences* explain the belligerence of both nations?

3. Can you make up something your instructor might say that would place you in a *double bind?* Under what conditions would this be merely laughable rather than frustrating?

4. At the start of this chapter, the interactional view is charted as a highly *interpretive theory* coming from the *cybernetic tradition*—a tradition mapped as relatively *objective* in Chapter 4. Can you resolve this apparent contradiction?

A SECOND LOOK

Recommended resource: Paul Watzlawick, Janet Beavin Bavelas, and Don Jackson, *Pragmatics of Human Communication,* W. W. Norton, New York, 1967.

Commitments of the Palo Alto Group: Codruta Porcar and Cristian Hainic, "The Interactive Dimension of Communication: The Pragmatics of the Palo Alto Group," *Journal for Communication and Culture,* Vol. 1, No. 2, 2011, pp. 4–19.

Original conception of the theory: Gregory Bateson, "Information and Codification," in *Communication,* Jurgen Ruesch and Gregory Bateson (eds.), W. W. Norton, New York, 1951, pp. 168–211.

System theory: B. Aubrey Fisher, "The Pragmatic Perspective of Human Communication: A View from System Theory," in *Human Communication Theory,* Frank E. X. Dance (ed.), Harper & Row, New York, 1982, pp. 192–219.

Relational control: L. Edna Rogers and Richard Farace, "Analysis of Relational Communication in Dyads: New Measurement Procedures," *Human Communication Research,* Vol. 1, 1975, pp. 222–239.

Relational control in families: L. Edna Rogers, "Relational Communication Theory: An Interactional Family Theory," in *Engaging Theories in Family Communication: Multiple Perspectives,* Dawn O. Braithwaite and Leslie A. Baxter (eds.), Sage, Thousand Oaks, CA, 2006, pp. 115–129.

Reframing: Paul Watzlawick, John H. Weakland, and Richard Fisch, *Change,* W. W. Norton, New York, 1974, pp. 92–160.

Whether one cannot not communicate: Theodore Clevenger Jr., "Can One Not Communicate? A Conflict of Models," *Communication Studies,* Vol. 42, 1991, pp. 340–353.

Social construction approach to therapy: Paul Watzlawick and Michael Hoyt, "Constructing Therapeutic Realities: A Conversation with Paul Watzlawick," in *Handbook of Constructive Therapies,* Michael Hoyt (ed.), Jossey-Bass, San Francisco, CA, 1997, pp. 183–196.

Theory adjustments: Janet Beavin Bavelas, "Research into the Pragmatics of Human Communication," *Journal of Strategic and Systemic Therapies,* Vol. 11, No. 2, 1992, pp. 15–29.

Current face of the theory: L. Edna Rogers and Valentin Escudero (eds.), *Relational Communication: An Interactional Perspective to Study Process and Form,* Lawrence Erlbaum, Mahwah, NJ, 2004.

Critique: Carol Wilder, "The Palo Alto Group: Difficulties and Directions of the Interactional View for Human Communication Research," *Human Communication Research,* Vol. 5, 1979, pp. 171–186.

For additional scholarly and artistic resources, click on
Further Resources under Theory Resources at
www.afirstlook.com.

I n f l u e n c e

Getting a person to play a role in an unfamiliar situation can be a powerful method of influence. To explore its effectiveness, Yale social psychologists Irving Janis and Leon Mann surveyed students at a women's college to find out their attitudes and behavior toward smoking—a practice quite resistant to change.[1] They later asked many who smoked to take part in a role play that supposedly assessed their acting ability. Each woman was to take the role of a patient who had gone to the doctor because of a continual cough. She was now back in his office to get the results of a battery of tests the doctor had ordered. She had no script to follow and could respond to the other actor in whatever way she desired.[2]

One researcher then ushered her into a room that was decked out with a scale, sterilizer, fluorescent light for reading X-rays, and a medical school diploma on the wall. The room even smelled of disinfectant. The second experimenter wore a white lab coat with a stethoscope around his neck. Speaking in an authoritative tone of voice, the "doctor" came right to the point. Her chest X-ray gave a positive indication of lung cancer and the diagnosis was confirmed by lab tests. Without question, this condition had developed over a long time. He then paused to let the young woman respond. Often she would say that she'd been smoking too much. Most students eventually asked what they could do.

The doctor wasn't optimistic: "We need to operate immediately. Can you be prepared to check into the hospital tomorrow afternoon?" The surgery only had a 50–50 chance of success of stopping the cancer's spread. At this point the minidrama could go in a number of directions. The student might express fear for her life, anguish over broken plans for graduation, hesitancy over what to tell her parents or fiancé, anger at God, or disbelief that it was happening to her. No matter how the dialogue went, the young woman got caught up in the situation and emotionally involved with the link between smoking and cancer.

Janis and Mann waited two weeks for the effects of the role play to take hold and then rechecked attitudes toward cigarette smoking. They found that role-play students expressed less favorable opinions toward smoking than they had before. They also discovered that the average cigarettes-per-day habit had dropped from 24 (more than a pack a day) to 14—a dramatic decrease in actual smoking behavior. The attitudes of smokers in the control group who didn't have the role-play experience remained the same as before. So did their 24 cigarettes-per-day habit.

Relapse is common when smokers try to cut back or quit cold turkey. Many find the force of nicotine addiction, cigarette advertising, and friends who smoke hard to resist. Yet after eight months the slippage was slight. On average, those who participated in the emotional role play lit up 15 times a day—only one cigarette more.

Why is role play so effective in this case? In their book, *New Techniques of Persuasion*, the late Gerald Miller (Michigan State University) and Michael Burgoon (University of Arizona) suggested three possibilities. Role play makes for *immediacy*. The cigarette–cancer connection becomes more real to the smoker when she can't get the image of the doctor delivering bad news out of her mind. There's also *personal involvement*. The smoker can no longer stand aloof from the

176   *INTERPERSONAL COMMUNICATION*

threat of cancer when she's actively stating her fears to the doctor. Finally, Miller and Burgoon suggested we consider the effect of *nonverbal messages,* such as the doctor pointing to the patient's X-ray. "The impact of this simple behavioral sequence may well transcend the effects of an extended medical lecture on the dangers of cigarette smoking."[3]

We've recounted this experiment because it illustrates and measures what influence theorists, researchers, and many practitioners value. Will a persuasive approach change people's inner attitudes—their beliefs, their emotional response, and what they intend to do? Will that shift in attitude be matched by a change in actual behavior? Are these changes so deep-seated that they will resist forces that tend to draw them back into old patterns of thinking and behavior? And will they last over time? The three theories that follow suggest different routes to this kind of effective interpersonal influence and, most important, explain why they work.

"I'm through playing doctor.
With insurance forms, co-payments,
and malpractice suits, it's just no fun!"

© Chris Wildt. Reprinted by permission of
www.CartoonStock.com

CHAPTER **14**

Social Judgment Theory
of Muzafer Sherif

My son, Jim, is an airline pilot—a job that has changed dramatically since the terrorist acts of September 11, 2001. When he walks through the airport he overhears a variety of comments about the safety of air travel. I've listed 11 statements that reflect the range of attitudes he's heard expressed. Read through these opinions and consider the diversity of viewpoints they represent.

a. Airlines aren't willing to spend money on tight security.

b. All life is risk. Flying is like anything else.

c. Anyone willing to die for a cause can hijack an airplane.

d. Air marshals with guns can deter terrorists.

e. There are old pilots and bold pilots; there are no old, bold pilots.

f. Pilots drink before they fly to quell their fears of skyjacking.

g. Getting there by plane is safer than taking the train or bus.

h. American pilots are trained to handle any in-flight emergency.

i. It's easy to get into the cockpit of a jet airplane.

j. Passenger screening is better with full-body scanners in place.

k. The odds of a plane crash are 1 in 10 million.

Take a few minutes to mark your reactions to these statements. If you follow each instruction before jumping ahead to the next one, you'll have a chance to experience what social judgment theory predicts.

1. To begin, read through the items again and underline the single statement that most closely represents your point of view.

2. Now look and see whether any other items seem reasonable. Circle the letters in front of those acceptable statements.

3. Reread the remaining statements and cross out the letters in front of any that are objectionable to you. After you cross out these unreasonable ideas, you may have marked all 11 statements one way or another. It's also possible that you'll leave some items unmarked.

THREE LATITUDES: ACCEPTANCE, REJECTION, AND NONCOMMITMENT

I've just taken you on paper through what social judgment theory says happens in our heads. We hear a message and immediately judge where it should be placed on the attitude scale in our minds. According to the late Muzafer Sherif, a social psychologist at the University of Oklahoma, this subconscious sorting of ideas occurs at the instant of perception. We weigh every new idea by comparing it with our present point of view. He called his analysis of attitudes the *social judgment–involvement approach,* but most scholars refer to it simply as *social judgment theory.*

**Social judgment–
involvement**
Perception and evaluation
of an idea by comparing
it with current attitudes.

Sherif believed that the three responses you made on the previous page are necessary to determine your attitude toward airline safety, or any other attitude structure. In all probability you circled a range of statements that seemed reasonable to you and crossed out a number of opinions you couldn't accept. That's why Sherif would see your attitude as a *latitude* rather than any single statement you underlined. He wrote that an "individual's stand is not represented adequately as a point along a continuum. Different persons espousing the same position may differ considerably in their tolerance around this point."[1]

He saw an attitude as an amalgam of three zones. The first zone is called the *latitude of acceptance.* It's made up of the item you underlined and any others you circled as acceptable. A second zone is the *latitude of rejection.* It consists of the opinions you crossed out as objectionable. The leftover statements, if any, define the *latitude of noncommitment.* These were the items you found neither objectionable nor acceptable. They're akin to marking *undecided* or *no opinion* on a traditional attitude survey. Sherif said we need to know the location and width of each of these interrelated latitudes in order to describe a person's attitude structure.

Latitude of acceptance
The range of ideas that a
person sees as reason-
able or worthy of consid-
eration.

Latitude of rejection
The range of ideas that a
person sees as unreason-
able or objectionable.

**Latitude of
noncommitment**
The range of ideas that
a person sees as neither
acceptable nor
objectionable.

Suppose Jim encounters Ned, a man in the airport who is complaining about the dangers of flight as evidenced by 9/11 terrorism. Assume Jim would like to persuade Ned that flying is absolutely safe, or at least much less risky than anxious Ned believes. Social judgment theory recommends that Jim try to figure out the location and breadth of the man's three latitudes before presenting his case. Figure 14–1 shows where Ned places those 11 statements along the mental yardstick he uses to gauge safety. As you will discover in the next few pages, if my son has a good idea of this cognitive map, he'll have a much better chance of crafting a message that will persuade Ned to be more optimistic about flying.

EGO-INVOLVEMENT: HOW MUCH DO YOU CARE?

There's one other thing about Ned's attitude structure that Jim needs to know—how *important* the issue of air safety is in Ned's life. Sherif called this concept *ego-involvement.* *Ego-involvement* refers to how crucial an issue is in our lives. Is it central to our well-being? Do we think about it a lot? Does our attitude on the matter go a long way toward defining who we are? In Figure 14–1, I've used an anchor to represent the position that most closely represents Ned's point of view—that flying is dangerous because fanatics are willing to die for their cause. Sherif said that's what our favored position does; it anchors all our other thoughts about the topic.

If air safety were only a casual concern for Ned, it would be fitting to represent his stance with a small anchor that could easily be dragged to a new position. That's probably the case for some of the nonfliers in the terminal who

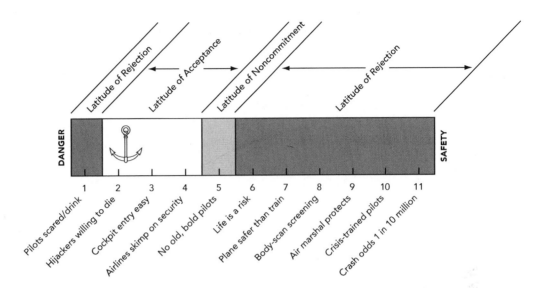

FIGURE 14–1 Ned's Cognitive Map Regarding Air Safety

are simply picking up a rental car, dropping off Aunt Juanita for her flight, or perhaps retrieving a lost bag for a friend. These folks are for safe flights and against crashes, but air safety doesn't present a major personal concern.

Despite the fact that images of airplanes slamming into the twin towers of the World Trade Center are stenciled into most people's minds, not everyone who flies dwells on the topic. Those people don't argue about it, stew over it, or get sweaty palms when their jet roars down the runway. As long as everything seems normal, their ego-involvement is moderate.

But for Ned and others like him, the issue is crucial. They are fearful fliers who swap horror stories of knowing someone who died on a hijacked plane. They experience panic when three swarthy men board their flight to Chicago. Others may experience only passing anxiety about flying, but since Ned's fear is deep-seated, the hefty anchor shown in Figure 14–1 is appropriate.

People with attitude profiles similar to Ned's are highly ego-involved. Some join the International Air Safety Association (IASA), an airline passenger association that lobbies for stricter safety regulations. One way Sherif defined high ego-involvement was *membership in a group with a known stand.* My son's pilot's license, Air Line Pilots Association union card, and employment with a major airline are indications that he's at least as ego-involved in the issue as Ned. Of course, his confidence in airline safety is at the other end of the spectrum.

Three features of Ned's attitude structure are typical of people with high ego-involvement in an issue. The first indication is that his latitude of noncommitment is almost nonexistent. People who don't care about an issue usually have a wide latitude of noncommitment, but Ned has only one statement in that category. He may not be sure about old, bold pilots, but he has definite opinions on everything else.

Second, Ned rejects all five statements that offer assurances of safety. According to social judgment theory, a wide latitude of rejection is a typical sign of high ego-involvement. Ned has intense feelings about the potential dangers of flying;

Ego-involvement
The importance or centrality of an issue to a person's life, often demonstrated by membership in a group with a known stand.

he sees safety as a black-and-white issue. People with low ego-involvement would probably see more gray area.

Finally, people who hold extreme opinions on either side of an issue almost always care deeply. While it's possible to feel passionate about middle-of-the-road positions, social judgment researchers find that massive attitude anchors are usually located toward the ends of the scale. Extreme positions and high ego-involvement go together. That's why religion, sex, and politics are traditionally taboo topics in the wardroom of a U.S. Navy ship at sea. When passions run deep, radical opinions are common, and there's little tolerance for diversity.

Steven Spielberg's film *Lincoln* illustrates Sherif's concepts of ego-involvement and attitudes as latitudes.[2] Against the advice of his cabinet, the president pushes Congress to pass a constitutional amendment abolishing slavery. A *yes* vote falls somewhere within each Republican's latitude of acceptance. But to get the needed two-thirds majority, Lincoln needs to switch the votes of 20 Democrats, whose party publicly opposes the amendment. Abolition appears to fall within their latitude of rejection.

Yet Lincoln's men see a window of opportunity. Leaving Congress are 39 lame-duck Democrats who now have weaker party ties. With that lower ego-involvement, these 39 men may have a wider latitude of noncommitment toward the amendment and could be encouraged to *abstain* rather than vote *no*. Some might be swayed to broaden their latitude of acceptance, making a *yes* vote possible. The film shows Lincoln's political operatives in the House balcony noting which Democrats are sweating or at least not cheering when their leaders lambast the amendment. The aides then use Lincoln's popularity, moral arguments, job offers, threats, and bribes to induce latitude change. The amendment passes and slavery is abolished by a two-vote margin.

Everything I've presented up to this point deals with the way social judgment theory describes the cognitive *structure* of a person's attitude. We now turn to the two-step mental *process* that Sherif said is triggered when a person hears or reads a message. Ned will first evaluate the content of the message to see where it falls vis-à-vis his own position—how far it is from his anchor. That's the *judgment* phase of social judgment theory. In the second stage of the process, Ned will adjust his anchored attitude toward or away from the message he's just encountered. The next two sections explain the way Sherif said the two stages of this influence process work.

JUDGING THE MESSAGE: CONTRAST AND ASSIMILATION ERRORS

Sherif claimed that we use our own anchored attitude as a comparison point when we hear a discrepant message. He believed there's a parallel between systematic biases in the judgments we make in the physical world and the way we determine other people's attitudes. I recently set up three pails of water in my class to illustrate this principle. Even though the contents looked the same, the water in the left bucket was just above freezing, the water in the right bucket was just below scalding, and the water in the middle bucket was lukewarm. A student volunteered to plunge her left hand into the left bucket and her right hand into the right bucket at the same time. Twenty seconds was about all she could take. I then asked her to plunge both hands into the middle bucket and judge the temperature of the water. Of course, this produced a baffling experience, because her left hand told her the water was hot, while her right hand sent a message that it was cold.

Sherif hypothesized a similar *contrast* effect when people who are hot for an idea hear a message on the topic that doesn't have the same fire. Judged by their standard, even warm messages strike them as cold. Sherif's *social judgment–involvement* label nicely captures the idea of a link between ego-involvement and perception. Highly committed people have large latitudes of rejection. Any message that falls within that range will be perceived by them as more discrepant from their anchor than it really is. The message is mentally pushed away to a position that is farther out—not within the latitude of acceptance. So the hearer doesn't have to deal with it as a viable option.

All of this is bad news for Jim as he tries to dispel Ned's fears. He'll probably address Ned's concerns head on:

Contrast
A perceptual error whereby people judge messages that fall within their latitude of rejection as farther from their anchor than they really are.

> Look, Ned, statistics show you're much safer flying than taking the train or bus. In fact, the most dangerous part of flying is the drive to the airport. I know you worry about terrorists, but with the new full-body scanners the TSA is using, there's no way that guns, knives, or explosives can get on board. And you should know there's been an undercover air marshal riding shotgun back in coach on my last three trips.

Jim hopes these points will be reassuring. If Ned hears them as they were intended, they will register at 7, 8, and 9 on his mental scale, where a 1 represents total danger and an 11 indicates complete safety. However, social judgment theory says Ned won't hear them that way. Because the message falls within Ned's latitude of rejection, he's likely to judge the words as even farther from his anchor, perhaps at 9, 10, and 11. The words will strike Ned as unbelievable, self-serving, pilot propaganda—a false guarantee of safety that he'll be quick to reject.

Contrast is a perceptual distortion that leads to polarization of ideas. But according to Sherif, it happens only when a message falls within the latitude of rejection. *Assimilation* is the opposite error of judgment. It's the rubberband effect that draws an idea toward the hearer's anchor so it seems that she and the speaker share the same opinion. Assimilation takes place when a message falls within the latitude of acceptance. For example, suppose Jim tells Ned that his airline isn't willing to spend money on effective security. Although that message is at 4 on Ned's cognitive map, he will hear it as more similar to his anchoring attitude than it really is, perhaps at 3.

Assimilation
A perceptual error whereby people judge messages that fall within their latitude of acceptance as less discrepant from their anchor than they really are.

Sherif was unclear about how people judge a message that falls within their latitude of noncommitment. Most interpreters assume that perceptual bias will not kick in and that the message will be heard roughly as intended.

DISCREPANCY AND ATTITUDE CHANGE

Judging how close or how far a message is from our own anchored position is the first stage of attitude change. Shifting our anchor in response is the second. Sherif thought that both stages of the influence process usually take place below the level of consciousness.

According to social judgment theory, once we've judged a new message to be within our latitude of acceptance, we will adjust our attitude somewhat to accommodate the new input. The persuasive effect will be positive but partial. We won't travel the whole distance, but there will be some measurable movement toward the speaker's perceived position. How much movement? Sherif wasn't specific, but he did claim that *the greater the discrepancy, the more hearers*

182   *INTERPERSONAL COMMUNICATION*

will adjust their attitudes. Thus, the message that persuades the most is the one that is most discrepant from the listener's position yet falls within his or her *latitude of acceptance* or *latitude of noncommitment.*

If we've judged a message to be within our *latitude of rejection,* we will also adjust our attitude, but in this case *away from* what we think the speaker is advocating. Since people who are highly ego-involved in a topic have a broad range of rejection, most messages aimed to persuade them are in danger of actually driving them further away. This predicted *boomerang effect* suggests that people are often *driven* rather than *drawn* to the attitude positions they occupy.

Boomerang effect
Attitude change in the opposite direction of what the message advocates; listeners driven away from rather than drawn to an idea.

The mental processes Sherif described are automatic. He reduced interpersonal influence to the issue of the distance between the message and the hearer's position:

> Stripped to its bare essential, the problem of attitude change is the problem of the degree of discrepancy from communication and the felt necessity of coping with the discrepancy.[3]

So the only space for volition in social judgment theory is the choice of alternative messages available to the person who's trying to persuade.

PRACTICAL ADVICE FOR THE PERSUADER

Sherif would have advised Jim to avoid messages that claim flying is safer than taking the bus or train. Ned simply won't believe them, and they may push him deeper into his anti-aviation stance. To make sure his words have a positive

"We think you could gain much wider support simply by re-languaging your bigotry."

© William Haefeli/The New Yorker Collection/www.cartoonbank.com

effect, Jim should select a message that falls at the edge of Ned's latitude of acceptance. Even after the perceptual process of assimilation kicks in, Ned will still judge Jim's message to be discrepant from his point of view and shift his attitude slightly in that direction.

> Ned, you're right. For years the airlines—mine included—didn't invest the money it takes to successfully screen passengers. But 9/11 has changed all that. Every ticket you buy has a surcharge to pay for tight security. And the days of the cowboy pilot are over. Because it's my job to protect hundreds of lives in a $100 million airplane, I do it by the book every flight. I know that if I get my butt there safely, yours will get there that way too.

Jim might try a riskier strategy to produce greater attitude shift. He could use the vague statement about there being no old, bold pilots, since ambiguity can often serve better than clarity. When George W. Bush started campaigning for president, he called himself a "compassionate conservative." Nobody knew exactly what the label meant, so the term stayed out of voters' latitude of rejection. If Jim goes that route and Ned presses for clarification on the absence of old, bold pilots, Jim can explain that rigorous cockpit checkrides weeded out those who take chances. But this approach could backfire and feed Ned's fears if the statement calls to mind an image of reckless pilots about to crash and burn.

The idea of crafting a message to fall within Ned's latitude of acceptance or noncommitment is frustrating to Jim. He wants more change than these strategies offer. But according to social judgment theory, limited change is all he can get in a one-shot attempt. If he were talking to an open-minded person with wide latitudes of acceptance and noncommitment, a bigger shift would be possible. Toby, a student in my class, saw himself that way over a broad range of issues:

> Time and time again I find myself easily persuaded. Afterward I wonder, *How did I get talked into this one?* Credit it to my flexibility, willingness to try, or naïve trust in people's motives. I always pay attention to advice given by a friend or an expert. Social judgment theory would say that I simply have a wide latitude of noncommitment. That's because I have low ego-involvement most of the time. The situation is not a hill to die on, so why should I get my pride involved?

Toby isn't typical. We're more likely to encounter people who are dogmatic on every issue. "Don't confuse me with the facts," they say. "My mind is made up." These cantankerous souls have wide latitudes of rejection. This probably doesn't describe Ned. His deeply skeptical attitude is likely limited to fear of flying. But when Jim is dealing with a highly ego-involved traveler, he has to work within a narrow range. True conversion from one end of the scale to the other is a rare phenomenon. The only way to stimulate large-scale change is through a series of small, successive movements. Persuasion is a gradual process.

It's also a *social* process. The lack of an interpersonal bond between Jim and Ned limits the amount of influence that's possible. If Ned heard strong reassurances of airline safety from his friends and family, it might occasion a major shift. Sherif noted that "most dramatic cases of attitude change, the most widespread and enduring, are those involving changes in reference groups with differing values."[4]

Reference groups
Groups that members use to define their identity.

184   *INTERPERSONAL COMMUNICATION*

ATTITUDES ON SLEEP, BOOZE, AND MONEY: EVIDENCE SUPPORTING SJT

Research on the predictions of social judgment theory (SJT) requires highly ego-involving issues where strong resistance to some persuasive messages is likely. The topics of sufficient sleep, alcohol consumption, and asking for money seem ripe for assessing the theory's validity.

Sufficient sleep. In an early experiment testing social judgment theory, psychologists Stephen Bochner (University of New South Wales) and Chester Insko (University of North Carolina at Chapel Hill) queried college students about how much sleep they thought a person should get each night.[5] Before the study, most college students accepted the conventional wisdom that the human body functions best with eight hours of sleep. They then read an article written by an expert in the field that claimed young adults actually need much less. The message was the same for all with one crucial difference. Some students were told they needed eight hours, some seven, some six, and so on, right down the line. The final group actually read that humans need no sleep at all! Then each group had a chance to give their opinions.

Sherif's theory suggests that the fewer hours recommended, the more students will be swayed, until they begin to regard the message as patently ridiculous. The results shown in Figure 14–2 confirm this prediction. Persuasion increased as the hours advocated were reduced to 3, a message that caused students to revise their estimate of optimum sleep down to 6.3 hours. Anything less than 3 hours apparently fell outside their latitude of acceptance and became progressively ineffective. But a highly credible speaker can shrink the hearer's latitude of rejection. When the "expert" in the sleep study was a Nobel Prize-winning physiologist rather than a YMCA director, persuasion increased.

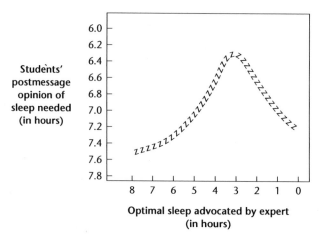

FIGURE 14–2 **Sleep Study Results**
Adapted from Bochner and Insko, "Communicator Discrepancy, Source Credibility and Opinion Change"

Pluralistic ignorance
The mistaken idea that everyone else is doing or thinking something that they aren't.

Alcohol consumption.   In the fall of 2004, Michigan State University communication professors Sandi Smith, Charles Atkin, and three other university colleagues measured students' perception of drinking behavior at the school.[6] They found a campus wide *pluralistic ignorance* of the actual amount of booze consumed by students who drink at a party. Whereas reported alcohol consumption averaged 5.3 drinks—with 63 percent downing five drinks or less—students thought the norm was closer to six drinks (5.9 percent). This gap concerned health center officials because perceived social norms affect behavior—in this case, the idea encouraged risky binge drinking. In preparation for a campus wide social norm campaign to correct the misperception and publicize the actual norm, Smith and Atkin measured student body latitudes of acceptance, noncommitment, and rejection of various messages. Based on their research they selected the following true phrase to be included in every communication about student drinking behavior: "Most (63 percent) drink zero to five when they party." The message fell within most students' latitude of noncommitment—as discrepant from campus opinion as possible while still being believable.

The intensive, three-month campaign involved posters across campus, table tents in the cafeteria, and multiple ads in the campus newspaper and in a news magazine handed out at orientation. Almost all students reported seeing the zero-to-five-drinks message many times. The campaign was a success. When Smith and Atkin measured perception of drinking in the spring, they found that students had lowered their estimate to 4.9—one drink less than they had thought in the fall. Even more impressive, the average of number of drinks consumed at a party during that time span fell from 5.3 to 4.5—almost a full glass or mug. Like the lung-cancer role-play experiment reported in the introduction to this section, this research validates an effective strategy to induce lasting change in beliefs and behavior, even when the issue is highly ego-involving.

Asking for money.   An anecdotal story of SJT in action comes from a university development director I know who was making a call on a rich alumnus. He anticipated that the prospective donor would give as much as $10,000. He made his pitch and asked what the wealthy businessman could do. The man protested that it had been a lean year and that times were tough—he couldn't possibly contribute more than $20,000. The fundraiser figured that he had seriously underestimated the giver's latitude of acceptance and that $20,000 was on the low end of that range. Without missing a beat he replied, "Trevor, do you really think that's enough?" The alumnus wrote a check for $25,000.

How do you feel about the fundraising ploy just described? The persuasive technique obviously worked, but the application of social judgment theory raises some thorny ethical questions. Is it OK for fundraisers to alter their pitch based on a potential donor's latitude of acceptance? Is it all right for politicians to be intentionally vague so that their message has broad appeal? Or consider my son's genuine desire to allay the fears of the flying public. The theory claims Jim will be more effective by presenting a soft-sell message at mid scale rather than stating his genuine conviction that flying is safer than driving. Are these choices you want to make, or want others to make when they try to influence you?

CRITIQUE: A THEORY WELL WITHIN THE LATITUDE OF ACCEPTANCE

The social norm campaign on alcohol consumption and the college fundraiser's appeal for a generous contribution demonstrate that social judgment theory has *practical utility*—one of the six criteria of a good scientific theory. The trick for the influence practitioner is figuring out where the other person's latitudes of acceptance, noncommitment, and rejection lie. That's what audience analysis, market research, and focus groups are all about, but it's hard to imagine Jim handing a questionnaire to every jittery traveler in the departure lounge.

Social judgment theory offers specific *predictions* about what happens in the mind of someone who hears or reads a message that falls within his or her latitude of acceptance or rejection. Sherif's appeal to the perceptual distortions of assimilation and contrast, as well as the crucial role of ego-involvement, offer a compelling *explanation* of what goes on behind the eyes. Yet like all cognitive explanations put forth in this section of the book, these mental structures and processes can't be seen. We can only infer what's going on inside the head by observing the input and the output—the message and a person's response. The SJT explanation of persuasion is complex, but given Sherif's claim that an attitude can't be identified by a single point on a continuum, it's hard to imagine a *simpler* account of what's happening.

As the studies I've described demonstrate, social judgment theory requires *quantitative research,* and that's the kind social scientists have designed. But compared to the hundreds of empirical studies run to test and refine other leading theories of persuasion, the research base of SJT is relatively small. That may be because it's hard to locate a wide range of experimental subjects who run the gamut of high to low ego-involvement and hold widely different opinions on the same topic. And once they are willing to participate, the process of locating their three latitudes can be tedious for everyone involved. Even so, specific predictions of SJT are *testable;* some have been supported and a few found to fail. For example, Bochner and Insko's sleep experiment confirms that as long as a message remains outside people's latitudes of rejection, the more discrepant it is from the anchor, the greater the attitude shift in the desired direction will be. On the other hand, the boomerang effect that SJT predicts can happen when a message is delivered in the latitude of rejection is not often found. (Students who read the bizarre claim that the body thrives with zero hours of sleep per night didn't then decide that eight hours were too few.)

Despite the questions that surround social judgment theory, it is an elegant conception of the persuasion process that falls well within my latitude of acceptance. There's an intuitive appeal to the idea of crafting a message just short of the latitude of rejection in order to be as effectively discrepant as possible. That would be my message to Jim as he confronts a variety of air travelers. I wonder in what latitude of attitude my advice will fall?

QUESTIONS TO SHARPEN YOUR FOCUS

1. How does the concept of *attitudes as latitudes* help you understand your attitude toward the various requirements of this course?

2. Suppose you find out that the fellow sitting next to you is *highly ego-involved* in the issue of gun control. Based on social judgment theory, what three predictions about his attitude structure would be reasonable to make?

3. What practical advice does social judgment theory offer if you want to ask your boss for a raise?

4. Do you have any *ethical qualms* about applying the wisdom of social judgment theory? Why or why not?

A SECOND LOOK

Recommended resources: Donald Granberg, "Social Judgment Theory," in *Communication Yearbook 6*, Michael Burgoon (ed.), Sage, Beverly Hills, CA, 1982, pp. 304–329; Daniel J. O'Keefe, "Social Judgment Theory," in *Persuasion: Theory and Research*, Sage, Newbury Park, CA, 1990, pp. 29–44.

Original conception: Muzafer Sherif and Carl Hovland, *Social Judgment: Assimilation and Contrast Effects in Communication and Attitude Change*, Yale University, New Haven, CT, 1961.

Further development: Carolyn Sherif, Muzafer Sherif, and Roger Nebergall, *Attitude and Attitude Change: The Social Judgment–Involvement Approach*, W. B. Saunders, Philadelphia, PA, 1965.

Attitudes as latitudes: Kenneth Sereno and Edward Bodaken, "Ego-Involvement and Attitude Change: Toward a Reconceptualization of Persuasive Effect," *Speech Monographs*, Vol. 39, 1972, pp. 151–158.

Ego-involvement: William W. Wilmot, "Ego-Involvement: A Confusing Variable in Speech Communication Research," *Quarterly Journal of Speech*, Vol. 57, 1971, pp. 429–436.

Assimilation and contrast: Alison Ledgerwood and Shelly Chaiken, "Priming Us and Them: Automatic Assimilation and Contrast in Group Attitudes," *Journal of Personality and Social Psychology*, Vol. 93, 2007, pp. 940–956.

Message discrepancy: Stan Kaplowitz and Edward Fink, "Message Discrepancy and Persuasion," in *Progress in Communication Sciences: Advances in Persuasion, Vol. 13*, George Barnett and Frank Boster (eds.), Ablex, Greenwich, CT, 1997, pp. 75–106.

Boomerang effect: Hilobumi Sakaki, "Experimental Studies of Boomerang Effects Following Persuasive Communication," *Psychologia*, Vol. 27, No. 2, 1984, pp. 84–88.

Sleep study: Stephen Bochner and Chester Insko, "Communicator Discrepancy, Source Credibility and Opinion Change," *Journal of Personality and Social Psychology*, Vol. 4, 1966, pp. 614–621.

Changing social norms for drinking on campus: Sandi Smith, Charles Atkin, Dennis Martell, Rebecca Allen, and Larry Hembroff, "A Social Judgment Theory Approach to Conducting Formative Research in a Social Norms Campaign," *Communication Theory*, Vol. 16, 2006, pp. 141–152.

Critique: Hee Sun Park, Timothy Levine, Catherine Y. K. Waterman, Tierney Oregon, and Sarah Forager, "The Effects of Argument Quality and Involvement Type on Attitude Formation and Attitude Change," *Human Communication Research*, Vol. 33, 2007, pp. 81–102.

CHAPTER 15

Objective   Interpretive

Socio-psychological tradition

Elaboration Likelihood Model

of Richard Petty & John Cacioppo

Like a number of women whose children are out of the home, Rita Francisco has gone back to college. Her program isn't an aimless sampling of classes to fill empty hours—she has enrolled in every course that will help her become a more persuasive advocate. Rita is a woman on a mission.

Rita's teenage daughter was killed when the car she was riding in smashed into a stone wall. After drinking three cans of beer at a party, the girl's 18-year-old boyfriend lost control on a curve while driving 80 miles per hour. Rita's son walks with a permanent limp as a result of injuries sustained when a high school girl plowed through the parking lot of a 7-Eleven on a Friday night. When the county prosecutor obtained a DUI (driving under the influence) conviction, it only fueled Rita's resolve to get young drinking drivers off the road. She has become active with Mothers Against Drunk Driving and works to convince anyone who will listen that zero-tolerance laws, which make it illegal for drivers under the age of 21 to have *any* measurable amount of alcohol in their system, should be strictly enforced. Rita also wants to persuade others that young adults caught driving with more than 0.02 percent blood alcohol content should automatically lose their driver's licenses until they are 21.

This is a tough sell on most college campuses. While her classmates can appreciate the tragic reasons underlying her fervor, few subscribe to what they believe is a drastic solution. As a nontraditional, older student, Rita realizes that her younger classmates could easily dismiss her campaign as the ranting of a hysterical parent. She's determined to develop the most effective persuasive strategy possible and wonders if she would have the most success by presenting well-reasoned arguments for enforcing zero-tolerance laws. Then again, couldn't she sway students more by lining up highly credible people to endorse her proposal?

THE CENTRAL AND PERIPHERAL ROUTES TO PERSUASION

Ohio State psychologist Richard Petty thinks Rita is asking the right questions. He conducted his Ph.D. dissertation study using the topic of teenage driving to test the relative effectiveness of strong-message arguments and high source credibility. He found that the results varied depending on which of two mental routes to attitude change a *listener* happened to use. Petty labeled the two cognitive processes the *central route* and the *peripheral route.* He sees the distinction as helpful in reconciling much of the conflicting data of persuasion research. Along with his University of Chicago colleague John Cacioppo, he launched an intensive program of study to discover the best way for a persuader to activate each route.

Central route

Message elaboration; the path of cognitive processing that involves scrutiny of message content.

The central route involves message elaboration. Elaboration is "the extent to which a person carefully thinks about issue-relevant arguments contained in a persuasive communication."[1] In an attempt to process new information rationally, people using the central route carefully scrutinize the ideas, try to figure out if they have true merit, and mull over their implications. Similar to Berger's characterization of strategic message plans, elaboration requires high levels of cognitive effort (see Chapter 9).

Message elaboration

The extent to which a person carefully thinks about issue-relevant arguments contained in a persuasive communication.

The peripheral route offers a mental shortcut path to accepting or rejecting a message "without any active thinking about the attributes of the issue or the object of consideration."[2] Instead of doing extensive cognitive work, recipients rely on a variety of cues that allow them to make quick decisions. Robert Cialdini of Arizona State University lists six cues that trigger a "click, whirr" programmed response.[3] These cues allow people hearing a persuasive appeal to fly the peripheral route on automatic pilot:

1. Reciprocation—"You owe me."
2. Consistency—"We've always done it that way."
3. Social proof—"Everybody's doing it."
4. Liking—"Love me, love my ideas."
5. Authority—"Just because I say so."
6. Scarcity—"Quick, before they're all gone."

Peripheral route

A mental shortcut process that accepts or rejects a message based on irrelevant cues as opposed to actively thinking about the issue.

Figure 15–1 shows a simplified version of Petty and Cacioppo's elaboration likelihood model (ELM) as it applies to Rita's situation. Although their model's twin-route metaphor seems to suggest two mutually exclusive paths to persuasion, the theorists stress that the central route and the peripheral route are poles on a cognitive processing continuum that shows the degree of mental effort a person exerts when evaluating a message.[4] The elaboration scale at the top represents effortful scrutiny of arguments on the left-hand side and mindless reliance on noncontent cues on the right. Most messages receive middle-ground attention between these poles, but there's always a trade-off. The more Rita's listeners work to discern the merits of strict zero-tolerance enforcement, the less they'll be influenced by peripheral factors such as their friends' scoffing laughter at her suggestion. Conversely, the more her hearers are affected by content-irrelevant factors such as Rita's age, accent, or appearance, the less they will be affected by her ideas. We'll work down the model one level at a time in order to understand Petty and Cacioppo's predictions about the likelihood of Rita's message being scrutinized by students at her college.

190   *INTERPERSONAL COMMUNICATION*

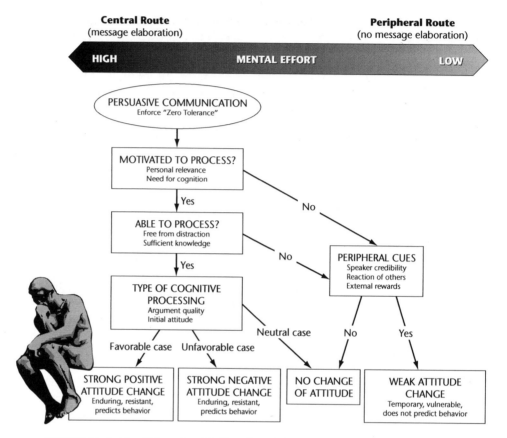

FIGURE 15–1   The Elaboration Likelihood Model
Adapted from Petty and Cacioppo, "The Elaboration Likelihood Model: Current Status and
Controversies"

MOTIVATION FOR ELABORATION: IS IT WORTH THE EFFORT?

Petty and Cacioppo assume that people are motivated to hold correct attitudes.
The authors admit that we aren't always logical, but they think we make a good
effort not to kid ourselves in our search for truth. We want to maintain reasonable positions.

But a person can examine only a limited number of ideas. We are exposed
to so many persuasive messages that we would experience a tremendous information overload if we tried to interact with every variant idea we heard or read
about. The only way to solve this problem is by being "lazy" toward most issues
in life. Petty and Cacioppo claim we have a large-mesh mental filter that allows
items we regard as less important to flow through without being carefully processed. But statements about things that are personally relevant get trapped and
tested. In the terminology of social judgment theory (see Chapter 14), we're
motivated to elaborate only ideas with which we are highly ego-involved.

There are few things in life more important to young Americans than the
right to drive. A license is the closest thing our society has to an adolescent rite

of passage; for some it is a passport to freedom. It seems unlikely, therefore, that students would regard Rita's zero-tolerance proposal as trivial. Yet threatening the loss of license may have less personal relevance to students who don't drink, or to those who already make sure they don't drive when they drink. And if students over 21 aren't worried about who's driving on the road, they too may feel that Rita's proposal has little to do with them. So ELM's authors would regard teenage students who drive after drinking a few beers as especially motivated to grapple with arguments about automatic driver's license suspension.

Petty and Cacioppo maintain that as long as people have a personal stake in accepting or rejecting an idea, they will be much more influenced by what a message says than by the characteristics of the person who says it. But when a topic is no longer relevant, it gets sidetracked to the periphery of the mind, where credibility cues take on greater importance. Without the motivation of personal relevance, there probably will be little elaboration.

The theorists do recognize, however, that some people have a need for cognitive clarity, regardless of the issue. In fact, they've developed a *Need for Cognition Scale* to identify individuals who are most likely to carefully consider message arguments.[5] Four of the items state:

Need for cognition
Desire for cognitive clarity; an enjoyment of thinking through ideas even when they aren't personally relevant.

I really enjoy a task that involves coming up with new solutions to problems.

I prefer my life to be filled with puzzles that I must solve.

I like tasks that require little thought once I've learned them.

Thinking is not my idea of fun.

If you substantially agree with the first two statements and take issue with the last two, Petty and Cacioppo would anticipate that you'd be a person who works through many of the ideas and arguments you hear.

ABILITY FOR ELABORATION: CAN THEY DO IT?

Once people have shown an inclination to think about the content of a message (motivation), the next issue is whether they are *able* to do so. Since Rita's immediate audience consists of young men and women who have duly impressed a college admissions officer with their ability to think, you would imagine that the question of ability would be moot. But issue-relevant thinking (elaboration) takes more than intelligence. It also requires concentration.

Distraction disrupts elaboration. Rita's classmates will be hard-pressed to think about her point of view if it's expressed amid the din of a student union snack bar where you can't hear yourself think. Or perhaps she presents her solution for highway safety when students are trying to concentrate on something else—an upcoming exam, a letter from home, or a mental replay of the winning shot in an intramural basketball game.

Rita may face the same challenge as television advertisers who have only the fleeting attention of viewers. Like them, Rita can use repetition to ensure that her main point comes across, but too much commotion will short-circuit a reasoned consideration of the message, no matter how much repetition is used. In that case, students will use the peripheral route and judge the message by cues that indicate whether Rita is a competent and trustworthy person.

TYPE OF ELABORATION: OBJECTIVE VERSUS BIASED THINKING

As you can see from the downward flow in the central path of their model (Figure 15–1), Petty and Cacioppo believe motivation and ability strongly increase the likelihood that a message will be elaborated in the minds of listeners. Yet as social judgment theory suggests, they may not process the information in a fair and objective manner. Rita might have the undivided attention of students who care deeply about the right to drive, but discover that they've already built up an organized structure of knowledge concerning the issue.

When Rita claims that the alcohol-related fatal crash rate for young drivers is double that of drivers over 21, a student may counter with the fact that teenagers drive twice as many miles and are therefore just as safe as adults. Whether or not the statistics are true or the argument is valid isn't the issue. The point is that those who have already thought a lot about drinking and driving safety will probably have made up their minds and be biased in the way they process Rita's message.

Biased elaboration
Top-down thinking in which predetermined conclusions color the supporting data.

Petty and Cacioppo refer to biased elaboration as top-down thinking in which a predetermined conclusion colors the supporting data underneath. They contrast this with objective elaboration, or bottom-up thinking, which lets facts speak for themselves. Biased elaboration merely bolsters previous ideas.

Objective elaboration
Bottom-up thinking in which facts are scrutinized without bias; seeking truth wherever it might lead.

Perhaps you've seen a picture of Rodin's famous statue *The Thinker*, a man sitting with his head propped in one hand. If the thinker already has a set of beliefs to contemplate, Petty and Cacioppo's research shows that additional thought will merely fix them in stone. Rita shouldn't assume that audience elaboration will always help her cause; it depends on whether it's biased elaboration or objective elaboration. It also depends on the quality of her arguments.

ELABORATED ARGUMENTS: STRONG, WEAK, AND NEUTRAL

If Rita manages to win an unbiased hearing from students at her school, Petty and Cacioppo say her cause will rise or fall on the perceived strength of her arguments. The two theorists have no absolute standard for what distinguishes a cogent argument from one that's specious. They simply define a strong message as one that generates favorable thoughts when it's heard and scrutinized.

Strong arguments
Claims that generate favorable thoughts when examined.

Petty and Cacioppo predict that thoughtful consideration of strong arguments will produce major shifts in attitude in the direction desired by the persuader. Suppose Rita states the following:

> National Safety Council statistics show that drivers in the 16–20 age group account for 15 percent of the miles driven in the United States, yet they are responsible for 25 percent of the highway deaths that involve alcohol.

This evidence could give students cause for pause. They may not be comfortable with the facts, but some of them might find the statistics compelling and a reason to reconsider their stance. According to ELM, the enhanced thinking of those who respond favorably will cause their change in position to *persist over time*, *resist counterpersuasion*, and *predict future behavior*—the "triple crown" of interpersonal influence.

However, persuasive attempts that are processed through the central route can have dramatically negative effects as well. If, despite her strong convictions, Rita isn't able to come up with a strong argument for changing the current law, her persuasive attempt might actually backfire. For example, suppose she makes this argument:

> When underage drinkers are arrested for violating zero-tolerance rules of the road, automatic suspension of their licenses would allow the secretary of state's office to reduce its backlog of work. This would give government officials time to check driving records so that they could keep dangerous motorists off the road.

This weak argument is guaranteed to offend the sensibilities of anyone who thinks about it. Rather than compelling listeners to enlist in Rita's cause, it will only give them a reason to oppose her point of view more vigorously. The elaborated idea will cause a boomerang effect that will last over time, defy other efforts to change it, and affect subsequent behavior. These are the same significant effects that the elaborated strong argument produces, but in the opposite direction.

Rita's ideas could also produce an ambivalent reaction. Listeners who carefully examine her ideas may end up feeling neither pro nor con toward her evidence. Their neutral or mixed response obviously means that they won't change their attitudes as a result of processing through the central route. For them, thinking about the pros and cons of the issue reinforces their original attitudes, whatever they may be.

PERIPHERAL CUES: AN ALTERNATIVE ROUTE OF INFLUENCE

Although the majority of this chapter has dealt with the central cognitive route to attitude change, most messages are processed on the less-effortful peripheral path. Signposts along the way direct the hearer to favor or oppose the persuader's point of view without ever engaging in what Petty and Cacioppo call "issue-relevant thinking."[6] There is no inner dialogue about the merits of the proposal.

As explained earlier, the hearer who uses the peripheral route relies on a variety of cues as an aid in reaching a quick decision. The most obvious cues are tangible rewards linked to agreement with the advocate's position. Food, sex, and money are traditional inducements to change. I once overheard the conclusion of a transaction between a young man and a college senior who was trying to persuade him to donate blood in order to fulfill her class assignment. "Ok, it's agreed," she said. "You give blood for me today, and I'll have you over to my place for dinner tomorrow night." Although this type of social exchange has been going on for centuries, Petty and Cacioppo would still describe it as peripheral. Public compliance to the request for blood? Yes. Private acceptance of its importance? Not likely.

For many students of persuasion, source credibility is the most interesting cue on the peripheral route. Four decades of research confirm that people who are likable and have expertise on the issue in question can have a persuasive impact regardless of what arguments they present. Rita's appearance, manner of talking, and background credentials will speak so loudly that some students won't really hear what she says. Which students? According to Petty and Cacioppo, those students who are unmotivated or unable to scrutinize her message and therefore switch to the peripheral path.

Listeners who believe that Rita's twin tragedies have given her wisdom beyond their own will shift to a position more sympathetic to her point of view. The same holds true for those who see her as pleasant and warm. But there are students who will regard her grammatical mistakes as a sign of ignorance, or they'll be turned off by a maternal manner that reminds them of a lecture from mom. These peripheral route critics will become more skeptical of Rita's position.

"In the interest of streamlining the judicial process, we'll skip the evidence and go directly to sentencing."

© J.B. Handelsman/The New Yorker Collection/www.cartoonbank.com

Note that attitude change on this outside track can be either positive or negative, but it lacks the robust persistence, invulnerability, or link to behavior we see in change that comes from message elaboration.

Nicely illustrating the fragility of peripheral route change, Holly wrote the following entry in her application log:

> In his short story "Salvation," Langston Hughes recounts his childhood experience at a religious revival in his town. For days the old ladies of the church had been praying for the conversion of all the "little lambs" of the congregation. After working the congregation to a fever pitch, the preacher gave an altar call aimed at the children, and one after another they cried and went forward to be saved from hell. The author and his friend didn't feel anything, but after what seemed like forever, his friend went up so all the hubbub would finally stop. Langston knew that his friend hadn't really been converted, but since God didn't smite him for lying, he figured it would be safe for him to fake it as well, which he did. When the revival was over, the congregation calmed down and everyone went home praising the Lord. Langston says that was the day he stopped believing in God.

The preacher relied on peripheral cues. Langston went forward because of the expectation of authority figures, heightened emotion, and conformity pressure. But there was no elaboration of the message, no grappling with the issue, and certainly no encounter with God. The result of this peripheral route processing was as ELM predicts—his "salvation" didn't even last through the night.

PUSHING THE LIMITS OF PERIPHERAL POWER

Understanding the importance of role models for persuasion, Rita scans the pages of *Rolling Stone* to see if singer Dave Matthews might have said something about teenage drivers. The music of the Dave Matthews Band is widely acclaimed by students at her college, and Matthews recently put on a live concert near the school. By somehow associating her message with credible people, she can achieve change in many students' attitudes. But it probably won't last long, stand up to attack, or affect their behavior. Petty and Cacioppo say a fragile change is all that can be expected through the peripheral route.

Yet what if Dave Matthews' tour bus were run off the road by a drunk teenage fan, and a band member met the same fate as Rita's daughter? Would that tragic death and Matthews' avowal that "friends don't let friends drive drunk" cue students to a permanent shift in attitude and behavior? Fortunately, the band is still intact, but a high-profile tragedy in the sports world suggests that even the effect of powerful peripheral cues is short-lived at best.

In 1991, basketball superstar Magic Johnson held a candid press conference to announce that he had tested positive for HIV. At the time, such a diagnosis seemed like a death sentence; the story dominated network news coverage for days. University of South Florida psychologists Louis Penner and Barbara Fritzsche had just completed a study showing that many people had little sympathy for AIDS victims who had contracted the disease through sexual transmission. When asked to volunteer a few hours to help a patient stay in school, a little more than half of the women and none of the men in the study volunteered. Penner and Fritzsche extended their study when they heard of Magic Johnson's illness.[7] They wondered if the tragedy that had befallen this popular star and his pledge to become an advocate for those with the disease would cause students to react more positively toward people with AIDS.

For a while it did. The week after Johnson's announcement, 80 percent of the men offered assistance. That number tapered off to 30 percent, however, within a few months. The proportion of women helping dipped below 40 percent in the same period. Penner and Fritzsche observed that people didn't grapple with the substance of Magic Johnson's message; rather, they paid attention to the man who was presenting it. Consistent with ELM's main thesis, the researchers concluded that "changes that occur because of 'peripheral cues' such as . . . being a well liked celebrity are less permanent than those that occur because of the substantive content of the persuasion attempt."[8]

Penner and Fritzsche could have added that the effects of star performer endorsements are subject to the sharp ups and downs of celebrity status. For example, the Dave Matthews Band has been so environmentally green that a Ben and Jerry's flavor of ice cream was named after one of the band's songs. Yet that image was besmirched when their tour bus dumped 80 gallons of human waste through a grated bridge over the Chicago River. Much of the foul-smelling sewage doused tourists having dinner on the deck of a sightseeing boat passing under the bridge. So any comment by Matthews on safe and sane driving might be treated with derision rather than help Rita's cause.[9] Nike feared the same reaction when Tiger Woods publicly fell from grace.

Although most ELM research has measured the effects of peripheral cues by studying credibility, a speaker's competence or character could also be a stimulus for effortful message elaboration. For example, the high regard that millions of sports fans had for Magic Johnson might for the first time have made it possible to scrutinize proposals for the prevention and treatment of AIDS without a moral stigma biasing each idea. Or the fact that Johnson's magic wasn't strong enough to repel HIV might cause someone to think deeply, "If it happened to a guy like Magic, it could happen to me." Even though Figure 15–1 identifies *speaker credibility, reaction of others,* and *external rewards* as variables that promote mindless acceptance via the peripheral route, Petty and Cacioppo emphasize that it's impossible to compile a list of cues that are strictly peripheral.[10]

To illustrate this point, consider the multiple roles that the *mood* of the person listening to Rita's message might play in her attempt to persuade. Rita assumes that her classmate Sam will be a more sympathetic audience if she can present her ideas when he's in a good mood. And she's right, as long as Sam processes her message through the peripheral route without thinking too hard about what she's saying. His positive outlook prompts him to see her proposal in a favorable light.

Yet if Sam is somewhat willing and able to work through her arguments (moderate elaboration), his upbeat mood could actually turn out to be a disadvantage. He was feeling up, but he becomes depressed when he thinks about the death and disfigurement Rita describes. The loss of warm feelings could bias him against Rita's arguments. Petty suggests that Sam might process her arguments more objectively if his original mood had matched the downbeat nature of Rita's experience.[11] Many variables like *perceived credibility* or the *mood of the listener* can act as peripheral cues. Yet if one of them motivates listeners to scrutinize the message or affects their evaluation of arguments, it no longer serves as a no-brainer. There is no variable that's always a shortcut on the peripheral route.

Speaker credibility
Audience perception of the message source's expertise, character, and dynamism; typically a peripheral cue.

CHOOSING A ROUTE: PRACTICAL ADVICE FOR THE PERSUADER

Petty and Cacioppo's advice for Rita (and the rest of us) is clear. She needs to determine the likelihood that her listeners will give their undivided attention to evaluating her proposal. If it appears that they have the motivation and ability to elaborate the message, she had best come armed with facts and figures to support her case. A pleasant smile, an emotional appeal, or the loss of her daughter won't make any difference.

Since it's only by thoughtful consideration that her listeners can experience a lasting change in attitude, Rita probably hopes they can go the central route. But even if they do, it's still difficult to build a compelling persuasive case. If she fails to do her homework and presents weak arguments, the people who are ready to think will shift their attitude to a more antagonistic position.

If Rita determines that her hearers are unable or unwilling to think through the details of her plan, she'll be more successful choosing a delivery strategy that emphasizes the package rather than the contents. This could include a heartrending account of her daughter's death, a smooth presentation, and an ongoing effort to build friendships with the students. Perhaps bringing homemade cookies to class or offering rides to the mall would aid in making her an attractive source. But as we've already seen, the effects will probably be temporary.

It's not likely that Rita will get many people to elaborate her message in a way that ends up favorable for her cause. Most persuaders avoid the central route because the audience won't go with them or they find it too difficult to generate compelling arguments. But Rita really doesn't have a choice.

Driver's licenses (and perhaps beer) are so important to most of these students that they'll be ready to dissect every part of her plan. They won't be won over by a friendly smile. Rita will have to develop thoughtful and well-reasoned arguments if she is to change their minds. Given the depth of her conviction, she thinks it's worth a try.

ETHICAL REFLECTION: NILSEN'S SIGNIFICANT CHOICE

ELM describes persuasion that's effective. University of Washington professor emeritus Thomas Nilsen is concerned with what's ethical. Consistent with the democratic values of a free society, he proposes that persuasive speech is ethical to the extent that it maximizes people's ability to exercise free choice. Since many political, religious, and commercial messages are routinely designed to bypass rather than appeal to a listener's rational faculties, Nilsen upholds the value of significant choice in unequivocal terms:

> When we communicate to influence the attitudes, beliefs, and actions of others, the ethical touchstone is the degree of free, informed, rational and critical choice—significant choice—that is fostered by our speaking.[12]

For Nilsen, truly free choice is the test of ethical influence because "only a self-determining being can be a moral being; without significant choice, there is no morality."[13] To support his claim, he cites two classic essays on the freedom of speech. John Milton's *Areopagitica*[14] argues against prior restraint of any ideas, no matter how heretical. John Stuart Mill's *On Liberty*[15] advocates a free marketplace of ideas because the only way to test an argument is to hear it presented by a true believer who defends it in earnest.

Philosophers and rhetoricians have compared persuasion to a lover making fervent appeals to his beloved—wooing an audience, for example. Nilsen's ethic of significant choice is nicely captured in the courtship analogy because true love cannot be coerced; it must be freely given. Inspired by Danish philosopher Søren Kierkegaard's description of the ethical religious persuader as lover,[16] I have elsewhere presented a typology of false (unethical) lovers:[17]

> *Smother lovers* won't take no for an answer; their persistence is obnoxious.
> *Legalistic lovers* have a set image of what the other should be.
> *Flirts* are in love with love; they value response, not the other person.

Seducers try deception and flattery to entice the other to submit.

Rapists use force of threats, guilt, or conformity pressure to have their way.

In differing degrees, all five types of unethical persuader violate the human dignity of the people they pursue by taking away choice that is informed and free.

Nilsen obviously would approve of persuasive appeals that encourage message elaboration through ELM's central route. But his standard of significant choice is not always easy to apply. Do emotional appeals seductively short-circuit our ability to make rational choices, or does heightened emotion actually free us to consider new options? Significant choice, like beauty and credibility, may be in the eye of the beholder.

CRITIQUE: ELABORATING THE MODEL

For the last 20 years, ELM has been a leading, if not *the* leading, theory of persuasion and attitude change. Petty, Cacioppo, and their students have published more than 100 articles on the model, and the dual-process conception has stimulated additional research, application, and critique that go beyond what I'm able to capture in a short chapter. Since the time they introduced the theory, Petty and Cacioppo have made it more complex, less predictive, and less able to offer definitive advice to the influence practitioner. This is not the direction in which a scientific theory wants to go.

Arizona State University communication researcher Paul Mongeau and communication consultant James Stiff illustrate one of the specific problems with the theory when they charge that "descriptions of the ELM are sufficiently imprecise and ambiguous as to prevent an adequate test of the entire model."[18] For example, ELM views strong arguments as strong if people are persuaded, but weak if folks remain unmoved. There's no way apart from the persuasive outcome to know whether an argument is strong or weak. Like my childhood friend described in Chapter 3, ELM seems to have its own "never-miss shot." Petty and Cacioppo would say that they never intended to focus on defining factors like strong and weak arguments, high and low source credibility, or highly attractive or unattractive persuaders.[19] That may be true, but it doesn't help much in testing the theory. Objective theories that can't be clearly tested lose some of their luster.

Despite the criticisms, ELM is impressive because it pulls together and makes sense out of diverse research results that have puzzled communication theorists for years. For example, why do most people pay less attention to the communication than they do to the communicator? And if speaker credibility is so important, why does its effect dissipate so quickly? ELM's explanation is that few listeners are motivated and able to do the mental work required for a major shift in attitude. The two-path hypothesis also helps clarify why good evidence and reasoning can sometimes have a life-changing impact, but usually make no difference at all.

Attitude-change research often yields results that seem confusing or contradictory. Petty and Cacioppo's ELM takes many disjointed findings and pulls them together into a unified whole. This integrative function makes it a valuable theory of influence.

QUESTIONS TO SHARPEN YOUR FOCUS

1. Can you think of five different words or phrases that capture the idea of *message elaboration?*

2. What *peripheral cues* do you usually monitor when someone is trying to influence you?

3. Petty and Cacioppo want to persuade you that their elaboration likelihood model is a mirror of reality. Do you process their arguments for its accuracy closer to your *central route* or your *peripheral route?* Why not the other way?

4. Students of persuasion often wonder whether *high credibility* or *strong arguments* sway people more. How would ELM theorists respond to that question?

A SECOND LOOK

Recommended resource: Richard E. Petty, John T. Cacioppo, Alan J. Strathman, and Joseph R. Priester, "To Think or Not to Think: Exploring Two Routes to Persuasion," in *Persuasion: Psychological Insights and Perspectives,* 2nd ed., Timothy Brock and Melanie Green (eds.), Sage, Thousand Oaks, CA, 2005, pp. 81–116.

Full statement: Richard E. Petty and John T. Cacioppo, *Communication and Persuasion: Central and Peripheral Routes to Attitude Change,* Springer-Verlag, New York, 1986.

Major developments in the history of ELM: Richard E. Petty and Pablo Briñol, "The Elaboration Likelihood Model," in *Handbook of Theories of Social Psychology, Vol. 1,* Paul van Lange and Arie Kruglanski (eds.), Sage, London, England, 2012, pp. 224–245.

Effect of involvement: Richard E. Petty and John T. Cacioppo, "Involvement and Persuasion: Tradition Versus Integration," *Psychological Bulletin,* Vol. 107, 1990, pp. 367–374.

Postulates and research: Richard E. Petty and John T. Cacioppo, "The Elaboration Likelihood Model of Persuasion," in *Advances in Experimental Social Psychology, Vol. 19,* Leonard Berkowitz (ed.), Academic Press, Orlando, FL, 1986, pp. 124–205.

Message arguments versus source credibility: Richard E. Petty, John T. Cacioppo, and R. Goldman, "Personal Involvement as a Determinant of Argument-Based Persuasion," *Journal of Personality and Social Psychology,* Vol. 41, 1981, pp. 847–855.

Effects of evidence: John Reinard, "The Empirical Study of the Persuasive Effects of Evidence: The Status After Fifty Years of Research," *Human Communication Research,* Vol. 15, 1988, pp. 3–59.

Effects of credibility: Richard E. Petty, "Multiple Roles for Source Credibility Under High Elaboration: It's All in the Timing," *Social Cognition,* Vol. 25, 2007, pp. 536–552.

Mindless cues: Robert B. Cialdini, *Influence: Science and Practice,* 4th ed., Allyn and Bacon, Needham Heights, MA, 2001.

Cues that affect elaboration: Duane Wegener and Richard E. Petty, "Understanding Effects of Mood Through the Elaboration Likelihood and Flexible Correction Models," in *Theories of Mood and Cognition: A User's Guidebook,* L. L. Martin and G. L. Clore (eds.), Lawrence Erlbaum, Mahwah, NJ, 2001, pp. 177–210.

Status and controversies: Richard E. Petty and Duane Wegener, "The Elaboration Likelihood Model: Current Status and Controversies," in Shelly Chaiken and Yaacov Trope (eds.), *Dual Process Theories in Social Psychology,* Guilford, New York, 1999, pp. 41–72.

Critiques of ELM: "Forum: Specifying the ELM," *Communication Theory,* Vol. 3, 1993. (Paul Mongeau and James Stiff, "Specifying Causal Relationships in the Elaboration Likelihood Model," pp. 65–72; Mike Allen and Rodney Reynolds, "The Elaboration Likelihood Model and the Sleeper Effect: An Assessment of Attitude Change over Time," pp. 73–82.)

CHAPTER **16**

Cognitive Dissonance Theory

of Leon Festinger

Aesop told a story about a fox that tried in vain to reach a cluster of grapes dangling from a vine above his head. The fox leaped high to grasp the grapes, but the delicious-looking fruit remained just out of reach of his snapping jaws. After a few attempts the fox gave up and said to himself, "These grapes are sour, and if I had some I would not eat them."[1]

DISSONANCE: DISCORD BETWEEN BEHAVIOR AND BELIEF

Aesop's fable is the source of the phrase *sour grapes*. The story illustrates what former Stanford University social psychologist Leon Festinger called *cognitive dissonance*. It is the distressing mental state that people feel when they "find themselves doing things that don't fit with what they know, or having opinions that do not fit with other opinions they hold."[2]

Cognitive dissonance
The distressing mental state caused by inconsistency between a person's two beliefs or a belief and an action.

The fox's retreat from the grape arbor clashed with his knowledge that the grapes were tasty. By changing his attitude toward the grapes, he provided an acceptable explanation for abandoning his efforts to reach them.

Festinger considered the need to avoid dissonance to be just as basic as the need for safety or the need to satisfy hunger. It is an *aversive drive* that goads us to be consistent. The tension of dissonance motivates us to change either our behavior or our belief in an effort to avoid that distressing feeling. The more important the issue and the greater the discrepancy between our behavior and our belief, the higher the magnitude of dissonance we will feel. In extreme cases cognitive dissonance is like our cringing response to fingernails being scraped on a blackboard—we'll do anything to get away from the awful sound.

HEALTH-CONSCIOUS SMOKERS: DEALING WITH DISSONANCE

When Festinger first published his theory in 1957, he chose the topic of smoking to illustrate the concept of dissonance. Although authoritative medical reports on the link between smoking and lung cancer were just beginning to surface, there was already general concern across the United States that cigarette smoking might cause cancer. Ten years prior, country-and-western singer Tex Williams recorded Capitol Records' first million-seller, "Smoke! Smoke! Smoke! (That Cigarette)." The gravelly voiced vocalist expressed doubt that smoking would affect his health, but the chorus was unambiguous:

> Smoke, smoke, smoke that cigarette
> Puff, puff, puff until you smoke yourself to death
> Tell St. Peter at the Golden Gate
> That you hate to make him wait
> But you just gotta have another cigarette.[3]

At the time, many smokers and nonsmokers alike laughingly referred to cigarettes as "coffin nails." But as the number and certainty of medical reports linking smoking with lung cancer, emphysema, and heart disease increased, humorous references to cigarettes no longer seemed funny. For the first time in their lives, a hundred million Americans had to grapple with two incompatible cognitions:

1. Smoking is dangerous to my health.

2. I smoke cigarettes.

Consider the plight of Cliff, a habitual smoker confronted by medical claims that smoking is hazardous to his health—an idea that strongly conflicts with his pack-a-day practice. Festinger said the contradiction is so clear and uncomfortable that something has to give—either the use of cigarettes or the belief that smoking will hurt him. "Whether the behavior or the cognition changes will be determined by which has the weakest resistance to change."[4] For Cliff it's no contest. He lights up and dismisses the health risk. In his discussion of smoking, Festinger suggested a number of mental gymnastics that Cliff might use to avoid dissonance while he smokes.[5]

Perhaps the most typical way for the smoker to avoid mental anguish is to trivialize or simply deny the link between smoking and cancer. *I think the research is sketchy, the results are mixed, and the warnings are based on junk science.* After the surgeon general's report on smoking was issued in 1964, denial became an uphill cognitive path to climb, but many smokers continue to go that route.

Smokers may counter thoughts of scary health consequences by reminding themselves of other effects they see as positive. *Smoking helps me relax, I like the taste, and it gives me a look of sophistication.* These were the motives cigarette advertising appealed to when Festinger first published his theory. For example, Old Gold was the primary radio sponsor for Chicago Cubs baseball: "We're tobacco men, not medicine men," their ads proclaimed. "For a treat instead of a treatment, try Old Gold. . . . There's not a cough in a carload."

Although it's hard for smokers to pretend they aren't lighting up, they can elude nagging thoughts of trauma by telling themselves that the dire warnings don't apply to them since they are *moderate* smokers, or because they'll soon quit. *My boyfriend is a chain smoker, but I smoke less than a pack a day. As soon as I finish school, I'll have no problem stopping.* Conversely, other smokers manage dissonance by disclaiming any ongoing responsibility for a habit they can't kick. *Let's face it, cigarettes are addictive. I'm hooked.* To be sure, most behaviors are not as difficult to change as the habit of smoking, but Festinger noted that almost all of our actions are more entrenched than the thoughts we have about them. Thus, the focus of his theory is on the belief and attitude changes that take place because of cognitive dissonance.

REDUCING DISSONANCE BETWEEN ACTIONS AND ATTITUDES

Festinger hypothesized three mental mechanisms people use to ensure that their actions and attitudes are in harmony. Dissonance researchers refer to them as *selective exposure, postdecision dissonance,* and *minimal justification.* I'll continue to illustrate these cognitive processes by referring to the practice of smoking, but they are equally applicable to other forms of substance abuse or addiction—alcohol, drugs, food, sex, pornography, gambling, money, shopping, work. Most of us can spot at least one topic on that list where we struggle with an inconsistency between our thoughts and our actions. So if smoking isn't an issue for you, apply these ways of reducing dissonance in an area that is.

Hypothesis 1: Selective Exposure Prevents Dissonance

Festinger claimed that people avoid information that's likely to increase dissonance.[6] This *selective exposure hypothesis* explains why staunch political conservatives watch Sean Hannity on Fox News whereas stalwart liberals catch Rachel Maddow on MSNBC. Not only do we tend to listen to opinions and select reading materials that are consistent with our existing beliefs, we usually choose to be with people who are like us. By taking care to "stick with our own kind," we can maintain the relative comfort of the status quo. Like-minded people buffer us from ideas that could cause discomfort. In that sense, the process of making friends is a way to select our own propaganda.

Selective exposure
The tendency people have to avoid information that would create cognitive dissonance because it's incompatible with their current beliefs.

Two communication researchers looked back over 18 experiments where people were put in dissonant situations and then had to choose what kind of information they would listen to or read. Dave D'Alessio (University of Connecticut–Stamford) and Mike Allen (University of Wisconsin–Milwaukee) discovered that the results consistently supported the selective exposure hypothesis.[7] People tended to select information that lined up with what they already believed and ignored facts or ideas that ran counter to those beliefs. But the strength of this tendency was relatively small. Selective exposure explained only about 5 percent of why they chose the information they did. That leaves 95 percent unexplained.

That modest finding hasn't deterred the sponsors of two media persuasion campaigns from taking the power of selective exposure quite seriously. A University of California–San Francisco survey taken in 2006 documented that 75 percent of Hollywood films show attractive actors smoking, and that this modeling encourages young teens raised in smoke-free homes to adopt the practice. With some success, Harvard School of Public Health researchers are now proactively challenging directors not to introduce smoking into their films. Nevertheless, a follow-up study by the same University of California group found that smoking incidences increased by 36 percent in 2011 for movies rated PG-13 and below. That includes more than 50 smoking incidents apiece in hit movies such as *The Help, Rango,* and *X-Men: First Class.*[8]

Entertainment is a tried-and-true way to get around people's selective exposure filters. Another way is humor. The "Don't Pass Gas" broadcast campaign of the American Legacy Foundation uses barnyard comedy to convince the public of the intrusiveness of putrid gas. Presented in the style of a Dr. Seuss rhyme, one ad goes:

> I will not pass gas on a train. I will not pass gas on a plane.
> I will not pass gas in my house. I will not pass gas near my spouse.
> I will not pass gas in a bar. I will not pass gas in a car.
> I will not pass gas where little ones are, no matter how near or how far.
> I will not pass gas in your face, because the gas I pass is worse than mace.[9]

Only after listeners are either laughing or totally grossed out by the image of passing gas are they told that the limerick refers to secondhand smoke. It's a message most people would tune out had it not been for the use of humor with a twist.

German psychologist Dieter Frey surveyed all the pertinent research on selective exposure and concluded that even when we know we're going to hear discrepant ideas, the avoidance mechanism doesn't kick in if we don't regard the dissonant information as a threat.[10] Warm personal relationships are probably the best guarantee that we'll consider ideas that would otherwise seem threatening.

Hypothesis 2: Postdecision Dissonance Creates a Need for Reassurance

According to Festinger, close-call decisions can generate huge amounts of internal tension after the decision has been made. Three conditions heighten *postdecision dissonance:* (1) the more important the issue, (2) the longer an individual delays in choosing between two equally attractive options, and (3) the greater the difficulty involved in reversing the decision once it's been made. To the extent that these conditions are present, the person will agonize over whether he or she made the right choice.[11] Sometimes referred to as "morning-after-the-night-before" regrets, the misgivings or second thoughts that plague us after a tough choice motivate us to seek reassuring information and social support for our decision.

Postdecision dissonance Strong doubts experienced after making an important, close-call decision that is difficult to reverse.

A classic example of postdecision dissonance is the mental turmoil a person experiences after signing a contract to buy a new car. The cost is high, there are many competing models from which to choose, and the down payment commits the customer to go through with the purchase. It's not unusual to find a customer examining *Consumer Reports* auto ratings *after* placing an order. The buyer is seeking information that confirms the decision already made and quiets nagging doubts.

Many who recover from multiple addictions testify that quitting smoking is harder than giving up booze. Just as countless alcoholics turn to Alcoholics Anonymous for social support, people who try to give up tobacco often need at least one friend, family member, romantic partner, or co-worker who's also going through the pangs of withdrawal. They can remind each other that it's worth the effort. Of course, the decision to stop smoking doesn't fulfill Festinger's third condition of a once-and-for-all, no-going-back, final choice. One can always go back to smoking. In fact, those who swear off cigarettes typically have a few lapses, and total relapses are common. Encouragement and social support are necessary to tamp down the doubts and fears that follow this tough decision.

Smokers who consciously decide *not* to quit face similar qualms and anxieties. They are bombarded with messages telling them they are putting their health at risk. People who care for them deeply urge them to stop, and nonsmokers look down on them because they don't. University of Kentucky communication professor Alan DeSantis describes the camaraderie he found among regular customers at a Kentucky cigar shop. Just as smoke from cigars drives some folks away, DeSantis concludes that the friendship and collective rationalization of those who smoke cigars together hold postdecision dissonance at bay. He also sees *Cigar Aficionado* as serving the same function. He writes that although the magazine professes to simply celebrate the good life, it actually serves "to relieve the cognitive dissonance associated with the consumption of a potentially dangerous product by adding cognitions, trivializing dissonant information, selectively exposing readers to pro-smoking information, and creating a social support network of fellow cigar smokers."[12]

Hypothesis 3: Minimal Justification for Action Induces Attitude Change

Suppose someone wanted to persuade an ex-smoker who is dying of lung cancer to stop publicly bashing the tobacco industry and to respect cigarette companies' right to market their product. That is one of the assignments given to Nick Naylor, chief spokesman for tobacco companies in the movie *Thank You for Smoking*. His job is to convince "Big Tobacco's" former advertising icon—the Marlboro Man—to switch from outspoken critic to silent partner. Before cognitive dissonance theory, conventional wisdom would have suggested that Naylor work first to change the bitter man's *attitude* toward the industry. If he could convince the cowboy that the cigarette companies are well-intentioned, then the man would change his communication *behavior*. It seemed natural to think of attitude and behavior as the beginning and end of a cause-and-effect sequence.

Attitude → Behavior

But Festinger's *minimal justification hypothesis* reversed the sequence. This hypothesis suggests that the best way for Naylor to change the Marlboro Man's attitude toward his former employers is to get him to quit speaking out against them.

Behavior → Attitude

Minimal justification hypothesis
A claim that the best way to stimulate an attitude change in others is to offer just enough incentive to elicit counterattitudinal behavior.

Festinger attached one important condition, however. Instead of giving the cowboy massive incentives to abandon his public critique ($100,000 in cash, lifetime health care for his wife, or a threat to harm his kids), Naylor should offer the minimum enticement necessary to induce him to quietly step off his soapbox. Festinger concluded:

> Thus if one wanted to obtain private change in addition to mere public compliance, the best way to do this would be to offer just enough reward or punishment to elicit overt compliance.[13]

Naylor doesn't follow Festinger's advice. Instead, he does it the old-fashioned way by throwing lots of money at the Marlboro Man. He goes to his rundown ranch with a briefcase filled with bundles of hundred-dollar bills, which he pours out on the floor. He labels the money a gift rather than a bribe, but makes it clear that the cowboy can't keep the money if he continues to denounce the tobacco companies. As it turns out, the offer is more than enough because the dying man is worried about how his family will manage after he's gone. So the Marlboro Man takes both the money and a vow of silence, but his antagonistic attitude toward his former employers hasn't changed. *Compliance* without inner conviction. For Naylor, that's enough.

Compliance
Public conformity to another's expectation without necessarily having a private conviction that matches the behavior.

There is, however, a brief moment in their discussion that suggests the potential of a minimal justification strategy. When the Marlboro Man looks longingly at the cash, he wonders out loud if he might keep half the money and still denounce the tobacco companies. His question reveals that somewhere between 50 percent and 100 percent of the cash on the floor there's a tipping point where the cowboy becomes willing to be bought off. Festinger predicted that if Naylor were to offer that "just-enough" amount, not only would the Marlboro Man alter his communication behavior, but the dissonance he would feel would also cause him to be less angry at the cigarette companies. Festinger's startling $1/$20 experiment shows how this might work.

A CLASSIC EXPERIMENT: "WOULD I LIE FOR A DOLLAR?"

There is nothing particularly radical about Festinger's first two hypotheses. His selective exposure prediction nicely explains why political rallies attract the party faithful and why the audience for religious radio and television tends to be made up of committed believers. As for postdecision dissonance, all of us have tried to convince ourselves that we've made the right choice after facing a close-call decision. But Festinger's minimal justification hypothesis is counterintuitive. Will a small incentive to act really induce a corresponding attitude change when heaping on the benefits won't? Festinger's famous $1/$20 experiment supported his claim that it will.

Festinger and social psychologist James Carlsmith recruited Stanford University men to participate in a psychological study supposedly investigating industrial relations.[14] As each man arrived at the lab, he was assigned the boring and repetitive task of sorting a large batch of spools into sets of 12 and turning square pegs a quarter turn to the right. The procedure was designed to be both monotonous and tiring. At the end of an hour the experimenter approached the subject and made a request. He claimed that a student assistant had failed to show up and that he needed someone to fill in. The experimenter wanted the subject to tell a potential female subject in the waiting room how much fun the experiment was. Dissonance researchers call this *counterattitudinal advocacy*. We'd call it lying.

Counterattitudinal advocacy
Publicly urging others to believe or do something that is opposed to what the advocate actually believes.

Some of the men were promised $20 to express enthusiasm about the task; others were offered only $1. After adjusting for inflation, that's $160 or $8 today.[15] It's comforting to know that six of the men refused to take part in the deception, but most students tried to recruit the young woman. The gist of the typical conversation was similar for both payment conditions:

SHE: "I heard it was boring."

HE: "Oh no, it's really quite fun."

What differed were the men's privately expressed attitudes after the study was over. Students who lied for $20 later confessed that they thought the task of sorting spools was dull. Those who lied for $1 maintained that it was quite enjoyable. (Festinger and Carlsmith practiced their own form of deception in the study—subjects never received the promised money.)

By now you should have a pretty good idea how Festinger analyzed the results. He noted that $20 was a huge sum of money at the time. If a student felt qualms about telling a "white lie," the cash was a ready justification. Thus, the student felt little or no tension between his action and his attitude. But the men who lied for a dollar had lots of cognitive work to do. The logical inconsistency of saying a boring task was interesting had to be explained away through an internal dialogue:

> I'm a Stanford man. Am I the kind of guy who would lie for a dollar? No way. Actually, what I told the girl was true. The experiment was a lot of fun.

Festinger said that $1 was just barely enough to induce compliance to the experimenter's request, and so the students had to create another justification. They changed their attitude toward the task to bring it into line with their behavior—in other words, to eliminate dissonance.

THREE STATE-OF-THE-ART REVISIONS: THE CAUSE AND EFFECT OF DISSONANCE

The $1/$20 study has been replicated and modified many times in an effort to figure out what creates dissonance and how people reduce it. Based on hundreds of experimental studies, most persuasion researchers today subscribe to one of three revisions of Festinger's original theory.

To illustrate these revisions, we'll consider the most famous American to struggle recently with smoking: President Barack Obama. Obama put away his cigarettes before his 2008 presidential bid, but relapsed during the campaign and his first two years in office. In 2011, however, Obama's doctors declared that he had broken his 30-year cigarette habit.[16] According to First Lady Michelle Obama, it seems that dissonance caused the president's decision to stop: "I think he didn't want to look his girls in the eye and tell them that they shouldn't do something that he was still doing."[17] That sounds like a straightforward explanation, but for cognitive dissonance theorists it isn't enough—they want to know what's going on in the mind of the president that generates and eliminates dissonance.

In order to understand each of the options described in the following sections, it will help you to picture the overall dissonance arousal and reduction process. Figure 16–1 shows that four-step sequence. So far we've discussed Festinger's belief that we experience dissonance when we face *logical inconsis-*

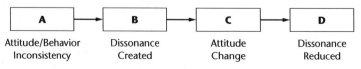

FIGURE 16–1   Festinger's Process Model of Cognitive Dissonance
Based on Festinger, *Cognitive Dissonance Theory*

tency, or beliefs and behaviors that don't quite add up. *(I value my health. My cigarette habit damages my health.)* That's a claim about the A → B link in the figure. Festinger further asserted that the way to reduce dissonance was to remove the logical inconsistency (point D). The three revisions question these assumptions, and each provides a somewhat different explanation for why Obama finally kicked his smoking habit.

1. Self-Consistency: The Rationalizing Animal

One of Festinger's early graduate students, University of California social psychologist Elliot Aronson, wasn't convinced that logical inconsistency produces dissonance. He noted that we sometimes find such inconsistencies curious or even amusing. For example, Andrew once received a university parking ticket in the mail dated several months after he'd graduated and moved out of the state. Two thoughts crossed his mind: *(1) I was not parked at the University of Kansas in October* and *(2) I have a parking ticket that says I was.* That's a logical inconsistency, and it made him feel mildly annoyed—but that's not the aversive discomfort Aronson claims is at the heart of dissonance.

Instead, Aronson thinks what produces dissonance is an inconsistency between a cognition and our *self-concept*—how we perceive ourselves. He interprets the $1/$20 experiment as a study of self-presentation.[18] The Stanford men were in a bind because they regarded themselves as decent, truthful human beings, in contrast to their deceptive behavior. In fact, the higher their opinion of their honesty, the more dissonance they would feel when they told the waiting woman that the study was fun. Conversely, if they had seen themselves as liars, cheats, or jerks, they would have felt no tension. As Aronson puts it, "If a person conceives of himself as a 'schnook,' he will be expected to behave like a 'schnook.'"[19]

Andrew's student Caitlin, a vegetarian, wrote about her feelings of guilt after eating meat. Clearly, she perceived that her choice was inconsistent with her self-concept:

> When I ate meat for the first time in a year, I was at a hibachi grill where the chef gave each of us a sample of steak. At first I tried just one piece, but that provoked my decision to order fried rice and steak. This choice violated my vegetarian beliefs, but I justified it because it was only a small amount of meat. The day after, I experienced postdecision dissonance: I had strong doubts, a guilty conscience about my decision, and a very upset stomach.

If Aronson is right, what's the best way to persuade someone like President Obama to stop smoking? Showing him studies of tobacco's negative health effects might not be the route to go. Even if Obama acknowledges that his cigarette use is inconsistent with that information, Aronson doesn't think logical inconsistency is enough. The president will only feel dissonance if he sees smoking as inconsistent with his self-concept. Given the first lady's explanation ("I think he didn't want to look his girls in the eye . . ."), Aronson might suggest that the president perceived an inconsistency between his smoking and his fatherly image. Maybe Obama also thought that lighting up contradicted his appearance as a health-conscious person who regularly exercises through pickup basketball games. Throwing away his cigarettes reduced dissonance by removing those psychological inconsistencies.

2. Personal Responsibility for Bad Outcomes (the New Look)

For Princeton psychologist Joel Cooper, both Festinger and Aronson miss the true cause of dissonance. He doesn't think inconsistency—whether logical or psychological—is the main motivating factor. In his *new look* model of cognitive dissonance, Cooper argues that we experience dissonance when we believe our actions have unnecessarily hurt another person. For example, in the minimal justification condition of the $1/$20 experiment, the Stanford men willingly "duped a fellow student to look forward to an exciting experience" while knowing "full well that the waiting participant was in for an immense letdown."[20]

Cooper concludes that dissonance is "a state of arousal caused by behaving in such a way as to feel personally responsible for bringing about an aversive event."[21] Note that the acceptance of personal *responsibility* requires that the person know ahead of time that his or her action will have negative consequences for someone else, and yet still choose to do the dirty deed. The reactions of participants in minimal justification experiments show that they often feel bad about the potential effects of their messages.

Purdue University social psychologists Richard Heslin and Michael Amo used a pro-smoking message prepared for junior high kids, but in this case the setup was more involving and potentially more harmful. The researchers encouraged college students in public speaking classes to deliver impromptu speeches to persuade uninformed and uncommitted seventh grade kids that smoking pot wouldn't hurt them. The speakers saw their recorded speeches and were reminded that they'd be identified as actually having pro-marijuana sentiments. The speakers were quite aware that their message might harm kids. One speaker pleaded, "Please don't use my speech. I don't want the course credit; just don't use my speech!"[22] Clearly they felt dissonance, and new look theorists would argue that's because they perceived their actions as harmful (rather than inconsistent). Nevertheless, the speakers actually changed their attitude in the direction of their advocacy—dissonance reduction by concluding that their actions weren't all that harmful.

New look theorists don't think inconsistency is enough to persuade someone like Obama to stop smoking. Sure, he may perceive that his actions are logically inconsistent with scientific research or psychologically inconsistent with his self-image. But if he only lights up in private—and he's never smoked publicly while president—he might believe his actions don't hurt anyone else. For Cooper, the first lady's explanation might suggest that the president thought his smoking could hurt their daughters. If Obama quit smoking because he was afraid Malia and Sasha would imitate him, or because he was concerned about their exposure to secondhand smoke, that's the new look in action.

3. Self-Affirmation to Dissipate Dissonance

While the revisions offered by Aronson (self-consistency) and Cooper (new look) address dissonance *creation* at the front end of Festinger's model (the link from A to B in Figure 16-1), Stanford psychologist Claude Steele's self-affirmation approach speaks to the question of dissonance *reduction* at the back end of the model—point D of the figure. Steele doesn't assume that dissonance always drives people to justify their actions by changing their attitudes. He thinks some fortunate people can call up a host of positive thoughts about themselves that will blot out a concern for restoring consistency. If he's right, high self-esteem is a resource for dissonance reduction.

According to Steele, most people are greatly motivated to maintain an overall self-image of moral adequacy. For a participant in the $1/$20 experiment, there's no question that lying to a fellow student makes it harder to preserve that favorable self-concept. But if the guy ignores the ethical slip and focuses instead on his good grades, athletic ability, social skills, and helpfulness to friends who are hurting, the dissonance will be only a blip on the radar screen of his mind and will quickly fade away. Thus, Steele believes that denial, forgetfulness, and trivialization of the incident are alternatives to attitude change, but only for the person who already has high self-esteem.

According to Steele's self-affirmation approach, Obama might have excused his smoking by reminding himself of his esteem-raising qualities, which include "gifted orator, award winning author, and proven intellect who was the first black president of the *Harvard Law Review*,"[23] not to mention president of the United States, winner of a Nobel Peace Prize, and the commander in chief who stopped Osama bin Laden for good. In light of these accomplishments, Obama might regard relapse as a minor inconsistency rather than a major contradiction. In Steele's view, the first lady's comment suggests that the president eventually couldn't rationalize that way anymore. As the son of a man who ignored his family obligations, perhaps Obama came to believe that smoking is a parenting flaw for which career success can't compensate.

Aronson, Cooper, and Steele offer their respective revisions as more accurate accounts of what goes on in people's heads than Festinger's original theory provided. But we don't have to pick one and trash the others. Self-consistency, personal responsibility for bad outcomes, and self-affirmation aren't mutually exclusive explanations. As Cooper suggests, "They each describe a distinct and important piece of the overall dissonance process and, in doing so, make a unique contribution to our understanding of how cognitions about the self mediate cognitive dissonance and arousal and reduction."[24]

THEORY INTO PRACTICE: PERSUASION THROUGH DISSONANCE

I've placed this chapter in the section on interpersonal influence because Festinger and his followers focused on attitude change as an end product of dissonance. Suppose you know someone named Sam who holds an opinion that you're convinced is harmful or wrong. What practical advice does the theory offer that might help you alter Sam's conviction?

For openers, don't promise lavish benefits if Sam abandons that attitude or warn of dire consequences if he doesn't. A massive reward–punishment strategy may gain behavioral compliance, but the hard sell seldom wins the heart or mind of the person being bribed or pressured. Instead, work to develop a friendly relationship with Sam. That way your own position will tend to bypass the *selective exposure* screen that Sam and the rest of us put up to avoid threatening ideas. And if Sam eventually adopts your viewpoint, an ongoing bond means you'll be around to offer reassurance when *postdecision dissonance* kicks in.

To be an effective agent of change, you should offer just enough encouragement *(minimal justification)* for Sam to try out novel behavior that departs from his usual way of thinking. Avoid making an offer that Sam can't refuse. As long as *counterattitudinal actions* are freely chosen and publicly taken, people are more likely to adopt beliefs that support what they've done. The greater the effort involved in acting this way, the greater the chance that their attitudes will change to match their actions.

Finally, as you seek to *induce compliance,* try to get Sam to count the cost of doing what you want and to grasp the potential downside of that behavior for others *(personal responsibility for negative outcomes)*. That kind of understanding will increase the probability that Sam's attitude will shift to be consistent with his actions. And if things turn sour, your relationship won't.

CRITIQUE: DISSONANCE OVER DISSONANCE

When Festinger died in 1989, his obituary in *American Psychologist* testified to the impact of his work:

> Like Dostoyevski and like Picasso, Festinger set in motion a *style* of research and theory in the social sciences that is now the common property of all creative workers in the field. . . . Leon is to social psychology what Freud is to clinical psychology and Piaget to developmental psychology.[25]

As the *Dilbert* cartoon in this chapter suggests, cognitive dissonance is one of the few theories in this book that has achieved name recognition within popular culture. Yet despite this wide influence, Festinger's original theory and its contemporary revisions contain a serious flaw. Like my boyhood friend's never-miss shot in his driveway basketball court (see Chapter 3), it's hard to think of a way the theory can be proved wrong.

Look again at the four stages of the dissonance process diagram in Figure 16–1. Almost all the creative efforts of dissonance researchers have been aimed at inducing counterattitudinal advocacy at point A—getting people to say something in public that is inconsistent with what they believe in private. When researchers find an attitude shift at point C, they automatically *assume* that dissonance was built up at point B and is gone by point D. But they don't test to see whether dissonance is actually there.

Festinger never specified a reliable way to detect the degree of dissonance a person experiences, if any. Psychologist Patricia Devine and her University of Wisconsin–Madison colleagues refer to such an instrument as a *dissonance thermometer*. They applaud researchers' occasional attempts to gauge the *arousal* component of dissonance through physiological measures such as galvanic skin response. (When our drive state increases, we have sweaty palms.) But they are even more encouraged at the possibility of assessing the *psychological discomfort* component of dissonance by means of a self-report measure of affect. Until some kind of dissonance thermometer is a standard part of dissonance research, we will never know if the distressing mental state is for real.

Dissonance thermometer A hypothetical, reliable gauge of the dissonance a person feels as a result of inconsistency.

Cornell University psychologist Daryl Bem doesn't think it is. He agrees that attitudes change when people act counter to their beliefs with minimal justification, but he claims that *self-perception* is a much simpler explanation than cognitive dissonance. He believes we judge our internal dispositions the same way others do—by observing our behavior.

Bem ran his own $1/$20 study to test his alternative explanation.[26] People heard a recording of a Stanford man's enthusiastic account of the spool-sorting, peg-turning task. Some listeners were told he received $1 for recruiting the female subject. Since he had little obvious reason to lie, they assumed he really liked the task. Other listeners were told the man received $20 to recruit the woman. These folks assumed the man was bored with the task and was lying to get the money. Bem's subjects didn't speculate about what was going on inside the Stanford man's head. They simply judged his attitude by looking at what he did under the circumstances. If people don't need an understanding of cognitive dissonance to forecast how the men would react, Bem asks, why should social scientists? Bem is convinced that cognitive dissonance theory is like the mouse-trap pictured on page 26—much too convoluted. He opts for simplicity.

Self-perception theory The claim that we determine our attitudes the same way outside observers do—by observing our behavior; an alternative to cognitive dissonance theory.

Advocates of cognitive dissonance in the field of communication counter that nothing about mental processes is simple. When we deal with what goes on behind the eyes, we should expect and appreciate complexity. Festinger's theory has energized scientifically oriented communication scholars for more than 50 years. I feel no dissonance by including cognitive dissonance theory in this text.

QUESTIONS TO SHARPEN YOUR FOCUS

1. Cognitive dissonance is a *distressing mental state*. When did you last experience this *aversive drive*? Why might you have trouble answering that question?

2. The results of Festinger's famous *$1/$20 experiment* can be explained in a number of different ways. Which explanation do you find most satisfying?

3. Suppose you want your friends to change their sexist attitudes. What advice does the *minimal justification hypothesis* offer?

4. I see cognitive dissonance theory as a "never-miss shot." What would it take to make the theory *testable*?

A SECOND LOOK

Recommended resource: Joel Cooper, *Cognitive Dissonance: 50 Years of a Classic Theory,* Sage, Thousand Oaks, CA, 2007, (see especially Chapter 1, "Cognitive Dissonance: In the Beginning," pp. 1–27, and Chapter 3, "The Motivational Property of Dissonance," pp. 42–61).

Original statement: Leon Festinger, *A Theory of Cognitive Dissonance,* Stanford University, Stanford, CA, 1957.

Toward a dissonance thermometer: Patricia G. Devine, John M. Turner, et al., "Moving Beyond Attitude Change in the Study of Dissonance Related Processes," Eddie Harmon-Jones and Judson Mills (eds.), *Cognitive Dissonance: Progress on a Pivotal Theory in Social Psychology,* American Psychological Association, Washington, DC, 1999, pp. 297-323.

Engaging account of theory's development: Elliot Aronson, "The Evolution of Cognitive Dissonance Theory: A Personal Appraisal," in *The Science of Social Influence: Advances and Future Progress,* Anthon Prankanis (ed.), Psychology Press, New York, 2007, pp. 115–135.

Selective exposure: Silvia Knobloch-Westerwick and Jingbo Meng, "Looking the Other Way: Selective Exposure to Attitude-Consistent and Counterattitudinal Political Information," *Communication Research,* Vol. 36, 2009, pp. 426–448.

Postdecision dissonance: Dave D'Alessio and Mike Allen, "Selective Exposure and Dissonance after Decisions," *Psychological Reports,* Vol. 91, 2002, pp. 527–532.

$1/$20 experiment: Leon Festinger and James Carlsmith, "Cognitive Consequences of Forced Compliance," *Journal of Abnormal and Social Psychology,* Vol. 58, 1959, pp. 203–210.

Self-consistency revision: Ruth Thibodeau and Elliot Aronson, "Taking a Closer Look: Reasserting the Role of the Self-Concept in Dissonance Theory," *Personality and Social Psychology Bulletin,* Vol. 18, 1992, pp. 591–602.

New-look revision: Joel Cooper and Russell Fazio, "A New Look at Dissonance Theory," in *Advances in Experimental Social Psychology, Vol. 17,* Leonard Berkowitz (ed.), Academic Press, Orlando, FL, 1984, pp. 229–262.

Self-affirmation revision: Claude Steele, "The Psychology of Self-Affirmation: Sustaining the Integrity of the Self," in *Advances in Experimental Social Psychology, Vol. 21,* Leonard Berkowitz (ed.), Lawrence Erlbaum, Hillsdale, NJ, 1988, pp. 261–302.

Role of weapons of mass destruction and dissonance in the invasion of Iraq: Jeff Stone and Nicholas Fernandez, "How Behavior Shapes Attitudes: Cognitive Dissonance Processes," in *Attitudes and Attitude Change,* William Crano and Radmila Prislin (eds.), Psychology Press, New York, 2008, pp. 313–334.

Critique: Daryl Bem, "Self-Perception: An Alternative Interpretation of Cognitive Dissonance Phenomena," *Psychological Review,* Vol. 74, 1967, pp. 183–200.

Critique: Daniel O'Keefe, "Cognitive Dissonance Theory," in *Persuasion: Theory and Research,* 2nd ed., Sage, Thousand Oaks, CA, 2002, pp. 77–100.

Experiencing cognitive dissonance may require a strong need for esteem.
To access a chapter on Abraham Maslow's theory of motivation,
click on Hierarchy of Needs in Archive under Theory Resources at
www.afirstlook.com.

DIVISION THREE

Group and Public Communication

Group   Communication

On the morning of January 28, 1986, the space shuttle *Challenger* blasted off from the Kennedy Space Center in Florida. For the first time, the flight carried a civilian schoolteacher, Christa McAuliffe, as part of the crew. Seventy-three seconds after liftoff, millions of schoolchildren watched on television as the rocket disintegrated in a fiery explosion, and the capsule with its crew of seven plunged into the Atlantic Ocean. For many Americans, the *Challenger* disaster marked the end of a love affair with space. As they learned in the months that followed, the tragedy could have been—and should have been—avoided.

An independent presidential commission identified the primary cause of the accident as failure in an O-ring that was supposed to seal a joint, thus allowing volatile rocket fuel to spew out during the "burn." But the commission also concluded that a highly flawed decision process was an important contributing cause of the disaster. Communication, as well as combustion, was responsible for the tragedy. The day before the launch, rocket engineers had talked about the flight being risky. They worried that the O-ring seals had never been tested below 53 degrees Fahrenheit. As one of them later testified, with launch-time temperature in the 20s, getting the O-rings to seal gaps would be like "trying to shove a brick into a crack versus a sponge."[1] Yet during the final "go/no-go" conference, all agreed that the rocket was ready to fly.

Yale social psychologist Irving Janis was convinced that this grievous error wasn't an isolated incident. He had spotted the same group dynamic in other tragic government and corporate decisions. Janis didn't regard chief executives or their advisors as stupid, lazy, or evil. Rather he saw them as victims of "groupthink." He defined *groupthink* as "a mode of thinking that people engage in when they are deeply involved in a cohesive in-group, when the members' strivings for unanimity override their motivation to realistically appraise alternative courses of action."[2] This concurrence-seeking tendency emerges only when the group is characterized by "a warm clubby atmosphere" in which members desire to maintain relationships within the group at all costs. As a result, they automatically apply the "preserve group harmony" test to every decision they face.[3] Janis maintained that the superglue of solidarity that bonds people together can also cause their mental processes to get stuck.

Janis' concept of groupthink highlights the accepted wisdom in the field that there are two functions communication needs to address in any group—a *task function* and a *relationship function*. Task-focused communication moves the group along toward its goal; relational communication holds the group together. Some people concentrate on getting the job done, while others are much more concerned about relationships within the group. Task-oriented individuals are the pistons that drive the group machine. Relationship-oriented members are the lubricant that prevents excessive friction from destroying the group. Good groups require both kinds of people.

Harvard social psychologist Robert Bales was an early theorist who formally made the connection between specific types of communication and accomplishing these two functions.[4] Bales said group locomotion won't happen unless members *ask for* as well as *offer* information, opinions, and suggestions on how the group should proceed. Bales claimed that the most effective groups are those in which the verbal requests and responses are roughly equal in number. If everyone is asking and nobody's offering answers, the group won't make progress toward the goal. If, on the other hand, no one asks and everyone declares, the group will still be stuck.

As for *socio-emotional* communication (Bales' label for relational concern), he regarded showing agreement, showing solidarity, and reducing tension by storytelling as positive forms of communication that make the group cohesive. He saw showing disagreement, antagonism, and tension as negative moves that tend to pull the group apart. Yet Bales found that groups make better decisions when there are a few negative voices. That squares with Janis' recommendation. He suggests that skepticism and blunt critiques are correctives to groupthink. That kind of communication might have saved the lives of the *Challenger* crew and Americans' support for the space shuttle program.[5]

"Now, let's hear it for good old Al, whose idea this Group Think was in the first place."

© Whitney Darrow, Jr./The New Yorker Collection/www.cartoonbank.com

CHAPTER **17**

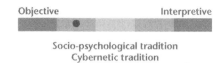
Functional Perspective on Group Decision Making

of Randy Hirokawa & Dennis Gouran

A cynic once said that a camel is a horse put together by a committee. Others upset by their experience with group decision making give voice to their frustration with equally disparaging quips:[1]

> "If you want something done, do it yourself."

> "Too many cooks spoil the broth."

> "A committee is a group that keeps minutes and wastes hours."

> "Committees lure fresh ideas down a cul-de-sac and quietly strangle them."

Randy Hirokawa (dean of liberal arts, University of Hawaii at Hilo) and Dennis Gouran (professor of communication, Pennsylvania State University) believe that these pessimistic views are unwarranted. Assuming that group members care about the issue, are reasonably intelligent, and face a challenging task that calls for more facts, new ideas, or clear thinking, Hirokawa and Gouran are convinced that group interaction has a positive effect on the final decision. Hirokawa seeks *quality* solutions.[2] Gouran desires decisions that are *appropriate*.[3] Both scholars regard talk as the social tool that helps groups reach better conclusions than they otherwise would. As the Hebrew proverb suggests, "Without counsel plans go wrong, but with many advisers they succeed."[4]

Functional perspective
A prescriptive approach that describes and predicts task-group performance when four communication functions are fulfilled.

The *functional perspective* specifies what communication must accomplish for jointly made decisions to be wise. Gouran laid the groundwork for the theory with his early writing on group decision making. Hirokawa developed the core principles of the theory during his graduate studies, and for 20 years his research tested and refined the theory. On the chance that you would be intrigued by a behind-the-scenes look at real-life group decisions made by college students living together, I'll illustrate the functional perspective by drawing on my experience conducting a two-week off-campus class that students called the "Island Course."

For 20 years I taught a group dynamics seminar limited to eight students on a remote island in northern Lake Michigan. Travel to and from the island was by a single-engine airplane, and we lived together in a cabin—the only structure on the island. Except when a few of us flew off the island to the mainland to get food, our sole communication was with each other. There's no cell phone service or Internet access on the island. Course alumni look back and consider our isolation as similar to *Survivor*, yet with a cooperative rather than a competitive agenda. No one was ever voted off the island.

The island course was primarily a venture in experiential education. We learned about group dynamics by studying our own interaction. I asked students to adopt the role of participant-observer. Whatever happened among us became a subject for group discussion. Still, the course maintained traditional academic features—four hours of class per day, assigned readings, and final grades. Within that hybrid framework, class members had to decide on a daily schedule, who would do each job necessary for group living, how limited funds for food and fuel would be spent, and on what basis I would assign grades. They understood that they had to live with their decisions for the first half of the course, but could change things for the second week.

As for my role, I let them know that I wouldn't be an active participant in the choices they made—they were free to decide as they saw fit. I'd provide any information they asked for, with the exception of revealing how other island-course groups had handled these issues or disclosing my own personal preferences. In the survey that alums filled out up to two decades after the course, Kelly's response reflected the general consensus:

> I remember Em's role best for what he didn't do. It was my first real experience with a leader who laid back intentionally so that we had to come to our own conclusion—a real democracy. It was refreshing to deal with someone in charge who didn't give all the answers. We were responsible for how things turned out.

As Hirokawa and Gouran predict, how things turned out hinged on the absence or presence of four types of communication.

FOUR FUNCTIONS OF EFFECTIVE DECISION MAKING

Consistent with the approach of Bales and other pioneer researchers, Hirokawa and Gouran draw an analogy between small groups and biological systems. Complex living organisms must satisfy a number of functions, such as respiration, circulation, digestion, and elimination of bodily waste, if they are to survive and thrive in an ever-changing environment. In like manner, Hirokawa and Gouran see the group decision-making process as needing to fulfill four task requirements if members are to reach a high-quality solution. They refer to these conditions as *requisite functions* of effective decision making—thus the "functional perspective" label.[5] The four functions are (1) problem analysis, (2) goal setting, (3) identification of alternatives, and (4) evaluation of positive and negative characteristics of each alternative.

Requisite functions
Requirements for positive group outcome; problem analysis, goal setting, identification of alternatives, and evaluation of pluses and minuses for each.

1. Analysis of the Problem

Is something going on that requires improvement or change? To answer that question, group members must take a realistic look at current conditions. Defenders of the status quo are fond of saying, "If it ain't broke, don't fix it." But, as Hirokawa warns, any misunderstanding of the situation tends to be compounded when the members make their final decision. He also notes that the clearest example of faulty analysis is the failure to recognize a potential threat when one really exists.[6] After people acknowledge a need to be addressed, they still must figure out the nature, extent, and probable cause(s) of the problem that confronts the group.

Problem analysis
Determining the nature, extent, and cause(s) of the problem facing the group.

The first night on the island, students faced the task of drawing up a daily schedule. Because that decision affected other choices, I'll describe how two groups in different summers handled problem analysis and how they fulfilled the other three requisite functions that Hirokawa and Gouran identify. I'll refer to them as the *blue group* and the *green group.*

The blue group never did any overt problem analysis. To them, scheduling seemed a simple matter. They jumped to pooling suggestions for what would make the two weeks ideal without ever considering the unique problems that island living posed. Their conversation centered on building in as much time as possible to go outside to enjoy the island during the day and each other at night. Most class members noted that sleeping in late was also an idea with great appeal.

Conversely, the green group started out by exploring what situational limitations they had to factor into their decision. The close quarters of the small cabin proved to be a problem because it provided no aural—and very little visual—privacy. A few light sleepers admitted that it would be impossible for them to get to sleep at night, or to stay asleep in the morning, if someone was talking or walking around. Before budgeting their limited funds for food and fuel, they also figured out the cost for each member to ride the all-terrain cycle (ATC) around the island for 30 minutes a day—something all were eager to do. Their figures showed that they'd run out of money before the end of the course unless they could limit the use of the diesel generator to no more than 10 hours a day. This problem analysis strongly informed the schedule they finally worked out.

2. Goal Setting

Because group members need to be clear on what they are trying to accomplish, Hirokawa and Gouran regard discussion of goals and objectives as the second requisite function of decision making. A group needs to establish criteria by which to judge proposed solutions. These criteria must set forth the minimal qualities that an acceptable solution must possess. If the group fails to satisfy this task requirement, it's likely that the decision will be driven by power or passion rather than reason.[7]

Goal setting
Establishing criteria by which to judge proposed solutions.

Even before they began discussing alternatives, the green group reached a consensus on the specific criteria their schedule had to meet. They agreed that the schedule should include four hours of class as well as windows wide enough for students to prepare and enjoy decent meals and clean up afterward. Members insisted that there be a minimum of six hours of free time to play, study, or chill out. They also specified a nighttime block of at least seven hours for sleeping, where both the generator and conversation in the cabin would be turned off. And based on their problem analysis, they wanted to craft an energy-sensitive schedule that wouldn't require the generator to be used for more than 10 hours a day. With the possible exceptions of *decent meals* and *energy sensitive*, these were measurable goals that could be used to gauge the quality of their final decision.

Unlike the green group, the blue group never spoke of goals, objectives, standards, targets, or criteria. Their discussion made it clear that fun in the sun and lots of casual time together were high priorities. But these overlapping desires are quite subjective and open to multiple interpretations. With no definitive goals to focus their discussion, it's difficult for group members to know whether they're making an appropriate decision. Or, as sports enthusiasts put it, *You don't know you're winning if you don't keep score.*

3. Identification of Alternatives

Hirokawa and Gouran stress the importance of marshaling a number of alternative solutions from which group members can choose:

Identification of alternatives
Generation of options to sufficiently solve the problem.

> If no one calls attention to the need for generating as many alternatives as is realistically possible, then relatively few may be introduced, and the corresponding possibility of finding the acceptable answer will be low.[8]

Both island-course groups wanted to schedule time when they could enjoy the island. Swimming, sunbathing, stone skipping, playing volleyball or soccer,

"Gentlemen, the fact that all my horses and all my men couldn't put Humpty together again simply proves to me that I must have more horses and more men."

© Dana Fradon/The New Yorker Collection/www.cartoonbank.com

trailblazing, riding the ATC, treasure hunting, bird watching, picking wild raspberries, building tree forts in the woods, and just lolling in the hammock were a few of the daylight activities suggested by blue and green course members alike. But the groups varied greatly on the number of options they generated for scheduling class and meals. The blue group seemed to have tunnel vision and could only picture a schedule with two hours of class in the morning and two hours at night. No other options were seriously considered. They were equally locked into the traditional practice of lunch at noon and dinner at six. One tentatively suggested alternative was shot down before it could be explained.

A girl in the green group had read an article on brainstorming before the course and urged classmates, "Let's see how many different ideas we can think of for when we'll eat." They took her up on it and suggested a dozen meal plans: late breakfast; no breakfast; brunch instead of breakfast and lunch; one big meal a day at noon; dinner at noon and light supper in the evening; a picnic snack to eat in the afternoon; four light meals a day; and a mix of these options.

The green group wasn't quite as creative with alternatives for class, yet they went beyond the two-hours-in-the-morning-and-two-at-night plan that seemed written in stone for the blue group. Different class members suggested three hours in the morning and one at night; four hours in the morning with two breaks; three class sessions of 80 minutes in the morning, afternoon, and night; three hours of class at night when the generator would be on anyway; all classes during daylight hours so the generator wouldn't have to be on. Their final decision turned out to be a combination of these ideas.

4. Evaluation of Positive and Negative Characteristics

After a group has identified alternative solutions, the participants must take care to test the relative merits of each option against the criteria they believe are important. This point-by-point comparison doesn't take place automatically. Hirokawa and Gouran warn that groups get sloppy and often need one member to remind the others to consider both the positive and negative features of each alternative.

Evaluation of positive and negative characteristics
Testing the relative merits of each option against the criteria selected; weighing the benefits and costs.

Because blue group members concentrated on only one schedule option, their evaluation of its characteristics was rather brief. They did a nice job of articulating the benefits they saw in their plan—a similarity to campus schedule, afternoons free for outdoor recreation, late-night opportunity to strengthen relationships, and a chance to sleep in before a late morning class. What's not to like? The blue group never addressed that issue. Hirokawa notes that some group tasks have a negative *bias* in that spotting the downside of each alternative is more important than identifying its positive qualities.[9] Since students were new to island living, it turned out that focusing on the disadvantages inherent in any plan would have been time well spent.

The green group discussed the pluses and minuses of every alternative. They concluded that late-night activity came at the cost of money they'd rather spend on food. They also saw that long class sessions in this idyllic setting could result in boredom and resentment. And for many of the meal plans they were considering, the amount of time spent in preparation, eating, and cleanup struck them as excessive. These realizations led them to adopt the novel schedule displayed on the bottom of Figure 17–1. Note that the three shorter classes meet in daylight hours. Since there are only two sit-down meals with prep and cleanup, there's

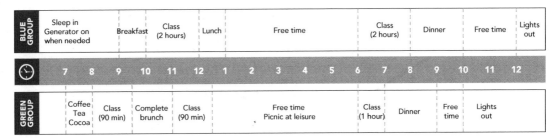

[The Green Group time line depicts their proposal before advancing it an hour to "Island Daylight Saving Time."]

FIGURE 17–1   Blue and Green Group Schedules for the Island Course

more free time for whatever people want to do. And there are more than eight hours of darkness for course members and the generator to be at rest.

When the green group members first looked at their schedule shown in Figure 17–1, some had second thoughts. For them, it seemed bizarre to be going to bed at 10 P.M., with some folks rising at 6:30 in the morning. But one girl suggested advancing all clocks, watches, and times on the schedule ahead by one hour. "We'll feel better about going to bed at 11, and our schedule will still be in sync with the sun," she explained. The others were intrigued by the elegant simplicity of her idea, so before turning in that night, we switched to Island Daylight Saving Time. Our body clocks were quick to adjust as well.

Predictable Outcomes

So what difference did Hirokawa and Gouran's four requisite functions make for these two island groups? Over the course of two weeks, how did these contrasting schedules turn out in practice? Both groups stuck to their plan for the first week, but by the fifth day, the class that didn't address the four functions was struggling. No one in the blue group went to sleep before midnight, and once someone got up early in the morning, no one else could sleep. Students slept only six or seven hours, and those who planned to sleep in were irritated at others who woke them up. The two-hour class at night became a real drag; no one looked forward to that time together.

Perhaps the biggest problem triggered by the blue group's decision was prolonged use of the generator. Extended activity in the cabin resulted in the generator running more than 12 hours a day, at a cost that took a big bite out of the food budget. The blue group made some adjustments the second week, but the menu for our last few meals seemed to consist of grubs and yucca roots. And there was no gas for the ATC.

On the other hand, the eight students in the green group were quite satisfied with the schedule they crafted. They saved time and energy by eating only two meals in the cabin, holding all classes during daylight hours, and preparing the afternoon picnic snack and the brunch at the same time. They had more time for fun in the sun than the blue group did, and looked forward to the abbreviated evening class as a lead-in to a relaxed dinner.

The well-rested green group took great pride in limiting generator use to eight hours per day and celebrated with a T-bone steak dinner the last night with the money they'd saved. In addition, there was enough room in the budget to guarantee unlimited rides on the ATC. As Hirokawa and Gouran suggest, it took

222   *GROUP AND PUBLIC COMMUNICATION*

discussion of all four requisite functions to hammer out a quality solution that was appropriate for the island course.

PRIORITIZING THE FOUR FUNCTIONS

The word *prioritizing* refers to addressing the four requisite functions in a logical progression. Hirokawa originally thought that no one sequence or group agenda does the job better. As long as the group ends up dealing with all four functions, the route its members take won't make much difference. Yet he's discovered the groups that successfully resolve especially difficult problems usually take a common decision-making path.[10]

The term *prioritizing* in the heading also refers to the question of which function is most important in order for a group to maximize the probability of a high-quality decision. Hirokawa and Gouran originally thought that no single function is inherently more important than any of the others.[11] But as Hirokawa admits, in a paper entitled, "To Err Is Human, To Correct for It Divine," they were wrong. The paper reports on a meta-analysis of 60 empirical research studies on the functional perspective. The study concludes that of the four functions, *evaluation of negative consequences of alternative solutions* is by far the most crucial to ensure a quality decision.[12] Perhaps to stress its importance, Hirokawa now splits up the evaluation of alternatives function into positive outcomes and negative outcomes for each option, and speaks of five requisite functions rather than four.

Figure 17–2 portrays the path that seems to offer the best problem-solving progression. Groups start with problem analysis, then deal with goal setting and identifying alternatives, and end by evaluating the positive and negative characteristics of each alternative before making a final choice. This decision-making flow parallels the advice I once heard on National Public Radio's *Car Talk*. Asked how car owners should handle close-call decisions on auto repair, mechanics Tom and Ray Magliozzi ("Click and Clack, the Tappet Brothers") gave a street-smart answer that ran something like this:

> First, figure out what's broke. Then, make up your mind how good you want to fix it. Or before that ask your mechanic to list the choices you've got. Either way, you gotta do both. Finally, weigh the bang-for-the-buck that each job gives. Then decide.

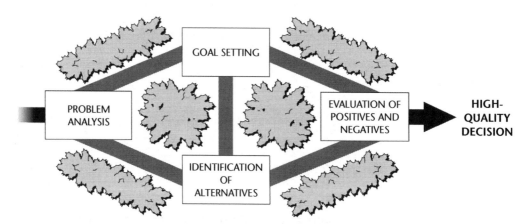

FIGURE 17–2   An Effective Decision-Making Path from the Functional Perspective

THE ROLE OF COMMUNICATION IN FULFILLING THE FUNCTIONS

Most communication scholars believe that discussion among members has a significant effect on the quality of group decisions. Traditional wisdom suggests that talk is the medium, channel, or conduit through which information travels between participants.[13] Verbal interaction makes it possible for members to (1) distribute and pool information, (2) catch and remedy errors, and (3) influence each other. But distractions and nonproductive conversation create channel noise causing a loss of information. Group researcher Ivan Steiner claimed that[14]

$$\frac{\text{Actual Group}}{\text{Productivity}} = \frac{\text{Potential}}{\text{Productivity}} - \frac{\text{Losses Due}}{\text{to Processes}}$$

It follows that communication is best when it doesn't obstruct or distort the free flow of ideas.

While not rejecting this traditional view, Hirokawa believes that communication plays a more active role in crafting quality decisions. Like social constructionists (see Chapters 6, 11, and 13), he regards group discussion as a tool or instrument that group members use to create the social reality in which decisions are made.[15] Discussion exerts its own impact on the end product of the group.

How does this work in practice? Think of the dark, wide lines in Figure 17–2 as safe trails through a dense thicket—paths that connect the four key task functions and lead ultimately to the goal of a high-quality group decision. Members can easily wander off that goal path and get caught up in a tangle of prickerbushes that thwart the group's progress. The bushes in this analogy represent distractions or barriers that hinder movement toward the goal. Hirokawa and Gouran list a number of thorny obstacles—ignorance of the issue, faulty facts, misguided assumptions, sloppy evaluation of options, illogical inferences, disregard of procedural norms, and undue influence by powerful members. They believe that people go astray through talk, but they also believe that communication has the power to pull them back onto the goal-directed path.

Consistent with these convictions, Hirokawa and Gouran outline three types of communication in decision-making groups:

1. Promotive—interaction that moves the group along the goal path by calling attention to one of the four requisite decision-making functions.
2. Disruptive—interaction that diverts, hinders or frustrates group members' ability to achieve the four task functions.
3. Counteractive—interaction that members use to get the group back on track.

Hirokawa and Gouran suggest that most comments from group members disrupt rather than promote progress toward the goal. They conclude, therefore, that "effective group decision-making is perhaps best understood as a consequence of the exercise of counteractive influence."[16] In other words, someone has to say something that will get the group back on track. After reading about these three types of communication in her comm theory course, Lydia recognized that her comments had been disruptive rather than counteractive during a crucial discussion:

I think group decision making is important, even vital, yet I am the worst at it. When I was in high school, I applied to be a foreign exchange student to

Germany. For our final selection task the six finalists had to come up with a solution to a problem, then present it to the directors. Based on the group process, the directors would select the four of us who would go. Judging by Hirokawa and Gouran's theory, I see why I never went to Germany. I'd like to say it's because I tend to promote different alternatives, however, I can see how my smart/sarcastic comments tend to disrupt and take away from the task of problem analysis and goal setting. I wish I had a chance to do it over—after my big personality change, of course.

FOICS

Function-Oriented Inter-action Coding System; a tool to record and clas-sify the function of utter-ances during a group's discussion.

Hirokawa has made repeated efforts to develop a conversational coding sys-tem that classifies the function of specific statements. Much like Bales' interaction categories outlined in the introduction to group communication, Hirokawa's *Function-Oriented Interaction Coding System (FOICS)* requires researchers to cate-gorize each *functional utterance*, which is "an uninterrupted statement of a single member that appears to perform a specified function within the group interaction process."[17]

Figure 17–3 shows a FOICS checklist that researchers might use to analyze communication within a group. As you can see, raters are asked to make two judgments: (1) Which of the four requisite functions, if any, does an utterance address? and (2) Does the remark facilitate (*promote*), inhibit (*disrupt*), or redirect (*counteract*) the group's focus on that function? Ideally, this 4×3 classification scheme provides 12 discrete categories of group discussion. With that informa-tion, researchers could determine the effect of communication on the quality of the decision the group makes.

Functional utterance

An uninterrupted state-ment of a single member that appears to perform a specific function.

In practice, however, analyzing the content of group discussion is fraught with difficulty. In the first place, independent raters find it hard to agree on how a statement should be coded. Extensive training boosts the reliability of their judg-ments, but Hirokawa is keenly aware that a single comment may serve multiple functions. In addition, words that appear helpful on the surface may have hidden power to disrupt, or vice versa. The process of coding comments has turned out to be an ongoing problem for all researchers who want to study the nature and effects of group communication.

	Problem Analysis	Goal Setting	Identification of Alternatives	Evaluation of Positives/Negatives
Promote				
Disrupt				
Counteract				

FIGURE 17–3   Function-Oriented Interaction Coding System (FOICS) Checklist

THOUGHTFUL ADVICE FOR THOSE WHO KNOW THEY ARE RIGHT

How can you and I use the functional perspective to facilitate better group deci-sions? We start with a healthy dose of humility concerning the wisdom of our own opinions. Hirokawa and Gouran report that groups often abandon the rational path due to the persuasive efforts of members who are convinced that they alone have the right answer. Their discussion style proclaims, "Don't confuse me with the facts; my mind's made up," and they wear down the opposition. We can make sure we don't come to the table with the sort of closed-minded attitude that torpedoes honest discussion. Additionally, we should be wary of pushing any "intuitive hunch" or "gut feeling" that we can't back up with reasonable evidence. These are errors to avoid.

We can also take proactive measures to promote clear thinking within the group. In almost every article they write, Hirokawa and Gouran acknowledge their intellectual debt to early-twentieth-century American pragmatist philosopher John Dewey.[18] Dewey's pragmatism was based on the hopeful assumption that practical decisions can be brought under more intelligent control through the process of rational inquiry.[19] He advocated a six-step process of *reflective thinking* that parallels a doctor's approach to treating a patient:[20]

1. Recognize symptoms of illness.
2. Diagnose the cause of the ailment.
3. Establish criteria for wellness.
4. Consider possible remedies.
5. Test to determine which solutions will work.

Reflective thinking
Thinking that favors rational consideration over intuitive hunches or pressure from those with clout.

6. Implement or prescribe the best solution.

Note that Hirokawa and Gouran's four requisite functions are almost exact replicas of steps 2, 3, 4, and 5 in Dewey's reflective-thinking process. Both lists recommend that group members discuss issues in a way that promotes problem analysis, goal setting, discovery of alternatives, and evaluation of these options. When we're tempted to make remarks that will detract from the process, Hirokawa and Gouran suggest we bite our tongues. And when others say things that sidetrack the group from fulfilling the four functional requisites, the theorists urge us to counter with a comment aimed at getting the group back on a rational path.

You may be hesitant to counteract the dubious logic of a powerful leader or a high-status member of the group, but Hirokawa and Gouran don't advocate direct criticism. Instead, they recommend a strategy of insisting on a careful process. By raising questions, calling for more alternatives, and urging a thorough evaluation of evidence, a low-status member can have a high-power impact on the quality of the final decision.

ETHICAL REFLECTION: HABERMAS' DISCOURSE ETHICS

German philosopher Jürgen Habermas suggests a rational group process through which people can determine right from wrong—a different kind of decision than Hirokawa and Gouran usually study. In order to develop guidelines for ethical action, the Frankfurt School critical theorist pictures a diverse group of people engaged in public discourse. Habermas' ethical approach seeks an after-the-fact discussion about what we did in a particular situation and why we decided to do it. Being ethical means being accountable.[21]

Habermas assumes that people within a given culture or community can pretty much agree on the good they want to accomplish, and that over time they've built up practical wisdom on how to achieve it. For example, your campus newspaper reporters assume that it's good for students to know more about

226 *GROUP AND PUBLIC COMMUNICATION*

what's going on within the school's administration ("the people's right to know") and that guaranteeing confidentiality to insiders is the best way to find out ("protecting their sources"). This newsroom common sense is a good place to start doing journalistic ethics, but reporters' justification of the practice typically lacks reflective rigor. It often doesn't take into account the interests of everyone affected by their stories.

Habermas' *discourse ethics* sets up a discursive test for the validity of any moral claim. The person who performed an act must be prepared to discuss in an open forum what he or she did and why he or she did it. This deliberative process is a two-stage process of justification and application. The actor must reveal the general ethical principle that he or she used to justify the action and then show why it was the appropriate thing to do in those particular circumstances. Habermas imagines an *ideal speech situation* where participants are free to listen to reason and speak their minds without fear of constraint or control.[22] He's convinced that the validity of any ethical consensus can be reached only to the extent that three requirements are met:[23]

(validity of any moral claim)

Discourse ethics
Jürgen Habermas' vision of the ideal speech situation in which diverse participants could rationally reach a consensus on universal ethical standards.

1. *Requirement for access.* All people affected by the ethical norm being debated can attend and be heard, regardless of their status. That means donors, administrators, professors, students, and minimum-wage staff at the school are welcome at the table without prejudice.

2. *Requirement for argument.* All participants are expected to exchange their points of view in the spirit of genuine reciprocity and mutual understanding. They aren't merely trying to advance their own interests but are trying to figure out whether an action serves the common good.

3. *Requirement for justification.* Everyone is committed to a standard of universalization. What makes ethical claims legitimate is their "acceptance not only among those who agree to live with and by them but by anyone *affected* by them."[24]

Ideal speech situation
A discourse on ethical accountability in which discussants represent all who will be affected by the decision, pursue discourse in a spirit of seeking the common good, and are committed to finding universal standards.

Habermas understands that thoroughly noncoercive dialogue is a utopian dream, yet he finds his conception of the ideal speech situation helpful in gauging the degree to which a discussion is rational. This, of course, is a major goal of Hirokawa's, Gouran's, and Dewey's. The trick is getting group members to do it.

CRITIQUE: IS RATIONALITY OVERRATED?

In their review of small-group communication literature, John Cragan and David Wright conclude that there are three leading theories.[25] One is Bormann's *symbolic convergence theory*, discussed in the next chapter. The second is Scott Poole's *adaptive structuration theory*, which you can read about in the theory list section of *www.afirstlook.com*. The third is Hirokawa and Gouran's functional perspective. In their critique of the functional perspective, communication professors Cynthia Stohl (University of California Santa Barbara) and Michael Holmes (Ball State University) explain why it is so highly regarded:

> The basic premise of the perspective, that communication serves task functions and the accomplishment of those functions should be associated with effective group decisions, is intuitively appealing and sensible. It also meets the standards of an objective theory in that it explains, is testable, simple, and practical.[26]

As a result, many communication scholars endorse the theory as a model for group discussion and decision making. One of my students is so convinced that he wrote, "A list of the four functions should be woven into the carpet of every committee room."

Yet Hirokawa's exclusive focus on rational talk may be the reason researchers get mixed results when they test his theory's predictions.[27] Note that the FOICS method of coding conversation all but ignores comments about relationships inside or outside the group. By treating relational statements as a distraction, Hirokawa commits the same mistake that the late Aubrey Fisher admitted he made in his own task-focused research:[28]

> The original purpose of the investigation . . . was to observe verbal task behavior free from the confounding variables of the socioemotional dimension. That purpose, of course, was doomed to failure. The two dimensions are interdependent.[29]

Stohl and Holmes' critique frames the same issue in a slightly different way. They contend that most real-life groups have a prior decision-making history and are embedded within a larger organization. They advocate adding a *historical function* that requires the group to talk about how past decisions were made. They also recommend an *institutional function* that is satisfied when members discuss the reality of power brokers and stakeholders who aren't at the table, but whose views clearly affect and are affected by the group decision.

Dennis Gouran has recently raised doubts about how useful the functional perspective may be for many small-group discussions.[30] He notes that almost all group dynamics research has dealt with decision making and problem solving. Although he and Hirokawa attempted to craft a one-size-fits-all model for group communication, he now believes it's beneficial for members to fulfill the four requisite functions only when they are addressing *questions of policy*. That's not always the case.

Investigative panels and juries deal with *questions of fact* such as "What happened?" or "Who's responsible?" College admission boards and product design teams face *questions of conjecture*, trying to figure out what's likely to happen in an uncertain future without any current way of knowing if their predictions are right. Religious groups and addiction recovery support groups face emotionally loaded *questions of value*, with members sharing or debating what they believe is acceptable, appropriate, ethical, or morally right. None of these questions has a discernable "right" or "high-quality" answer. Gouran doesn't believe that these alternative group goals invalidate the functional perspective, but he does suggest their existence shows that the theory isn't relevant in every situation. The scope of the functional perspective is more limited than first believed.

QUESTIONS TO SHARPEN YOUR FOCUS

1. Hirokawa and Gouran claim that small groups are like living *systems*. Do you see parallels between the four *functional requisites* of task groups and the body's need for respiration, circulation, digestion, and elimination?

2. Given that the functional theory focuses on *decision-making* and *problem-solving* groups, why is its silence on *relationship* issues a problem?

228   *GROUP AND PUBLIC COMMUNICATION*

3. Think of a time when you've been part of a task group that strayed from the *goal path*. What *counteractive statement* could you have made that might have brought it back on track?

4. Why might you find it frustrating to use Hirokawa's *Function-Oriented Interaction Coding System (FOICS)* to analyze a group discussion?

SELF-QUIZ

For chapter self-quizzes, go to the book's Online Learning Center at
www.mhhe.com/griffin9e

CONVERSATIONS

View this segment online at
www.mhhe.com/griffin9e or
www.afirstlook.com.

As you might expect from an objective theorist discussing a rational theory, Randy Hirokawa gives clear, concise responses to my opening questions about group decision making. Is it possible he will find a yet undiscovered requisite function? Are jokes a form of disruptive communication? But as the conversation continues, Hirokawa voices ideas not usually heard from thoroughgoing empiricists. He refers to the irony of questionable motives producing beneficial actions, a subjective standard to determine whether a decision is good, and his belief that there are no guarantees in life. Many students consider this conversation the best of the bunch.

A SECOND LOOK

Recommended resource: Dennis Gouran, Randy Hirokawa, Kelly Julian, and Geoff Leatham, "The Evolution and Current Status of the Functional Perspective on Communication in Decision-Making and Problem-Solving Groups," in *Communication Yearbook 16*, Stanley Deetz (ed.), Sage, Newbury Park, CA, 1993, pp. 573–600.

Original statement: Dennis Gouran and Randy Hirokawa, "The Role of Communication in Decision-Making Groups: A Functional Perspective," in *Communications in Transition*, Mary Mander (ed.), Praeger, New York, 1983, pp. 168–185.

Research review: Randy Hirokawa, "From the Tiny Pond to the Big Ocean: Studying Communication and Group Decision-Making Effectiveness from a Functional Perspective," 1999 B. Aubrey Fisher Memorial Lecture, Department of Communication, University of Utah, Salt Lake City, UT.

Role of communication: Randy Hirokawa and Dirk Scheerhorn, "Communication in Faulty Group Decision-Making," in *Communication and Group Decision-Making*, Randy Hirokawa and M. Scott Poole (eds.), Sage, Beverly Hills, CA, 1986, pp. 63–80.

Coding group interaction: Randy Hirokawa, "Functional Approaches to the Study of Group Discussion," *Small Group Research*, Vol. 25, 1994, pp. 542–550.

Additional propositions: Dennis Gouran and Randy Hirokawa, "Effective Decision Making and Problem Solving in Groups: A Functional Perspective," in *Small Group Communication: Theory and Practice*, 8th ed., Randy Hirokawa, Robert Cathcart, et al. (eds.), Roxbury, Los Angeles, CA, 2003, pp. 27–38.

Survey of group theories taking a functional perspective: Andrea B. Hollingshead, Gwen Wittenbaum, et al., "A Look at Groups from the Functional Perspective," in *Theories of Small Groups: Interdisciplinary Perspectives,* M. Scott Poole and Andrea B. Hollingshead (eds.), Sage, London, 2005, pp. 21–62.

Requisite functions accomplished face-to-face vs. CMC: Shu-Chu Sarrina Li, "Computer-Mediated Communication and Group Decision Making: A Functional Perspective," *Small Group Research,* Vol. 38, 2007, pp. 593–614.

Equivocal evidence that communication changes group decisions: Dean E. Hewes, "The Influence of Communication Processes on Group Outcomes: Antithesis and Thesis," *Human Communication Research,* Vol. 35, 2009, pp. 249–271.

Critique: Cynthia Stohl and Michael Holmes, "A Functional Perspective for Bona Fide Groups," *Communication Yearbook 16,* 1993, pp. 601–614.

Theorist's assessment of limited scope: Dennis Gouran, "Reflections on the Type of Question as a Determinant of the Form of Interaction in Decision-Making and Problem-Solving Discussions," *Communication Quarterly,* Vol. 53, 2003, pp. 111–125.

To access a chapter on Irving Janis' Groupthink,
click on Archive under Theory Resources at
www.afirstlook.com.

CHAPTER **18**

Objective   Interpretive

Rhetorical tradition
Socio-psychological tradition

Symbolic Convergence Theory

of Ernest Bormann

In the introduction to this section on group communication, I refer to Harvard social psychologist Robert Bales' work to categorize comments made in small-group discussions. On the basis of his research with zero-history problem-solving groups in his lab, Bales discovered that *dramatizing* was a significant type of communication that often fostered group cohesiveness.[1] The late University of Minnesota communication professor Ernest Bormann picked up on Bales' finding and undertook a more extensive study of newly formed groups to examine leadership emergence, decision making, norms, cohesiveness, and a number of other features of group life.[2]

Similar to Bales, Bormann and his team of colleagues observed that group members often dramatized events happening outside the group, things that took place at previous meetings, or what might possibly occur among them in the future. Sometimes these stories fell flat and the discussion moved in a different direction. But at other times group members responded enthusiastically by adding on to the story or chiming in with their own matching narratives. When the drama was enhanced in this way, members developed a common group consciousness and drew closer together. On the basis of extensive case studies, Bormann set forth the central explanatory principle of symbolic convergence theory (SCT):

Sharing group fantasies creates symbolic convergence.[3]

When she read about Bormann's theory, Maggie had no difficulty illustrating this core claim. Two weeks before her communication course began, she served as a student leader in the Wheaton Passage program for new freshmen that's held at a camp in Wisconsin's Northwoods. One of the stated goals of this optional offering is to build intentional community. In her application log, Maggie wrote of unplanned communication that achieved this end.

Cabin 8 was the rustic, run-down cabin that my group of Passage students was assigned to live in for the week. My co-leader and I decked the cabin out with decorations by hanging Christmas lights and origami doves, yet there was no escaping the massive holes in the screens, sticky messes in the drawers, and the spiders residing in the rafters. The night students arrived, we walked our group of girls past the brand new cabins, arrived at our old cabin, and presented Cabin 8—their home for a week. Needless to say, they were less than pleased.

The next day as our group was trekking to our morning activity, one of the girls brought up what she thought the perfect cabin would look like. Others jumped in with their ideas. For 10 minutes, each girl contributed something to the discussion of the fantasy cabin. Hot tubs, screened-in porches, soft carpet, lounge chairs, and a glass roof for stargazing were all mentioned as features in their ideal cabin. Looking back on this experience, I see how this shared fantasy played a role in our cabin bonding. As the week went on, our dream cabin became a running joke within our group that helped students develop a sense of closeness—what they deemed "hardcoreness." While living in the crummy cabin, they frequently revisited the image of the ideal cabin they created in their conversation.

DRAMATIZING MESSAGES: CREATIVE INTERPRETATIONS OF THERE-AND-THEN

Many comments in task-oriented discussion groups offer lines of argument, factual information, members' opinions, and suggestions for how the group should proceed. That's the kind of member contribution Hirokawa and Gouran's functional perspective values (see Chapter 17). Advocates of rational discussion believe it's usually disruptive and counterproductive when someone cracks a joke, describes a movie, or starts talking about plans for the upcoming weekend. Not so for Bormann. SCT classifies these examples and many other forms of speaking as *dramatizing messages* and believes that conversations about things outside of what's going on right now can often serve the group well.

A dramatizing message is one that contains imaginative language such as a pun or other wordplay, figure of speech (e.g., metaphor, simile, personification), analogy, anecdote, allegory, fable, narrative, story, or other creative expression of ideas. Whatever the form, the dramatizing message describes events occurring somewhere else and/or at some time other than the here-and-now.[4]

Dramatizing message
Imaginative language by a group member describing past, future, or outside events; creative interpretations of there-and-then.

Notice first that a group member's words must paint a picture or call to mind an image in order to be labeled a dramatizing message. A comment that groups need conflict in order to make good decisions might stimulate discussion among members, but that's not dramatizing in the way Bormann used the term. Second, a vivid message qualifies as dramatizing if it either describes something outside the group or portrays an event that has happened within the group in the past or might happen to the group in the future. Comments that have no imagery or those that refer to what's currently going on in the group make up the bulk of most group discussions. They aren't dramatizing messages.

When Maggie's girls started to verbally construct their ideal cabin, they were using imaginative language to talk about what they'd like to see in the future, probably wishing it would magically appear that night. If in a darker tone one of the girls expressed her hope that someone would set fire to the cabin before they returned, that message would also be dramatizing. But if the group of girls sat around in the cabin grousing about the spiders, mosquitoes, and sticky goo in the drawers, those comments would be about the here-and-now and wouldn't be defined as dramatizing messages.

Why is this distinction so important to Bormann and SCT advocates? Because dramatizing messages are interpretive. They aren't knee-jerk responses to

232   *GROUP AND PUBLIC COMMUNICATION*

experiences of the moment. "Dramatizing accounts of past occurrences artistically organize what are usually more complex, ambiguous, and chaotic experiences."[5] They help the speaker, and sometimes the listeners, make sense out of a confusing situation or bring some clarity to an uncertain future. Whether or not other group members connect with their imagery, dramatizing messages are creative interpretations of the there-and-then.

FANTASY CHAIN REACTIONS: UNPREDICTABLE SYMBOLIC EXPLOSIONS

Some people use the term *fantasy* to refer to children's literature, sexual desire, or things "not true." Bormann, however, reserved the term *fantasy* for dramatizing messages that are enthusiastically embraced by the whole group. Most dramatizing messages don't get that kind of reaction. They often fall on deaf ears, or group members listen but take a ho-hum attitude toward what was said. Of course, an embarrassing silence or a quick change of subject makes it obvious that the dramatizing message has fallen flat. As the cartoon below illustrates, there may even be group members who openly oppose what was said. Yet as Bormann noted, "Some dramatizing messages cause a symbolic explosion in the form of a chain reaction in which members join in until the entire group comes alive."[6] He described what he had seen when a fantasy chains out in this way:

> The tempo of the conversation would pick up. People would grow excited, interrupt one another, blush, laugh, forget their self-consciousness. The tone of the meeting, often quiet and tense immediately prior to the dramatizing, would

"Pardon us, Harrison, if the board fails to share your enthusiasm for the foliage up in Darien."

become lively, animated, and boisterous, the chaining process, involving both the verbal and nonverbal communication, indicating participation in the drama.[7]

A concrete example of a fantasy chain and its results may be helpful. University of Kentucky communication professor Alan DeSantis asks us to picture a group of Kentucky-born, middle-aged white guys sitting around a cigar store smoking hand-rolled imported cigars. As the topic shifts from college basketball to the risk of smoking, the owner tells the story of a heart surgeon who came into the shop after having been on duty for 36 hours. After lighting up, the doctor blew out a big mouthful of smoke and said, "This is the most relaxed I have felt in days. Now how can that be bad for you?"[8]

Whether or not the doctor really said this isn't the issue. Symbolic convergence theory is concerned with the group's response to the tale. In this case the patrons chuckle in appreciation, nod in agreement, or say "You've got it!" to punctuate the narrative. Some vie to tell their own stories that dismiss the harm of cigar smoking, a pastime they consider a benign hobby. Bormann said that we can spot a *fantasy chain* through a common response to the imagery. DeSantis, who was a cigar-smoking participant-observer among the shop's regular customers, affirms that the group's response to the owner's story paralleled Bormann's description above.

Symbolic convergence researchers have had little success predicting when a fantasy will ignite and trigger a chain reaction. They've found there's a better chance of a fantasy chaining out when the group is frustrated (as were Maggie's girls) or when they are bogged down in an effort to solve a thorny problem. Also, members with rhetorical skill seem to have a better chance of providing the spark, but there's no guarantee that their words will ignite others. And even when a skillful image-maker does spark a fantasy chain, he or she has little control over where the conversation will go. Fantasy chains seem to have a life of their own. But once a fantasy chain catches fire, symbolic convergence theory predicts that the group will converge around a fantasy theme.

Fantasy chain
A symbolic explosion of lively agreement within a group in response to a member's dramatizing message.

FANTASY THEMES—CONTENT, MOTIVES, CUES, TYPES

Bormann's technical definition of *fantasy* is "the creative and imaginative shared interpretation of events that fulfills a group's psychological or rhetorical needs."[9]

Think of a *fantasy theme* as the *content* of the dramatizing message that successfully sparks a fantasy chain. As such, it's the theory's basic unit of analysis. Because fantasy themes reflect and create a group's culture, all SCT researchers seek to identify the fantasy theme or themes that group members share. When spotted, fantasy themes are consistently ordered, always interpretive, and they inevitably put the group's slant on things. That is, fantasy themes act as a rhetorical means to sway doubters or naysayers.

Fantasy
The creative and imaginative shared interpretation of events that fulfills a group's psychological or rhetorical needs.

When a fantasy chains out among core patrons in the cigar store, we would expect to see that same theme run throughout multiple narratives. Perhaps the hero of every man's account is a famous cigar smoker who lived into old age without ill effects—think George Burns, Winston Churchill, or Fidel Castro. Or maybe each image reflects a meddling government bureaucrat who wants to limit their right to enjoy a cigar in a public place. Along with examples of long-lived smokers, group fantasies might focus on the difference between cigars and cigarettes, safety in moderation, inconsistent scientific findings concerning

Fantasy theme
Content of the fantasy that has chained out within a group; SCT's basic unit of analysis.

cancer, the greater risks of everyday living, and the health benefits of relaxation that come from smoking a good cigar. All of these fantasies have the same basic theme—*cigar smoking is safe.*

Bormann suggested that group members' *meanings, emotions, motives,* and *actions* are apparent in their fantasy themes. We can see all four of these in DeSantis' description of the angst that the core group of patrons experienced at the premature death of their friend Greg. Like the rest of the store's regulars who sat around smoking, Greg had scoffed at the health risks of their practice. Now they were confronted with the sobering fact of his fatal heart attack. Within a week of the funeral, however, his smoking buddies had constructed a verbal collage of images depicting Greg's stressful lifestyle. The store owner voiced their consensus: "Smoking had nothing to do with his death. He lived, drank and played hard and it took a toll on him at the end."[10] *Meaning:* Hard living killed Greg. *Emotion:* Reduction of fear; relief. *Motive:* Desire to smoke with buddies. *Action:* Not going to quit. Fantasy themes create a group's social reality.

Bormann and symbolic convergence theory advocates have found that many fantasy themes are indexed by a *symbolic cue.* A symbolic cue is "an agreed-upon trigger that sets off the group members to respond as they did when they first shared the fantasy."[11] It could be a code word, nonverbal gesture, phrase, slogan, inside joke, bumper sticker, or any shorthand way of re-establishing the full force of shared fantasy. In the Kentucky smoke shop where these fantasy themes were voiced, any mention of criticism of cigar smoking from family or friends was the cue that set off a new round of protest among store regulars. Their emotional reaction was captured on a T-shirt sold at the store that satirized the surgeon general's cautionary statement: "Warning—Harassing me about my smoking can be hazardous to your health."[12]

The meaning of a given fantasy theme is quite specific. Since clusters of related fantasy themes sometimes surface again and again in different groups, Bormann found it helpful to have a label to classify this phenomenon when it occurs. He used the term *fantasy type* to describe these well-worn symbolic paths. Fantasy types are "greater abstractions incorporating several concrete fantasy themes" and they exist "when shared meaning is taken for granted."[13] The cigar store group's fantasy theme of family and friends criticizing their smoking could be considered part of a larger "get-off-my-case" fantasy type. Perhaps that's a fantasy type that you and your friends have drawn upon when talking about your lifestyle, even if you've never smoked a cigar. Or students at your school may share stock fantasy types about Saturday night parties, the food on campus, professors who never seem to be in their offices, or the guy who always bails out at the last minute on a group project.

Symbolic cue
An agreed-upon trigger that sets off group members to respond as they did when they first shared the fantasy.

Fantasy type
A cluster of related fantasy themes; greater abstractions incorporating several concrete fantasy themes that exist when shared meaning is taken for granted.

SYMBOLIC CONVERGENCE: GROUP CONSCIOUSNESS AND OFTEN COHESIVENESS

The discussion of dramatizing messages, fantasy chains, and fantasy themes has dealt with the first part of SCT's core principle: *Sharing group fantasies creates symbolic convergence.* We're now ready to look at what that sharing creates—symbolic convergence. For Bormann, *symbolic convergence* meant the way in which "two or more private symbol worlds incline toward each other, come more closely together, or even overlap."[14] As those worlds intersect, group members develop a unique group consciousness. No longer do members think in terms of

Symbolic convergence
Two or more private symbol worlds incline toward each other, come more closely together, or even overlap; group consciousness, cohesiveness.

I, me, and *mine.* As symbolic overlap takes place, they begin to think and speak about *we, us,* and *ours.*

Do shared fantasies really cause this group transformation? Bormann insisted they do. Some limited commonality of words and images may naturally occur when group members interact often enough over a long period of time. But the process is accelerated and extended way beyond what otherwise might happen when members participate in one or more fantasy chains that create joint fantasy themes. Bormann used a variety of terms to portray the effect of group consciousness—*common ground, meeting of the minds, mutual understanding, groupiness, common social reality,* and *empathic communion.*

Once a group experiences symbolic convergence, Bormann suggested it's important for members to memorialize their group consciousness with a name and recorded history (*saga*) that recalls moments when fantasies chained out. He did that with his University of Minnesota colleagues who met in the Bormann home every Wednesday night to discuss the ideas that make up symbolic convergence theory. They called themselves the *Turtle Racers*—presumably based on an illustrated poster with the caption "Behold the turtle who makes progress only when he sticks his neck out." The image of a turtle race seemed doubly appropriate to their history of theory building when Bormann described the work going forward in fits and starts.

Symbolic convergence usually results in heightened group *cohesiveness*—members attracted to each other and sticking together through thick and thin. But not always. Bormann regarded symbolic convergence as usually a necessary but not sufficient cause of cohesiveness.

> Groups that do little fantasizing are seldom highly attractive and cohesive. Such groups tend to be boring and ordinary. The cohesive groups have usually done considerable fantasizing, but not all groups that fantasize a lot are rewarding and cohesive. The fantasies that chain may contribute to creating a social reality that is warm, friendly and hard working, that provides the group with a strong identity and self image, and that gives members a sense of purpose and meaning for their group's work. On the other hand, the fantasies may develop a group climate that is fascinating, frustrating, and punishing.[15]

Bormann went on to say that fantasy themes in those negative groups are riddled with conflict and that the humor expressed tends to be satire, ridicule, or sarcasm. I was in such a group my sophomore year of college, and he was right—it was fascinating. Fortunately I had enough sense to bail out.

RHETORICAL VISION: A COMPOSITE DRAMA SHARED BY A RHETORICAL COMMUNITY

Up to this point in the chapter, my description and illustration of symbolic convergence theory has focused on shared fantasies in small-group settings. That's where SCT was spawned. But early in the theory's development, the Turtle Racers discovered that shared fantasies weren't confined to a small-group context. As Bormann explained, "Fantasies that begin in small groups often are worked into public speeches, become picked up by mass media and 'spread out across larger publics.'"[16] Once attuned to the basic concepts of SCT, these scholars spotted swirling batches of related fantasy themes and types in all sorts of communication texts. Bormann coined the term *rhetorical vision* to designate "a composite drama that catches up large groups of people into a common symbolic reality."[17] He called the wide-ranging body of people who share that reality a *rhetorical community.*

The majority of research conducted using SCT has been aimed at capturing the rhetorical visions of dispersed rhetorical communities and figuring out how their communication created their unified fantasies. Researchers don't have the benefit of sitting in a room with the whole community while waiting for a fantasy to chain out as evidence of a fantasy theme. So Bormann and his colleagues developed a procedure called *fantasy theme analysis* to discover fantasy themes and rhetorical visions that have already been created.

Rhetorical vision
A composite drama that catches up large groups of people into a common symbolic reality.

Fantasy Theme Analysis

Fantasy theme analysis is a specific type of rhetorical criticism that's built on two basic assumptions. First, people create their social reality—a premise shared by many interpretive theorists (see Chapters 5, 6, 11, and 13). Second, people's meanings, motives, and emotions can be seen in their rhetoric. So when a dispersed community embraces the same rhetorical vision, that's reality for them. They aren't pretending.

A rhetorical critic using fantasy theme analysis looks for recurring fantasy themes in the text. If found, the critic should then discern if these shared fantasies are woven together into a rhetorical vision. In addition to using the basic SCT concepts already discussed, Bormann suggested that the critic look for at least four features that are present in all rhetorical visions.[18]

Fantasy theme analysis
A type of rhetorical criticism used to detect fantasy themes and rhetorical visions; the interpretive methodology of SCT.

1. **Characters:** Are there heroes to root for and villains to despise?
2. **Plot lines:** Do characters act in a way consistent with the rhetorical vision?
3. **Scene:** How do descriptions of time and place increase the drama's impact?
4. **Sanctioning agent:** Who or what legitimates the rhetorical vision?

I'll describe a fantasy theme analysis of Internet websites to demonstrate how these tools can reveal a rhetorical vision and show how that vision is created and sustained within a dispersed rhetorical community.

The Symbolic Creation of a Pro-Eating Disorder Rhetorical Vision

For those who are anorexic and/or bulimic, the world of face-to-face communication can be a lonely place. Afraid of condemnation if they reveal their eating disorder, they often live a life of secrecy, deception, and guilt. Although 12-step programs extend social support to those who want to overcome their disease, not all people with food disorders want to change. The Internet offers hundreds of pro-eating disorder websites where those who resist recovery can anonymously interact with like-minded others. Wayne State University communication professor Jessi McCabe conducted a fantasy theme analysis to "explore how group exchanges on these websites redefine a reality largely rejected by the cultural norm and what elements contribute to creating this worldview."[19] She chose the 12 most active pro-food disorder sites for her analysis. The message boards on the three most popular sites—Blue Dragon Fly, Pro-Ana Suicide Society, and Fragile Innocence—had a combined membership of more than 25,000 users.

Fantasy types are an SCT category midway between specific fantasy themes and an overall rhetorical vision. McCabe found that two contrasting fantasy types emerged in her analysis—a positive one and a negative one. She labeled the positive fantasy type "The humorous world of Ana and Mia." Within this world, fantasy chains reinforce site users' eating habits and shared reality. Across the message boards, members personify their disorders as characters in an ongoing drama.

> Members depict their own goals, struggles, and emotions through the personification of Ana and Mia. Anorexia and bulimia are given life and attributed human-like emotions and qualities, which are justified by the sanctioning agent, humor. The most favorable depiction is a girl named Ana (anorexia), who represents the goal of the group, the idolization of perfection in this reality. Perfection is about having self-control and being thin. Personified through Ana is a yearning for being untouchable and perfect.[20]

Message-board users write about Ana as their hero. ("Ana knows what to say to make me feel better."[21]) They also confess lapses and seek her forgiveness. ("Dear Ana, I am sorry that I failed you. . . . Not only did I fail you but I binged."[22])

Unlike Ana, Mia (bulimia) isn't seen as perfect. Her role in the drama is to stir up the emotions users feel as they struggle to get down to the elusive perfect weight. Site users rarely describe Mia in positive terms. One post complains, "Mia is SO loud and annoying . . . my Mom heard Mia because she can't keep her [stinking] mouth shut!"[23] Yet other messages reluctantly suggest Mia is needed. "Sometimes she is all right . . . she lets me eat . . . keeps my body pure."[24] The third character in this ongoing drama is the villainous ED (eating disorder). He represents the social norm of moderation and recovery from addiction. McCabe explains why he's so feared: "Members not only try to avoid ED for fear of recovery but the group knows that accepting ED means a loss of community and a reentry into a reality in which eating disorders are a negative attribute."[25]

The discussion of these three characters constructs an alternative world where high-risk dieters aren't hassled. Despite the lurking presence of ED, who reminds everyone of another reality "out there," this positive fantasy type is a closed world where anorexics and bulimics feel safe. McCabe sees humor as the *sanctioning agent* that makes this constructed reality legitimate for site users. The satirical exchange of experiences turns discussion of a deadly disease into a game that validates what these users are doing, saying, and living.

Conversely, the negative fantasy type portrayed on these message boards is "Surviving encounters with The Real World," a distressing place for those who visit these websites. McCabe notes that almost all users log on to get tips on "safe" foods and how to hide their eating habits and symptoms from friends and family. The *scene* of the struggle in "the real world" is almost always part of this fantasy type. Many posts include references to time and space.

> I hate coming home at night. . . . I am with Ana all day and I cannot eat . . . but when I get home Ana stays at the door and I just binge.[26]

> How can I live with Mia if we are sharing community bathrooms in our dorm?[27]

McCabe doesn't explicitly address *plot lines* in her fantasy theme analysis, but from her rich description two plots seem paramount. The first is acting in multiple ways to reduce weight—dieting, exercising, and purging. The second plot is doing whatever one has to do to keep the extent of this obsession with food a secret from those who don't share it.

McCabe concludes that the rhetorical vision of the pro-eating disorder community is the uneasy coexistence of these two contrasting fantasy types—*The humorous world of Ana and Mia* and *Surviving encounters with The Real World*. She writes, "The rhetorical vision shared by this group is the effort to maintain a disease within settings where their belief is challenged and get back to the state where the personification of the disease can proliferate."[28]

THEORY INTO PRACTICE: ADVICE TO IMPROVE YOUR COLLEGE EXPERIENCE

As you've gained an understanding of symbolic convergence theory, you've hopefully thought about its implications for a group in which you take part. No matter what your role in the group, Bormann has offered the following advice:[29]

- When the group begins to share a drama that in your opinion would contribute to a healthy culture, you should pick up the drama and feed the chain.

- If the fantasies are destructive, creating group paranoia or depression, cut the chain off whenever possible.

- To build cohesiveness, use personification to identify your group.

- Be sure to encourage the sharing of dramas depicting your group history early in your meetings.

- Remember that a conscious rhetorical effort on your part can succeed in igniting a chain reaction, but the fantasy may take an unexpected turn.

Bormann and his followers have also used fantasy theme analysis to improve organizational communication, conduct market research, and assess public opinion. To illustrate the pragmatic value of the methodology, John Cragan (University of St. Thomas—Minnesota) and Donald Shields (University of Missouri–St. Louis) require students in their applied research classes to analyze the way high school seniors talk about college. They find that most rhetorical visions employ one of three competing master analogues—a righteous vision, a social vision, or a pragmatic vision.[30]

Potential applicants who embrace a *righteous* vision are interested in a school's academic excellence, the reputation of its faculty, and special programs it offers. Those who adopt a *social* vision view college as a means of getting away from home, meeting new friends, and joining others in a variety of social activities. High school seniors who buy into a *pragmatic* vision are looking for a marketable degree that will help them get a good job. (What was your vision when you entered college?) Knowledge of these distinct visions could help admissions officers at your school develop a strategy to appeal to prospective students who would most appreciate the character of your campus. That knowledge could also help you figure out if you're at a school that can best meet your needs.

CRITIQUE: JUDGING SCT AS BOTH A SCIENTIFIC AND INTERPRETIVE THEORY

Ernest Bormann claimed that symbolic convergence theory is both objective and interpretive. The theory's basic explanatory hypothesis—*sharing group fantasies creates symbolic convergence*—is framed as a universal principle that holds for all people, in any culture, at any time, in any communication context.[31] Definitely objective. But the methodology of determining fantasy themes, fantasy types, and rhetorical visions is rhetorical criticism—a humanistic approach that's undeniably interpretive. Perhaps this unusual mix has stimulated many of the 1,000 original research studies that have examined and applied the theory over the last 40 years.[32] Bormann wryly noted that one positive result from SCT has been the collaboration between "muddleheaded anecdotalists and hardheaded empiricists."[33] When the six standards for judging a social science theory and the six criteria for evaluating an interpretive theory are applied to SCT, the theory stacks up remarkably well. I'll single out four of these benchmarks for further discussion.

1. *A good objective theory explains what occurs and why it happened.* The concept of symbolic convergence can help us make sense of chaotic group discussions. Even though group leaders urge members to *speak one at a time* and *stick to the point*, participants often go off on verbal tangents. According to SCT, graphic digressions and boisterous talk aren't signs of a flawed process; rather, they are evidence that the group is chaining out a fantasy and developing a group consciousness. This explanation of how groups become cohesive is a strength of the theory. However, University of Oklahoma communication professor James Olufowote doesn't believe Bormann's explanation goes far enough. In a sympathetic critique aimed at making the theory better, he contends that "SCT does not sufficiently explain why humans are predisposed to dramatizing reality and sharing fantasy in the first place."[34]

2. *A good objective theory predicts what's going to happen.* SCT clearly predicts that when a fantasy chain erupts among members, symbolic convergence will occur. The theory even suggests that without shared fantasies, there will be little or no cohesiveness. But as discussed earlier in the chapter, SCT researchers have had minimal success predicting when a dramatizing message will trigger a chain reaction. On that point, Bormann noted that uncertainty about the future isn't bothersome in other scientific theories. He saw symbolic convergence theory as similar to Darwin's biological theory of evolution in that respect.

> An evolutionary theory can explain the way modern humans evolved from earlier humanoid individuals. But, such theories cannot predict the future path of evolution. . . . SCT involves a careful cataloguing of group consciousness through time. The theory also includes a description of the dynamic forces that provide a necessary and sufficient set of causes to explain the discovered communication patterns. For an evolution theory the dynamic may be the survival of the fittest. For SCT the dynamic is the process of group sharing.[35]

3. *A good interpretive theory clarifies people's values.* There's no doubt that fantasy theme analysis uncovers the values of a rhetorical community. It does that well. But Olufowote is concerned about the unexamined values that undergird SCT.[36] One concern is an ideology of convergence. The terms that describe its effects—*common ground, meeting of the minds, empathic communion,* etc.—make it clear that the theory has a pro-social bias. Shall we look at the convergence of hate groups or pro-eating disorder websites as a positive outcome?

A second concern Olufowote expresses is an egalitarian assumption that ignores issues of power within groups. For example, do all members of a group benefit equally when a fantasy chains out? Does an *inside joke* become a symbolic cue at the expense of one of the members? A final concern is about the way members of a rhetorical community are characterized. The communities described come across as conflict-free. Differences among members are ignored, and there's little discussion of the inner tension a member feels when the multiple rhetorical visions he or she embraces don't mesh.

4. *A good interpretive theory offers a new understanding of people.* SCT's method of fantasy theme analysis does this exceptionally well by directing rhetorical critics to focus on symbolic language. A few scholars charge that the best fantasy theme analyses are the result of critics' astute perception or acumen rather than the method they use.[37] Bormann acknowledged that some critics do it better than others. But he noted that regardless of how perceptive the critic, the method used makes a huge difference. For example, a Marxist critique looks for economic exploitation; a feminist critique looks for patterns of male dominance. Think how different the analyses of cigar store smokers or pro-eating disorder message-board users would be if DeSantis or McCabe hadn't zeroed in on imaginative language. With that lens in place, fantasy theme analysts uncover rhetorical visions as varied as the communities they study. When I read a well-written fantasy theme analysis, I gain a greater appreciation for the fascinating diversity within the human race.

QUESTIONS TO SHARPEN YOUR FOCUS

1. As a rhetorically sensitive scholar, Bormann defined SCT terms carefully. Can you distinguish between *dramatizing messages* and *fantasies?* Do you understand why it's a difference that makes a difference?

2. Some critics dismiss SCT as a cookie-cutter approach to group analysis. Could this be said of most social science theories? Bormann regarded the charge as a compliment.[38] Can you figure out why he was pleased rather than offended?

3. Bormann insisted that SCT is an objective theory that's valid *any time* and in *any culture*, but that its methodology, *fantasy theme analysis*, is interpretive. Do you regard SCT as a better *objective* or *interpretive* theory? Why?

4. Bormann was intrigued with a T-shirt that proclaims, "I have given up my search for truth. Now I want to find a good fantasy."[39] Based on what you've read, does this slogan reflect the *symbolic world* of SCT advocates? Does it reflect yours?

A SECOND LOOK

Recommended resource: Ernest G. Bormann, John Cragan, and Donald Shields, "Three Decades of Developing, Grounding, and Using Symbolic Convergence Theory (SCT)," in *Communication Yearbook 25*, William Gudykunst (ed.), Lawrence Erlbaum, Mahwah, NJ, 2001, pp. 271–313.

Brief summary: Ernest Bormann, "Symbolic Convergence Theory," in *Small Group Communication Theory & Practice: An Anthology*, 8th ed., Randy Hirokawa, Robert Cathcart, Larry Samovar, and Linda Henman (eds.), Roxbury, Los Angeles, CA, 2003, pp. 39–47.

Early statement of the theory: Ernest G. Bormann, "Fantasy and Rhetorical Vision: The Rhetorical Criticism of Social Reality," *Quarterly Journal of Speech*, Vol. 58, 1972, pp. 396–407.

Small-group context: Ernest G. Bormann and Nancy C. Bormann, *Effective Small Group Communication,* 5th ed., Burgess, Edina, MN, 1992, pp. 105–126.

Organizational context: Ernest G. Bormann, "Symbolic Convergence: Organizational Communication and Culture," in *Communication and Organizations: An Interpretive Approach,* Linda Putnam and Michael Pacanowsky (eds.), Sage, Beverly Hills, CA, 1983, pp. 99–122.

Fantasy theme analysis: Sonja K. Foss, *Rhetorical Criticism: Exploration and Practice,* 4th ed., Waveland, Prospect Heights, IL, 2009, pp. 97–136.

Practical applications of assessing rhetorical visions: John F. Cragan and Donald C. Shields, *Symbolic Theories in Applied Communication Research: Bormann, Burke, and Fisher,* Hampton, Cresskill, NJ, 1995, pp. 161–198.

Cigar store ethnography: Alan D. DeSantis, "Smoke Screen: An Ethnographic Study of a Cigar Shop's Collective Rationalization," *Health Communication,* Vol. 14, 2002, pp. 167–198.

Symbolic convergence in a neighborhood watch group: Cheryl Broom and Susan Avanzino, "The Communication of Community Collaboration: When Rhetorical Visions Collide," *Communication Quarterly,* Vol. 58, 2010, pp. 480–501.

Pro-eating disorder website analysis: Jessi McCabe, "Resisting Alienation: The Social Construction of Internet Communities Supporting Eating Disorders," *Communication Studies,* Vol. 60, 2009, pp. 1–15.

Small-group fantasies becoming rhetorical visions: Ernest Bormann, "The Critical Analysis of Seminal American Fantasies," in *The Force of Fantasy: Restoring the American Dream,* Southern Illinois University, Carbondale, IL, 2001, pp. 1–25.

Early critique: G. P. Mohrmann, "An Essay on Fantasy Theme Criticism" and "Fantasy Theme Criticism: A Peroration," *Quarterly Journal of Speech,* Vol. 68, 1982, pp. 109–132, 306–313.

Response to early critics: Ernest G. Bormann, John Cragan, and Donald Shields, "In Defense of Symbolic Convergence Theory: A Look at the Theory and Its Criticisms After Two Decades," *Communication Theory,* Vol. 4, 1994, pp. 259–294.

Contemporary critique: James O. Olufowote, "Rousing and Redirecting a Sleeping Giant: Symbolic Convergence Theory and Complexities in the Communicative Constitution of Collective Action," *Management Communication Quarterly,* Vol. 19, 2006, pp. 451–492.

Will our group stay like this or will it change?
Poole's Adaptive Structuration Theory answers this question.
Click on Archive under Theory Resources at
www.afirstlook.com.

Organizational Communication

What do the following organizations have in common—the *United States Navy, McDonald's, General Motors,* and the *Green Bay Packers?* The first three are gigantic organizations, the middle two sell a tangible product, and the last three are publicly owned corporations that try to make a profit. But in terms of organizational communication, their most important common feature is that each is a prime example of *classical management theory* in action. Figure OC–1 lists some of the principles of this traditional approach to management.

Classical management theory places a premium on productivity, precision, and efficiency. As York University (Toronto) professor Gareth Morgan notes, these are the very qualities you expect from a well-designed, smoothly running machine. Morgan uses the mechanistic metaphor because he finds significant parallels between mechanical devices and the way managers traditionally think about their organizations.[1] In classical management theory, workers are seen as cogs in vast machines that function smoothly as long as their range of motion is clearly defined and their actions are lubricated with an adequate hourly wage.

Machines repeat straightforward, repetitive tasks, just as McDonald's workers have cooked billions of hamburgers, each one in exactly the same way. Machines have interchangeable parts that can be replaced when broken or worn out, just as a National Football League coach can insert a new player into the tight-end slot when the current starter is injured or begins to slow down. A new Chevy Tahoe comes with a thick operator's manual that specifies how the van should be driven, but the GM employee handbook is thicker and contains even more detailed instructions on how things are done within the company. As for the U.S. Navy, the fleet is an integral part of the country's war machine, and officers at every level are most comfortable when it runs like one.

Unity of command—an employee should receive orders from only one superior.

Scalar chain—the line of authority from superior to subordinate, which runs from top to bottom of the organization; this chain, which results from the unity-of-command principle, should be used as a channel for communication and decision making.

Division of work—management should aim to achieve a degree of specialization designed to achieve the goal of the organization in an efficient manner.

Authority and responsibility—attention should be paid to the right to give orders and to exact obedience; an appropriate balance between authority and responsibility should be achieved.

Discipline—obedience, application, energy, behavior, and outward marks of respect in accordance with agreed rules and customs.

Subordination of individual interest to general interest—through firmness, example, fair agreements, and constant supervision.

FIGURE OC–1   Selected Principles of Classical Management Theory
Excerpted from Gareth Morgan, "Organizations as Machines," in *Images of Organizations*

"Bad news, hon. I got replaced by an app."

The three theories in this section view classical management theory as outmoded and reject the idea that organization members are like replaceable parts. Each approach searches for ways of thinking about organizations other than as machines. The *cultural approach* looks for stories and shared meanings that are unique to a given organization. The *constitutive approach* believes communication itself is the essence of any organization. And the *critical approach* looks at organizations as political systems where conflict and power should be negotiated openly. Above all, the theorists who employ these approaches are committed to developing humane ways of talking about people and the organizational tasks they do.

CHAPTER **19**

Objective   Interpretive

Socio-cultural tradition
Semiotic tradition

Cultural Approach to Organizations

of Clifford Geertz & Michael Pacanowsky

The late Princeton anthropologist Clifford Geertz wrote that "man is an animal suspended in webs of significance that he himself has spun."[1] He pictured culture as those webs. In order to travel across the strands toward the center of the web, an outsider must discover the common interpretations that hold the web together. Culture is shared meaning, shared understanding, shared sensemaking.

Geertz conducted field research in the islands of Indonesia and on the Moroccan highlands, rural settings remote from industrial activity. His best-known monograph is an in-depth symbolic analysis of the Balinese cockfight. Geertz never wrote a treatise on the bottom line, never tried to decipher the significance of the office Christmas party, and never met a payroll—a disqualifying sin in the eyes of many business professionals. Despite his silence on the topic of big business, Geertz' interpretive approach has proved useful in making sense of organizational activity.

In the field of communication, former University of Colorado professor Michael Pacanowsky has applied Geertz' cultural insights to organizational life. He says that if culture consists of webs of meaning that people have spun, and if spun webs imply the act of spinning, "then we need to concern ourselves not only with the structures of cultural webs, but with the process of their spinning as well."[2] That process is communication. It is communication that "creates and constitutes the taken-for-granted reality of the world."[3]

CULTURE AS A METAPHOR OF ORGANIZATIONAL LIFE

The use of culture as a root metaphor was undoubtedly stimulated by Western fascination with the economic success of Japanese corporations in the 1970s and 1980s. Back then, when American business leaders traveled to the Far East to study methods of production, they discovered that the superior quantity and quality of

Japan's industrial output had less to do with technology than with workers' shared cultural value of loyalty to each other and to their corporation. Organizations look radically different depending on how people in the host culture structure meaning. Communal face-saving in Japan is foreign to the class antagonism of Great Britain or the we're-number-one competitive mindset of the United States.

Today the term *corporate culture* means different things to different people. Some observers use the phrase to describe the surrounding environment that constrains a company's freedom of action. (U.S. workers would scoff at singing a corporate anthem at the start of their working day.) Others use the term to refer to a quality or property of the organization. (Acme Gizmo is a friendly place to work.) They speak of *culture* as synonymous with *image, character,* or *climate.* But Pacanowsky is committed to Geertz' symbolic approach and thus considers culture as more than a single variable in organizational research:

> Organizational culture is not just another piece of the puzzle; it is the puzzle. From our point of view, culture is not something an organization has; a culture is something an organization is.[4]

WHAT CULTURE IS; WHAT CULTURE IS NOT

Geertz admitted that the concept of culture as *systems of shared meaning* is somewhat vague and difficult to grasp. Though popular usage equates culture with concerts and art museums, he refused to use the word to signify *less primitive.* No modern anthropologist would fall into the trap of classifying people as high- or low-culture.

Culture
Webs of significance; systems of shared meaning.

Culture is not whole or undivided. Geertz pointed out that even close-knit societies have subcultures and countercultures within their boundaries. For example, employees in the sales and accounting departments of the same company may eye each other warily—the first group calling the accountants *number crunchers* and *bean counters,* the accountants in turn labeling members of the sales force *fast talkers* and *glad-handers.* Despite their differences, both groups may regard the blue-collar bowling night of the production workers as a strange ritual compared with their own weekend ritual of a round of golf.

For Pacanowsky, the web of organizational culture is the residue of employees' performance—"those very actions by which members constitute and reveal their culture to themselves and to others."[5] He notes that job performance may play only a minor role in the enactment of corporate culture.

Cultural performance
Actions by which members constitute and reveal their culture to themselves and others; an ensemble of texts.

> People do get the job done, true (though probably not with the singleminded task-orientation communication texts would have us believe); but people in organizations also gossip, joke, knife one another, initiate romantic involvements, cue new employees to ways of doing the least amount of work that still avoids hassles from a supervisor, talk sports, arrange picnics.[6]

Geertz called these cultural performances "an ensemble of texts . . . which the anthropologist strains to read over the shoulder of those to whom they properly belong."[7] The elusive nature of culture prompted Geertz to label its study a *soft science.* It is "not an experimental science in search of law, but an interpretive one in search of meaning."[8] The corporate observer is one part scientist, one part drama critic.

The fact that symbolic expression requires interpretation is nicely captured in a story about Pablo Picasso recorded by York University (Toronto) professor Gareth Morgan.[9] A man commissioned Picasso to paint a portrait of his wife. Startled by the nonrepresentational image on the canvas, the woman's husband complained, "It isn't how she really looks." When asked by the painter how she really looked, the man produced a photograph from his wallet. Picasso's comment: "Small, isn't she?"

THICK DESCRIPTION: WHAT ETHNOGRAPHERS DO

Geertz referred to himself as an *ethnographer,* one whose job is to sort out the symbolic meanings of people's actions within their culture. Just as geographers chart the physical territory, ethnographers map out social discourse. They do this "to discover who people think they are, what they think they are doing, and to what end they think they are doing it."[10] There's no shortcut for the months of participant observation required to collect an exhaustive account of interaction. Without that raw material, there would be nothing to interpret.

Ethnography
Mapping out social discourse; discovering who people within a culture think they are, what they think they are doing, and to what end they think they are doing it.

Geertz spent years in Indonesia and Morocco, developing his deep description of separate cultures. Pacanowsky initially invested nine months with W. L. Gore & Associates, best known for its Gore-Tex line of sports clothing and equipment. Like Geertz, he was completely open about his research goals, and during the last five months of his research he participated fully in problem-solving conferences at the company. Later, Pacanowsky spent additional time at the W. L. Gore plants in Delaware as a consultant. In order to become intimately familiar with an organization *as members experience it,* ethnographers must commit to the long haul. Pacanowsky did commit to the long haul of working full time at Gore, this despite his earlier caution against "going native." He had previously advised ethnographers to assume an attitude of "radical naïveté" that would make it possible for them to "experience organizational life as 'strange.'" This stance of wonder would help them get past taken-for-granted interpretations of what's going on and what it means to insiders. When Pacanowsky went to work for Gore, he no longer had that opportunity.[11]

Thick description
A record of the intertwined layers of common meaning that underlie what a particular people say and do.

The daily written accounts of intensive observation invariably fill the pages of many ethnographic notebooks. The visual image of these journals stacked on top of each other would be sufficient justification for Geertz to refer to ethnography as *thick description.* The term, however, describes the intertwined layers of common meaning that underlie what a particular people say and do. Thick descriptions are powerful reconstructions, not just detailed observations.[12] After Geertz popularized the concept, most ethnographers realized their task is to:

1. Accurately describe talk and actions and the context in which they occur.
2. Capture the thoughts, emotions, and web of social interactions.
3. Assign motivation, intention, or purpose to what people say and do.
4. Artfully write this up so readers feel they've experienced the events.
5. Interpret what happened; explain what it means within this culture.[13]

Thick description is tracing the many strands of a cultural web and tracking evolving meaning. No matter how high the stack of an ethnographer's notes, without interpretation, they would still be *thin* description.

Thick description starts with a state of bewilderment. *What the devil's going on?* Geertz asked himself as he waded into a new culture. The only way to reduce the puzzlement is to observe as if one were a stranger in a foreign land. This can be difficult for a manager who is already enmeshed in a specific corporate culture. He or she might overlook many of the signs that point to common interpretation. Worse, the manager might assume that office humor or the company grapevine has the same significance for people in this culture as it does for those in a previous place of employment. Geertz said it will always be different.

Behaviorists would probably consider employee trips to the office watercooler or coffee machine of little interest. If they did regard these breaks worth studying, they would tend to note the number of trips and length of stay for each worker. Ethnographers would be more interested in the significance this seemingly mundane activity had for these particular employees. Instead of a neat statistical summary, they'd record pages of dialogue while workers were standing around with a cup in their hands. Pacanowsky fears that a frequency count would only bleach human behavior of the very properties that interest him. Classifying performances across organizations would yield superficial generalizations at the cost of localized insight. He'd rather find out what makes a particular tribal culture unique.

Although Pacanowsky would pay attention to all cultural performances, he would be particularly sensitive to the imaginative language members used, the stories they told, and the nonverbal rites and rituals they practiced. Taken together, these three forms of communication provide helpful access to the unique shared meanings within an organization.

METAPHORS: TAKING LANGUAGE SERIOUSLY

Metaphor
Clarifies what is unknown or confusing by equating it with an image that's more familiar or vivid.

When used by members throughout an organization (and not just management), *metaphors* can offer the ethnographer a starting place for accessing the shared meaning of a corporate culture. Pacanowsky records a number of prominent metaphors used at W. L. Gore & Associates, none more significant than the oft-heard reference within the company to Gore as a *lattice organization.*[14] If one tried to graph the lines of communication at Gore, the map would look like a lattice rather than the traditional pyramid-shaped organizational chart. The crosshatched lines would show the importance of one-on-one communication and reflect the fact that no person within the company needs permission to talk to anyone else. Easy access to others is facilitated by an average plant size of 150 employees and a variety of electronic media that encourage quick responses.

This lack of hierarchical authority within the lattice organization is captured in the egalitarian title of *associate* given to every worker. People do have differential status at Gore, but it comes from technical expertise, a track record of good judgment, and evidence of follow-through that leads to accomplishment.

The company's stated objective (singular) is "to make money and have fun."[15] The founder, Bill Gore, was famous for popping into associates' offices and asking, "Did you make any money today? Did you have any fun today?" But work at Gore is not frivolous. The *waterline* operating principle makes it clear that associates should check with others before making significant decisions:

Each of us will consult with appropriate Associates who will share the responsibility of taking any action that has the potential of serious harm to the reputation, success, or survival of the Enterprise. The analogy is that our Enterprise is like a ship that we are all in together. Boring holes above the waterline is not serious, but below the waterline, holes could sink us.[16]

When Kevin read about the emphasis Pacanowsky placed on metaphors, he analyzed their use among fellow computer-savvy student employees at Wheaton:

> As a student worker at ResNet, the technical support branch of our campus Internet service provider, I have become aware of our corporate culture. One thing I have noticed is we often talk about our department using the metaphor of a fortress wall. Computing Services makes decisions and institutes policy, and it's our responsibility to handle the waves of students with resulting problems. We talk about "stemming the flow" of students with problems and "manning the phones" or "manning the desk." We also talk about how we "take the blow" for the decisions of our superiors.

This realization later served Kevin and Wheaton students well when, after graduation, Kevin was hired as manager of the ResNet program. Desiring to change the fortress mentality that had permeated the organization, Kevin in effect "lowered the drawbridge" to give students easy access to computer help. He extended hours into the evening, established help desks in each of the dorms, and did away with the keypad locked door that had prevented face-to-face contact with frustrated users. Two years later, ResNet workers talked about themselves as guiding students on paths through a jungle—a more proactive metaphor that suggests the culture has changed.

Pacanowsky suggests that "fictional descriptions, by the very nature of their implicitness and impressionism can fully capture . . . both the bold outlines and the crucial nuances of cultural ethos."[17] Many TV critics believe the show *Mad Men* reliably reflects the culture of a 1960s New York advertising agency, not just in the retro style of clothing and cars, but in the dialogue. If so, the metaphors these men employ should reveal the shared meaning within their organizational culture.

In the very first episode of the series, Pete Campbell, a junior account executive, sucks up to Don Draper, creative director at the Sterling Cooper ad agency: "A man like you, I'd follow you into combat blindfolded and I wouldn't be the first. Am I right, buddy?" Don responds, "Let's take it a little slower. I don't want to wake up pregnant."[18] The obvious meaning is for Pete to back off, and Pete's muttered curse as Don walks away shows he gets the message. But there are overlapping layers of meaning within the *wake-up-pregnant* imagery that reflect the underlying culture that's Sterling Cooper.

Sexual allusions are present in almost every conversation among men at the agency, regardless of whether women are present. So is power. The self-described *mad men* are all highly competitive. Despite a surface backslapping camaraderie, in this ad game, it's every man for himself. Men at Sterling Cooper score by winning the multimillion dollar account or sleeping with a pretty associate. Losing is getting pregnant, which doesn't happen to men. And if it happens to you physically or metaphorically, you're on your own. So a guy has to be on guard lest he come to the office one morning and discover he's been screwed.

Can these multiple meanings really be teased out of a single metaphor heard only once? Probably not without other symbolic clues to collaborate the interpretation. Yet regular viewers of *Mad Men* who listen and watch with an ethnographer's mindset can look back on this first episode and realize that Draper's *wake-up-pregnant* metaphor is both a lens into the culture they've come to know and an artifact of it.

THE SYMBOLIC INTERPRETATION OF STORY

Stories that are told over and over provide a convenient window through which to view corporate webs of significance. Pacanowsky asks, "Has a good story been told that takes you to the heart of the matter?"[19] He focuses on the scriptlike qualities of narratives that portray an employee's part in the company play. Although workers have room to improvise, the anecdotes provide clues to what it means to perform a task in this particular theater. Stories capture memorable performances and convey the passion the actor felt at the time.

Pacanowsky suggests three types of narrative that dramatize organizational life. *Corporate stories* carry the ideology of management and reinforce company policy. Every McDonald's franchisee hears about the late Ray Kroc, who, when he was chairman of the board, picked up trash from the parking lot when he'd visit a store.

Personal stories are those that employees tell about themselves, often defining how they would like to be seen within the organization. If you've seen reruns of NBC's *The Office*, you've witnessed Dwight Schrute's interviews with the camera crew. During these interviews, he talks about his excellence as an employee and how he deserves the respect of others in the Dunder Mifflin paper company. These are Dwight's personal accounts.

Collegial stories are positive or negative anecdotes told about others in the organization. When the camera crew interviews Dwight's colleagues Jim and Pam, we hear stories of Dwight's eccentricity and lack of basic social awareness. These collegial stories describe Dwight as someone who is not to be taken seriously. Since these tales aren't usually sanctioned by management, collegial accounts convey how the organization "really works."

Corporate stories
Tales that carry management ideology and reinforce company policy.

Personal stories
Tales told by employees that put them in a favorable light.

Collegial stories
Positive or negative anecdotes about others in the organization; descriptions of how things "really work."

Stories at Dixie

Throughout most of my life, I've had access to some of the cultural lore of Dixie Communications, a medium-size corporation that operates a newspaper and a television station in a Southern city. Like so many other regional companies, Dixie has been taken over by an out-of-state corporation that has no local ties. The following three narratives are shorthand versions of stories heard again and again throughout the company.

> Although the original publisher has been dead for many years, old-timers fondly recall how he would spend Christmas Eve with the workers in the press room. Their account is invariably linked with reminders that he initiated health benefits and profit sharing prior to any union demand. (Corporate story)

> The current comptroller is the highest-ranking "local boy" in the corporation. He often tells the story about the first annual audit he performed long before computers were installed. Puzzled when he ran across a bill for 50 pounds of pigeon feed, he discovered that the company used homing pigeons to send in news copy and circulation orders from a town across the bay. The story usually concludes with an editorial comment about pigeons being more reliable than the new machines. His self-presentation reminds listeners that he has always been cost-conscious, yet it also aligns him with the human side of the "warm people versus cold machines" issue. (Personal story)

> Shortly after the takeover, a department head encouraged the new publisher to meet with his people for a few minutes at the end of the day. The new boss

declined the invitation on the grounds of efficiency: "To be quite candid, I don't want to know about a woman's sick child or a man's vacation plans. That kind of information makes it harder to fire a person." Spoken in a cold, superior tone, the words *quite candid* are always part of the story. (Collegial story)

Both Geertz and Pacanowsky caution against any analysis that says, "This story means. . . ." Narratives contain a mosaic of significance and defy a simplistic, one-on-one translation of symbols. Yet taken as a whole, the three stories reveal an uneasiness with the new management. This interpretation is consistent with repeated metaphorical references to the old Dixie as *family* and the new Dixie as *a faceless computer*.

RITUAL: THIS IS THE WAY IT'S ALWAYS BEEN AND ALWAYS WILL BE

Geertz wrote about the Balinese rite of cockfighting because the contest represented more than a game. "It is only apparently cocks that are fighting there. Actually it is men." The cockfight is a dramatization of status. "Its function is interpretive: It is a Balinese reading of Balinese experience, a story they tell themselves about themselves."[20]

Ritual
Texts that articulate multiple aspects of cultural life, often marking rites of passage or life transitions.

Pacanowsky agrees with Geertz that some rituals (like the Balinese cockfight) are "texts" that articulate *multiple* aspects of cultural life.[21] These rituals are nearly sacred, and any attempt to change them meets with strong resistance. Although the emphasis on improvisation and novelty reduces the importance of ritual at Gore, organizational rites at more traditional companies weave together many threads of corporate culture.

More than a generation ago, workers in the classified advertising department at Dixie created an integrative rite that survives to the present. The department is staffed by more than 50 telephone sales representatives who work out of a large common room. At Dixie, these representatives not only take the "two lines/two days/two dollars" personal ads over the phone, they also initiate callbacks to find out if customers were successful and might want to sell other items. Despite the advent of eBay and other online sites for buying and selling, classified advertising at Dixie is a major profit center with low employee turnover. The department continues to have the *family atmosphere* of premerger Dixie. Most of the phone representatives are women under the age of 40. They regard Max, the male manager who has held his position for 35 years, as a *father confessor*—a warm, nonjudgmental person who has genuine concern for their lives. Whenever a female employee has a baby, Max visits her in the hospital and offers help to those at home preparing for her return. Women announce their pregnancy by taping a dime within a large picture frame on the outer wall of Max' office, inscribing their name and anticipated day of delivery. This rite of integration serves multiple functions for the women:

> At a time of potential anxiety, it is an occasion for public affirmation from the larger community.

> The rite is a point of contact between work and those outside Dixie. Employees often take pride in describing the ritual to customers and friends.

> Although the dime-on-the-wall practice originated with the workers, the authorized chronicle of decades of expected births proclaims a sense of permanence. It says, in effect: "The company doesn't consider motherhood a liability; your job will be here when you get back."

From the management's standpoint, the rite ensures there will be no surprises. Max has plenty of time to schedule the employee's maternity leave, arrange for another salesperson to cover her accounts, and anticipate stresses she might be encountering.

It is tempting to read economic significance into the fact that employees use dimes to symbolize this major change in their lives. But the women involved refer to the small size of the token rather than its monetary value. Geertz and Pacanowsky would caution that this is *their* story; we should listen to *their* interpretation.

CAN THE MANAGER BE AN AGENT OF CULTURAL CHANGE?

The popularity of the cultural metaphor when it was first introduced to the corporate world in the 1980s was undoubtedly due to business leaders' desire to shape interpretation within the organization. Symbols are the tools of management. Executives don't operate forklifts or produce widgets; they cast vision, state goals, process information, send memos, and engage in other symbolic behavior. If they believe culture is the key to worker commitment, productivity, and sales, the possibility of changing culture becomes a seductive idea. Creating favorable metaphors, planting organizational stories, and establishing rites would seem an ideal way to create a corporate myth that would serve managerial interests.

But once a corporate culture exists, can it be altered by a manager? Geertz regarded shared interpretations as naturally emerging from all members of a group rather than consciously engineered by leaders. In *The Office,* Jim, Pam, Stanley, and Phyllis all play a part in developing their corporate culture. And you'll notice that, despite his best efforts, manager Michael Scott can't alter it single-handedly. Managers may articulate a new vision in a fresh vocabulary, but it is the workers who smile, sigh, snicker, or scoff. For example, Martin Luther King's "I Have a Dream" speech, which will be discussed in Chapter 22, was powerful because he struck a chord that was already vibrating within millions of listeners.

Shared meanings are hard to dispel. Symbol watchers within a company quickly discount the words of management if they don't square with performance. But even if culture *could* be changed, there still remains the question of whether it *should* be. Symbolic anthropologists have traditionally adopted a nonintrusive style appropriate to examining fine crystal—look, admire, but don't touch. So managers

who regard themselves as agents of cultural change create bull-in-a-china-shop fears for ethnographers who have ethical concerns about how their corporate analyses might be used. University of Massachusetts management professor Linda Smircich notes that ethnographers would draw back in horror at the idea of using their data to extend a tribal priest's control over the population, yet most communication consultants are hired by top management to do just that.[22]

CRITIQUE: IS THE CULTURAL APPROACH USEFUL?

The cultural approach adopts and refines the qualitative research methodology of ethnography to gain a new understanding of a specific group of people. A crucial part of that understanding is a clarification of values within the culture under study. Today, however, there isn't the excitement about the cultural approach to organizations that there was when interpretive scholars introduced it in the 1980s. Perhaps that's because many researchers trained in organizational communication are hired as consultants by corporate managers who are looking for change. By now you understand that Geertz would regard the quest to alter culture as both inappropriate and virtually impossible. This purist position exposes him and his admirers within our discipline to criticism from corporate consultants who not only desire to understand organizational communication, but also want to influence it. That was certainly Kevin's ambition when he was hired to manage the ResNet technical support program at Wheaton.

If a thick description of the web of meanings within an organization can't be used to change the culture, how can the cost in time and money of an ethnographic study be justified? Better employee recruitment is one answer. Traditionally, companies stress their attractive features and downplay characteristics that potential hires would find disturbing. So it's only after the firm has spent about $15,000 to recruit, assess, orient, and train a new employee that the newcomer finds out if he or she is suited for the job. Early resignations are costly and leave everyone disgruntled.

Managers are learning that they can cut costs and avoid hassles by providing a realistic job preview right from the start.[23] Offering recruits a sensitive analysis of the culture they'd be entering gives potential hires the chance to make an informed decision as to whether they will fit within it or not. And for those who take the plunge, the shared knowledge of what means what within the organization will reduce mistakes and misunderstandings. W. C. Gore's subsequent hiring of Pacanowsky shows the high regard the founder placed on the theorist's thick description.

A different kind of objection comes from critical theorists who fault the cultural approach because interpretive scholars like Geertz and Pacanowsky refuse to evaluate the customs they portray. For example, if Pacanowsky were to discover that female associates at Gore hit a glass ceiling when they try to advance, these advocates insist he should *expose* and *deplore* this injustice rather than merely *describe* and *interpret* it for readers.[24] For researchers who take a cultural approach to organizational life, this criticism misses the point of their work. The purpose of ethnography is not to pass moral judgment or reform society. The goal of symbolic analysis is to create a better understanding of what it takes to function effectively within a culture.

Anthropologist Adam Kuper is critical of Geertz for his emphasis on interpretation rather than behavioral observation. Because if, as Geertz claimed, "we begin with our own interpretations of what our informants are up to or think they are up to and then systematize those,"[25] who's to say the meaning assigned by the ethnographer is right?[26] Kuper is afraid that the past experiences and biases of interpretive researchers will shape the conclusions they reach. But for Geertz, members within the culture are the ones who verify a thick description. Participant-observers need to check out their interpretation with the "natives" in their study. It's their culture. They should recognize the "truth" of the story told about them.[27] In organizational research, that means members affirming the ethnographer's construction of what's going on. (*Right. You've got it. That's what this means.*)

There might be another reason why interest in the cultural approach has waned in recent years. In Chapter 3, I cited *aesthetic appeal* as one of the criteria for a good interpretive theory. The force of an ethnographic analysis depends in large measure on the prose in which it's couched. In the *Times Literary Supplement* (U.K.), T. M. Luhrmann gives testimony to the compelling power of Geertz' writing: "Rarely has there been a social scientist who has also been so acute a writer; perhaps there has never been one so quotable."[28] Indeed, Geertz' interpretation of a Balinese cockfight reads like an engrossing novel that the reader can't put down. Though Pacanowsky writes well, it may not be until a perceptive ethnographer with Geertz' compelling way with words focuses on organizational life that the cultural approach to organizations will spark renewed interest.

QUESTIONS TO SHARPEN YOUR FOCUS

1. Based on the concept of organizational culture as a system of *shared meaning*, how would you describe the culture at your school to a prospective student?

2. Anthropologists say, "We don't know who discovered water, but we know it wasn't the fish." Does this adage suggest that it's foolish to ask members of a culture to verify or challenge an *ethnographer's interpretation*?

3. Think of your extended family as an *organizational culture*. What family *ritual* might you analyze to *interpret* the webs of significance you share for someone visiting your home?

4. What favorite *story* do you tell others about your most recent place of employment? Is it a *corporate*, *personal*, or *collegial* narrative?

SELF-QUIZ   For chapter self-quizzes, go to the book's Online Learning Center at
www.mhhe.com/griffin9e

A SECOND LOOK   *Recommended resource:* Clifford Geertz, *The Interpretation of Cultures*, Basic Books, New York, 1973. (See especially "Thick Description: Toward an Interpretive Theory of Culture," pp. 3–30; and "Deep Play: Notes on the Balinese Cockfight," pp. 412–453.)

Culture as performance: Michael Pacanowsky and Nick O'Donnell-Trujillo, "Organizational Communication as Cultural Performance," *Communication Monographs*, Vol. 50, 1983, pp. 127–147.

Nonmanagerial orientation: Michael Pacanowsky and Nick O'Donnell-Trujillo, "Communication and Organizational Cultures," *Western Journal of Speech Communication*, Vol. 46, 1982, pp. 115–130.

Thick description: Joseph G. Ponterotto, "Brief Note on the Origins, Evolution, and Meaning of the Qualitative Research Concept 'Thick Description,'" *The Qualitative Report*, Vol. 11, 2006, pp. 538–549.

Cultural metaphor: Gareth Morgan, "Creating Social Reality: Organizations as Cultures," in *Images of Organization*, Sage, Newbury Park, CA, 1986, pp. 111–140.

Corporate ethnography: Michael Pacanowsky, "Communication in the Empowering Organization," in *Communication Yearbook 11*, James Anderson (ed.), Sage, Newbury Park, CA, 1988, pp. 356–379.

Corporate stories: Joanne Martin, Martha Feldman, Mary Jo Hatch, and Sim Sitkin, "The Uniqueness Paradox in Organizational Stories," *Administrative Science Quarterly*, Vol. 28, 1983, pp. 438–453.

Rites: Harrison Trice and Janice Beyer, "Studying Organizational Cultures Through Rites and Ceremonials," *Academy of Management Review*, Vol. 9, 1984, pp. 653–669.

Interpretive vs. objective approach: Linda L. Putnam, "The Interpretive Perspective: An Alternative to Functionalism," in *Communication and Organizations: An Interpretive Approach*, Linda L. Putnam and Michael Pacanowsky (eds.), Sage, Newbury Park, CA, 1982, pp. 31–54.

Brief autobiography: Clifford Geertz, "A Life of Learning" (ACLS Occasional Paper No. 45), American Council of Learned Societies, New York, 1999.

Webs of shared meaning in sports: Nick Trujillo, "Reflections on Communication and Sport: On Ethnography and Organizations," *Communication and Sport*, Vol. 1, 2013, pp. 68–75.

Fiction as scholarship: Michael Pacanowsky, "Slouching Towards Chicago," *Quarterly Journal of Speech*, Vol. 74, 1988, pp. 453–469.

Interpretive research: Bryan Taylor and Nick Trujillo, "Qualitative Research Methods," in *The New Handbook of Organizational Communication*, Fredric Jablin and Linda L. Putnam (eds.), Sage, Thousand Oaks, CA, 2001, pp. 161–194.

History and critique of Geertz: Adam Kuper, *Culture: The Anthropologists' Account*, Harvard University, Cambridge, MA, 1999, pp. 75–121.

For links to relevant websites and YouTube videos,
click on Links under Theory Resources at
www.afirstlook.com.

P u b l i c   R h e t o r i c

Aristotle defined rhetoric as "an ability, in each particular case, to see the available means of persuasion."[1] That designation centers attention on the intentional act of using words to have an effect. I use the term *public rhetoric* in this section to refer to a speaking context in which the orator has an opportunity to monitor and adjust to the response of his or her immediate audience.

For citizens of ancient Greece, knowing how to speak in public was part of their democratic responsibility. Later on, when Rome ruled the world, rhetorical ability was a survival skill in the rough-and-tumble politics of the forum. Rhetoricians have always had a special interest in judicial argument, legislative debate, political rallies, religious sermons, and speeches given at celebrations. In each setting, teachers and practitioners champion the art of rhetoric as a means of ensuring that speakers of truth are not at a disadvantage when trying to win the hearts and minds of an audience.

The Greeks and Romans distinguished five parts, or divisions, of the study of rhetoric:

1. *Invention*—discovery of convincing arguments
2. *Arrangement*—organization of material for best impact
3. *Style*—selection of compelling and appropriate language
4. *Delivery*—coordination of voice and gestures
5. *Memory*—mastery and rehearsal of content

With the possible exception of memory, these concerns of rhetoric require that a speaker first analyze and then adapt to a specific group of listeners. We can, of course, react to the idea of audience adaptation in two different ways. If we view speakers who adjust their message to fit a specific audience in a positive light, we'll praise their rhetorical sensitivity and flexibility. If we view them negatively, we'll condemn them for their pandering and lack of commitment to the truth. Rhetorical thought across history swings back and forth between these two conflicting poles. The words of most rhetoricians reflect the tension they feel between "telling it like it is" and telling it in such a way that the audience will listen.

Greek philosopher Plato regarded rhetoric as mostly flattery. Far from seeing it as an art, he described rhetoric as a *knack*—similar to the clever use of cosmetics. Both are attempts to make things seem better than they really are.[2] In spite of his scorn, Plato imagined an ideal rhetoric based on a speaker's understanding of listeners with different natures and dispositions.

Plato's ideal discourse was an elite form of dialogue meant for private, rather than public, consumption. This philosophic, one-on-one mode of communication is known as *dialectic* (a different meaning for the term than its use in Baxter and Montgomery's relational dialectics). Unlike typical oratory in Athens, where speakers addressed large audiences on civic issues, Plato's dialectic focused on exploring eternal Truths in an intimate setting.

Although Plato hoped that philosophic dialectic would supplant public rhetoric, his best student, Aristotle, rejuvenated public rhetoric as a serious academic subject. More than 2,000 years ago, Aristotle's *Rhetoric* systematically explored the topics

282 *GROUP AND PUBLIC COMMUNICATION*

"I found the old format much more exciting."

© Arnie Levin/The New Yorker Collection/www.cartoonbank.com

of speaker, message, and audience. His ideas have stood the test of time and form a large portion of the advice presented in contemporary public speaking texts. But even though Aristotle defined rhetoric as the art of discovering all available means of persuasion, this conception doesn't solve the problem of how to get audiences to listen to hard truths.

Religious rhetors face the same paradox. In many ways the apostle Paul seemed to personify the lover of diverse souls that Plato had earlier described. In his first letter to the Corinthians, Paul reminds the people of Corinth that he made a conscious decision to let his message speak for itself: "My speech and my proclamation were not with plausible words of wisdom."[3] Yet further on in the same letter he outlines a conscious rhetorical strategy: "I have become all things to all people, that I might by all means save some."[4] Four centuries later, Augustine continued to justify the conscious use of rhetoric by the church. Why, he asked, should defenders of truth be long-winded, confusing, and boring, when the speech of liars was brief, clear, and persuasive?

The tension between the logic of a message and the appeal it has for an audience isn't easily resolved. British philosopher Francis Bacon sought to integrate the two concerns when he wrote that "the duty of rhetoric is to apply Reason to Imagination for the better moving of the will."[5]

The three rhetoricians I introduce in this section face the dilemma that rhetoricians have struggled with since Plato: "How do you move an audience without changing your message or losing your integrity?" As you read, see which theorist comes up with an answer that is most satisfying for you.

CHAPTER 22

Objective   Interpretive

Rhetorical tradition

The Rhetoric

of Aristotle

Aristotle was a student of Plato's in the golden age of Greek civilization, four centuries before the birth of Christ. He became a respected instructor at Plato's Academy but disagreed with his mentor over the place of public speaking in Athenian life.

Ancient Greece was known for its traveling speech teachers called Sophists. Particularly in Athens, those teachers trained aspiring lawyers and politicians to participate effectively in the courts and deliberative councils. In hindsight, they appear to have been innovative educators who offered a needed and wanted service.[1] But since their advice was underdeveloped theoretically, Plato scoffed at the Sophists' oratorical devices. His skepticism is mirrored today in the negative way people use the term *mere rhetoric* to label the speech of *tricky* lawyers, *mealy-mouthed* politicians, *spellbinding* preachers, and *fast-talking* salespeople.

Aristotle, like Plato, deplored the demagoguery of speakers using their skill to move an audience while showing a casual indifference to the truth. But unlike Plato, he saw the tools of rhetoric as a neutral means by which the orator could either accomplish noble ends or further fraud: ". . . by using these justly one would do the greatest good, and unjustly, the greatest harm."[2] Aristotle believed truth has a moral superiority that makes it more acceptable than falsehood. But unscrupulous opponents of the truth may fool a dull audience unless an ethical speaker uses all possible means of persuasion to counter the error. Speakers who neglect the art of rhetoric have only themselves to blame when their hearers choose falsehood. Success requires wisdom *and* eloquence.

Both the *Politics* and the *Ethics* of Aristotle are polished and well-organized books compared with the rough prose and arrangement of his text on rhetoric. The *Rhetoric* apparently consists of Aristotle's reworked lecture notes for his course at the academy. Despite the uneven nature of the writing, the *Rhetoric* is a searching study of audience psychology. Aristotle raised rhetoric to a science by systematically exploring the effects of the speaker, the speech, and the audience. He regarded the speaker's use of this knowledge as an art. Quite likely, the text your communication department uses for its public speaking classes is basically a contemporary recasting of the audience analysis provided by Aristotle more than two thousand years ago.

RHETORIC: MAKING PERSUASION PROBABLE

Rhetoric
Discovering all possible
means of persuasion.

Aristotle saw the function of *rhetoric* as the discovery in each case of "the available means of persuasion." He never spelled out what he meant by persuasion, but his concern with noncoercive methods makes it clear that he ruled out force of law, torture, and war. His threefold classification of speech situations according to the nature of the audience shows that he had affairs of state in mind.

The first in Aristotle's classification is courtroom (forensic) speaking, which addresses judges who are trying to render a just decision about actions alleged to have taken place in the *past*. The closing arguments presented by the prosecution and defense in the trial of George Zimmerman for killing an unarmed Trayvon Martin are examples of judicial rhetoric centered on guilt or innocence. The second, ceremonial (epideictic) speaking, heaps praise or blame on another for the benefit of *present-day* audiences. For example, Rev. Al Sharpton's eulogy for Michael Jackson gave fans an opportunity to celebrate the life of the conflicted rock star. The third, political (deliberative) speaking, attempts to influence legislators or voters who decide *future* policy. The 2012 presidential debates gave Barack Obama and Mitt Romney a chance to sway undecided voters. These different temporal orientations could call for diverse rhetorical appeals.

Because his students were familiar with the question-and-answer style of Socratic dialogue, Aristotle classified rhetoric as a counterpart or an offshoot of dialectic. Dialectic is one-on-one discussion; rhetoric is one person addressing many. Dialectic is a search for truth; rhetoric tries to demonstrate truth that's already been found. Dialectic answers general philosophical questions; rhetoric addresses specific, practical ones. Dialectic deals with certainty; rhetoric deals with probability. Aristotle saw this last distinction as particularly important: rhetoric is the art of discovering ways to make truth seem more probable to an audience that isn't completely convinced.

RHETORICAL PROOF: *LOGOS, ETHOS, PATHOS*

Inartistic proofs
External evidence
the speaker doesn't
create.

According to Aristotle, the available means of persuasion can be artistic or inartistic. *Inartistic* or external proofs are those the speaker doesn't create. They would include testimonies of witnesses or documents such as letters and contracts. *Artistic* or internal proofs are those the speaker creates. There are three kinds of artistic proofs: logical (*logos*), ethical (*ethos*), and emotional (*pathos*). Logical proof comes from the line of argument in the speech, ethical proof is the way the speaker's character is revealed through the message, and emotional proof is the feeling the speech draws out of the hearers. Some form of *logos, ethos,* and *pathos* is present in every public presentation, but perhaps no other modern-day speech has brought all three appeals together as effectively as Martin Luther King Jr.'s "I Have a Dream," delivered in 1963 to civil rights marchers in Washington, DC. In the year 2000, American public address scholars selected King's "I Have a Dream" as the greatest speech of the twentieth century. We'll look at this artistic speech throughout the rest of the chapter to illustrate Aristotle's rhetorical theory.

Artistic proofs
Internal proofs that
contain logical, ethical,
or emotional appeals.

Case Study: "I Have a Dream"

At the end of August 1963, a quarter of a million people assembled at the Lincoln Memorial in a united march on Washington. The rally capped a long, hot summer of sit-ins protesting racial discrimination in the South. (The film

Mississippi Burning portrays one of the tragic racial conflicts of that year.) Two months before the march, President John F. Kennedy submitted a civil rights bill to Congress that would begin to rectify segregation and other racial injustices, but its passage was seriously in doubt. The organizers of the march hoped it would put pressure on Congress to outlaw segregation in the South, but they also wanted the demonstration to raise the national consciousness about economic exploitation of blacks around the country.

Martin Luther King shared the platform with a dozen civil rights leaders, each limited to a five-minute presentation. King's successful Montgomery bus boycott, freedom rides across the South, and solitary confinement in a Birmingham jail set him apart in the eyes of demonstrators and TV viewers. The last of the group to speak, King had a dual purpose. In the face of a Black Muslim call for violence, he urged blacks to continue their nonviolent struggle without hatred. He also implored white people to get involved in the quest for freedom and equality, to be part of a dream fulfilled rather than contribute to an unjust nightmare.

A few years after King's assassination, I experienced the impact his speech continued to have upon the African-American community. Teaching public address in a volunteer street academy, I read the speech out loud to illustrate matters of style. The students needed no written text. As I came to the last third of the speech, they recited the eloquent "I have a dream" portion word for word with great passion. When we finished, all of us were teary-eyed.

David Garrow, author of the Pulitzer Prize–winning biography of King, called the speech the "rhetorical achievement of a lifetime, the clarion call that conveyed the moral power of the movement's cause to the millions who watched the live national network coverage."[3] King shifted the burden of proof onto those who opposed racial equality. Aristotle's three rhetorical proofs can help us understand how King made the status quo of segregation an ugly option for the moral listener.

Logical Proof: Lines of Argument That Make Sense

Logos
Logical proof, which comes from the line of argument in a speech.

Aristotle focused on two forms of *logos*—the *enthymeme* and the *example.* He regarded the enthymeme as "the strongest of the proofs."[4] An enthymeme is merely an incomplete version of a formal deductive syllogism. To illustrate, logicians might create the following syllogism out of one of King's lines of reasoning:

Major or general premise: *All people are created equal.*
Minor or specific premise: *I am a person.*
Conclusion: *I am equal to other people.*

Typical enthymemes, however, leave out a premise that is already accepted by the audience. *All people are created equal. . . . I am equal to other people.* In terms of style, the enthymeme is more artistic than a stilted syllogistic argument. But as University of Wisconsin rhetorician Lloyd Bitzer notes, Aristotle had a greater reason for advising the speaker to suppress the statement of a premise the listeners already believe.

> Because they are jointly produced by the audience, enthymemes intuitively unite speaker and audience and provide the strongest possible proof. . . . The audience itself helps construct the proof by which it is persuaded.[5]

Most rhetorical analysis looks for enthymemes embedded in one or two lines of text. In the case of "I Have a Dream," the whole speech is one giant enthymeme.

286   *GROUP AND PUBLIC COMMUNICATION*

Enthymeme
An incomplete version of a formal deductive syllogism that is created by leaving out a premise already accepted by the audience or by leaving an obvious conclusion unstated.

If the logic of the speech were to be expressed as a syllogism, the reasoning would be as follows:

Major premise: *God will reward nonviolence.*
Minor premise: *We are pursuing our dream nonviolently.*
Conclusion: *God will grant us our dream.*

King used the first two-thirds of the speech to establish the validity of the minor premise. White listeners are reminded that blacks have been "battered by the storms of persecution and staggered by winds of police brutality." They have "come fresh from narrow jail cells" and are "veterans of creative suffering." Blacks are urged to meet "physical force with soul force," not to allow "creative protest to degenerate into physical violence," and never to "satisfy our thirst for freedom by drinking from the cup of bitterness and hatred." The movement is to continue to be nonviolent.

King used the last third of the speech to establish his conclusion; he painted the dream in vivid color. It included King's hope that his four children would not be "judged by the color of their skin, but by the content of their character." He pictured an Alabama where "little black boys and black girls will be able to join hands with little white boys and white girls as sisters and brothers." And in a swirling climax, he shared a vision of all God's children singing, "Free at last, free at last. Thank God Almighty, we are free at last." But he never articulated the major premise. He didn't need to.

King and his audience were already committed to the truth of the major premise—that God would reward their commitment to nonviolence. Aristotle stressed that audience analysis is crucial to the effective use of the enthymeme. The centrality of the church in American black history, the religious roots of the civil rights protest, and the crowd's frequent response of "My Lord" suggest that King knew his audience well. He never stated what to them was obvious, and this strengthened rather than weakened his logical appeal.

The enthymeme uses deductive logic—moving from global principle to specific truth. Arguing by example uses inductive reasoning—drawing a final conclusion from specific cases. Since King mentioned few examples of discrimination, it might appear that he failed to use all possible means of logical persuasion. But pictures of snarling police dogs, electric cattle prods used on peaceful demonstrators, and signs over drinking fountains stating "Whites only" appeared nightly on TV news. As with the missing major premise of the enthymeme, King's audience supplied its own vivid images.

Ethical Proof: Perceived Source Credibility

According to Aristotle, it's not enough for a speech to contain plausible argument. The speaker must *seem* credible as well. Many audience impressions are formed before the speaker even begins. As poet Ralph Waldo Emerson cautioned more than a century ago, "Use what language you will, you can never say anything but what you are."[6] Some who watched Martin Luther King on television undoubtedly tuned him out because he was black. But surprisingly, Aristotle said little about a speaker's background or reputation. He was more interested in audience perceptions that are shaped by what the speaker does or doesn't say. In the *Rhetoric* he identified three qualities that build high source credibility—*intelligence, character,* and *goodwill.*

1. Perceived Intelligence. The quality of intelligence has more to do with practical wisdom (phronesis) and shared values than it does with training at

"Trust me, at this point it's the only way we can boost your numbers on likability."

© David Sipress/The New Yorker Collection/www.cartoonbank.com

Plato's Academy. Audiences judge intelligence by the overlap between their beliefs and the speaker's ideas. ("My idea of an agreeable speaker is one who agrees with me.") King quoted the Bible, the United States Constitution, the patriotic hymn "My Country, 'Tis of Thee," Shakespeare's *King Lear*, and the Negro spiritual "We Shall Overcome." With the exception of violent terrorists and racial bigots, it's hard to imagine anyone with whom he didn't establish strong value identification.

2. Virtuous Character. Character has to do with the speaker's image as a good and honest person. Even though he and other blacks were victims of "unspeakable horrors of police brutality," King warned against a "distrust of all white people" and against "drinking from the cup of bitterness and hatred." It would be difficult to maintain an image of the speaker as an evil racist while he was being charitable toward his enemies and optimistic about the future.

3. Goodwill. Goodwill is a positive judgment of the speaker's intention toward the audience. Aristotle thought it possible for an orator to possess extraordinary intelligence and sterling character yet still not have the listeners' best interest at heart. King was obviously not trying to reach "the vicious racists" of Alabama, but no one was given reason to think he bore them ill will. His dream included "black men and white men, Jews and Gentiles, Protestants and Catholics."

Although Aristotle's comments on *ethos* were stated in a few brief sentences, no other portion of his *Rhetoric* has received such close scientific scrutiny. The results of sophisticated testing of audience attitudes show that his three-factor

Ethos
Perceived credibility, which comes from the speaker's intelligence, character, and goodwill toward the audience, as these personal characteristics are revealed through the message.

theory of source credibility stands up remarkably well.[7] Listeners definitely think in terms of competence (intelligence), trustworthiness (character), and care (goodwill). As Martin Luther King spoke in front of the Lincoln Memorial, most listeners perceived him as strong in all three.

Emotional Proof: Striking a Responsive Chord

Recent scholarship suggests that Aristotle was quite skeptical about the emotion-laden public oratory typical of his era.[8] He preferred the reason-based discussion characteristic of relatively small councils and executive deliberative bodies. Yet he understood that public rhetoric, if practiced ethically, benefits society. Thus, Aristotle set forth a theory of *pathos*. He offered it not to take advantage of an audience's destructive emotions, but as a corrective measure that could help a speaker craft emotional appeals that inspire reasoned civic decision making. To this end, he cataloged a series of opposite feelings, then explained the conditions under which each mood is experienced, and finally described how the speaker can get an audience to feel that way. Aristotle scholar and translator George Kennedy claims that this analysis of pathos is "the earliest systematic discussion of human psychology."[9] If Aristotle's advice sounds familiar, it may be a sign that human nature hasn't changed much in the last 2,300 years.

Pathos
Emotional proof, which comes from the feelings the speech draws out of those who hear it.

    Anger versus Mildness. Aristotle's discussion of anger was an early version of Freud's frustration–aggression hypothesis. People feel angry when they are thwarted in their attempt to fulfill a need. Remind them of interpersonal slights, and they'll become irate. Show them that the offender is sorry, deserves praise, or has great power, and the audience will calm down.

    Love or Friendship versus Hatred. Consistent with present-day research on attraction, Aristotle considered similarity the key to mutual warmth. The speaker should point out common goals, experiences, attitudes, and desires. In the absence of these positive forces, a common enemy can be used to create solidarity.

    Fear versus Confidence. Fear comes from a mental image of potential disaster. The speaker should paint a vivid word picture of the tragedy, showing that its occurrence is probable. Confidence can be built up by describing the danger as remote.

    Indignation versus Pity. We all have a built-in sense of fairness. As the producers of *60 Minutes* prove weekly, it's easy to arouse a sense of injustice by describing an arbitrary use of power upon those who are helpless.

    Admiration versus Envy. People admire moral virtue, power, wealth, and beauty. By demonstrating that an individual has acquired life's goods through hard work rather than mere luck, admiration will increase.

THE FIVE CANONS OF RHETORIC

Although the organization of Aristotle's *Rhetoric* is somewhat puzzling, scholars and practitioners synthesize his words into four distinct standards for measuring the quality of a speaker: the construction of an argument (invention), ordering of material (arrangement), selection of language (style), and techniques of delivery. Later writers add memory to the list of skills the accomplished speaker must master. As previewed in the introduction to this section on public rhetoric, the

Canons of rhetoric
The principle divisions of the art of persuasion established by ancient rhetoricians—invention, arrangement, style, delivery, and memory.

Invention
A speaker's "hunt" for arguments that will be effective in a particular speech.

five canons of rhetoric have set the agenda of public address instruction for more than 2,000 years. Aristotle's advice strikes most students of public speaking as surprisingly up-to-date.

Invention.   To generate effective enthymemes and examples, the speaker draws on both specialized knowledge about the subject and general lines of reasoning common to all kinds of speeches. Imagining the mind as a storehouse of wisdom or an informational landscape, Aristotle called these stock arguments *topoi*, a Greek term that can be translated as "topics" or "places." As Cornell University literature professor Lane Cooper explained, "In these special regions the orator hunts for arguments as a hunter hunts for game."[10] When King argued, "We refuse to believe that there are insufficient funds in the great vaults of opportunity of this nation," he marshaled the specific American topic or premise that the United States is a land of opportunity. When he contended that "many of our white brothers, as evidenced by their presence here today, have come to realize that their destiny is tied up with our destiny," he established a causal connection that draws from Aristotle's general topics of cause/effect and motive.

Arrangement.   According to Aristotle, you should avoid complicated schemes of organization. "There are two parts to a speech; for it is necessary first to state the subject and then to demonstrate it."[11] The introduction should capture attention, establish your credibility, and make clear the purpose of the speech. The conclusion should remind listeners what you've said and leave them feeling good about you and your ideas. Like public address teachers today, Aristotle decried starting with jokes that have nothing to do with the topic, insisting on three-point outlines, and waiting until the end of the speech to reveal the main point.

Style.   Aristotle's treatment of style in the *Rhetoric* focuses on metaphor. He believed that "to learn easily is naturally pleasant to all people" and that "metaphor most brings about learning."[12] Furthermore, he taught that "metaphor especially has clarity and sweetness and strangeness."[13] But for Aristotle, metaphors were more than aids for comprehension or aesthetic appreciation. Metaphors help an audience visualize—a "bringing-before-the-eyes" process that energizes listeners and moves them to action.[14] King was a master of metaphor:

> The Negro lives on a *lonely island* of poverty in the midst of a *vast ocean* of material prosperity.
> To rise from the *dark and desolate valleys* of segregation to the *sunlit path* of racial justice.

King's use of metaphor was not restricted to images drawn from nature. Perhaps his most convincing imagery was an extended analogy picturing the march on Washington as people of color going to the federal bank to cash a check written by the Founding Fathers. America had defaulted on the promissory note and had sent back the check marked "insufficient funds." But the marchers refused to believe that the bank of justice was bankrupt, that the vaults of opportunity were empty. These persuasive images gathered listeners' knowledge of racial discrimination into a powerful flood of reason:

> Let justice roll down like waters
> and righteousness like a mighty stream.[15]

Delivery.   Audiences reject delivery that seems planned or staged. Naturalness is persuasive; artifice just the opposite. Any form of presentation that calls attention to itself takes away from the speaker's proofs.

Memory.   Aristotle's students needed no reminder that good speakers are able to draw upon a collection of ideas and phrases stored in the mind. Still, Roman teachers of rhetoric found it necessary to stress the importance of memory. In our present age of word processing and teleprompters, memory seems to be a lost art. Yet the stirring I-have-a-dream litany at the end of King's speech departed from his prepared text and effectively pulled together lines he had used before. Unlike King and many Athenian orators, most of us aren't speaking in public every day. For us, the modern equivalent of memory is rehearsal.

ETHICAL REFLECTION: ARISTOTLE'S GOLDEN MEAN

Aristotle's *Rhetoric* is the first known systematic treatise on audience analysis and adaptation. His work therefore begs the same question discussed in the introduction to this section on public rhetoric: *Is it ethical to alter a message to make it more acceptable for a particular audience?*

The way I've phrased the question reflects a Western bias for linking morality with behavior. Does an act produce benefit or harm? Is it right or wrong to do a certain deed? Aristotle, however, spoke of ethics in terms of character rather than conduct, inward disposition instead of outward behavior. He took the Greek admiration for moderation and elevated it to a theory of virtue.

When Barry Goldwater was selected as the Republican Party's nominee for president in 1964, he boldly stated, "Extremism in the defense of liberty is no vice . . . moderation in the pursuit of justice is not virtue."[16] Aristotle would have strongly disagreed. He assumed virtue stands between the two vices.[17] Aristotle saw wisdom in the person who avoids excess on either side. Moderation is best; virtue develops habits that seek to walk an intermediate path. This middle way is known as the *golden mean*. That's because out of the four cardinal virtues—courage, justice, temperance, and practical wisdom—temperance is the one that explains the three others.

Golden mean
The virtue of moderation; the virtuous person develops habits that avoid extremes.

As for audience adaptation, Aristotle would have counseled against the practice of telling people only what they want to hear, pandering to the crowd, or "wimping out" by not stating what we really think. He would be equally against a disregard of audience sensitivities, riding roughshod over listeners' beliefs, or adopting a take-no-prisoners, lay-waste-the-town rhetorical belligerence. The golden mean would lie in winsome straight talk, gentle assertiveness, and adaptation.

Whether the issue is truth-telling, self-disclosure, or risk-taking when making decisions, Aristotle's golden mean suggests other middle-way communication practices:

Extreme	Golden Mean	Extreme
Lies	Truthful statements	Brutal honesty
Secrecy	Transparency	Soul-baring
Cowardice	Courage	Recklessness

The golden mean will often prove to be the best way to persuade others. But for Aristotle, that was not the ethical issue. Aristotle advocated the middle way because it is the well-worn path taken by virtuous people.

CRITIQUE: STANDING THE TEST OF TIME

For many teachers of public speaking, criticizing Aristotle's *Rhetoric* is like doubting Einstein's theory of relativity or belittling Shakespeare's *King Lear*. Yet the Greek philosopher often seems less clear than he urged his students to be. Scholars are puzzled by Aristotle's failure to define the exact meaning of *enthymeme*, his confusing system of classifying metaphor according to type, and the blurred distinctions he made between deliberative (political) and epideictic (ceremonial) speaking. At the beginning of the *Rhetoric*, Aristotle promised a systematic study of *logos, ethos,* and *pathos,* but he failed to follow that three-part plan. Instead, it appears that he grouped the material in a speech-audience-speaker order. Even those who claim there's a conceptual unity to Aristotle's theory admit the book is "an editorial jumble."[18] We must remember, however, that Aristotle's *Rhetoric* consists of lecture notes rather than a treatise prepared for the public. To reconstruct Aristotle's meaning, scholars must consult his other writings on philosophy, politics, ethics, drama, and biology. Such detective work is inherently imprecise.

Some present-day critics are bothered by the *Rhetoric's* view of the audience as passive. Speakers in Aristotle's world seem to be able to accomplish any goal as long as they prepare their speeches with careful thought and accurate audience analysis. Other critics wish Aristotle had considered a fourth component of rhetoric—the situation. Any analysis of King's address apart from the context of the march on Washington would certainly be incomplete.

Referring to Aristotle's manuscript in a rare moment of sincere appreciation, French skeptic Voltaire declared what many communication teachers would echo today: "I do not believe there is a single refinement of the art that escapes him."[19] Despite the shortcomings and perplexities of this work, it remains a foundational text of our discipline—a starting point for social scientists and rhetoricians alike.

QUESTIONS TO SHARPEN YOUR FOCUS

1. For most people today, the term *rhetoric* has unfavorable associations. What synonym or phrase captures what Aristotle meant yet doesn't carry a negative connotation?

2. What *enthymemes* have advocates on each side of the abortion issue employed in their public *deliberative rhetoric*?

3. Aristotle divided *ethos* into issues of *intelligence, character,* and *goodwill*. Which quality is most important to you when you hear a campaign address, sermon, or other public speech?

4. Most scholars who define themselves as rhetoricians identify with the humanities rather than the sciences. Can you support the claim that Aristotle took a *scientific approach to rhetoric*?

292 *GROUP AND PUBLIC COMMUNICATION*

SELF-QUIZ 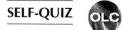 *www.mhhe.com/griffin9e*

A SECOND LOOK

Recommended resource: Aristotle, *On Rhetoric: A Theory of Civil Discourse*, George A. Kennedy (ed. and trans.), Oxford University, New York, 1991.

Key scholarship: Richard Leo Enos and Lois Peters Agnew (eds.), *Landmark Essays on Aristotelian Rhetoric*, Lawrence Erlbaum, Mahwah, NJ, 1998.

Rhetoric as art: George A. Kennedy, "Philosophical Rhetoric," in *Classical Rhetoric*, University of North Carolina, Chapel Hill, NC, 1980, pp. 41–85.

Rhetoric as science: James L. Golden, Goodwin F. Berquist, and William E. Coleman, *The Rhetoric of Western Thought*, Kendall/Hunt, Dubuque, IA, 1976, pp. 25–39.

Twenty-first-century interpretation: Alan Gross and Arthur Walzer (eds.), *Rereading Aristotle's Rhetoric*, Southern Illinois University, Carbondale, IL, 2000.

Enthymeme: Lloyd F. Bitzer, "Aristotle's Enthymeme Revisited," *Quarterly Journal of Speech*, Vol. 45, 1959, pp. 399–409; also in Enos and Agnew, pp. 179–191.

Metaphor: Sara Newman, "Aristotle's Notion of 'Bringing-Before-the-Eyes': Its Contributions to Aristotelian and Contemporary Conceptualizations of Metaphor, Style, and Audience," *Rhetorica*, Vol. 20, 2002, pp. 1–23.

Measuring ethos: James McCroskey and Jason Teven, "Goodwill: A Reexamination of the Construct and Its Measurement," *Communication Monographs*, Vol. 66, 1999, pp. 90–103.

Ethos and oral morality: Charles Marsh, "Aristotelian Ethos and the New Orality: Implications for Media Literacy and Media Ethics," *Journal of Mass Media Ethics*, Vol. 21, 2006, pp. 338–352.

Rhetoric and ethics: Eugene Garver, *Aristotle's Rhetoric: An Art of Character*, University of Chicago, Chicago, IL, 1994.

History of rhetoric: Thomas Conley, *Rhetoric in the European Tradition*, Longman, New York, 1990.

Analysis of King's speech: Alexandra Alvarez, "Martin Luther King's 'I Have a Dream,'" *Journal of Black Studies*, Vol. 18, 1988, pp. 337–357.

March on Washington: David J. Garrow, *Bearing the Cross*, William Morrow, New York, 1986, pp. 231–286.

For a twentieth century theory of rhetoric, click on
I. A. Richards' Meaning of Meaning in
Archive under Theory Resources at
www.afirstlook.com.

CHAPTER 24

Objective   Interpretive

Rhetorical tradition

Narrative Paradigm

of Walter Fisher

People are storytelling animals. This simple assertion is Walter Fisher's answer to the philosophical question *What is the essence of human nature?*

Many of the theorists discussed in preceding chapters offer different answers to this key question of human existence. For example, Thibaut and Kelley's social exchange theory operates on the premise that humans are rational creatures. Berger's uncertainty reduction theory assumes that people are basically curious. More pertinent for students of communication, Mead's symbolic interactionism insists that our ability to use symbols is what makes us uniquely human. (See Chapters 8, 9, and 5.)

Fisher doesn't argue against any of these ideas, but he thinks that human communication reveals something more basic than rationality, curiosity, or even symbol-using capacity. He is convinced that we are narrative beings who "experience and comprehend life as a series of ongoing narratives, as conflicts, characters, beginnings, middles, and ends."[1] If this is true, then all forms of human communication that appeal to our reason need to be seen fundamentally as stories.[2]

Walter Fisher is a professor emeritus at the University of Southern California's Annenberg School of Communication. Throughout his professional life he has been uncomfortable with the prevailing view that rhetoric is only a matter of evidence, facts, arguments, reason, and logic that has its highest expression in courts of law, legislatures, and other deliberative bodies. In 1978, he introduced the concept of *good reasons,* which led to his proposal of the narrative paradigm in 1984.[3] He proposed that offering good reasons has more to do with telling a compelling story than it does with piling up evidence or constructing a tight argument.

Fisher soon became convinced that all forms of communication that appeal to our reason are best viewed as stories shaped by history, culture, and character. When we hear the word *story,* most of us tend to think of novels, plays, movies, TV sitcoms, and yarns told sitting around a campfire. Some of us also call to mind accounts of our past—tales we tell to others in which we are the central character. But with the exception of jokes, *Hi, How are you?* greetings, and other forms of *phatic communication,* Fisher regards almost *all* types of communication as story. Obviously, he sees differences in form between a Robert Frost poem, a *Harry Potter* book, or a performance of *As You Like It* on the one hand, and a philosophical essay, historical report, political debate, theological discussion, or

Phatic communication
Communication aimed at maintaining relationships rather than passing along information or saying something new.

scientific treatise on the other. But if we want to know whether we should believe the "truth" each of these genres proclaims, Fisher maintains that all of them can and should be viewed as narrative. He uses the term *narrative paradigm* to highlight his belief that there is no communication of ideas that is purely descriptive or didactic.

TELLING A COMPELLING STORY

Most religious traditions are passed on from generation to generation through the retelling of stories. The faithful are urged to "tell the old, old story" to encourage believers and convince those in doubt. American writer Frederick Buechner takes a fresh approach to passing on religious story. His book *Peculiar Treasures* retells the twelfth-century B.C. biblical story of Ruth's devotion to Naomi, her mother-in-law, in twenty-first-century style.[4] Buechner's account of true friendship provides a vehicle for examining Fisher's narrative paradigm in the rest of this chapter. The story begins after the death of Naomi's husband and two sons:

> Ruth was a Moabite girl who married into a family of Israelite transplants living in Moab because there was a famine going on at home. When her young husband died, her mother-in-law, Naomi, decided to pull up stakes and head back for Israel where she belonged. The famine was over by then, and there was no longer anything to hold her where she was, her own husband having died about the same time that Ruth's had. She advised Ruth to stay put right there in Moab and to try to snag herself another man from among her own people.
>
> She was a strong-willed old party, and when Ruth said she wanted to go to Israel with her, she tried to talk her out of it. Even if by some gynecological fluke she managed to produce another son for Ruth to marry, she said, by the time he was old enough, Ruth would be ready for the geriatric ward. But Ruth had a mind of her own too, besides which they'd been through a lot together what with one thing and another, and home to her was wherever Naomi was. "Where you go, I go, and where you live, I live," Ruth told her, "and if your God is Yahweh, then my God is Yahweh too" (*Ruth 2:10–17*). So Naomi gave in, and when the two of them pulled in to Bethlehem, Naomi's home town, there was a brass band to meet them at the station.
>
> Ruth had a spring in her step and a fascinating Moabite accent, and it wasn't long before she caught the eye of a well-heeled farmer named Boaz. He was a little long in the tooth, but he still knew a pretty girl when he saw one, and before long, in a fatherly kind of way, he took her under his wing. He told the hired hands not to give her any trouble. He helped her in the fields. He had her over for a meal. And when she asked him one day in her disarming Moabite way why he was being so nice to her, he said he'd heard how good she'd been to Naomi, who happened to be a distant cousin of his, and as far as he was concerned, she deserved nothing but the best.
>
> Naomi was nobody's fool and saw which way the wind was blowing long before Ruth did. She was dead-set on Ruth's making a good catch for herself, and since it was obvious she'd already hooked old Boaz whether she realized it or not, all she had to do was find the right way to reel him in. Naomi gave her instructions. As soon as Boaz had a good supper under his belt and had polished off a nightcap or two, he'd go to the barn and hit the sack. Around midnight, she said, Ruth should slip out to the barn and hit the sack too. If Boaz's feet just happened to be uncovered somehow, and if she just happened to be close enough to keep

them warm, that probably wouldn't be the worst thing in the world either (*Ruth 3:1–5*). But she wasn't to go too far. Back in Jericho, Boaz's mother, Rahab, had had a rather seamy reputation for going too far professionally, and anything that reminded him of that might scare him off permanently.

Ruth followed her mother-in-law's advice to the letter, and it worked like a charm. Boaz was so overwhelmed that she'd pay attention to an old crock like him when there were so many young bucks running around in tight-fitting jeans that he fell for her hook, line and sinker, and after a few legal matters were taken care of, made her his lawful wedded wife.

They had a son named Obed after a while, and Naomi came to take care of him and stayed on for the rest of her life. Then in time Obed had a son of his own named Jesse, and Jesse in turn had seven sons, the seventh of whom was named David and ended up as the greatest king Israel ever had. With Ruth for his great-grandmother and Naomi for his grandfather's nurse, it was hardly a wonder.[5]

NARRATION AND PARADIGM: DEFINING THE TERMS

Fisher defines *narration* as "symbolic actions—words and/or deeds—that have sequence and meaning for those who live, create, or interpret them."[6] Ruth's life and Buechner's account of it clearly qualify as narrative. But Fisher's definition is broad and is especially notable for what it doesn't exclude. On the basis of his further elaboration,[7] I offer this expanded paraphrase of his definition:

> Narration is communication rooted in time and space. It covers every aspect of our lives and the lives of others in regard to character, motive, and action. The term also refers to every verbal or nonverbal bid for a person to believe or act in a certain way. Even when a message seems abstract—devoid of imagery—it is narration because it is embedded in the speaker's ongoing story that has a beginning, middle, and end, and it invites listeners to interpret its meaning and assess its value for their own lives.

Narration
Symbolic actions—words and/or deeds—that have sequence and meaning for those who live, create, or interpret them.

Under this expanded definition, Ruth's *my God is Yahweh* statement is as much a story of love and trust as it is a declaration of belief. Framed in the context of King David's genealogy, it is also an early episode in the *Greatest Story Ever Told.* Those who identify with the human love, trust, loyalty, and commitment described in the narrative can't help but feel the solidarity of an extended family of faith.

Fisher uses the term *paradigm* to refer to a *conceptual framework*—a widely shared perceptual filter. Perception is not so much a matter of the physics of sight and sound as it is one of interpretation. Meaning isn't inherent in events; it's attached at the workbench of the mind. A paradigm is a universal model that calls for people to view events through a common interpretive lens.

Paradigm
A conceptual framework; a universal model that calls for people to view events through a common interpretive lens.

In *The Structure of Scientific Revolutions,* Thomas Kuhn argues that an accepted paradigm is the mark of a mature science.[8] Responding to this challenge, communication scientists in the 1970s sought to discover a universal model that would explain communication behavior. Fisher's narrative paradigm is an interpretive counterpart to their efforts. Fisher offers a way to understand all communication and to direct rhetorical inquiry. He doesn't regard the narrative paradigm as a specific rhetoric. Rather, he sees it as "the foundation on which a complete rhetoric needs to be built. This structure would provide a comprehensive explanation of the creation, composition, adaptation, presentation, and reception of symbolic messages."[9]

PARADIGM SHIFT: FROM A RATIONAL-WORLD PARADIGM TO A NARRATIVE ONE

Fisher begins his book *Human Communication as Narration* with a reference to the opening line of the Gospel of John: "In the beginning was the word (*logos*)." He notes that the Greek word *logos* originally included story, reason, rationale, conception, discourse, thought—all forms of human communication. Imagination and thought were not yet distinct. So the story of Naomi and Ruth was *logos*.

According to Fisher, the writings of Plato and Aristotle reflect the early evolution from a generic to a specific use of *logos*—from story to statement. *Logos* had already begun to refer only to philosophical discourse, a lofty enterprise that relegated imagination, poetry, and other aesthetic concerns to second-class status. Rhetoric fell somewhere between *logos* and *mythos*. As opposed to the abstract discourse of philosophy, it was practical speech—the secular combination of pure logic on the one hand and emotional stories that stir up passions on the other. The Greek citizen concerned with truth alone should steer clear of rhetoric and consult an expert on wisdom—the philosopher.

Fisher says that 2,000 years later the scientific revolution dethroned the philosopher–king. In the last few centuries, the only knowledge that seems to be worth knowing in academia is that which can be spotted in the physical world. The person who wants to understand the way things are needs to check with a doctor, a scientist, an engineer, or another technical expert. Despite the elevation of technology and the demotion of philosophy, both modes of decision making are similar in their elitist tendencies to "place that which is not *formally* logical or which is not characterized by *expertise* within a somehow subhuman framework of behavior."[10] Fisher sees philosophical and technical discussion as scholars' standard approach to knowledge. He calls this mindset the *rational-world paradigm*. Hirokawa and Gouran's functional perspective on group decision making is a perfect example (see Chapter 17).

Fisher lists five assumptions of the prevailing rational-world paradigm. See if they match what you've been taught all along in school.[11]

Rational-world paradigm
A scientific or philosophical approach to knowledge that assumes people are logical, making decisions on the basis of evidence and lines of argument.

1. People are essentially rational.
2. We make decisions on the basis of arguments.
3. The type of speaking situation (legal, scientific, legislative) determines the course of our argument.
4. Rationality is determined by how much we know and how well we argue.
5. The world is a set of logical puzzles that we can solve through rational analysis.

Viewed through the rational-world paradigm, the story of Ruth is suspect. Ruth ignores Naomi's argument, which is based on uncontestable biological facts of life. Nor does Ruth offer any compelling rationale for leaving Moab or for worshiping Yahweh. Once they are back in Israel, Naomi's scheme for Ruth to "reel in" Boaz has nothing to do with logic and everything to do with emotional bonds. Other than the Old Testament passage, the author offers no evidence that Naomi and Ruth are historical characters, that any kind of god exists, or that a book about friendship, kinship, and romance deserves a place in the Old Testament canon. Thus, from a rational-world perspective, the story makes little sense.

Fisher is convinced that the assumptions of the rational-world paradigm are too limited. He calls for a new conceptual framework (a paradigm shift) in order to better understand human communication. His *narrative paradigm* is built on five assumptions similar in form to the rational-world paradigm, but quite different in content.[12]

1. People are essentially storytellers.

2. We make decisions on the basis of good reasons, which vary depending on the communication situation, media, and genre (philosophical, technical, rhetorical, or artistic).

3. History, biography, culture, and character determine what we consider good reasons.

4. Narrative rationality is determined by the coherence and fidelity of our stories.

5. The world is a set of stories from which we choose, and thus constantly re-create, our lives.

Narrative paradigm
A theoretical framework that views narrative as the basis of all human communication.

Viewing human beings as storytellers who reason in various ways is a major conceptual shift. For example, in a logical system, values are emotional nonsense. From the narrative perspective, however, values are the stuff of stories. Working from a strictly logical standpoint, aesthetic proof is irrelevant, but within a narrative framework, style and beauty play a pivotal role in determining whether we get into a story. Perhaps the biggest shift in thinking has to do with who is qualified to assess the quality of communication. Whereas the rational-world model holds that only experts are capable of presenting or discerning sound arguments, the narrative paradigm maintains that, armed with a bit of common sense, almost any of us can see the point of a good story and judge its merits as the basis for belief and action. No one taught us how to do this. It's an inherent awareness that's honed by life experience. Fisher would say that each of us will make a judgment about Buechner's account of Ruth (or any story) based upon *narrative rationality.*

NARRATIVE RATIONALITY: COHERENCE AND FIDELITY

Narrative rationality
A way to evaluate the worth of stories based on the twin standards of narrative coherence and narrative fidelity.

According to Fisher, not all stories are equally good. Even though there's no guarantee that people won't adopt a bad story, he thinks everybody applies the same standards of *narrative rationality* to whatever stories they hear: "The operative principle of narrative rationality is identification rather than deliberation."[13] Will we accept a cross-cultural tale of a young widow's total commitment to her mother-in-law and of Naomi's enthusiastic efforts to help Ruth remarry and have children by another man? Fisher believes that our answer depends on whether Buechner's account meets the twin tests of *narrative coherence* and *narrative fidelity.* Together they are measures of a story's truthfulness and humanity.

Narrative Coherence: Does the Story Hang Together?

Narrative coherence has to do with how probable the story sounds to the hearer. Does the narrative *hang together?* Do the people and events it portrays seem to be of one piece? Are they part of an organic whole or are there obvious contradictions among them? Do the characters act consistently?

308   *GROUP AND PUBLIC COMMUNICATION*

"I know what you're thinking, but let me offer a competing narrative."

© Harry Bliss/The New Yorker Collection/www.cartoonbank.com

Narrative coherence
Internal consistency with characters acting in a reliable fashion; the story hangs together.

Buechner's version of Ruth and Naomi's relationship translates an ancient tale of interpersonal commitment into a contemporary setting. To the extent that his modern-day references to a brass band at the station, polishing off a nightcap, and young bucks running around in tight-fitting jeans consistently portray the present, the story has structural integrity. Fisher regards the internal consistency of a narrative as similar to lines of argument in a rational-world paradigm. In that sense, his narrative paradigm doesn't discount or replace logic. Instead, Fisher lists the test of reason as one, but only one, of the factors that affect narrative coherence.

Stories hang together when we're convinced that the narrator hasn't left out important details, fudged the facts, or ignored other plausible interpretations. Although the TV series *Lost* and the re-imagined *Battlestar Galactica* garnered critical acclaim throughout their runs, their final episodes were roundly panned by fans and critics because they didn't meet those criteria. At the end, both shows lacked narrative coherence.

We often judge the coherence of a narrative by comparing it with other stories we've heard that deal with the same theme. How does Buechner's account of feminine wiles used to move an older man toward marriage without going "too far" stack up against the blatant seduction scenes in the TV series *House of Lies* or the typical daytime soap opera? To the extent that Ruth's ploy seems more believable, we'll credit Buechner's biblical update with coherence.

For Fisher, the ultimate test of narrative coherence is whether we can count on the characters to act in a reliable manner. We are suspicious of accounts where characters behave uncharacteristically. We tend to trust stories of people who show continuity of thought, motive, and action. Whether you regard Buechner's Naomi as a wise matchmaker or an overcontrolling mother-in-law, her consistent concern that Ruth find a man to marry is a thread that gives the fabric of the story a tight weave.

Narrative Fidelity: Does the Story Ring True and Humane?

Narrative fidelity is the quality of a story that causes the words to strike a responsive chord in the life of the listener. A story has fidelity when it rings true with the hearers' experiences—it squares with the stories they might tell about themselves.[14]

Narrative fidelity
Congruence between values embedded in a message and what listeners regard as truthful and humane; the story strikes a responsive chord.

Have we, like Boaz, done special favors for a person we found especially attractive? Like Naomi, have we stretched the rules of decorum to help make a match? Or, like Ruth, have we ever experienced a bond with a relative that goes beyond obligation to family? To the extent that the details of this 3,000-year-old story portray the world we live in today, the narrative has fidelity.

Fisher's book *Human Communication as Narration* has the subtitle *Toward a Philosophy of Reason, Value, and Action*. He believes a story has fidelity when it provides good reasons to guide our future actions. When we buy into a story, we buy into the type of character we should be. Thus, values are what set the narrative paradigm's logic of good reasons apart from the rational-world paradigm's mere logic of reasons.

The *logic of good reasons* centers on five value-related issues. Fisher says we are concerned with (1) the values embedded in the message, (2) the relevance of those values to decisions made, (3) the consequence of adhering to those values, (4) the overlap with the worldview of the audience, and (5) conformity with what the audience members believe is "an ideal basis for conduct."[15] The last two concerns—congruity with the listeners' values and the actions they think best—form the basis of Fisher's contention that people tend to prefer accounts that fit with what they view as truthful and humane. But what specific values guide audiences as they gauge a story's truth or fidelity? Fisher suggests there is an *ideal audience* or permanent public that identifies the humane values a good story embodies:

> It appears that there is a permanent public, an actual community existing over time, that believes in the values of truth, the good, beauty, health, wisdom, courage, temperance, justice, harmony, order, communion, friendship, and oneness with the Cosmos—as variously as those values may be defined or practiced in "real" life.[16]

Ideal audience
An actual community existing over time that believes in the values of truth, the good, beauty, health, wisdom, courage, temperance, justice, harmony, order, communion, friendship, and oneness with the cosmos.

Fisher admits that other communities are possible—ones based on greed or power, for example. But he maintains that when people are confronted by "the better part of themselves," these less-idealistic value systems won't be "entirely coherent or true to their whole lives, or to the life that they would most like to live."[17] Fisher believes, then, that the humane virtues of the ideal audience shape our logic of good reasons. They help us pick which stories are reliable and trustworthy. If we are convinced that this audience of good people would scoff at Boaz' protection of Ruth or squirm in discomfort at her midnight visit to the barn, Buechner's version of the biblical narrative will lack fidelity. But inasmuch as we think that these ideal auditors would applaud Ruth's rarified devotion to Naomi—while appreciating the older woman's down-to-earth approach to courtship—Buechner's words will have the ring of truthfulness and humanity.

According to Fisher, when we judge a story to have fidelity, we are not merely affirming shared values. We are ultimately opening ourselves to the possibility that those values will influence our beliefs and actions. For example, many engaged couples for whom the love of Ruth rings true have adopted her words to Naomi as a model for their wedding vows:

> I will go wherever you go and live wherever you live.
> Your people will be my people, and your God will be my God.[18]

I have employed the age-old story of Ruth to illustrate features of the narrative paradigm. In like manner, most of my students—like Chris below—pick a book or a film to demonstrate their application of Fisher's theory.

> Beginning with *The Lion, The Witch, and the Wardrobe* in *The Chronicles of Narnia*, C. S. Lewis presents a coherent set of stories. While the characters, places, and events may not be "of this world"—the rational world we live in—Lewis has constructed a set of relationships and rules so consistent that it makes the fictional world seem plausible. The stories also have fidelity because Lewis skillfully creates parallels to our common human reality. The characters relate directly to people in my life (including me). For instance, I can identify with "doubting" Susan as she grows out of her childlike faith. Yet I long for the innocent passion of Lucy and the nobleness of Peter.

A good story is a powerful means of persuasion. Fisher would remind us, however, that almost *all* communication is narrative, and that we evaluate it on that basis. This chapter and all the others in this book are story. According to his narrative paradigm, you can (and will) judge whether they hang together and ring true to the values held by the people who make up your ideal audience.

CRITIQUE: DOES FISHER'S STORY HAVE COHERENCE AND FIDELITY?

Fisher's narrative paradigm offers a fresh reworking of Aristotelian analysis, which has dominated rhetorical thinking in the field of communication. His approach is strongly democratic—people usually don't need specialized training or expertise to figure out if a story holds together or offers good reasons for believing it to be true. There's still a place for experts to provide information and explanation in specialized fields, but when it comes to evaluating coherence and fidelity, people with ordinary common sense are competent rhetorical critics.

In *Human Communication as Narration*, Fisher applies the principles of narrative coherence and narrative fidelity to analyze various types of communication. He explains why a sometimes illogical President Ronald Reagan was aptly known as "The Great Communicator." He examines the false values of Willy Loman that lead to his downfall in *Death of a Salesman*. And he explores the consequences of adopting the rival philosophies embedded in the stories of two Greek thinkers—Socrates and Callicles. According to Fisher, the fact that the narrative paradigm can be applied to this wide range of communication genres provides strong evidence for its acceptance. And unlike a value-neutral scientific or rational-world approach, Fisher's narrative paradigm is clear about the motives, actions, and outcomes that make a story good.

Of course, Fisher's theory is itself a story, and as you might expect, not everyone accepts his tale. For example, many critics charge that he is overly optimistic when, similar to Aristotle, he argues that people have a natural tendency to prefer the true and the just. Challenging Fisher's upbeat view of human nature, rhetorical critic Barbara Warnick at the University of Pittsburgh calls attention to the great communicative power of evil or wrongheaded stories such as Hitler's *Mein Kampf*. Fisher declares that Hitler's opus "must be judged a bad story,"[19] but as Warnick notes, it "struck a chord in an alienated, disunited, and despairing people."[20] Hitler's success in scapegoating the Jews ranks as one of history's most notorious acts of rhetoric, yet in its time and place it achieved both coherence and fidelity. Fisher thinks Warnick is confusing Hitler's *effective* discourse with the *good* discourse people tend to prefer. But he grants that evil can overwhelm that tendency and thinks that's all the more reason to identify and promote the humane values described by the narrative paradigm.

William Kirkwood at East Tennessee State University claims there is another problem with the logic of good reasons. Kirkwood says a standard of narrative rationality implies that good stories cannot and perhaps should not go beyond what people already believe and value. He charges that the logic of good reasons encourages writers and speakers to adjust their ideas to people rather than people to their ideas, and thus denies the "rhetoric of possibility," the chance to be swayed by that which is unfamiliar or radically different.[21]

University of Rhode Island communication professor Kevin McClure agrees with Kirkwood, and argues that Fisher's understanding of probability and fidelity are too tightly linked with normative concepts of rationality. He reminds us that Fisher wrote that "the operative principle of narrative rationality is identification."[22] If Fisher would concentrate on Kenneth Burke's understanding of identification as "an aesthetic and poetic experience, and thus a relational experience or encounter with the symbolic rather than an encounter with rational argument," McClure believes the narrative paradigm could easily explain how improbable stories that "lack a sense of fidelity are accepted and acted on."[23]

Fisher thinks these critiques are ridiculous. He explicitly states that people have the capacity to "formulate and adopt new stories that better account for their lives or the mystery of life itself."[24] In a somewhat wry fashion, Fisher credits his detractors for demonstrating the wisdom of the narrative paradigm:

> I want to thank my critics, for they cannot but substantiate the soundness of my position. They do this in two ways: whatever line of attack they may take, they end up criticizing either the coherence or fidelity of my position, or both. And whatever objections they may make, the foundation for their objections will be a rival story, which, of course, they assume to be coherent and which has fidelity.[25]

Is most communication story, and do we judge every message we hear on the basis of whether it hangs together and rings true with our values? If you take Fisher's ideas seriously, you won't need me or a trained rhetorician to give you the final word. Like everyone else, you can spot the difference between a good story and a bad one.

QUESTIONS TO SHARPEN YOUR FOCUS

1. Using Fisher's definition of *narration,* can you think of any types of communication other than jokes or phatic communication that don't fit within the *narrative paradigm?*

2. Fisher claims that the *rational-world paradigm* dominates Western education. Can you list college courses you've taken that adopt the assumptions of this conceptual framework?

3. What is the difference between *narrative coherence* and *narrative fidelity?*

4. You apply a *logic of good reasons* to the stories you hear. What are the *values* undergirding Buechner's story of Ruth? Which one do you most admire? What *values* do you hold that cause you to ultimately accept or reject his narrative?

312   *GROUP AND PUBLIC COMMUNICATION*

A SECOND LOOK

Recommended resource: Walter R. Fisher, *Human Communication as Narration: Toward a Philosophy of Reason, Value, and Action,* University of South Carolina, Columbia, 1987.

Original statement: Walter R. Fisher, "Narration as a Human Communication Paradigm: The Case of Public Moral Argument," *Communication Monographs,* Vol. 51, 1984, pp. 1–22.

Storytelling and narrativity in communication research: Journal of Communication, Vol. 35, No. 4, 1985, entire issue.

Scientific communication as story: Walter R. Fisher, "Narration, Knowledge, and the Possibility of Wisdom," in *Rethinking Knowledge: Reflections Across the Disciplines,* Robert F. Goodman and Walter R. Fisher (eds.), State University of New York, Albany, 1995, pp. 169–197.

Narrative ethics: Walter R. Fisher, "The Ethic(s) of Argument and Practical Wisdom," in *Argument at Century's End,* Thomas Hollihan (ed.), National Communication Association, Annandale, VA, 1999, pp. 1–15.

Telling the old story in a new way: Frederick Buechner, *Peculiar Treasures,* Harper & Row, New York, 1979.

Coherent life stories: Dan McAdams, "The Problem of Narrative Coherence," *Journal of Constructivist Psychology,* Vol. 19, 2006, pp. 109–125.

Ethics as story: Richard Johannesen, "A Rational World Ethic Versus a Narrative Ethic for Political Communication," in *Ethics in Human Communication,* 6th ed., Waveland, Prospect Heights, IL, 2008, pp. 254–262.

Empirical measure of believability: Robert Yale, "Measuring Narrative Believability: Development and Validation of the Narrative Believability Scale (NBS-12)," *Journal of Communication,* Vol. 63, 2013, pp. 578–599.

Critique: Barbara Warnick, "The Narrative Paradigm: Another Story," *Quarterly Journal of Speech,* Vol. 73, 1987, pp. 172–182.

Critique: Robert Rowland, "On Limiting the Narrative Paradigm: Three Case Studies," *Communication Monographs,* Vol. 56, 1989, pp. 39–54.

Response to critics: Walter R. Fisher, "Clarifying the Narrative Paradigm," *Communication Monographs,* Vol. 56, 1989, pp. 55–58.

Suggested revision: Kevin McClure, "Resurrecting the Narrative Paradigm: Identification and the Case of Young Earth Creationism," *Rhetoric Society Quarterly,* Vol. 39, 2009, pp. 189–211.

Are you convinced you can detect when a story is false?
Click on Interpersonal Deception Theory in
Archive under Theory Resources at
www.afirstlook.com.

DIVISION FOUR

Mass Communication

M e d i a   E f f e c t s

In 1940, before the era of television, a team of researchers from Columbia University, headed by Paul Lazarsfeld, descended on Erie County, Ohio, an area that had reflected national voting patterns in every twentieth-century presidential election. By surveying people once a month from June to November, the interviewers sought to determine how the press and radio affected the people's choice for the upcoming presidential election.[1]

Contrary to the then-accepted *magic-bullet* model of direct media influence, the researchers found little evidence that voters were swayed by what they read or heard. Political conversions were rare. The media seemed merely to reinforce the decisions of those who had already made up their minds.

Lazarsfeld attributed the lack of media effect to *selective exposure* (see Chapter 16). Republicans avoided articles and programs that were favorable to President Franklin Roosevelt; Democrats bypassed news stories and features sympathetic to Republican Wendell Willkie. The principle of selective exposure didn't always test out in the laboratory, where people's attention was virtually guaranteed, but in a free marketplace of ideas it accounted for the limited, short-term effects of mass communication.

The Erie County results forced media analysts to recognize that friends and family affect the impact of media messages. They concluded that print and electronic media influence masses of people only through an indirect *two-step flow of communication.* The first stage is the direct transmission of information to a small group of people who stay well informed. In the second stage, those opinion leaders pass on and interpret the messages to others in face-to-face discussion.

The two-step flow theory surfaced at a time of rapid scientific advancement in the fields of medicine and agriculture. The model accurately described the diffusion of innovation among American doctors and farmers in the 1950s, but the present era of saturation television and Internet news has made alterations necessary. The first step of the *revised two-step theory* of media influence is the transmission of information to a mass audience. The second step is validation of the message by people the viewer respects.[2]

By the 1970s, empirical studies on viewer response to television had re-established belief in a *powerful-effects* model of media influence, and the explanatory links between the two were becoming clear. The possible connection between violence on the screen and subsequent viewer aggression was of particular interest to media theorists, and remains an important research focus today.

In the 1980s and 1990s, theorists continued to study how media content affects behavior, but expanded their focus to include thoughts and feelings. Dolf Zillmann, professor emeritus at the University of Alabama, used his *excitation transfer theory* to highlight the role of physiological arousal when we react to media.[3] According to the theory, emotional reactions like fear, anger, joy, and lust all generate heightened arousal that takes a while to dissipate after media exposure. The leftover excitation can amplify any mood we feel afterward. If a man becomes angry at his wife, the arousal he experiences from watching televised aggression can fuel his anger and lead to domestic violence. But Zillmann says that arousal from an erotic bedroom scene or a protagonist's joyful triumph can cause the same effect.

352　*MASS COMMUNICATION*

Excitation transfer can account for violent acts performed immediately after TV viewing. But Stanford psychologist Albert Bandura's *social learning theory* takes the findings a step further and predicts that the use of force modeled on television today may erupt in antisocial behavior years later.[4] Although Bandura's theory can explain imitation in many contexts, most students of his work apply it specifically to the vicarious learning of aggression through television.

Social learning theory postulates three necessary stages in the causal link between television and the actual physical harm we might inflict on another some time in the future. The three-step process is attention, retention, and motivation. Video violence grabs our *attention* because it's simple, distinctive, prevalent, useful, and depicted positively. If you doubt that last quality, remember that television draws in viewers by placing attractive people in front of the camera. There are very few overweight bodies or pimply faces on TV. When the winsome star roughs up a few hoods to rescue the lovely young woman, aggression is given a positive cast.

Without any risk to ourselves, watching media violence can expand our repertoire of behavioral options far beyond what we'd discover on our own through trial-and-error learning. For example, we see a knife fighter holding a switchblade at an inclined angle of 45 degrees and that he jabs up rather than lunging down. This kind of street smarts is mentally filed away as a visual image. But Bandura says *retention* is strongest when we also encode vicarious learning into words: *Hold the pistol with both hands. Don't jerk the trigger; squeeze it. Aim six inches low to compensate for recoil.*

Without sufficient *motivation*, we may never imitate the violence we saw and remember. But years later we may be convinced that we won't go to jail for shooting a prowler lurking in our backyard or that we might gain status by punching out a jerk who is hassling a friend. If so, what we learned earlier and stored in our memory bank is now at our disposal.

Communication scholars are playing catch-up trying to document the effects of the rapid changes brought by new media technology. We need to be patient before a strong consensus forms about some of the effects. A few researchers blame Facebook content for increasing feelings of depression,[5] while others find no such relationship.[6] Still others tout the social network's benefits for keeping us closely connected to friends.[7] Theorists are busy attempting to scope out the conditions that might explain these divergent findings.

CALVIN AND HOBBES 1995 © Watterson. Distributed by Universal UCLICK. Used by permission. All rights reserved.

CHAPTER **28**

Uses and Gratifications

of Elihu Katz

Paul and Alex are college sophomores who have roomed together since freshman year. At the end of their first year, Paul notices that Alex is spending more and more time playing *Call of Duty: Modern Warfare*, an online game in which many players join together in a common mission. During their second year, the gaming gets even more intense. Paul becomes concerned that his roommate's game playing is draining time from his studies and ruining his social life.

Thinking about Alex, Paul remembers what he heard in his media class about the case of Lien Wen-cheng. The 27-year-old Taiwanese man died of exhaustion in 2002 after playing a video game for 32 straight hours.[1] And in 2005 in South Korea, a man died after playing a game for 50 consecutive hours. Authorities said the man had hardly eaten during his game playing and hadn't slept.[2] While Paul knows that these deaths happened in Asian countries where addiction to video games has been a greater problem than in the United States,[3] he wonders if he should try to have a serious talk with Alex about his game playing. He feels especially motivated to talk with Alex after reading about Chris Staniforth, the 20-year-old British man who died in 2011 after playing *Halo* on his Xbox. Staniforth sat for 12 hours straight while playing the game and developed a blood clot in his leg that eventually hit his heart and killed him.[4]

Whether or not you spend time playing video games like Alex does, you do make daily choices to consume different types of media. In the late 1950s, when communication scholar Elihu Katz began his work on uses and gratifications theory (commonly referred to as *uses & grats*), no one was playing video games on campus. But newspapers, magazines, radio, and movies were well established, and 80 percent of American households had a TV. There were plenty of media to choose from.

Katz thought studying all of those media choices was so important that it could save the entire field of communication.[5] He made his argument about saving the field in response to another communication scholar, Bernard Berelson, who had just published an influential essay arguing that the future of communication research was bleak.[6] Berelson based his case on the study of the persuasive power of radio during the 1940 presidential campaign[7]—research described in the introduction to this section. The study showed that media didn't do anything to change people's attitudes. Berelson reasoned that if media weren't persuasive, the field of communication research would simply wither away.

Katz, who is now a professor emeritus of both sociology and communication at The Hebrew University of Jerusalem, introduced a different logic. In order to prevent the disintegration of the field, he suggested that scholars change the question used to generate their research. Instead of asking, "What do media do to people?" Katz flipped the question around to ask, "What do people do with media?"[8] In retrospect, the field of communication was hardly on its deathbed. Berelson's perspective was overly pessimistic and, by focusing only on media effects, it was overly narrow as well. Though Katz' theory didn't "save" the discipline, it was still valuable because it encouraged scholars to think about mass communication in a different way. As it turns out, uses & grats has endured for more than 50 years and still inspires cutting-edge research.

The theory attempts to make sense of the fact that people consume a dizzying array of media messages for all sorts of reasons, and that the effect of a given message is unlikely to be the same for everyone. The driving mechanism of the theory is need gratification. By understanding the particular needs of media consumers, the reasons for media consumption become clear. Particular media effects, or lack of effects, can also be clarified. For example, radio listeners in 1940 may have been so loyal to their political party that they had little need to listen to the opposing party's campaign ads. If they didn't attend to the ads, the ads couldn't have any effect. Let's look more closely at the five key assumptions that underlie uses & grats.

PEOPLE USE MEDIA FOR THEIR OWN PARTICULAR PURPOSES

The theory's fundamental assumption was revolutionary at the time Katz proposed it: *The study of how media affect people must take account of the fact that people deliberately use media for particular purposes.* Prior to this proposal, scholars thought that audiences were passive targets waiting to be hit by a magic bullet (the media message) that would affect everyone in the same way. In uses & grats, audiences are seen as anything but passive. They decide which media they want to use and what effects they want the media to have.

Consider an example: When Game 6 of the 2010 NHL Stanley Cup Finals was on TV, I (Glenn) wanted to watch it in hopes of seeing the Chicago Blackhawks become hockey champions. I wasn't a big fan of the sport, but after talking with Em, a hockey aficionado, I got sucked into the series. When I sat down to watch I was already prepared to celebrate. My wife, Cheri, who would ordinarily choose to watch *anything* instead of hockey, decided that the clacking of hockey sticks was exactly what she needed to prevent her from stumbling upon the depressing CNN videos of oil gushing into the Gulf of Mexico from the exploded BP oil well. So we decided to watch the game together—each for very different reasons and with very different effects. For me, watching the game resulted in happiness as I basked in the Blackhawks' victory. For her, the game provided a boring, but safe, distraction from unpleasant news she wanted to avoid. According to uses & grats, audiences are strong; they play a pivotal role in determining how any influence of media will play out. When Cheri and I each decided to watch that hockey game for different reasons, we behaved in a way that was consistent with the theory.

Fast-forward to 2013 with the Blackhawks again trying to win the Stanley Cup in Game 6 but trailing the Boston Bruins 2 to 1 with just 76 seconds left in the game. When the Hawks scored two goals in 17 seconds to win the championship, I was once again basking in their success. But this time around, Cheri wasn't viewing just to hear the clack of hockey sticks. She had become a fan and her excitement for the Blackhawks matched mine. This illustrates an underlying premise of uses and gratifications theory: reasons to consume media—even the same type of media—can change over time.

In the history of media theory, uses & grats is known for its deliberate shift away from the notion that powerful media messages have uniform effects on large audiences (passive receivers). Instead, the theory emphasizes the personal media choices consumers make to fulfill different purposes at different times. The *uniform-effects model* does not easily account for Paul's and Alex' very different behavior surrounding video games. But uses & grats assumes that the two roommates make deliberate choices that result in different patterns of media use and different effects. The uniform-effects view of media evokes the image of a parent who force-feeds the kids with a prepared formula that's guaranteed to have the same effect on each child. Uses & grats rejects that image and replaces it with one of adults in a cafeteria deciding what to eat based on individual yearnings at particular times. You might compare Alex' obsession with playing video games to someone craving the same food for every meal.

Uniform-effects model
The view that exposure to a media message affects everyone in the audience in the same way; often referred to as the "magic-bullet" or "hypodermic-needle" model of mass communication.

PEOPLE SEEK TO GRATIFY NEEDS

Just as people eat in order to satisfy certain cravings, uses & grats assumes people have needs that they seek to gratify through media use.[9] Note the close connection between the concepts of *media use* and *gratification from media.* The deliberate choices people make in using media are presumably based on the gratifications they seek from those media. Thus, *uses* and *gratifications* are inextricably linked. By taking this position, Katz was swimming against the tide of media theory at the time. In 1974, he wrote an essay with Jay Blumler and Michael Gurevitch, two scholars often considered co-creators of the theory. The essay states:

> In the mass communication process much initiative in linking need gratification and media choice lies with the audience member. This places a strong limitation on theorizing about any form of straight-line effect of media content on attitudes and behavior.[10]

Straight-line effect of media
A specific effect on behavior that is predicted from media content alone, with little consideration of the differences in people who consume that content.

A *straight-line effect of media* is a specific effect on behavior that is predicted from media content alone, with little consideration of the differences in people who consume that content. A theory predicting this sort of effect might guess that *both* Cheri and I would have become excited watching the Blackhawks win the Stanley Cup in 2010. But Katz thought the key to understanding media depended upon which need(s) a person was trying to satisfy when selecting a media message. One reason that hockey game affected Cheri and I differently is that we were watching the game to satisfy different needs.

MEDIA COMPETE FOR YOUR ATTENTION AND TIME

One of Paul's concerns as he watches Alex spend so much time playing video games is that gaming is ruining Alex' social life. From Paul's perspective, the technology that permits Alex to interact with other gamers online is competing with opportunities to interact with peers on campus. The uses & grats approach directly acknowledges the competition. Not only do media compete with each other for your time, they compete with other activities that don't involve media exposure.

While Paul evaluates Alex' situation as unhealthy, uses & grats first attempts to understand exactly what needs motivate Alex' use of video games. Why does he choose to spend his time gaming instead of socializing with Paul and the other guys who live in the dorm? Some of the more recent attempts to understand these sorts of choices might provide an answer. Uses & grats researchers have discovered that some people experience high levels of anxiety when they think about talking face-to-face; they don't enjoy these sorts of interactions or find them rewarding.[11] Meeting in person just doesn't gratify their needs. In contrast, extroverts express a clear preference for one-on-one conversations over spending time with media.[12]

The notion that media compete for attention and time is only an initial step in understanding the choices people eventually make. The more interesting question is *why* some people choose to watch TV while others decide to play a video game or read a book, and still others decide to have coffee with a friend. On any given day, the number of ways we can choose to spend our time is nearly limitless. According to uses & grats, we won't understand the media choices we make unless we first recognize the underlying needs that motivate our behavior. Paul's well-intentioned concern might cause him to overlook the needs Alex has that are gratified by playing video games. Helping Alex get a good grasp of the reasons he plays may be the key to helping him alter his behavior.

MEDIA AFFECT DIFFERENT PEOPLE DIFFERENTLY

One of the core concepts of uses and gratifications theory is that the same media message doesn't necessarily affect everyone the same way. That's because media audiences are made up of people who are not identical to each other. In terms of media effects, the differences matter.

My own studies on the effects of frightening media have confirmed this central tenet of uses & grats. Assuming that Hollywood makes so many scary movies because of the popularity of the genre, journalists often ask me, "Why do people enjoy watching scary movies?" My first response to this question is always the same and echoes the fundamental point of uses & grats: Not everyone *does* enjoy scary movies. Some people systematically avoid them and can suffer for days if they become emotionally upset from what they see in a film.

As it turns out, few people voluntarily expose themselves to scary movies in order to experience fear. Fear is a negative emotion and, in general, people want to avoid it. However, some people are willing to tolerate fear in order to ooh and aah at high-tech special effects they can't see anywhere else. Others are willing to endure fear to experience a sense of mastery over something threatening— much like the effect of riding a roller coaster. Still others might actually enjoy the adrenaline rush that accompanies a scary movie and the intense relief that comes when the film is over.[13] Current research seeks to understand the factors that lead some individuals to shun frightening entertainment and others to seek it out. Media effects scholarship lends strong support to the uses & grats claim that media affect different people differently.

PEOPLE CAN ACCURATELY REPORT THEIR MEDIA USE AND MOTIVATION

If uses & grats was to have any future as a theory, researchers had to find a way to uncover the media that people consumed and the reasons they consumed it. For these purposes, the most obvious way to collect data involved asking people directly and recording their answers. There is now a long tradition in mass communication research that asks people to report the amount of time they devote to different kinds of media. The early research on uses & grats can take a good deal of the credit for starting that practice.[14]

The controversial aspect of this measurement strategy is whether or not people are truly capable of discerning the reasons for their media consumption. It may be easy for us to report the reason why we watch a local weather forecast, but it might be more difficult to know exactly why we're so willing to kill a few hours each day playing a game like *Angry Birds* on our smart phones.

If Paul were to ask Alex why he spends so much time playing video games, Alex might simply say, "Because I like it." Scholars attempting to arrive at the best scientific explanation for Alex' behavior might question that response. Is it possible, for example, that Alex is playing the games to avoid having to talk with others face-to-face? If so, would he necessarily be aware of that motivation? While some scholars have attempted to show that we can trust people's reports of the reasons for their media consumption,[15] this assumption of the theory continues to be debated. Sometimes assumptions turn out to be wrong.

A TYPOLOGY OF USES AND GRATIFICATIONS

What are the reasons people give for their media consumption? For the last 50 years, uses & grats researchers have compiled various lists of the motives people report. These studies are designed to construct a *typology* of the major reasons why people voluntarily expose themselves to different media. A typology is simply a classification scheme that attempts to sort a large number of specific instances into a more manageable set of categories.

One of the most comprehensive typologies of media uses and gratifications was proposed by communication scholar Alan Rubin in 1981.[16] Rubin claims that his typology of eight motivations can account for most explanations people give for why they watch television. Notice that each category describes both a reason for TV *use* as well as a potential *gratification* experienced from that use.

1. **Passing time.** Consider the waiting room at the doctor's office. The primary reason for watching TV is to simply pass the time until you're called in for your appointment.

2. **Companionship.** When sports fans get together to watch the big game, some fans are there primarily for the chance to get together with friends. Watching the game is secondary.

3. **Escape.** Instead of focusing on that anxiety-causing term paper due in two weeks, a college student might just turn on the tube to escape the pressure.

4. **Enjoyment.** Many report that the main reason they watch a TV show is that they find the whole experience enjoyable. This might be the most basic motivation to consume any media.

358   *MASS COMMUNICATION*

5. **Social interaction.** TV viewing provides a basis for connecting to others. If I make sure to watch the most recent episode of a series like *Game of Thrones*, I may find that I have more opportunities to start a conversation with someone else who saw the same show.

6. **Relaxation.** After working all day, many people report that they find watching TV to be relaxing. Today, many households have at least one bedroom with a TV set. People sometimes report that watching TV relaxes them so much that they have difficulty falling asleep any other way.

7. **Information.** News junkies report that watching TV is all about keeping up with the latest information of the day. If they don't get to watch TV for several days, they report feeling uncomfortable about the information they know they've missed.

8. **Excitement.** Sometimes media consumers are after an intense sense of excitement. This could be one reason why media violence is a staple of TV entertainment. Conflict and violence generate a sense of excitement that few other dramatic devices can match.

When you look at Rubin's eight categories, it's easy to see that the examples filed under any one label don't have to be identical. While some people look for violence to gratify their need for excitement, others, like Alex, look for a competitive online game. Still others might seek out a movie with erotic content in order to provide a sense of sexual excitement. Excitement can be subdivided into sexual excitement, competitive excitement, and excitement that arises from a suspenseful story line. But if each of Rubin's eight categories were subdivided into three more, the resulting typology of 24 categories would seem unwieldy and inelegant. Remember that relative simplicity is a valuable asset for objective theories.

Rubin claims that his typology captures *most* of the explanations people give for their media consumption. There may well be others. When Bradley Greenberg studied uses and gratifications among British children back in 1974, he discovered that many kids reported they watched TV simply because they had developed a *habit* of doing so that was difficult to break.[17] Rubin discussed habitual viewing under the "passing time" category. If he were doing his research today, he'd find habitual texting or Facebook use as common activities. Of course, kids aren't the only ones who cite habit as the main reason they use media. In "Television

Typology
A classification scheme that attempts to sort a large number of specific instances into a more manageable set of categories.

Addiction Is No Mere Metaphor," a 2002 *Scientific American* cover story, communication researchers Robert Kubey and Mihaly Csikszentmihalyi present hard evidence of TV's habit-forming nature.[18] Maintaining that habit feels good. Breaking it is agony. Paul may realize that if he asks Alex to simply stop playing video games, his roommate will balk at the request. Alex may have developed a habitual behavior that is no longer volitional.

PARASOCIAL RELATIONSHIPS: USING MEDIA TO HAVE A FANTASY FRIEND

Using media to gratify a habitual urge may not be the only motivation to consider as an additional category for Rubin's typology. Years ago, actor Robert Young played the lead role in the hit TV series *Marcus Welby, M.D.* As the ideal physician who combined kindness with authority and expertise, he attracted millions of weekly viewers who were curious about how Dr. Welby would solve the next medical mystery. As the popularity of the series grew, something strange started to happen—the actor began receiving personal letters from viewers asking him for medical advice. In fact, according to one researcher who wrote a book on the "psychology of fame and celebrity," Robert Young received more than 250,000 such letters during the first five years of the program.[19] Why did so many viewers come to believe that a Hollywood actor with no medical credentials was a good source of medical advice?

The answer to that intriguing question is now best understood in terms of what researchers refer to as the *parasocial relationship.* According to Rubin, a parasocial relationship is basically a sense of friendship or emotional attachment that develops between TV viewers and media personalities. This relationship can be measured by asking viewers some basic questions about their involvement with popular characters. Rubin says these relationships are experienced in different ways, including ". . . seeking guidance from a media persona, seeing media personalities as friends, imagining being part of a favorite program's social world, and desiring to meet media performers."[20] While Rubin doesn't suggest that desire for a parasocial relationship might count as another category in his typology, it certainly seems to be a candidate.

Parasocial relationship A sense of friendship or emotional attachment that develops between TV viewers and media personalities.

Knowing which media consumers will form parasocial relationships can help researchers predict how media will affect different viewers in different ways. An illustration is found in the surprising aftermath of an episode of the old TV series *Happy Days.*[21] Shortly after the episode where "The Fonz" applied for a library card was broadcast, library card applications around the country increased 500 percent. By applying uses & grats, a researcher might hypothesize that viewers who were more deeply involved in a parasocial relationship with The Fonz would be the ones most likely to apply for a card.

In the same way that uses & grats could be used to analyze TV viewing, it also holds potential for studying social media. For example, the theory could be applied to make sense of the huge number of people who felt the urge to share their grief online after the death of Cory Monteith in July 2013. Monteith, a star on the TV show *Glee,* died suddenly and tragically from a lethal mix of heroin and alcohol. Weeks later, tribute pages with thousands of followers continued to percolate with activity. In fact, Monteith's followers on Twitter increased by over a half million *after* he was gone.[22] Who would start subscribing to the Twitter feed of a dead person? A uses & grats theorist might suggest that signing up for the Twitter feed is a way of expressing a deep parasocial involvement with Monteith.

Although fans who feel attached to celebrities aren't able to express their grief by going to the funeral and hugging grieving family members, they *are* able to use social media to show they care. Following the Twitter feed of the deceased may serve the same function as paying respects at the funeral home to the family members of a personal acquaintance. In both cases, the expression shows appropriate concern.

In his review of some of the current directions of research on uses & grats, Rubin notes several studies that utilize the existence of parasocial relationships to predict differential effects of media content on viewers.[23] For example, after basketball star Magic Johnson announced in 1991 that he had tested positive for HIV, one study compared college students who may have had a parasocial relationship with Johnson to those who said they had only heard of him. News reports of Johnson's disease affected the two groups differently. Those who may have had a parasocial relationship said they were more concerned about HIV among heterosexuals and expressed an intention to reduce risky sexual behavior. Students who had only heard of Magic Johnson weren't affected by the news reports in the same way.[24]

CRITIQUE: HEAVY ON DESCRIPTION AND LIGHT ON PREDICTION?

In Chapter 3 you read that a good objective theory explains the past and present and predicts the future. These two criteria are called the "twin objectives of scientific knowledge." One criticism of uses & grats is that its major contribution is a *descriptive* typology of media uses and gratifications. For some, the emphasis on description rather than *explanation* and *prediction* is one of the theory's weak spots. This criticism might be countered by pointing out that studies such as the one on reactions to reports of Magic Johnson's contracting HIV offer more than just description; they enable researchers to predict which media will affect consumers in particular ways, and they offer an explanation for the data observed.

Jiyeon So, a communication professor at the University of Georgia, recently published an article that tackles the "description–prediction" critique head-on.[25] She notes that uses and gratifications theory was never intended to be merely descriptive; it was originally designed to offer specific predictions about media effects. But for whatever reason, the research on uses & grats has emphasized description. She goes on to explain that the theory can be used to predict different media effects by first understanding why people are consuming a particular media message. If her article helps set a new course for uses & grats research, the standard critique about prediction should fade away.

How well does uses & grats measure up against the other criteria mentioned in Chapter 3: *relative simplicity, testability, practical utility,* and *quantitative research?* There's nothing overly complex about the theory. The propositions that people use media to gratify particular needs and that those needs can be succinctly described using eight categories have the ring of *relative simplicity.* On the other hand, scholars continue to question the extent to which people can accurately report the reasons for their media use.[26] If they can't, the theory's *testability* is jeopardized. While people may be able to report with reasonable accuracy *what* media they consume, who is to say *why* they consume it? Depth psychologists from Freud to present-day therapists would suggest that the average media user is probably in one of the *worst* positions to explain his or her choices. There may also be a logical contradiction between the habit motive for consuming media and the theory's notion that media choices are conscious and deliberate. To the extent that Alex plays video games out of a deeply ingrained habit, he may not reflect on how he spends his time before he sits down to play. If so, his failure to reflect creates a problem for testing a theory that takes such reflection for granted.

To their credit, uses & grats scholars don't just dig in and defend the theory. They've tried to respond to critics by making changes. Instead of staying with the simple assertion that media audiences are uniformly active and making conscious choices, Rubin modified uses & grats by claiming that activity is actually a variable in the theory.[27] Though some consumers exemplify the highly active audience member described in early versions of the theory, others consume media passively, out of habit, or with little conscious deliberation. Still others fall somewhere in between—or even at different points of the continuum at different times or in different situations. When Alex returns from class and unthinkingly slumps into his chair to play *Call of Duty*, he's on the passive end of the continuum. When he makes arrangements with his friends to meet online to play the game together, he's much more active.

As a student of communication theory and an expert in your own personal media consumption, you may be in the best position to evaluate the *practical utility* of uses & grats. What implications does the theory have for you? At the very least, you might think of uses & grats as raising your own personal consciousness about the media you consume and the reasons you consume it. By reflecting on your media use, you could come to a new realization of your needs and how you choose to gratify them. And this self-awareness can lead to more satisfying choices in the long run. If Alex realizes his game playing is based on a habitual urge that's threatening his health, he might be more inclined to take the advice of a concerned friend like Paul and seek help to curtail his habit.

Katz' notion in the 1950s that the theory of uses and gratifications could save the entire field of communication turned out to be an extreme exaggeration. Perhaps that was his way of getting scholars to pay attention to a new idea. A view that emphasizes what people do with media instead of what media do to people seemed like a strange theoretical twist. But despite the fact that Katz may have initially overplayed his hand, the theory has fared well. Uses & grats has generated a large body of *quantitative research*. It's also poised to serve as one of the main theories guiding media research well into the twenty-first century.

QUESTIONS TO SHARPEN YOUR FOCUS

1. To what extent can we give an *accurate report* of the media content we consume? Are we always aware of the reasons we choose the media we do? Why or why not?

2. Consider Facebook and other *social networking sites.* Have you heard others express reasons for using Facebook that aren't reflected in the typology proposed by Alan Rubin?

3. Do you think many people have *parasocial relationships* with media characters? Were the people who wrote letters to Robert Young seeking medical advice genuinely confused about whether he was an actor or a doctor?

4. Think of a specific example of how two individuals might use *media content* to gratify different needs. How will those individuals experience very different *media effects?*

A SECOND LOOK

Recommended resource: Elihu Katz, Jay G. Blumler, and Michael Gurevitch, "Utilization of Mass Communication by the Individual," in *The Uses of Mass Communications: Current Perspectives on Gratifications Research,* Jay G. Blumler and Elihu Katz (eds.), Sage, Beverly Hills, CA, 1974, pp. 19–32.

Current update and overview: Alan M. Rubin, "Uses-And-Gratifications Perspective on Media Effects," in *Media Effects: Advances in Theory and Research,* 3rd ed., Jennings Bryant and Mary Beth Oliver (eds.), Lawrence Erlbaum, New York, 2009, pp. 165–184.

Parasocial relationships: Alan M. Rubin and Mary M. Step, "Impact of Motivation, Attraction, and Parasocial Interaction on Talk Radio Listening," *Journal of Broadcasting & Electronic Media,* Vol. 44, 2000, pp. 635–654.

Using media as a substitute for face-to-face relationships: Will Miller and Glenn Sparks, *Refrigerator Rights: Creating Connections and Restoring Relationships,* Perigree, New York, 2002.

Validity of self-reports in uses & grats research: Jack M. McLeod and Lee B. Becker, "Testing the Validity of Gratification Measures Through Political Effects Analysis," in *The Uses of Mass Communications,* pp. 137–164.

Related theory: Dolf Zillmann, "Mood Management: Using Entertainment to Full Advantage," *Communication, Social Cognition, and Affect,* Lewis Donohew, Howard E. Sypher, and E. Tory Higgins (eds.), Lawrence Erlbaum, Hillsdale, NJ, 1988.

Gender differences in media use: Silvia Knobloch-Westerwick, "Gender Differences in Selective Media Use for Mood Management and Mood Adjustment," *Journal of Broadcasting & Electronic Media,* Vol. 51, 2007, pp. 73–92.

New media: Isolde Anderson, "The Uses and Gratifications of Online Care Pages: A Study of CaringBridge," *Health Communication,* Vol. 26, 2011, pp. 546–559.

Policy implications: Harold Mendelsohn, "Some Policy Implications of the Uses and Gratifications Paradigm," in *The Uses of Mass Communications,* pp. 303–318.

Comprehensive critique: Philip Elliott, "Uses and Gratifications Research: A Critique and a Sociological Alternative," in *The Uses of Mass Communications,* pp. 249–268.

Uses & grats is a theory describing needs and interests.
For another theory of motivation, click on Hierarchy of Needs
in Archive under Theory Resources at
www.afirstlook.com.

CHAPTER **29**

Cultivation Theory

of George Gerbner

What are the odds that you'll be involved in some kind of violent act within the next seven days? 1 out of 10? 1 out of 100? 1 out of 1,000? 1 out of 10,000?

According to Hungarian-born George Gerbner, the answer you give may have more to do with how much TV you watch than with the actual risk you face in the week to come. Gerbner, who died in 2005, was dean emeritus of the Annenberg School for Communication at the University of Pennsylvania and founder of the Cultural Environment Movement. He claimed that because TV contains so much violence, people who spend the most time in front of the tube develop an exaggerated belief in a *mean and scary world*. The violence they see on the screen can cultivate a social paranoia that counters notions of trustworthy people or safe surroundings.

Like Marshall McLuhan, Gerbner regarded television as the dominant force in shaping modern society. But unlike McLuhan, who viewed the medium as the message, Gerbner was convinced that TV's power comes from the symbolic content of the real-life drama shown hour after hour, week after week. At its root, television is society's institutional storyteller, and a society's stories give "a coherent picture of what exists, what is important, what is related to what, and what is right."[1]

Until the advent of broadcast media, the two acceptable storytellers outside the home were schools and faith communities. Today, the TV set is a key member of the household, with virtually unlimited access to every person in the family. Television dominates the environment of symbols, telling most of the stories, most of the time. Gerbner claimed that people now watch television as they might attend church, "except that most people watch television more religiously."[2]

What do they see in their daily devotions? According to Gerbner, violence is one of the major staples of the TV world. He wrote that violence "is the simplest and cheapest dramatic means to demonstrate who wins in the game of life and the rules by which the game is played."[3] Those who are immersed in the world of TV drama learn these "facts of life" better than occasional viewers do.

Most people who decry violence on television are worried that it affects receptive young viewers by encouraging aggressive *behavior*. Gerbner was more concerned that it affects viewers' *beliefs* about the world around them and the *feelings* connected to those beliefs. If viewers come to believe that the world around them is filled with crime, they're also likely to feel scared about the prospect of engaging in that crime-filled world. Gerbner thought that watching television violence might result in viewers wanting to own guard dogs, double-bolt locks, and home security systems. He was concerned that television violence convinces viewers that it is indeed "a jungle out there."

Gerbner's general expertise in the field of communication was widely acknowledged. He served as editor of the *Journal of Communication*, and for almost two decades he spearheaded an extensive research program that monitored the level of violence on television, classified people according to how much TV they watch, and compiled measures of how viewers perceive the world around them. He was especially interested in how viewers' consumption of TV violence increased their perceptions of risk for crime, and most of his research sought to gather support for that idea.

But cultivation theory isn't limited to TV violence. Other scholars have used it to theorize about how TV affects perceptions about the health risks of smoking, the popularity of various political positions, and appropriate gender roles. The ways that TV might affect views of social reality are probably too many to count. Partly because of Gerbner's credentials and partly because of the intuitive appeal of the theory itself, his cultivation explanation of his research findings remains one of the most popular and controversial theories of mass communication.

Gerbner introduced the theory of cultivation as part of his "cultural indicators" paradigm. As you'll recall from Fisher's *narrative paradigm* (see Chapter 24), a paradigm is a conceptual framework that calls for people to view events through a common interpretive lens. You might think of Gerbner's framework as a three-pronged plug leading to a TV set, with each of the prongs uniquely equipped to tell us something different about the world of TV.[4] Each of the three prongs is associated with a particular type of analysis that Gerbner considers a critical component in understanding the effects of television on its viewers.

INSTITUTIONAL PROCESS ANALYSIS—THE FIRST PRONG

The first prong of the plug represents scholars' concern for the reasons why media produce the messages they do. Gerbner labeled the research addressing this concern *institutional process analysis*. Scholars who do this type of research penetrate behind the scenes of media organizations in an effort to understand what policies or practices might be lurking there. For example, Gerbner believed that one reason there is so much violence on TV is that Hollywood is mainly concerned with how to export its product globally for maximum profit at minimum cost. Since violence is cheap to produce and speaks in a language that is universally understood, studios adopt policies that call for their shows to include lots of violent content.

Institutional process analysis
Scholarship that penetrates behind the scenes of media organizations in an effort to understand what policies or practices might be lurking there.

It would be difficult for a scholar to discover institutional policy without conducting in-depth interviews with media producers, accountants, and studio executives. When scholars conduct these sorts of interviews, they are engaging in institutional process analysis. Gerbner was fond of promoting his own views about the inner workings of Hollywood, but it isn't always clear whether those views were based on systematic scholarship. Cultivation theory is far better known for the concerns represented by the second and third prongs of the plug.

MESSAGE SYSTEM ANALYSIS—THE SECOND PRONG

If TV cultivates perceptions of social reality among viewers, it becomes essential to know exactly what messages TV transmits. The only way to know for sure is to undertake careful, systematic study of TV content—*message system analysis.* For Gerbner, that involved employing the method of quantitative *content analysis,* which resulted in numerical reports of exactly what the world of television contained.

Message system analysis
Scholarship that involves careful, systematic study of TV content, usually employing content analysis as a research method.

While Gerbner designed most of his content analyses to reveal how much violence was on TV and how that violence was depicted, this method can be used to focus on any type of TV content. For example, scholars who thought that TV cultivated perceptions about smoking behavior and appropriate gender roles used content analysis to document the prevalence of smoking and the different roles played by males and females in prime time. Other researchers have examined depictions of marriage and work, attitudes about science, depictions of the paranormal, treatment of various political views, and ways environmental issues are handled. Before one can examine how certain messages might affect perceptions of social reality, however, it's important to know exactly what those messages contain.

An Index of Violence

As the opening paragraphs of the chapter reveal, Gerbner devoted most of his research to studying the cultivating impact of media violence. His content analysis was designed to uncover exactly how violence was depicted on TV. Of course, that required Gerbner to clearly specify what he meant by violence. He defined *dramatic violence* as "the overt expression of physical force (with or without a weapon, against self or others) compelling action against one's will on pain of being hurt and/or killed or threatened to be so victimized as part of the plot."[5]

Dramatic violence
The overt expression or serious threat of physical force as part of the plot.

The definition rules out verbal abuse, idle threats, and pie-in-the-face slapstick. But it includes the physical abuse presented in a cartoon format. When the coyote pursuing the roadrunner is flattened by a steamroller or the *Mighty Morphin Power Rangers* crush their enemies, Gerbner would label the scene violent. He also counted auto crashes and natural disasters. From an artistic point of view, these events are no accident. The screenwriter inserted the trauma for dramatic effect. Characters die or are maimed just as effectively as if they'd taken a bullet in the chest.

For more than two decades, Gerbner's team of researchers randomly selected a week during the fall season and videotaped every prime-time (8 to 11 p.m.) network show. They also recorded programming for children on Saturday and Sunday (8 a.m. to 2 p.m.). After counting up the incidents that fit their description, they gauged the overall level of violence with a formula that included the ratio of programs that scripted violence, the rate of violence in those programs, and the percentage of characters involved in physical harm and killing. They found that the annual index was both remarkably stable and alarmingly high.

Equal Violence, Unequal Risk

One indisputable fact to emerge from Gerbner's analysis is that the cumulative portrayal of violence varies little from year to year. More than half of prime-time programs contain actual bodily harm or threatened violence. *The Big Bang Theory* and *Two and a Half Men* are not typical. Dramas that include violence average five traumatic incidents per viewing hour. Almost all the weekend children's shows major in mayhem. They average 20 cases an hour. By the time the typical TV viewer graduates from high school, he or she has observed 13,000 violent deaths.

On any given week, two-thirds of the major characters are caught up in some kind of violence. Heroes are just as involved as villains, yet there is great inequality as to the age, race, and gender of those on the receiving end of physical force. Old people and children are harmed at a much greater rate than are young or middle-aged adults. In the pecking order of "victimage," African Americans and Hispanics are killed or beaten more than their Caucasian counterparts. Gerbner noted that it's risky to be "other than clearly white." It's also dangerous to be female. The opening lady-in-distress scene is a favorite dramatic device to galvanize the hero into action. And finally, blue-collar workers "get it in the neck" more often than do white-collar executives.

The symbolic vulnerability of minority-group members is striking, given their gross underrepresentation in TV drama. Gerbner's analysis of the world of television recorded that 50 percent of the characters are white, middle-class males, and women are outnumbered by men 3 to 1. Although one-third of our society is made up of children and teenagers, they appear as only 10 percent of the characters on prime-time shows. Two-thirds of the United States labor force have blue-collar or service jobs, yet that group constitutes a mere 10 percent of the players on television. African Americans and Hispanics are only occasional figures, but the elderly are by far the most excluded minority. Less than 3 percent of the dramatic roles are filled by actors over the age of 65. If insurance companies kept actuarial tables on the life expectancy of television characters, they'd discover that the chance of a poor, elderly black woman's avoiding harm for the entire hour is almost nil.

"You do lovely needlepoint, grandma, but . . ."

Reproduced by permission of Punch Ltd., www.punch.co.uk

In sum, Gerbner's content analyses reveal that people on the margins of American society are put in symbolic double jeopardy. Their existence is understated, but at the same time their vulnerability to violence is overplayed. When written into the script, they are often made visible in order to be victims. Not surprisingly, these are the very people who exhibit the most fear of violence when the TV set is turned off.

CULTIVATION ANALYSIS—THE THIRD PRONG

Most devotees of cultivation theory subscribe to the notion that *message system analysis* is a prerequisite to the third prong of the plug: *cultivation analysis*. It's important to recognize the difference between the two. Message system analysis deals with the content of TV; cultivation analysis deals with how TV's content might affect viewers—particularly the viewers who spend lots of time glued to the tube.

It might be helpful to think of cultivation analysis as the prong that carries the most electrical current in the theory. This is the part of the paradigm where most of the action takes place. Gerbner's research associates, Michael Morgan, James Shanahan, and Nancy Signorielli, offer a clear definition of *cultivation:*

> The concept of "cultivation" thus refers to the independent contribution television viewing makes to audience members' conceptions of social reality. Television viewing cultivates ways of seeing the world—those who spend more time "living" in the world of television are more likely to see the "real world" in terms of the images, values, portrayals and ideologies that emerge through the lens of television.[6]

Cultivation analysis Research designed to find support for the notion that those who spend more time watching TV are more likely to see the "real world" through TV's lens.

After watching an episode of *Law & Order: Special Victims Unit*, Em's student Jeremy found the idea of cultivation perfectly plausible when it comes to watching media violence and developing a fear of real-world crime. His description of the episode and his conclusion about cultivation are worth noting:

> In the episode, a child found the dead bodies of both his nanny and his mom. His nanny was killed by someone she met online and his mom was killed by his dad a few days later because she was having an affair and wanted to leave him. At the end of the episode, a detective and the wife of another detective were in a car accident. Of the nine central characters in the episode, three were victims of violent crime and two were perpetrators of violent crime. Two of the four remaining characters were involved in the car crash, so only two people made it out of the episode unscathed. I can see how heavy viewers of such shows would get the idea that the world is mean and scary.

CULTIVATION WORKS LIKE A MAGNETIC OR GRAVITATIONAL FIELD

If Gerbner is right that heavy TV watching influences viewers' beliefs about the world, how can we understand exactly how this happens? It's tempting to think of cultivation as a linear *push* process, where TV content influences viewers much like the cue ball on a billiard table pushes the other balls to new locations upon impact. But cultivation researchers aren't fond of that metaphor. Michael Morgan and his co-authors point out that the cultivation process is much more like the *pull* of a gravitational field.[7]

As a researcher who majors in media effects and has published research on media cultivation,[8] I (Glenn) like to extend the metaphor of gravity to magnetism. Imagine a table of billiard balls that are made of metal, with the cue ball (representing TV) possessing powerful magnetic properties. Regardless of where the other balls (representing individual viewers) are positioned on the table, they will be affected by the magnetic pull of the cue ball and tend to move closer to it. Depending on the initial position of the balls on the table, they won't all move toward the magnetic cue ball at the same angle and at the same speed—but they will all be susceptible to the pull of the magnet to some degree. In the same way, although the magnitude of TV's influence is not the same for every viewer, all are affected by it.

While metaphors like the magnetic cue ball can shed light on a theoretical process like cultivation, some scholars see them as limited in terms of explaining what's really going on. L. J. Shrum, a professor of marketing at the University of Texas at San Antonio, offers insight into the "black box" of the mind so we can better understand how watching TV affects judgments of the world around us. Shrum relies on the *accessibility principle* in explaining TV's cultivating impact.[9] This principle states that when people make judgments about the world around them, they rely on the smallest bits of information that come to mind most quickly—the information that is most accessible.

Accessibility principle
When people make judgments about the world around them, they rely on the smallest bits of information that come to mind most quickly.

For those who consume lots of TV, the most accessible information for making judgments is more likely to come from TV shows than anywhere else. Heavy TV viewing keeps messages from the screen at the top of the mind's vast bin of information. If you're a heavy TV viewer and someone asks you about your odds of being involved in a violent act, the most accessible information about crime that you will use to construct your answer could come from your steady diet of *CSI.*

Gerbner seemed content to leave scholars like Shrum with the task of explaining exactly how the cultivation process works. In the meantime, he was busy spinning out more specific propositions to test. The two main propositions that guided his thinking about cultivation were *mainstreaming* and *resonance.*

MAINSTREAMING: BLURRING, BLENDING, AND BENDING OF ATTITUDES

Mainstreaming is Gerbner's term to describe the process of "blurring, blending, and bending" that those with heavy viewing habits undergo. He thought that through constant exposure to the same images and labels, heavy viewers develop a commonality of outlook that doesn't happen with radio. Radio stations segment the audience to the point where programming for left-handed truck drivers who bowl on Friday nights is a distinct possibility. But instead of *narrowcasting* their programs, TV producers *broadcast* in that they seek to "attract the largest possible audience by celebrating the moderation of the mainstream."[10] Television homogenizes its audience so that those with heavy viewing habits share the same orientations, perspectives, and meanings with each other.

Mainstreaming
The blurring, blending, and bending process by which heavy TV viewers from disparate groups develop a common outlook through constant exposure to the same images and labels.

Think of the metaphor of the metal billiard balls scattered on the pool table and visualize the magnetic cue ball in the center. Despite the fact that the individual metal balls are located in many different positions on the table, each one is drawn closer to the magnetic cue ball and, in the process, all of the balls become closer to each other—assuming positions on the table that are more alike than before the magnet had its effect. In a similar way, as TV mainstreams people, it pulls those who might initially be different from each other into a common perception of reality that resembles the TV world. We needn't ask how close this common perception of the way the world works is to the mainstream of culture. According to Gerbner, the "television answer" *is* the mainstream.

Gerbner illustrated the mainstreaming effect by showing how heavy TV viewers blur economic and political distinctions. TV glorifies the middle class, and those with heavy viewing habits assume that label, no matter what their income. But those with light viewing habits who have blue-collar jobs accurately describe themselves as working-class people.

In like fashion, those with heavy viewing habits label themselves political *moderates*. Most characters in TV dramas frown on political extremism—right or left. This nonextremist ethic is apparently picked up by the constant viewer. It's only from the ranks of sporadic TV users that Gerbner found people who actually label themselves *liberal* or *conservative*.

Social scientists have come to expect political differences between rich and poor, blacks and whites, Catholics and Protestants, city dwellers and farmers. Those distinctions still emerge when sporadic television viewers respond to the survey. But Gerbner reported that traditional differences diminish among those with heavy viewing habits. It's as if the light from the TV set washes out any sharp features that would set them apart.

Even though those with heavy viewing habits call themselves moderates, Gerbner and his associates studying cultural indicators noted that their positions on social issues are decidedly conservative. Heavy viewers consistently voice opinions in favor of lower taxes, more police protection, and stronger national defense. They are against big government, free speech, the Equal Rights Amendment, abortion, open-housing legislation, and affirmative action. The *mainstream* is not *middle of the road*. The magnetic cue ball isn't sitting in the middle of the table—it's distinctly skewed to the right.

RESONANCE: THE TV WORLD LOOKS LIKE MY WORLD, SO IT MUST BE TRUE

Resonance
The condition that exists when viewers' real-life environment is like the world of TV; these viewers are especially susceptible to TV's cultivating power.

To understand the resonance process, consider again the billiard metaphor. The balls closest to the magnetic cue ball are like TV viewers whose real-world environment is very much like the world of TV. They might be viewers who live in the inner city and are accustomed to violent attacks, police chases, and losing friends to violent crime. The balls farthest away from the cue ball are like viewers who live in a world that doesn't resemble TV at all. Which of the balls on the table are most affected by the magnetic cue ball? If you remember how magnets behave and you have a clear image of the billiard table, the answer is clear: the closest balls are the ones that will be most affected. In fact, if they are extremely close to the cue ball, they will be pulled in quickly and end up firmly attached. Although Gerbner didn't use this metaphor, I think he would have seen it as illustrative of the *resonance* process. He thought the cultivating power of TV's messages would be especially strong over viewers who perceived that the world depicted on TV was a world very much like their own. He thought of these viewers as ones who get a "double dose" of the same message.[11]

For three years Em was a volunteer advocate in a low-income housing project. Although he felt relatively safe walking through the project, police and social workers told stories of shootings and stabbings. Even peace-loving residents

370   *MASS COMMUNICATION*

were no strangers to violence. Em can't recall ever entering an apartment where the TV was turned off. Gerbner would expect that the daily diet of symbolic savagery would reinforce people's experience of doorstep violence, making life even more frightening. The hesitation of most tenants to venture outside their apartments is consistent with his resonance assumption.

RESEARCH ON CULTIVATION ANALYSIS

Cultivation takes time. Gerbner viewed the process as one that unfolds gradually through the steady accumulation of TV's messages. Consequently, he shunned the experimental method many researchers used to study the effects of TV violence on aggressive behavior. According to Gerbner, these experiments couldn't possibly detect the sort of changes he sought to document. Change due to cultivation takes place over months and years; most experiments measure change that takes place over 30 or 60 minutes. That's why the strategy for performing *cultivation analysis* relies on surveys instead of experiments.

Gerbner's basic prediction was that heavy TV viewers would be more likely than light viewers to see the social world as resembling the world depicted on TV. The strategy for testing this notion was simple. Survey respondents were asked two types of questions: one type focused on reports of TV exposure so that Gerbner could distinguish between heavy and light viewers; the second focused on perceptions of social reality that he thought media might cultivate. Once measured, the responses could be correlated to find out if heavy viewers perceive the world as a scarier place than light viewers do.

Heavy viewers
TV viewers who report that they watch at least four hours per day; television types.

Based on the data from survey questionnaires on TV viewing, most of Gerbner's work established a self-report of two hours a day as the upper limit of light viewing. He labeled *heavy viewers* as those who watch four hours or more. He also referred to the heavy viewer as the *television type,* a more benign term than *couch potato* with its allusion to either a steady diet of television and potato chips or a vegetable with many eyes. There are more heavy viewers than light viewers, but each group makes up about one-fourth of the general population. People whose viewing habits are in the two- to four-hour midrange make up the other half, but Gerbner wanted to compare people with distinctly different patterns of television exposure.

THE MAJOR FINDINGS OF CULTIVATION ANALYSIS

Cultivation differential
The difference in the percentage giving the "television answer" within comparable groups of light and heavy TV viewers.

Believing that violence is the backbone of TV drama and knowing that people differ in how much TV they watch, Gerbner sought to discover the *cultivation differential.* That's his term for "the difference in the percent giving the 'television answer' within comparable groups of light and heavy viewers."[12] He referred to *cultivation differential* rather than *media effects* because the latter term implies a comparison between *before*-TV exposure and *after*-TV exposure. Gerbner believed there is no before-television condition. Television enters people's lives in infancy. His surveys have revealed some provocative findings:

1. *Positive correlation between TV viewing and fear of criminal victimization.* In most of the surveys Gerbner conducted, the results reveal a small but statistically significant relationship between TV consumption and fear about becoming the victim of a crime. The question at the start of the chapter is illustrative:

Those with light viewing habits predict their weekly odds of being a victim are 1 out of 100; those with heavy viewing habits fear the risk to be 1 out of 10. Actual crime statistics indicate that 1 out of 10,000 is more realistic. Not surprisingly, more women than men are afraid of dark streets. But for both sexes, the fear of victimization correlates with time spent in front of the tube. People with heavy viewing habits tend to overestimate criminal activity, believing it to be 10 times worse than it really is. In actuality, muggers on the street pose less bodily threat to pedestrians than does injury from cars.

Meta-analysis
A statistical procedure that blends the results of multiple empirical and independent research studies exploring the same relationship between two variables (e.g., TV viewing and fear of violence).

Because so many cultivation studies have been published, it is possible to compute an overall average effect based on the correlations from all the individual surveys. Such a study is called a *meta-analysis*. One meta-analysis estimated the average correlation over 82 different studies to be consistently small, but positive ($r = +0.09$)—indicating that as TV viewing increases, there is a tendency for fear of victimization to increase as well.[13] Since correlations can range from 0.0 to 1.0, a value of 0.09 is certainly on the small side. But in most of the studies, the correlation was large enough to conclude that the relationship was not just a chance finding. TV viewing is definitely related to fear of criminal victimization.

2. *Perceived activity of police.* People with heavy viewing habits believe that 5 percent of society is involved in law enforcement. Their video world is populated with police officers, judges, and government agents. People with light viewing habits estimate a more realistic 1 percent. Gerbner's television type assumes that cops draw their guns almost every day, which isn't true.

3. *General mistrust of people.* Those with heavy viewing habits are suspicious of other people's motives. They subscribe to statements that warn people to expect the worst:

"Most people are just looking out for themselves."

"In dealing with others, you can't be too careful."

"Do unto others before they do unto you."

Mean world syndrome
The cynical mindset of general mistrust of others subscribed to by heavy TV viewers.

Gerbner called this cynical mindset the *mean world syndrome.* The evidence suggests that the minds of heavy TV viewers are fertile ground for sowing thoughts of danger.

CRITIQUE: HOW STRONG IS THE EVIDENCE IN FAVOR OF THE THEORY?

For most observers, Gerbner's claim that the dramatic content of television creates a fearful climate makes sense. How could the habitual viewer watch so much violence without it having a lasting effect? Yet over the last 30 years, communication journals have been filled with the sometimes bitter charges and countercharges of critics and supporters. Opponents have challenged Gerbner's definition of violence, the programs he selected for content analysis, his decision to lump together all types of dramatic programs (action, soap operas, sitcoms, and so on), his assumption that there is always a consistent television answer, his nonrandom methods of selecting respondents, his simple hours-per-day standard of categorizing viewers as *light* or *heavy*, his multiple-choice technique of measuring their perceived risk of being mugged, his statistical method of analyzing the data, and his interpretation of correlational data.

Perhaps the most daunting issue to haunt cultivation research is how to clearly establish the causal claim that heavy TV viewing leads a person to perceive the world as mean and scary. Because cultivation researchers shun the experimental method in favor of the survey, they are stuck with a method that is incapable of establishing clear evidence of causality. Critics are quick to point out that the correlation between TV viewing and fear of criminal victimization can be interpreted plausibly in more than one way. The correlation could indicate, as Gerbner contended, that TV viewing cultivates or causes fear of crime. But it could make just as much sense to interpret the relationship the other way—fear of crime causes people to watch more TV. After all, most TV shows depict a just world in which the bad guys get caught in the end. Perhaps those most afraid of crime are the ones most motivated to tune in to TV to become assured that justice will ultimately triumph.

With correlational data, the only way to distinguish what causes what is to collect data from the same people on more than one occasion over a longer period of time. *Longitudinal studies* like these can help determine which of the two variables comes before the other. Unfortunately, longitudinal research typically takes many months or years to complete. Scholars who live by the adage "publish or perish" are not usually attracted to projects that require them to wait around that long to collect data. As a result, cultivation studies of this type are virtually nonexistent. This state of affairs causes some critics to give cultivation theory low marks on the criterion of *testability* that you read about in Chapter 3.

Another possibility is that the relationship between TV viewing and fear of crime is like the relationship between a runny nose and a sore throat. Neither one causes the other—they are both caused by something else. Just as the cold virus is a common cause of runny noses *and* sore throats, some critics suggest that the neighborhoods people live in could be the common cause of TV viewing *and* fear of crime.[14] People who live in high-crime areas may fear crime for good reason. They also tend to stay inside to avoid victimization. While indoors, they pass the time by watching TV. In contrast, people who live in low-crime areas don't fear crime as much and so they tend to go outside more frequently, which leads to less TV consumption. If researchers ignore where people live—and most cultivation researchers do—they might miss the role played by this variable or others that weren't included in their questionnaires.

Scholars have another reservation about the evidence: cultivation effects tend to be statistically small. Imagine an entire pie that represents all the fear of crime that is measured in a cultivation questionnaire. The amount of the pie that researchers can attribute to watching TV might be just a single bite. On the other hand, champions of the theory point out that tiny statistical effects can be crucial. Consider the fact that a 1 percent swing in voting patterns in 3 of the last 14 presidential elections would have resulted in a different person being elected (Kennedy–Nixon in 1960; Nixon–Humphrey in 1968; Bush–Gore in 2000). Or reflect on the fact that a change in the average temperature of just a single degree could have catastrophic consequences for our planet.

Issues of statistical size aside, Gerbner's defenders would emphasize the *importance* of the issue at hand. Fear of violence is a paralyzing emotion. As Gerbner repeatedly pointed out, worry can make people prisoners in their own homes, change the way they vote, affect how they feel about themselves, and dramatically lower their quality of life. Even if the effect of TV viewing on these factors is relatively small, the consequences at stake make TV's message one that we should be concerned about.

But what is TV's message? When Gerbner formulated his theory decades ago, there were only three major networks. The vast offerings of today's cable and satellite menu were unimaginable. Critics contend that Gerbner's original assumption that TV viewers are constantly exposed to the same images and labels is no longer true. While there may not yet be a channel for left-handed truck drivers who bowl on Friday nights, the TV environment seems to be moving in that direction. The choices between such channels as the Food Network, the Golf Channel, and C-SPAN permit a level of viewing selectivity that cultivation theory doesn't acknowledge. If the theory is to continue to exert influence, many critics maintain that it will have to adapt to the new media environment.

Compared to most of the other theories in this text, the "critique" section of cultivation theory is much longer. Does this mean it's a bad theory? Not necessarily. Consider the fact that cultivation theory has generated research for almost a half-century. Theories that have been around that long sustain more attacks than ones recently hatched. It's also important to keep in mind that amid all the criticism, few theories in the area of mass communication have generated as many studies. In addition to its tremendous contribution to research, the theory has influenced at least three generations of scholars to think about media in a particular way. Most theorists would love to have even a fraction of the recognition that cultivation theory has managed to garner.

As for Gerbner, in 1996 he founded the Cultural Environment Movement, a coalition of organizations and social activists who believe it's vitally important who gets to tell the stories within a culture, and whose stories don't get told. They are committed to changing the stories that American television tells and are convinced this will happen only when the public wrests control of the airwaves from media conglomerates. Gerbner underscored the movement's agenda with repeated references to a line from Scottish patriot Andrew Fletcher:

> "If a man were permitted to make all the ballads, he need not care who should make the laws of a nation."[15]

QUESTIONS TO SHARPEN YOUR FOCUS

1. How would you change Gerbner's definition of *dramatic violence* so that his index of TV violence would measure what you think is important?

2. What types of people are underrepresented in television drama? What types of people are overrepresented? Who are the victims of symbolic violence on the screen?

3. How do your *political* and *social values* differ from, or coincide with, the *mainstream* attitudes of Gerbner's *television type?*

4. The *meta-analysis* finding of a +0.09 relationship between TV exposure and worldview can be seen as *significant, small,* and/or *important.* How do these interpretations differ? Which impresses you most?

A SECOND LOOK

Recommended resource: Michael Morgan, James Shanahan, and Nancy Signorielli, "Growing Up with Television," in *Media Effects: Advances in Theory & Research,* 3rd ed., Jennings Bryant and Mary Beth Oliver (eds.), Routledge, New York, 2009, pp. 34–49.

Primary sources: Michael Morgan (ed.), *Against the Mainstream: The Selected Works of George Gerbner,* Peter Lang, New York, 2002.

Violence index: George Gerbner, Larry Gross, Marilyn Jackson-Beeck, Suzanne Jeffries-Fox, and Nancy Signorielli, "Cultural Indicators: Violence Profile No. 9," *Journal of Communication,* Vol. 28, No. 3, 1978, pp. 176–207.

Violence update: Amir Hetsroni, "Four Decades of Violent Content on Prime-Time Network Programming: A Longitudinal Meta-Analytic Review," *Journal of Communication,* Vol. 57, No. 4, 2007, pp. 759–784.

Introduction to key concepts: George Gerbner, "Cultivation Analysis: An Overview," *Mass Communication & Society,* Vol. 1, 1998, pp. 175–194.

Profile of Gerbner: Scott Stossel, "The Man Who Counts the Killings," *Atlantic,* May 1997, pp. 86–104.

Mainstreaming and resonance: George Gerbner, Larry Gross, Michael Morgan, and Nancy Signorielli, "The 'Mainstreaming' of America: Violence Profile No. 11," *Journal of Communication,* Vol. 30, No. 3, 1980, pp. 10–29.

Mainstreaming and resonance research: L. J. Shrum and Valerie D. Bischak, "Mainstreaming, Resonance, and Impersonal Impact: Testing Moderators of the Cultivation Effect for Estimates of Crime Risk," *Human Communication Research,* Vol. 27, 2001, pp. 187–215.

Research review and meta-analysis: Michael Morgan and James Shanahan, "Two Decades of Cultivation Research: An Appraisal and a Meta-Analysis," in *Communication Yearbook 20,* Brant Burleson (ed.), Sage, Thousand Oaks, CA, 1997, pp. 1–45.

Television news violence: Daniel Romer, Kathleen Hall Jamieson, and Sean Aday, "Television News and the Cultivation of Fear of Crime," *Journal of Communication,* Vol. 53, 2003, pp. 88–104.

Computer game violence: Dmitri Williams, "Virtual Cultivation: Online Worlds, Offline Perceptions," *Journal of Communication,* Vol. 56, 2006, pp. 69–87.

Causality with correlation data: Constanze Rossmann and Hans-Bernd Brosius, "The Problem of Causality in Cultivation Research," *Communications,* Vol. 29, 2004, pp. 379–397.

How Cultivation Works: L. J. Shrum, Jaehoon Lee, James Burroughs, and Aric Rindfleisch, "An Online Process Model of Second-Order Cultivation Effects: How Television Cultivates Materialism and Its Consequences for Life Satisfaction," *Human Communication Research,* Vol. 37, No. 1, 2011, pp. 34–57.

Critique: Dolf Zillmann and Jacob Wakshlag, "Fear of Victimization and the Appeal of Crime Drama," in *Selective Exposure to Communication,* Dolf Zillmann and Jennings Bryant (eds.), Lawrence Erlbaum, Hillsdale, NJ, 1985, pp. 141–156.

To access a chapter that predicts when and how viewers will imitate TV violence, click on Social Learning Theory in Archive under Theory Resources at *www.afirstlook.com.*

CHAPTER 30

Objective   Interpretive

Socio-psychological tradition

Agenda-Setting Theory
of Maxwell McCombs & Donald Shaw

For some unexplained reason, in June 1972, five unknown men broke into the Democratic National Committee headquarters looking for undetermined information. It was the sort of local crime story that rated two paragraphs on page 17 of *The Washington Post*. Yet editor Ben Bradlee and reporters Bob Woodward and Carl Bernstein gave the story repeatedly high visibility even though the public initially seemed to regard the incident as trivial.

President Nixon dismissed the break-in as a "third-rate burglary," but over the following year Americans showed an increasing public awareness of Watergate's significance. Half the country became familiar with the word *Watergate* over the summer of 1972. By April 1973, that figure had risen to 90 percent. When television began gavel-to-gavel coverage of the Senate hearings on the matter a year after the break-in, virtually every adult in the United States knew what Watergate was about. Six months after the hearings President Nixon still protested, "I am not a crook." But by the spring of 1974, he was forced from office because the majority of citizens and their representatives had decided that he was.

THE ORIGINAL AGENDA: NOT WHAT TO *THINK,* BUT WHAT TO THINK *ABOUT*

Journalism professors Maxwell McCombs and Donald Shaw regard Watergate as a perfect example of the agenda-setting function of the mass media. They were not surprised that the Watergate issue caught fire after months on the front page of *The Washington Post*. McCombs and Shaw believe that the "mass media have the ability to transfer the salience of items on their news agendas to the public agenda."[1] They aren't suggesting that broadcast and print personnel make a deliberate attempt to influence listener, viewer, or reader opinion on the issues. Most reporters in the free world have a deserved reputation for independence and fairness. But McCombs and Shaw say that we look to news professionals for cues on where to focus our attention. "*We* judge as important what the *media* judge as important."[2]

Although McCombs and Shaw first referred to the agenda-setting function of the media in 1972, the idea that people desire media assistance in determining political reality had already been voiced by a number of current events analysts. In an attempt to explain how the United States had been drawn into World War I, Pulitzer Prize–winning author Walter Lippmann claimed that the media act as a mediator between "the world outside and the pictures in our heads."[3] McCombs and Shaw also quote University of Wisconsin political scientist Bernard Cohen's observation concerning the specific function the media serve: "The press may not be successful much of the time in telling people what to think, but it is stunningly successful in telling its readers what to think about."[4]

Agenda-setting hypothesis
The mass media have the ability to transfer the salience of issues on their news agenda to the public agenda.

Starting with the Kennedy–Nixon contest in 1960, political analyst Theodore White wrote the definitive account of four presidential elections. Independent of McCombs and Shaw, and in opposition to then-current wisdom that mass communication had limited effects upon its audience, White came to the conclusion that the media shaped those election campaigns:

> The power of the press in America is a primordial one. It sets the agenda of public discussion; and this sweeping political power is unrestrained by any law. It determines what people will talk and think about—an authority that in other nations is reserved for tyrants, priests, parties and mandarins.[5]

A THEORY WHOSE TIME HAD COME

McCombs and Shaw's agenda-setting theory found an appreciative audience among mass communication researchers. The prevailing selective-exposure hypothesis claimed that people would attend only to news and views that didn't threaten their established beliefs. The media were seen as merely stroking preexistent attitudes. After two decades of downplaying the influence of newspapers, magazines, radio, and television, the field was disenchanted with this limited-effects approach. Agenda-setting theory boasted two attractive features: it reaffirmed the power of the press while maintaining that individuals were free to choose.

McCombs and Shaw's agenda-setting theory represents a back-to-the-basics approach to mass communication research. Like the initial Erie County voting studies,[6] the focus is on election campaigns. The hypothesis predicts a cause-and-effect relationship between media content and voter perception. Although later work explores the conditions under which media priorities are most influential, the theory rises or falls on its ability to show a match between the media's agenda and the public's agenda later on. McCombs and Shaw supported their main hypothesis with results from surveys they took while working together at the University of North Carolina at Chapel Hill.[7] (McCombs is now at the University of Texas.) Their analysis of the 1968 race for president between Richard Nixon and Hubert Humphrey set the pattern for later agenda-setting research. The study provides an opportunity to examine in detail the type of quantitative survey research that Stuart Hall and other critical theorists so strongly oppose.

MEDIA AGENDA AND PUBLIC AGENDA: A CLOSE MATCH

Media agenda
The pattern of news coverage across major print and broadcast media as measured by the prominence and length of stories.

McCombs and Shaw's first task was to measure the *media agenda*. They determined that Chapel Hill residents relied on a mix of nine print and broadcast sources for political news—two Raleigh papers, two Durham papers, *Time, Newsweek,* the out-of-state edition of *The New York Times,* and the CBS and NBC evening news.

They established *position* and *length* of story as the two main criteria of prominence. For newspapers, the front-page headline story, a three-column story on an inside page, and the lead editorial were all counted as evidence of significant focus on an issue. For news magazines, the requirement was an opening story in the news section or any political issue to which the editors devoted a full column. Prominence in the television news format was defined by placement as one of the first three news items or any discussion that lasted more than 45 seconds.

Because the agenda-setting hypothesis refers to substantive issues, the researchers discarded news items about campaign strategy, position in the polls, and the personalities of the candidates. The remaining stories were then sorted into 15 subject categories, which were later boiled down into 5 major issues. A composite index of media prominence revealed the following order of importance: foreign policy, law and order, fiscal policy, public welfare, and civil rights.

Public agenda
The most important public issues as measured by public opinion surveys.

In order to measure the *public's agenda*, McCombs and Shaw asked Chapel Hill voters to outline what each one considered the key issue of the campaign, regardless of what the candidates might be saying. People who were already committed to a candidate were dropped from the pool of respondents. The researchers assigned the specific answers to the same broad categories used for media analysis. They then compared the aggregate data from undecided voters with the composite description of media content. The rank of the five issues on both lists was nearly identical.

WHAT CAUSES WHAT?

McCombs and Shaw believe that the hypothesized agenda-setting function of the media is responsible for the almost perfect correlation they found between the media and public ordering of priorities:

Media Agenda ⟶ Voters' Agenda

But as critics of cultivation theory remind us, correlation is not causation. It's possible that newspaper and television coverage simply reflects public concerns that already exist:

Voters' Agenda ⟶ Media Agenda

The results of the Chapel Hill study could be interpreted as providing support for the notion that the media are just as market-driven in their news coverage as they are in programming entertainment. By themselves, McCombs and Shaw's findings were impressive, but equivocal. A true test of the agenda-setting hypothesis must be able to show that public priorities lag behind the media agenda. I'll briefly describe two research studies that provide evidence that the media agenda is, in fact, the *cause*, while the public agenda is its somewhat delayed *effect*.

Critics have suggested that *both* the media agenda and the public agenda merely reflect current events as they unfold; it's just that news professionals become aware of what's happening sooner than the rest of us do. To examine that possibility, communication researcher Ray Funkhouser, now retired from Pennsylvania State University, undertook an extensive *historical* review of stories in news magazines from 1960 to 1970.[8] He charted the rise and fall of media attention on issues and compared these trends with annual Gallup poll responses to a question about "the most important problem facing America." Funkhouser's results make it clear that the twin agendas aren't mere reflections of reality. For example, the number of American troops in Vietnam increased until 1968, but news coverage peaked two years before that. The same was true of urban violence and campus unrest. Press interest cooled down while cities and colleges were still heating up. It appears that Walter Lippmann was right—the actual environment and the pictures in our mind are two different worlds.

This historical study provides strong support for McCombs and Shaw's basic agenda-setting hypothesis. But it took a tightly controlled *experiment* run by Yale researchers to establish a cause-and-effect chain of influence from the media agenda to the public agenda.[9] Political scientists Shanto Iyengar, Mark Peters, and Donald Kinder spliced previously aired news features into tapes of current network newscasts. For four days straight, three groups of New Haven residents came together to watch the evening news and fill out a questionnaire about their own concerns. Each group saw a different version—one version contained a daily story on environmental pollution, another had a daily feature on national defense, and a third offered a daily dose of news about economic inflation. Viewers who saw the media agendas that focused on pollution and defense elevated those issues on their own lists of concerns—definite confirmation of a cause-and-effect relationship between the media agenda and the public agenda. (As it turned out, inflation was already an important topic for most participants, so there wasn't any room for that issue to move up on the third group's agenda.)

WHO IS MOST AFFECTED BY THE MEDIA AGENDA?

Even in their original Chapel Hill study, McCombs and Shaw understood that "people are not automatons waiting to be programmed by the news media."[10] They suspected that some viewers might be more resistant to the media's political priorities than others—that's why they filtered out the responses of voters who were already committed to a candidate. In follow-up studies, McCombs and Shaw turned to the *uses and gratifications* approach, which suggests that viewers are selective in the kinds of TV programs they watch (see Chapter 28). The theorists sought to discover exactly what kind of person is most susceptible to the media agenda. They concluded that people who have a willingness to let the media shape their thinking have a high *need for orientation*. Others refer to it as an *index of curiosity*.

Index of curiosity
A measure of the extent to which individuals' need for orientation motivates them to let the media shape their views.

Need for orientation arises from high *relevance* and *uncertainty*. For example, because I'm a dog and cat owner, any story about cruelty to animals always catches my attention (high relevance). However, I don't really know the extent to which medical advances require experimentation on live animals (high uncertainty). According to McCombs and Shaw, this combination would make me a likely candidate to be influenced by media stories about vivisection. If the news editors of *Time* and ABC think it's important, I probably will too.

FRAMING: TRANSFERRING THE SALIENCE OF ATTRIBUTES

Until the 1990s, almost every article about the theory included a reiteration of the agenda-setting mantra—*the media aren't very successful in telling us what to think, but they are stunningly successful in telling us what to think about*. In other words, the media make some issues more *salient*. We pay greater attention to those issues and regard them as more important. By the mid-1990s, however, McCombs was saying that the media do more than that. They do, in fact, influence the way we think. The specific process he cites is one that many media scholars discuss—*framing*.

James Tankard, one of the leading writers on mass communication theory, defines a media frame as "the central organizing idea for news content that supplies a context and suggests what the issue is through the use of *selection, emphasis, exclusion,* and *elaboration*."[11] The final four nouns in that sentence suggest that the media not only set the agenda for what issues, events, or candidates are most important, they also transfer the salience of specific attributes belonging to those potential objects of interest. My own "final four" experience may help explain the distinction.

I'm writing this section while visiting relatives in St. Petersburg, Florida. The *St. Petersburg Times* is filled with stories about the finals of the NCAA men's basketball tournament that starts here tomorrow. The field of 64 teams has now been narrowed to 4, and it's hard to imagine anything the newspaper or television stations could do to make this Final Four event more prominent for local residents. No one seems to talk about anything else.

What is it about the Final Four extravaganza that captures people's attention? For some it's the high quality of basketball play they expect to see. For others it's a rooting interest for a particular team. But beyond these inherent characteristics of a basketball tournament, there are many other potential features of the event that might come to mind:

Gambling—there's more money bet on this game than on the Super Bowl.

Party scene—a guy leans out the window and yells, "This is where it's at."

Local economy—this is the weekend that could keep Florida green.

Exploitation of players—how many of these guys will ever graduate?

Beach forecast—it will be sunny and warm both today and tomorrow.

"Your royal command has been obeyed, Highness. Every town crier in the land is crying: 'Old King Cole is a merry ole soul.' Before nightfall we'll have them all believing it."

Cartoon by Ed Frascino. Reprinted by permission.

The morning paper carried separate stories on each of these features, but coverage on benefits to the local economy and the gambling angle were front-page features that ran five times as long as the brief article on player exploitation buried inside.

We see, therefore, that there are two levels of agenda setting. The first level, according to McCombs, is the transfer of salience of an *attitude object* in the mass media's pictures of the world to a prominent place among the pictures in our head. The Final Four becomes important to us. This is the agenda-setting function that survey researchers have traditionally studied.

Framing
The selection of a restricted number of thematically related attributes for inclusion on the media agenda when a particular object or issue is discussed.

The second level of agenda setting is the transfer of salience of a dominant set of *attributes* that the media associate with an attitude object to the specific features of the image projected on the walls of our minds.[12] Now when I think of the Final Four, I imagine money changing hands for a variety of reasons. I don't think about GPAs or diplomas. According to McCombs, the agenda setting of attributes mirrors the process of framing that Robert Entman describes in his article clarifying the concept:

> To frame is to select some aspects of a perceived reality and make them more salient in a communication text, in such a way as to promote a particular problem definition, causal interpretation, moral evaluation and/or treatment recommendation for the item described.[13]

NOT JUST WHAT TO THINK ABOUT, BUT HOW TO THINK ABOUT IT

Is there evidence that the process of framing as defined by agenda-setting theorists actually alters the pictures in the minds of people when they read the newspaper or tune in to broadcast news? Does the media's construction of an agenda with a cluster of related attributes create a coherent image in the minds of subscribers, listeners, and viewers? McCombs cites national election studies in Spain, Japan, and Mexico that show this is how framing works.[14] I also find compelling evidence in another framing study conducted by Salma Ghanem for her doctoral dissertation under McCombs' supervision at the University of Texas.[15]

Ghanem, now dean of communication at Central Michigan University, analyzed the changing percentage of Texans who ranked crime as the most important problem facing the country between 1992 and 1995. The figure rose steadily from 2 percent of respondents in 1992 to 37 percent in 1994, and then dipped down to a still high 21 percent a year later. Ironically, even as public concern about crime was on the rise the first two years, the actual frequency and severity of unlawful acts were going down. On the basis of many first-level agenda-setting studies like the Chapel Hill research, Ghanem assumed that the increased salience of crime was driven by media that featured crime stories prominently and often. She found a high correlation (+0.70) between the amount of media coverage and the depth of public concern.

Ghanem was more interested in tracking the transfer of salience of specific crime attributes—the second level of agenda setting. Of the dozen or so media frames for stories about crime, two bundles of attributes were strongly linked to the public's increasing alarm. The most powerful frame was one that cast crime as something that could happen to anyone. The stories noted that the robbery took place in broad daylight, or the shooting was random and without provocation.

The second frame was where the crime took place. Out-of-state problems were of casual interest, but when a reported felony occurred locally or in the state of Texas, concern rose quickly. Note that both frames were features of news stories that shrank the psychological distance between the crimes they described and the average citizens who read or heard about them. Many concluded, "I could be next." The high correlations (+0.78, +0.73) between these media frames and the subsequent public concern suggest that attribute frames make compelling arguments for the choices people make after exposure to the news.

Framing is not an option. Reporters inevitably frame a story with the personal attributes of public figures they select to describe. For example, the media continually reported on the "youthful vigor" of John F. Kennedy while he was alive but made no mention of his extramarital affairs, which were well known to the White House press corps. The 1988 presidential race was all but over after *Time* framed the contest between George H. W. Bush and Michael Dukakis as "the Nice Man vs. the Ice Man." In 1996 Republican spin doctors fought an uphill battle positioning their candidate once media stories focused on Bob Dole's lack of passion—"Dead Man Walking" was the quip of commentator Mark Shields. And the press picked up on George W. Bush's claim to be a "compassionate conservative" in the 2000 presidential election, whereas Senator John Kerry, his opponent in 2004, was repeatedly described as "flip-flopping" on the issues. In all of these cases it's easy to spot the affective tone of the attribute.

For the last decade, researchers seeking to determine the public's agenda during an election campaign have asked potential voters, "Suppose one of your friends has been away a long time and knows nothing about the candidates. . . . What would you tell your friend about _____?" They take note of each attribute mentioned and later sort them into content categories such as experience, competence, personality, and morality. They then code each attribute as positive, neutral, or negative. Summing all of these affective aspects of attributes gives researchers a reliable measure of voters' attitudes toward the candidate. In most studies, the voters' agenda mirrors the media's agenda in substance and in tone, and also predicts the outcome of the election.[16]

McCombs and Shaw no longer subscribe to Bernard Cohen's classic remark about the media's limited agenda-setting role. They now headline their work with a revised and expanded version that describes agenda setting as a much more powerful media function:

> The media may not only tell us what to think about, they also may tell us how and what to think about it, and perhaps even what to do about it.[17]

BEYOND OPINION: THE BEHAVIORAL EFFECT OF THE MEDIA'S AGENDA

Most of the research studies on agenda setting have measured the effect of media agendas on public *opinion*. But some intriguing findings suggest that media priorities also affect people's *behavior*. Craig Trumbo, a professor of journalism and technical communication at Colorado State University, monitored the headlines for stories about the flu virus in 32 different newspapers between 2002 and 2008.[18] He also had access to the regular flu reports issued by the Centers for Disease Control and Prevention. Those reports showed the number of visits to doctors for flu-like symptoms as well as the actual number of cases of the flu. It would certainly make sense that with more actual flu cases, doctor visits would increase and journalists would be more likely to cover the story. But Trumbo found that even when he took account of the actual flu cases, there was still an agenda-setting effect. The amount of media coverage on the flu during one week predicted the number of doctor visits the next week. There was no evidence of a reverse effect. Patient visits to the doctor for flu symptoms didn't predict later media coverage about the virus. Trumbo's study provides evidence that the agenda-setting effect extends to behavior.

Nowhere is the behavioral effect of the media agenda more apparent than in the business of professional sports. In his book *The Ultimate Assist,* John Fortunato explores the commercial partnership between network television's agenda and the National Basketball Association's (NBA).[19] Television dramatically raised the salience of the sport (the first level of agenda setting) by scheduling games in prime-time viewing slots. It also put basketball's best attributes forward (the second level of agenda setting) by selecting the teams with the premier competitors to play in those games and focusing on those players. During the peak years of Michael Jordan's basketball career, it was "all Michael, all the time."

Television shaped an attractive picture of the NBA in viewers' minds through a series of off-court frames. Interviews with select players and coaches, color commentary, graphics, and instant replays of players' spectacular moves all created a positive image of the NBA. As for the rape accusation against L.A. Lakers superstar Kobe Bryant, and later his feud with teammate Shaquille O'Neal that split the team, the media cooperated in downplaying those attributes that tarnish the NBA's image. As McCombs and other researchers have discovered by analyzing multiple presidential elections, it's the cumulative effect of long-term attribute salience that can alter attitudes and behavior.[20]

This 30-year effort to shape the public agenda has not only had a spectacular effect on fan behavior, it has also altered the face of popular culture. From 1970 to 2000, the number of NBA teams and the number of games doubled. The number of fans going to games quadrupled. But the astronomical difference is in the money. In 1970, television provided $10 million in revenue to the NBA. In 2000, the payout was $2 billion, and in 2012 it was $5 billion—no small change. McCombs' comment: "Agenda setting the theory can also be agenda setting the business plan."[21]

WHO SETS THE AGENDA FOR THE AGENDA SETTERS?

News doesn't select itself. So who sets the agenda for the agenda setters? One view regards a handful of news editors as the guardians, or "gatekeepers," of political dialogue. Nothing gets put on the political agenda without the concurrence of a few select people—the operations chiefs of the Associated Press, *The New York Times, The Washington Post, Time, Newsweek,* ABC, NBC, CBS, CNN, Fox, and MSNBC. Although there is no evidence to support right-wing conservative charges that the editors are part of a liberal, eastern-establishment conspiracy, when one of them features an issue, the rest of the nation's media tend to pick up the story.

An alternative view regards candidates and office holders themselves as the ultimate source of issue salience. George H. W. Bush put the tax issue on the table with his famous statement "Read my lips: no new taxes." But he was unable to get the issue off the table when he broke that pledge. He also tried to dismiss the economic recession as a "mild technical adjustment." The press and the populace decided it was major.

Current thinking on news selection focuses on the crucial role of public relations professionals working for government agencies, corporations, and interest groups. Even prestigious newspapers with large investigative staffs such as *The Washington Post* and *The New York Times* get more than half of what they print straight from press releases and press conferences.[22]

Interest aggregations are becoming increasingly adept at creating news that must be reported. This term refers to clusters of people who demand center stage for their one overriding concern, whatever it might be—anti-abortion, antiwar, anti-communism, antipollution, anti-immigration, anti-same-sex-marriage. As the examples indicate, these groups usually rally around a specific action that they oppose. They stage demonstrations, marches, and other media events so that television and the press will be forced to cover their issue. The prominence of the Tea Party's campaign against government spending and taxes is a striking example. The media seem to pay attention to those who grab it.

Interest aggregations
Clusters of people who demand center stage for their one overriding concern; pressure groups.

On rare occasions, news events are so compelling that editors have no choice but to feature them for extended periods of time. The month-long Florida recount in 2000 to determine whether George W. Bush or Al Gore would be president was one such case. And, of course, the 9/11 terrorist attack totally dominated U.S. print and broadcast news, pushing almost every other story off the front page and television screen for the rest of the year. Stories like these clearly reveal what McCombs has referred to recently as *intermedia* agenda setting. Editors at most newspapers are influenced to some extent by what other news outlets are covering. When many news sources continue to feature the same story, it's tough for an editor to ignore the trend. There's more than one answer to the question of who sets the agenda for the agenda setters. The gatekeepers, interest aggregations, and the media themselves all play a role.[23]

WILL NEW MEDIA STILL SHAPE THE AGENDA, OPINIONS, AND BEHAVIOR?

Ironically, the power of agenda setting that McCombs and Shaw describe may be on the wane. In a creative experiment, University of Illinois researchers Scott Althaus and David Tewksbury predicted that traditional print media would be more effective than new electronic media in setting a reader's agenda.[24] They reasoned that people who are reading a newspaper know that editors consider a long, front-page article under a banner headline more important than a short story buried on an inside page. Not only are these comparative cues absent on the computer screen, but online readers can click on links to similar stories and never see accounts of events that paper readers see as they thumb through the pages.

Althaus and Tewksbury recruited students to spend 30 to 60 minutes a day for 5 days reading either a print version or an online version of *The New York Times* under controlled conditions. For both groups it was their only exposure to news that week. On the sixth day, the researchers tested recognition and recall of the week's stories and assessed which problems facing the country students personally regarded as most important. Not only did those who read the traditional paper remember more content, they also selected a higher percentage of international issues as more important to them, thus aligning closer to the prioritized agenda of the *Times'* editors. The researchers concluded that "by providing users with more content choices and control over exposure, new technologies may allow people to create personalized information environments that shut them off from larger flows of public information in a society."[25] Abby's application log illustrates this point.

I confess to being an online newsreader who only clicks on links that interest me. I easily bypass information and headlines on my computer that I couldn't avoid when reading a print version of the news. This caught up with me in my class in American politics. Our assignment was to stay informed about worldwide current events by reading *The New York Times*. I chose to read the paper online—to my detriment. I found myself clicking on stories of personal interest and didn't even notice headlines on other issues. My weekly quiz grades let me know that my study agenda didn't match the media agenda.

McCombs wouldn't be surprised that Abby chose to get news online rather than through newspapers or news broadcasts. In a study reported in 2007, he and Renita Coleman, a colleague at the University of Texas, found that most of the younger generation (18 to 34) relied on the Internet for news, middle-aged viewers (35 to 54) tended to favor TV, and older readers (55+) preferred newspapers. The correlation between the media agenda and the younger generation was somewhat lower than for boomers or the older generation, but at 0.70, it was still high. These results are consistent with a 2013 study by Adam Shehata and Jesper Strömbäck, media professors at Mid Sweden University. While these researchers discovered that the size of the agenda-setting effect is shrinking as people rely more on a variety of online news outlets, it certainly hasn't vanished.[26] McCombs thinks that's because "most Internet news sources are subsidiaries of traditional news media, and there is a high degree of redundancy in the media agendas even on diverse media."[27] He does note, however, that young adults are also learning what's important from late-night comedians like Jon Stewart on *The Daily Show*. It's not yet clear if the news they parody parallels the agenda of other media outlets.

ETHICAL REFLECTION: CHRISTIANS' COMMUNITARIAN ETHICS

Clifford Christians is the former director of the Institute of Communications Research at the University of Illinois at Urbana–Champaign and the lead author of *Good News: Social Ethics and the Press*.[28] Although he values free speech, he doesn't share the near-absolute devotion to the First Amendment that seems to be the sole ethical commitment of many journalists. Christians rejects reporters' and editors' insistence on an absolute right of free expression that is based on the individualistic rationalism of John Locke and other Enlightenment thinkers. In our age of ethical relativism where *continue the conversation* is the best that philosophy has to offer,[29] Christians believes that discovering the truth is still possible if we are willing to examine the nature of our humanity. The human nature he perceives is, at root, personhood in community.[30]

Christians agrees with Martin Buber that the relation is the cradle of life. ("In the beginning is the relation."[31]) He is convinced, therefore, that mutuality is the essence of humanness. People are most fully human as "persons-in-relation" who live simultaneously for others and for themselves.

> A moral community demonstrates more than mere interdependence; it is characterized by mutuality, a will-to-community, a genuine concern for the other apart from immediate self-interest. . . . An act is morally right when compelled by the intention to maintain the community of persons; it is wrong if driven by self-centeredness.[32]

Communitarian ethics
A moral responsibility to promote community, mutuality, and persons-in-relation who live simultaneously for others and for themselves.

Christians understands that a commitment to mutuality would significantly alter media culture and mission. His *communitarian ethics* establish civic transformation rather than objective information as the primary goal of the press. Reporters' aim would thus become a revitalized citizenship shaped by community norms—morally literate and active participants, not just readers and audiences provided with data.[33] Editors, publishers, and owners—the gatekeepers of the media agenda—would be held to the same standard. Christians insists that media criticism must be willing to reestablish the idea of moral right and wrong. Selfish practices aimed at splintering community are not merely misguided; they are evil.[34]

Christians' communitarian ethics are based on the Christian tradition of *agape love*—an unconditional love for others because they were created in the image of God. He believes journalists have a social responsibility to promote the sacredness of life by respecting human dignity, truthtelling, and doing no harm to innocents.[35] With an emphasis on establishing communal bonds, alienated people on the margins of society receive special attention from communitarians. Christians ultimately judges journalists on the basis of how well they use the media's power to champion the goal of social justice. For example, Christians asks:

> Is the press a voice for the unemployed, food-stamp recipients, Appalachian miners, the urban poor, Hispanics in rural shacks, the elderly, women discriminated against in hiring and promotion, ethnic minorities with no future in North America's downsizing economy?[36]

If the media sets that kind of agenda and features attributes that promote community, he believes they are fulfilling their communitarian responsibility.

Agape love
An unconditional love for others because they were created in the image of God.

CRITIQUE: ARE THE EFFECTS TOO LIMITED, THE SCOPE TOO WIDE?

When McCombs and Shaw first proposed the agenda-setting hypothesis, they saw it as a sharp break from the limited-effects model that had held sway in media research since Paul Lazarsfeld introduced the concept of *selective exposure* (see the introduction to Media Effects). Although not reverting to the old magic-bullet conception of media influence, McCombs and Shaw ascribed to broadcast and print journalism the significant power to set the public's political priorities. As years of careful research have shown, however, agenda setting doesn't always work. Perhaps the best that could be said until the mid-1990s was that the media agenda affects the salience of some issues for some people some of the time. So in 1994, McCombs suggested that "agenda setting is a theory of limited media effects."[37] That would be quite a comedown from its original promise.

The new dimension of framing reasserts a powerful media-effects model. As Ohio State University journalism professor Gerald Kosicki states,

> Media "gatekeepers" do not merely keep watch over information, shuffling it here and there. Instead, they engage in active construction of the messages, emphasizing certain aspects of an issue and not others.[38]

But Kosicki questions whether framing is even a legitimate topic of study under an agenda-setting banner. He sees nothing in McCombs and Shaw's original model that anticipates the importance of interpretive frames.

As McCombs is fond of pointing out, the evidence is there. In the lead article of a 1977 book that he and Shaw edited, they clearly previewed the current "New Frontiers" of agendas of attributes and framing:

> Agenda setting as a concept is not limited to the correspondence between salience of topics for the media and the audience. We can also consider the saliency of various attributes of these objects (topics, issues, persons or whatever) reported in the media. To what extent is our view of an object shaped or influenced by the picture sketched in the media, especially by those attributes which the media deem newsworthy?[39]

386   *MASS COMMUNICATION*

McCombs' definition of framing appears to be quite specific: "Framing is the selection of a restricted number of thematically related attributes for inclusion on the media agenda when a particular object is discussed."[40] In contrast, the popularity of framing as an *interpretive* construct in media studies has resulted in diverse and ambiguous meanings. The way Stuart Hall and other critical theorists use the term is so elastic that the word seems to refer to anything they don't like. Thus, I regard a narrow view of framing as a distinct advantage for empirically based media-effects research.

As for the six criteria for evaluating a social science theory, agenda setting fares well. It *predicts* that the public's agenda for the salience of attitude objects and key attributes will follow the media's lead, and it *explains* why some people are more susceptible to media influence than others. Those predictions are *testable* by using content analysis to establish the media agenda, surveys to determine public opinion, and *quantitative* statistical tests to determine the overlap. More than 400 empirical studies have supported and refined the theory. Even with the theorists' added concern for the affective tone of attributes, their theory remains relatively simple. And as for *practical utility,* agenda setting tells journalists, advertisers, political operatives, and media scholars not only what to look for, but how they might alter the pictures in the heads of those who read, view, or listen to the news.

QUESTIONS TO SHARPEN YOUR FOCUS

1. If the media aren't telling you what to think, why is their ability to tell you *what to think about* so important?

2. What *type of person* under what *type of circumstances* is most susceptible to the media's *agenda-setting function*?

3. Sarah Palin is one of the most controversial public figures in America. What *dominant set of attributes* could you use to *frame* her visit to a children's hospital to make her look good? How could you make her look bad?

4. Is there a recent issue that *news reporters and commentators* are now talking about daily that you and the people you know don't care about? Do you think you'll still be unconcerned two months from now?

CONVERSATIONS

View this segment online at
www.mhhe.com/griffin9e or
www.afirstlook.com.

In our conversation, Max McCombs discusses the process of framing and how this concept has changed the scope of his theory. He also answers questions posed by my students: How many issues can a person focus on at one time? If he ran the classic Chapel Hill study today, would he use CNN as a media outlet that sets the public agenda? Do TV entertainment shows have an agenda-setting function? I wanted to know how he saw potential media bias. Are all news stories delivered with a spin? Does he see anything sinister about intentionally framing a story? Is there a liberal bias in the national media? I think you'll be surprised by his direct responses.

A SECOND LOOK

Recommended resource: Maxwell McCombs and Amy Reynolds, "How the News Shapes our Civic Agenda," in *Media Effects: Advances in Theory and Research,* Jennings Bryant and Dolf Zillmann (eds.), Routledge, New York, 2009, pp. 1–16.

Comprehensive summary of theory and research: Maxwell McCombs, *Setting the Agenda,* Polity, Cambridge, UK, 2004.

Historical development: Maxwell McCombs and Tamara Bell, "The Agenda-Setting Role of Mass Communication," in *An Integrated Approach to Communication Theory and Research,* Michael Salwen and Donald Stacks (eds.), Lawrence Erlbaum, Hillsdale, NJ, 1996, pp. 93–110.

Five stages of agenda-setting research and development: Maxwell McCombs, "A Look at Agenda-Setting: Past, Present and Future," *Journalism Studies,* Vol. 6, 2005, pp. 543–557.

Prototype election study: Maxwell McCombs and Donald Shaw, "The Agenda-Setting Function of the Mass Media," *Public Opinion Quarterly,* Vol. 36, 1972, pp. 176–187.

Framing: Maxwell McCombs and Salma Ghanem, "The Convergence of Agenda Setting and Framing," in *Framing Public Life,* Stephen Reese, Oscar Gandy Jr., and August Grant (eds.), Lawrence Erlbaum, Mahwah, NJ, 2001, pp. 67–81.

Relationship among agenda setting, framing, and priming: Dietram Scheufele and David Tewksbury, "Framing, Agenda Setting, and Priming: The Evolution of Three Media Effects Models," *Journal of Communication,* Vol. 57, 2007, pp. 9–20.

Bundles of attributes: Maxwell McCombs, "New Frontiers in Agenda Setting: Agendas of Attributes and Frames," *Mass Comm Review,* Vol. 24, 1997, pp. 4–24.

Anthology of earlier agenda-setting research: Maxwell McCombs, Donald Shaw, and David Weaver, *Communication and Democracy: Exploring the Intellectual Frontiers in Agenda-Setting Theory,* Lawrence Erlbaum, Mahwah, NJ, 1997.

Israeli election study: Meital Balmas and Tamir Sheafer, "Candidate Image in Election Campaigns: Attribute Agenda Setting, Affective Priming, and Voting Intentions," *International Journal of Public Opinion Research,* Vol. 22, 2010, pp. 204–229.

Focus on the theorist: William Davie and T. Michael Maher, "Maxwell McCombs: Agenda-Setting Explorer," *Journal of Broadcasting and Electronic Media,* Vol. 50, 2006, pp. 358–364.

Critique: Gerald Kosicki, "Problems and Opportunities in Agenda-Setting Research," *Journal of Communication,* Vol. 43, No. 2, 1993, pp. 100–127.

For a theory that explains the role of media in shaping public opinion, click on Spiral of Silence in Archive under Theory Resources in *www.afirstlook.com.*

INDEX

Bormann, Nancy, 240
Boster, Frank, 36, 187
Bostrom, Robert, 23, 470
Bottom-line accounting, 147, 244, 269, 444
Bottom-up thinking, 192, 265
Boulding, Kenneth, 325
Boundary(ies)
    fuzzy, 159–160
    intentional breach of, 159–160
    linkage, 156, 158–162
    permeability, 151, 156, 158–160
    relational, 83–85
    turbulence, 151, 157, 159–163
Bowling, communication as, 52–53
Bracken, Bruce, 482
Bradac, James J., 402, 443
Brain, 57–58, 320
Brainstorming, 220, 405
Braithwaite, Dawn O., 93, 119, 132, 150, 153, 174
Breadth and depth of self-disclosure, 98–99, 104, 106, 111, 127
Briñol, Pablo, 199
Brizendine, Louann, 434
Broadcast media, 267, 363
Broom, Cheryl, 241
Brosius, Hans-Bernd, 374
Brown, Barbara, 107
Brown, Penelope, 408
Browning, Larry, 262
Buber, Martin, 76–77, 80, 384, 440
Buechner, Frederick, 304–305, 307–309, 312
Buller, David, 93, 312
Burgoon, Judee, 2–4, 81-91, 93, 312, A–1
Burgoon, Michael, 175–176, 187
Burke, Kenneth, 11, 293–302, 311, A–4
Burleson, Brant R., 374, 442–443, 482
Burnett, Ann, 464–465, 468
Burroughs, James, 374
Bush, George H. W., 381–382
Bush, George W., 182–183, 295, 330, 332, 372, 383

C

Cacioppo, John, 188–193, 195–196, 198–199, A–3
Calabrese, Richard, 112, 119
Call of Duty: Modern Warfare, 353, 361
Canary, Daniel, 135, 443
Canons of rhetoric, 281, 288–289
Capitalism, 19, 54, 103, 271, 275, 315, 335–336
Carbaugh, Donal, 280, 389
Care, 99, 101, 279, 345, 399, 440, 448
Caregiving, 63, 447, 451–452, 464
Caring, 42, 74–75, 77, 93–94, 101, 142, 172, 204, 279, 345, 399, 440, 448
Carlsmith, James, 205, 212
Carnivalesque view, 146
Casmir, Fred, 4
Categorical imperative, 92–93, 440
Categorization, 166, 230, 239, 357–358, 377, 407, 431, 433 (*See also* Classification)
Cause-and-effect relationships, 17, 28, 30, 38, 55, 73, 83, 86, 131, 165, 168, 173, 204, 218, 235, 289, 295, 329, 336, 339, 351, 372, 374, 376–378, 381, 396
Cautions, 86, 430, 472

Cell phone, 7, 14, 122, 278
Censorship, 272, 347, 459
Center for Contemporary Cultural Studies, 340, 349
Central route of mind, 188–193, 195–199, 414
Centrifugal force, 137
Centripetal force, 137
Certainty, 79, 145, 284
Certainty–uncertainty dialectic, 138–141, 144
Chaffee, Steven, 36
Chaiken, Shelly, 187, 199
Challenger disaster, 214–215
Chandler, Daniel, 338
Change, 138, 140–141, 145, 149, 170–171, 217, 251, 257, 263, 316–323, 325, 340, 349, 361, 422, 426, 463
Channel of communication, 66, 125, 127–128, 132, 165, 173, 223, 242, 268, 317
Chapel Hill study, 376–378, 380
Characteristics, personal, 48, 75, 88, 95, 109, 196, 236–237, 245, 284, 296, 298, 303, 305, 435, 453, 466
Charades, communication as, 52–54
Chase, Kenneth, 299
Chicago School of Sociology, 62, 65
Choi, Charles W., 403
Choice, 5, 7, 17–19, 21, 60, 71, 131, 182, 197–198, 217–218, 222, 293, 297, 307, 361, 452, 458, 460, 470, 473 (*See also* Free will)
Christianity, 314, 325
Christians, Clifford, 349, 384–385
Cialdini, Robert, 189, 199
Cicero, 40
Circumstances, 83, 92, 116, 147, 226, 296, 319, 345, 386, 466
Cissna, Kenneth, 482
Civic transformation, 384
Civility, 74, 274
Civil rights, 300
Clarification of values, standard for interpretive theory, 29–31, 35, 77, 148, 161, 239, 252
Clarity, 28, 31, 64, 74, 182, 228, 282, 300, 400, 425, 465–466
Class, economic, 245, 341, 369, 419, 445–446, 467
Classical management theory, 242–243
Classification, 38, 162, 224, 284, 329, 335–337, 357, 381(*See also* Categorization)
Clevenger, Theodore, 174
Clinton, Bill, 452
Close relationships, 38–45, 60, 94–95, 105, 107, 116, 119, 121–122, 125, 134–139, 145–146, 148–149, 151–152, 158, 409, 422–425 (*See also* Intimacy; Personal relationships)
Closed-mindedness, 225, 394–395
CMM Institute for Personal and Social Evolution, 66, 69, 78, 119, 166
Co-cultural theory, 465–466, 468
Code-switching, 421
Codetermination, 269, 275
Coding, 169, 224, 227, 385, 389–390, 419–421, 423, 425, 431, 438, 458
Cognitive dissonance theory, 22, 25, 200–211, 474, 476, A–3
Cognitive processing, 2, 57–58, 113, 115, 138, 161, 189–192, 197, 201–202, 204–206, 211 (*See also* Thinking; Message elaboration)
Cohen, Bernard, 376, 381
Coherence, narrative, 70, 307–312
Cohesiveness, 214, 230, 234–235, 238, 265, 397